LET US HAVE PEACE

Let

Us

Have

Peace

Ulysses S. Grant
and the Politics
of War and
Reconstruction,
1861–1868

Brooks D. Simpson

The University of

North Carolina Press

Chapel Hill & London

© 1991 The University of
North Carolina Press
All rights reserved

Library of Congress Cataloging-in-
Publication Data
Simpson, Brooks D.
  Let us have peace : Ulysses S. Grant
and the politics of war and
reconstruction, 1861–1868 / Brooks D.
Simpson.
      p. cm.
  Includes bibliographical references
and index.
  ISBN 0-8078-1966-2 (alk. paper)
  1. Grant, Ulysses S. (Ulysses Simpson),
1822–1885.   2. United States—Politics
and government—Civil War, 1861–1865.
3. Reconstruction.   4. United States—
Politics and government—1865–1869.
I. Title.
E672.S6   1991
973.7—dc20   91-50256
                CIP

Manufactured in the United States of
America

Parts of this book have appeared in
somewhat different form and are
reprinted here with permission of the
publishers.

"Butcher? Racist? An Examination of
William S. McFeely's *Grant: A Biography*."
Civil War History 33 (March 1987):
63–83.

"'The Doom of Slavery': Ulysses S.
Grant, War Aims, and Emancipation,
1861–1863." *Civil War History* 36 (March
1990): 36–56.

"Grant's Tour of the South Revisited."
Journal of Southern History 54 (August
1988): 425–48.

TO MY PARENTS

CONTENTS

ACKNOWLEDGMENTS

In the course of preparing this book, I have incurred debts personal and professional. E. Arthur Gilcreast of the Phillips Exeter Academy planted the seed for this endeavor when he challenged me to do some research on the Appomattox agreement. At the University of Virginia, Robert Brugger, Michael Holt, Robert Cross, and Charles McCurdy fostered my interest in Grant. Along the way, other historians have encouraged me, including LaWanda Cox, James Mohr, Roger Bridges, Albert Castel, Charles Wynes, Emory Thomas, and Bill McFeely, who had some helpful words of advice.

I would like to thank the staffs of the following institutions for assisting me in using their collections: the University of Virginia's Alderman Library, the Illinois State Historical Society, the Newberry Library, Yale University's Sterling Library, Princeton University's Firestone Library, the Chicago Historical Society, and the Library of Congress. At the National Archives, Sara Dunlap Jackson was a source of encouragement, support, and information. The staffs of the State Historical Society of Wisconsin, Hoskins Library at the University of Tennessee, and the Sandor Tezler Library at Wofford College have provided warm havens for research.

At the University of Wisconsin-Madison, my fellow graduate students supported me in countless ways. Chris Berkeley, Nathan Peters, Kitty Kameon, Janice Steinschneider, Nancy Isenberg, Earl Mulderink, and Peter Knupfer always lent their ears and their hearts. Chris and Nathan deserve special praise for their sportsmanship, for the Bruins and Rangers never had a chance against Bryan Trottier and the four-time Stanley Cup champions, the New York Islanders. Thanks also go to Judy Cochran, who eased my way through the ordeal of dissertation completion, and to David Ecker, who put me up and put up with me during my first research trip to Washington. My three years at the Andrew Johnson Project at the University of Tennessee-Knoxville were memorable in many ways, but no more so than in the enduring friendships I formed with Pat Anthony, Marion Smith, Milton Klein, and John Muldowny. At Wofford College, Dan Maultsby was always supportive of my efforts, while Bill May offered not only his friendship and ever-ready ear but also a lay reader's perspective. The staff of the Papers of Ulysses S. Grant—John Y. Simon, David Wilson, and, during the years 1984–85, Wendy Hamand—responded to my queries, provided hospitality at Carbondale, and encouraged my work. At the University of North Carolina Press, Lewis Bateman took an early interest in this project; under extremely unusual circumstances Sandy Eisdorfer did an excellent job in turning a manuscript into a book; and Linda Pickett's expert eye caught many an error, some of them twice.

I especially wish to thank Edith Grant Griffiths, the general's great-granddaughter, for allowing me access to family papers not available for public use.

I have been blessed with some fine teachers at the University of Wisconsin-Madison. Stanley Kutler, in his own inimitable way, has provided me with opportunities to gain valuable professional exposure. Paul Boyer demonstrated anew his eclectic interests by serving on my dissertation committee, as did Leon Epstein. At the last moment, Edward Coffman generously agreed to survey the manuscript with his practiced eye. Allan Bogue, whether bemoaning the fate of the Cubs, speculating on the Islanders' chances, or in just talking shop, opened up a world of warm collegiality I will always treasure. And Richard Sewell has been a model mentor. Others know of his skills at pruning prose and slaying excess verbiage; I will add that I enjoyed working with him as a teaching assistant and that I remain extremely grateful for his valued counsel and assistance in many areas.

Finally, there are those to whom I owe my most personal thanks. Misha has always been there, although she doesn't have the foggiest idea why. My sister Joy needled me incessantly, but she always made up for it in other ways, most notably by getting hockey tickets. My wife Jean has been a wonderful partner, giving time and energy that might have been devoted to her own scholarship. Finally, I want to thank my parents. I hope they can take satisfaction in whatever I achieve, because they have done all they could to make it possible.

April 9, 1990   Cold Spring Harbor, New York

INTRODUCTION

Most Americans know two Ulysses S. Grants. Celebrated as one of the Republic's greatest generals, he is denigrated as one of its worst presidents, an image summed up in Henry Adams's terse statement, "A great soldier might be a baby politician."[1] After nearly forty years of obscurity and frustration, Grant rose in four years to command the armies of the United States, capturing three Confederate armies on the road to ultimate victory. And, so the traditional story goes, Appomattox marked the high point of his life; even the usually critical William McFeely begrudgingly admitted, "No matter how much one might find fault with Grant, one could always look back and be restored by this hour of his undoubted greatness—his finest hour."[2] But, as Bruce Catton remarked, once Grant reached this crest, "any road he took would lead downward." The abyss of Reconstruction and the White House awaited the unwary war hero. "His overwhelming success," Catton observed, "meant that other jobs would be given to him, and they would be radically different. They would, in fact, demand qualities quite the opposite of the ones that had brought him to his present high place."[3]

This dichotomy of good general/bad politician, with Appomattox as the dividing line, prevails in the literature about Grant. Of course, some have dissented. Catton, McFeely, and T. Harry Williams suggested that Grant demonstrated political shrewdness as a general in handling superiors and subordinates, an argument summed up in Williams's statement that Grant "appreciated the vital relationship in a democracy between war and politics." More recently, several historians—notably Morton Keller, David Donald, William R. Brock, and William Gillette (developing an interpretation first offered by William B. Hesseltine)—have accorded to Grant some political skill, although in each case they define it as the art of survival and maneuver as practiced by the practical professional politician. But the idea of the general as opposed to the politician, of war as opposed to peace, of military as opposed to civil affairs, persists in both the popular and scholarly imagination. Catton marveled at "the incomprehensible manner in which the endowment that wins a noble victory is never the endowment that can use the victory after it has been won."[4]

This study questions such distinctions in Grant's military career. It offers a new understanding of Grant's actions between 1861 and 1868 by delineating the interrelationship of warmaking and peacemaking during that period. Essential to this argument is the understanding that the American Civil War was first and foremost a civil war, and that the North's chief aim was to preserve the Union by subduing a Southern rebellion. Conquering the Confederacy was but one step of the Union effort; reintegrating the defeated South into the reunited states was of equal importance. Reconstruction began at Fort Sumter; Appomattox, although an essential step, left much unsettled. The struggle for reunion spanned both war and peace. Moreover, it soon became apparent that military victory was impossible without the eradication of slavery, an issue that complicated and transformed the process of reconciliation. To strike at the "peculiar institution" would not only spark a social revolution of untold dimensions but would also embitter already disgruntled white Southerners. After emancipation, protecting blacks from violence, intimidation, and discrimination worked at cross-purposes with attempts to renew white loyalty. To engage simultaneously in revolution and restoration proved a difficult task. In facing these problems in war and peace, Ulysses S. Grant was both warrior and statesman from 1861 to 1868. To him, the Civil War and Reconstruction were part of the same long struggle to preserve the Union, destroy slavery, and establish a durable peace to secure what Grant's contemporaries called "the fruits of victory."

Grant's fellow generals understood that warmaking and peacemaking were part of a continuum. "We never can have peace or quiet," asserted Philip Sheridan, "until the States which were in rebellion surrender their attempts at political power as absolutely as Lee surrendered the Military strength of the rebellion at Appomattox Court House." William T. Sherman agreed. "Reconstruction was a corol[l]ary of the war," he declared. Grant, he continued, was both "Hero in War" and "Leader in the Reconstruction," playing a key if not the central role during these years. To understand how Grant faced the challenges of war and peace is to gain greater insight into these critical years.[5]

Historians have often characterized Grant as the unconscious disciple of the Prussian military theorist Carl von Clausewitz, claiming that Grant's overall grasp of strategy exemplified Clausewitz's description of "total war." The comparison is apt, but not entirely for the right reasons; Clausewitz was not an unquestioning advocate of "total war," as any examination of the oft-cited but seldom-read *On War* will reveal. Other historians, who evaluate Grant's military operations according to Clausewitz's principles of strategy, come closer to the truth, although they grasp only part of the connection between the two men. Rather, Grant's wartime career embodied Clausewitz's most important maxim: "War is merely the continuation of policy by other means." As Clausewitz reminds us, "the political object is the goal, war is the means of reaching it, and means can never be considered in isolation from their purpose." Grant understood Clausewitz's argument that "the first, the supreme, the most far-reaching act of judgment that the statesman and commander have to make" is that "the kind of war on which they are embarking" is shaped by the goals of policy.[6]

Grant broadened Clausewitz's famed maxim in one crucial respect. He understood that the cessation of formal hostilities did not by itself mark the realization of the North's war aims. If the Civil War was politics by other means, then Reconstruction was in some sense a continuation of the struggle to achieve through political means the aims for which the war was fought. The Civil War and Reconstruction can best be understood as parts of the struggle for reunion, complicated and transformed by the emergence of emancipation and its consequences. As one of Grant's earliest biographers put it, after Appomattox, "the contest was simply transferred from the field of battle to the field of politics." To Grant, warmaking and peacemaking were part of the same larger political act of reuniting the Republic on a lasting basis. Like Clausewitz, he understood that at the highest levels "strategy and policy coalesce: the commander-in-chief is simultaneously a statesman."[7]

Nor was this the only way in which Grant instinctively understood Clausewitz. The Prussian noted that "the original political objects can greatly alter during the course of the war and may finally change entirely since they are influenced by events and their probable consequences."[8] Such was the case with emancipation. Originally outside the scope of Union war aims, the destruction of slavery inevitably became entwined with them. The reasons for this are many and varied, as Grant's wartime experience makes clear. Moreover, the surrender at Appomattox did not provide an answer as to what emancipation meant beyond the mere end of legalized enslavement. That would have to wait for the hammering out of a final settlement. Yet, for all the recent attention paid by historians to the revolutionary impact of emancipation on American society, one must remember that to people at the time the need to achieve a lasting reconciliation and "bind up the nation's wounds" was at least as important. Restoring amity between Northern and Southern whites while providing justice for the freedmen would have taxed the wisdom and ingenuity of any American, especially since one goal often seemed achievable only at the expense of the other.

This study offers a different perspective on Grant as warrior and statesman in the years between the opening of civil war and Grant's election as president. It weaves together threads of arguments presented by others, and adds some of its own, to offer an understanding of Grant that unites the themes of war and peace, stability and change, and policy and politics during his military career. Several themes inform the narrative, including the interplay between military means and political ends, Grant's understanding of politics, and the subordination of the military to civil rule. It is also essential to realize that Grant reacted to events as much as he shaped them and to place him in the context of the world in which he moved.

The relationship between military means and political ends is especially crucial in subduing a rebellion. Unlike military operations against a foreign foe, conquest is not an end in itself but the means to the end of reintegrating the insurrectionary areas into the nation-state. How one achieves victory is as important as victory itself; how the war is waged shapes the conditions under which a peace settlement, not just military triumph, will be achieved. Understanding this, Grant calibrated his conduct of operations according to the interplay of military and political matters. The intensity of Southern resistance, the behavior of the civilian population, the political environment both North and South, the prospects of battlefield triumph—all influenced his considerations of how and why to wage war. As Grant issued orders, made appointments, and planned strategy, he had to gauge the relative impact of partisan infighting, public opinion, and electoral contests on military operations—and vice versa. He did not have to be reminded that the war was political in fundamental ways. Charles A. Dana and James H. Wilson acknowledged this when they observed that the tasks Grant confronted "were of such a complex character that their successful performance demanded the talents of a statesman not less than those of a warrior."[9] The same concerns also shaped his approach toward postwar reconstruction, when military supervision became entangled with political debate on the proper course to pursue toward the defeated South and the freedmen.

Grant clearly defined politics on two levels, corresponding to the roles of statesman and politician. Statesmen served the public good, standing above partisan considerations to do what was best for all in a dispassionate and fair-minded manner. Politicians, on the other hand, were selfish, narrow-minded, calculating, manipulative, and always looking out for themselves. Although such notions might strike one as overly simplistic, Grant adhered to them until he became president. He deeply distrusted politicians. They had brought on the war through agitation; after the war, their continued bickering endangered the achievements of the statesmanlike Lincoln and the generals—who were, of course, no politicians. It was in large part to rescue Reconstruction from the politicians that Grant became involved in politics, although he always preferred to see himself as detached from the partisan fray.

If one reason for Grant's reluctance to enter party politics was his dislike of politicians, another was his strict observance of the subordination of the military to civil rule. Time and again, in his letters, he sounded the refrain of the soldier's duty selflessly to obey orders and to follow the policy outlined by his civil superiors. This conviction reflected practical wisdom as well as principle, for Grant observed how generals who made clearly known their dissent from administration policy were soon removed from command. Fortunately for Grant, there was little tension between principle and pragmatism under Lincoln, for the two men moved almost in step on the proper war aims to pursue. But Grant's concept of duty proved more burdensome when Andrew Johnson took over. Aware that he overshadowed Lincoln's successor in the public eye, Grant sought to support him even as he found himself disagreeing over administration policy. Increasingly, he tried to evade or circumvent Johnson's directives, justifying his decisions by claiming that Johnson was pandering to partisan ends and by citing his obligation to secure the peace and ensure that the Union dead had not died in vain. Still, he remained outwardly obedient. The cracks that began to appear in the relationship as early as 1866 and then widened during 1867 did not shatter the fiction of cooperation until early 1868.

In these eight years, Grant reacted to events as much as he initiated policies. He did not pursue any one policy single-mindedly. Rather, he sought to establish an equilibrium among ends, between means and ends, and between social change and social order. During the war, one such balance was established between war aims, the conduct of military operations, and the response of the enemy: after armed conflict had ceased, he weighed reconciliation with whites against justice for blacks. Whatever disturbed these equilibriums attracted his attention and drew a response, as did the changing boundaries of the scope of the war and the peace. Grant often discovered that military operations inevitably affected political ends. His military operations, and the means used to carry them out, were shaped by his understanding of political as well as strategic ends. As he grasped this truth, Grant increasingly took the initiative politically as well as militarily to ensure the realization of his vision of a reunited country, even as that vision was transformed by events. Much the same can be said of his attitude toward postwar reconstruction, as he reinterpreted his role in the policy process to preserve the fruits of victory from defiant Southerners and a reactionary chief executive.

Circumstances affected policy as much as policy shaped circumstances, which becomes abundantly apparent in any study of Grant in the 1860s. The interdependence of the variables of policy and circumstance form a major theme of this study. The escalation of war aims was due to the disruptive impact of the war upon Southern social institutions, the intensity and means of Confederate resistance, and policy decisions in Washington. Whatever Grant's early interest in maintaining order and keeping the war within certain conventional and limited bounds to enhance reconciliation, he accepted the broadening of war aims to include emancipation and social change because of the persistence of Southern resistance. A similar process characterized Grant's attitude toward postwar reconstruction. His initial interest in promoting reunification between Northern and Southern whites as the best way to restore order eroded when obdurate former Confederates, encouraged by Andrew Johnson's acquiescence and apathy, turned to discriminatory statutes and terrorism to fight emancipation and its consequences—demonstrating that they did not accept the verdict of Appomattox. Once again, escalating resistance bred revolution. Grant concluded that changes in the Constitution and in the postwar status of the freedmen were essential to preserve and protect the victory of the Union. Efforts to restore an old order, whether by war or by peace, had failed. In its place rose a new order created through revolutionary processes undertaken willingly by those, including Grant, whose initial reluctance to massive transformations had been worn away by the intensity, scope, and persistence of Southern resistance to any change whatsoever.[10]

Finally, there are the issues of identity and purpose, both for Grant and for the nation he worked to reunite. In 1861, Grant told his father that, whatever his previous feelings, "I have one sentiment now. That is we have a Government, and laws and a flag and they must all be sustained." The crusade to save the Union became the formative experience in Grant's life, giving it a meaning that transcended the personal. As savior of the Union, his reputation was inexorably tied to the fate of the nation. Had his efforts been in vain? Moreover, Grant felt a moral commitment to his men, both living and dead, to make sure that what was won on the battlefield was not frittered away by the politicians. Otherwise, those four long years of terrible bloodshed, that struggle that had given meaning, direction, and a higher purpose to the nation and to Grant's own life, would have been for naught. Echoing in Grant's mind were Lincoln's eloquent words at Gettysburg: "It is for us, the living, rather to be dedicated here to the unfinished work . . . the great task remaining before us—that from these honored dead we take increased devotion to that cause for which they here gave the last full measure of devotion—that we here highly resolve that these dead shall not have died in vain—that this nation, under God, shall have a new birth of freedom." The identity of the nation, as well as of Ulysses S. Grant, was at stake during Reconstruction.[11]

A word about the parameters of this study. Although it touches upon Grant's military strategy, it is not an exhaustive examination of it. That task has been performed elsewhere. And, since this is an exploration of Grant's political actions during his military career, it does not pursue Grant's approach to reconstruction as president. The nature of reconstruction policy on the federal level changed fundamentally during Grant's first year in office, and Grant's accession to the presidency placed him in a fundamentally different position. Rather, this study is concerned with General Grant and the issues of war and reconstruction during his military career, attempting to understand them as Grant did.

PROLOGUE

"THE SOUTH

WILL FIGHT"

Long before the outbreak of hostilities on April 12, 1861, Ulysses S. Grant's life had been shaped by sectionalism, slavery, and politics. Southerners were not faceless beings but close wartime comrades, men of integrity worth having as friends. Grant disregarded propaganda about blacks and slavery because he had worked alongside hired slaves and had owned and freed one. Sectional arguments sounded all too familiar to him: his father, an avowed opponent of slavery, and his father-in-law, a proud proponent of it, had relentlessly exposed him to both sides of the debate, perhaps lending a personal edge to his hatred of extremists. Indeed, the stresses of sectional politics had thwarted his personal advancement. As a result, Ulysses S. Grant understood something of both sides of the argument that was to divide the nation. His life had become entangled in the issues of sectional strife long before the secession crisis, despite his efforts to navigate a middle course.

Born on April 27, 1822, in the little hamlet of Point Pleasant on the north shore of the Ohio River, some twenty miles upriver from Cincinnati, Ulysses Grant grew up in southwest Ohio. His father, Jesse Root Grant, a local businessman who operated a tannery, was active in local politics as a newspaper editor, mayor, and antislavery Whig. As a young man, Jesse gave up a job in a Kentucky tannery because he would neither own slaves nor live where slavery existed. Returning to Ohio, he first worked at a tannery owned by Owen Brown, a

1

Connecticut-born abolitionist. Few would remember Owen, but many would hear one day of his slavery-hating son, John Brown. Jesse would count among his later associates Thomas Morris, a local congressman who was the vice presidential nominee of the Liberty party in 1844.[1]

But not all of young Ulysses's relatives shared his father's point of view. He had twenty-six cousins in Virginia and Kentucky and only eleven in Ohio. Jesse didn't care much for the Southern side of the family, complaining that they "depended too much on slave labor" and that their children had not the slightest idea how to fend for themselves. Even Ulysses's playmates were affected by slavery. Daniel Ammen, two years older than Ulysses, had migrated with his family from Virginia to Ohio to escape slavery. They had shared a house with Presbyterian preacher John Rankin, who assisted runaway slaves fleeing north from Kentucky. One escape was especially dramatic: a black man, his wife, and a child crossed the river by hopping from one piece of ice to another—a story Harriet Beecher Stowe later immortalized in *Uncle Tom's Cabin*.[2]

Ulysses had opportunities to judge things for himself as he traveled through northwest Virginia and Kentucky, although he left no record of his thoughts about slavery and the South. In 1836 he went to a private academy in Maysville, Kentucky; two years later, he attended another school in Ripley, Ohio, presided over by Rankin. This schooling prepared him for West Point. Entering the academy in 1839, he spent the next four years waiting to leave. Many of the cadets who helped him endure the endless routine were Southerners. Some became close associates. South Carolinian James "Pete" Longstreet and Georgian Lafayette McLaws befriended Ulysses early, Longstreet marveling at the way Grant handled horses. In 1840 Kentuckian Simon B. Buckner arrived to join the group. None of these fellows seemed staunch advocates of the peculiar institution in comparison to Patrick Calhoun, son of South Carolina's sectional spokesman, who was two years ahead of Grant. In his final year, Grant roomed with Missourian Frederick Dent, son of a slaveholder. Truman Seymour, who graduated three years after Grant, asserted that the cadets never discussed slavery: other cadets, however, recalled that sparks once flew between Grant and Dent as they engaged in a heated discussion on the topic. They almost came to blows before Grant burst out laughing at the pointlessness of the debate.[3]

Within two years of his graduation from West Point in 1843 as a brevet second lieutenant of infantry, Grant traveled with his regiment to the Rio Grande to confront the Mexican army. The following year, he participated in the first battles of the Mexican War, which he believed to be an unjust act of unwarranted aggression waged on behalf of the interests of Southern slaveholders. Betraying his Whig roots, Grant blamed President James K. Polk's eagerness to pursue the expansionist schemes of the Southern "slave power" for commencing a war he denounced as "wicked." The annexation of Texas was "a conspiracy to acquire territory out of which slave states might be formed for the American Union."[4] But if the Mexican War reinforced Grant's distaste for the impact of slavery on the political process, it ironically allowed him to form even closer ties with many Southern-born officers. He grew to admire Gen. Zachary Taylor to the point of imitating Taylor's plain uniform and demeanor. Longstreet and Tennessean Cadmus Wilcox fought by his side, and he met Virginian Henry Heth—and, as Heth recalled, "We took quite a fancy to each other." Certainly his reservations about the war did not interfere with these relationships.[5]

Perhaps the most obvious way in which Grant distinguished between slavery and Southerners was in his courtship of Julia Dent, the sister of his West Point roommate. Julia's father, "Colonel" Frederick Dent, was a fiery slaveholding Democrat who held sway over eighteen slaves, eleven of them old enough to work. But this did not deter Grant's heart, and upon the end of the Mexican War in 1848 he returned to St. Louis to marry Julia, with Longstreet and Wilcox in attendance. Peacetime life proved trying for the Grants. He moved from post to post and even spent two years on the Pacific coast. Finally, he resigned from the army in 1854 and returned home, possibly financing the journey in part through a loan from his old friend Buckner. He and Julia settled outside of St. Louis on land provided by her father.[6]

In Missouri, Grant was surrounded by slavery. He worked with slaves, including the four young servants owned by Julia. Biographer Albert D. Richardson later reported that "they were more trouble than help to him. He was too kind-hearted to enforce unpaid and reluctant labor with severity." And Grant was no businessman when it came to hiring black help. One of his workers, an old free black named Uncle Jason, reported in later years: "He used ter pay us several cents more a cord for cuttin' wood than anyone else paid, and some of the white men cussed about it, but Cap'n he jis' kep' right on a-payin' for er work jis' er same." No wonder Uncle Jason decided that Grant "was the kindest man he ever worked for." A white neighbor agreed that Grant paid his free blacks too much, "a-spoiling them, sir, spoiling them." Another neighbor, Jefferson Sappington, reported, "Grant was helpless when it came to making slaves work"; Mrs. Henry Boggs, the wife of one of Julia's cousins, later recalled, "He was no hand to manage negroes. He couldn't force them to do anything. He wouldn't whip them." Grant's treatment of his hired hands and Julia's slaves suggests that he accepted the basic humanity of blacks and did not mind working alongside them. But, as biographer Hamlin Garland concluded after interviewing Grant's neighbors, the use of slaves "was a source of irritation and shame" to him. In letters to his family, Grant never referred to the blacks around him as slaves, but only as "negro men" or "servants," as if to conceal the fact that they were slaves.[7]

For Grant, the question of slavery, at least on a personal level, became tangled with his concern for his wife and his need to maintain relations with his in-laws. Neighbors recalled that Grant objected to the institution of slavery on principle and opposed its expansion. However, he assailed abolitionists as agitators who, in advocating immediate abolition, imperiled the Union. And, as one of Julia's sisters commented, "I do not think that Grant was such a rank Abolitionist that Julia's slaves had to be forced upon him." His slaveholding father-in-law went to the other extreme, proclaiming slavery's virtues in debates with his son-in-law. Julia, of course, saw nothing wrong with slavery. She was so used to the joys of having servants that the family told her she could not do without them. She must have been displeased to hear her husband say within earshot of her father's servants that "he wanted to give his wife's slaves their freedom as soon as possible."[8]

In 1858, Grant finally gave up on farming and decided to set up a real estate and debt collection business with one of Julia's cousins,

Henry Boggs, in St. Louis. But, if he was finally free of farming and of Dents, slavery continued to follow him—Julia brought along her four servants. At least in one instance, Grant did what he could to distance himself from the peculiar institution. During his stay with the Dents, he had purchased a slave, a mulatto named William Jones, from his brother-in-law Fred. By 1859, William, some thirty-five years old, was probably worth $1,000, which to a still-struggling Grant represented a substantial sum. With that kind of money, he could probably pay off his debts and start out fresh. Yet, on March 29, 1859, with opportunity staring him in the face, Grant took William to the St. Louis Circuit Court and declared, "I do hereby manumit, emancipate & set free said William from slavery forever."[9]

Why did Grant do this? He was not adverse to making some money for hiring out Julia's slaves—the previous year he had raised the possibility of renting out Julia's new slave, "a very smart, active boy, capable of making anything," for $3 a month. He certainly needed the money. Perhaps he found slave trading distasteful; he knew he could not guarantee that William would enjoy the same easy master he had doubtlessly found in Grant. The former army captain had fought old man Dent over slavery. Perhaps it was time to do what was both right and expedient by freeing William, thus clearing his conscience at the same time he cut expenses.[10]

St. Louis proved a struggle for Grant. His search for secure employment became entangled with sectional politics. Some potential employers and clients objected to his Yankee heritage. Mrs. Boggs recalled that Grant was "gentle and dignified and uncomplaining," but that he "was in despair" when he arrived in St. Louis. "In those disturbed times he found it difficult to find employment. He had no trade, no profession, and he was a Northerner. That must never be left out of the account." Others pointed to his association with the Dents as proof of his sympathy with slavery. When his partnership with Boggs did not work out, he applied for the post of county engineer for St. Louis, gathering some thirty-five endorsements. Professors, lawyers, and businessmen signed his application. So did leaders of both parties—including Daniel M. Frost, a Democratic state senator who had served with Grant in the army, and George W. Fishback, part-owner of the pro-Republican *Missouri Democrat*. Nevertheless, Grant's connections with the Dent family marked him as a Democrat.

The Board of County Commissioners was controlled by Republicans, and they preferred German immigrant Charles E. Salomon. Politics overrode friendship: Grant was friends with one of the Republican commissioners, Dr. William Taussig, who later explained that Grant's kinship with the proslavery Dent family cost him his vote.[11]

"You may judge from the result of the action of the County Commissioners that I am strongly identified with the Democratic party! Such is not the case," Grant assured his father. "I never voted an out and out Democratic ticket in my life." Once a staunch supporter of the Whig party and its leader, Henry Clay, during the 1850s Grant drifted about politically. At one point, he joined a Know-Nothing lodge, but the secrecy and ceremony of the nativist order offended him, and he stopped attending meetings within a week. He eventually became a Democrat by default. The new Republican organization, with its agitation of the slavery issue, worried him. If it ever got into power, the nation would be forced to confront the slavery issue once more. Just as Grant cared little for wars on behalf of expanding slavery, so too did he have little use for the disruptive tendencies of the Republican party.[12]

Grant's vote in the 1856 presidential contest illustrated his reasoning. As an army officer, always on the move he had never voted in a presidential contest. He would have nothing to do with Millard Fillmore, despite the ex-president's Whig and Know-Nothing roots, leaving him to choose between Democrat James Buchanan and Republican John C. Frémont. Grant later recalled that, as election day drew near, "party feeling began to run high." Many Southerners spoke of their fears should Frémont win. Slavery, they declared, would be in peril with a Republican in the White House. Some even threatened secession. Grant did not share these fears, but the reaction of Southerners alarmed him. "Under the circumstances I preferred the success of a candidate whose election would prevent or postpone secession, to seeing the country plunged into a war the end of which no man could foretell," he later explained.[13]

If Grant thought this would stall the drive for secession, he was wrong. In fact, he needed only to talk to his friend Henry T. Blow to find out about the next flash point of sectional conflict. Blow and his brother Taylor were very interested in a case pending before the Supreme Court in the winter of 1856–57. Their father had once sold a slave named Dred Scott to Dr. John Emerson, an army surgeon. Now Dred was claiming that he was free because Emerson had taken him into areas that did not sanction slavery. The Supreme Court had decided to rule on Dred's status. Its decision, released on March 6, 1857, not only ruled that Scott was still a slave but also pronounced the Missouri Compromise unconstitutional. The decision served only to reinforce the polarization of American politics along sectional lines. Several months later, Taylor Blow obtained ownership of Scott and freed him.[14]

During the next several years, Grant worried a great deal about political questions. Reading accounts of the Lincoln-Douglas debates in 1858, he concluded that "it was a nice question to say who got the best of the argument." Neighbors, remarking that Grant seemed "thoroughly informed" on political issues, recalled that he was "opposed to slavery on principle . . . against its further extension," but "deplored the agitation of its abolition." He often appeared to be in a somber mood, contemplating the fate of the country. "I could not endure the thought of the Union separating," he said later. "It made my blood run cold to hear friends of mine, Southern men—as many of my friends were—deliberately discuss the dissolution of the Union as though it were a tariff bill."[15]

The debate also affected his personal relationships. He enjoyed discussing politics with Republican editor Fishback, but his Democratic friends criticized him so heavily that he ceased to visit them. The Boggses, thinking that he was too Northern in his preferences, began to talk behind his back. Yet he feared taking Julia and their four children to visit his father because Julia would want a servant to come along; what would happen if they touched free soil? And what would Jesse say? In the past, Jesse Grant had offered to help his son out, although Ulysses had refused previous offers because they required that he leave his family. Jesse, of course, wanted his eldest boy to leave the South. Rumor had it that Jesse told his son, "Ulysses, when you are ready to come North I will give you a start, but so long as you make your own home among a tribe of slave-owners I will do nothing." But, by 1860, Ulysses was desperate, and his father, abandoning any notion of separating Ulysses and Julia, approached him with the chance to help run the family general store at Galena, Illinois. This time the former army officer accepted the offer. St. Louis had not

worked out for him: he was too Northern to be accepted by Southerners but had too many Southern connections to be embraced by
Northerners. One day he encountered Fishback on the street. Would
the editor, a known antislavery man, either buy or hire one of Julia's
slaves? Having decided to go north, Grant's odd request was a way of
making sure that Julia's slaves would remain in good hands. Understandably, Fishback backed away from the proposed transaction, so
Grant had to leave the servants behind when his family moved to
Galena in the summer of 1860.[16]

In his new hometown, Grant at first tried to stay out of political
discussions, announcing, "I don't know anything of party politics, and
I don't want to." But he could not help but observe that this time the
Republicans, led by Lincoln, had an excellent shot at capturing the
presidency. "The fact is I think the Democratic party want a little
purifying and nothing will do it so effectually as a defeat," he told a
St. Louis friend after hearing of a Republican triumph in a Missouri
election. "The only thing is I don't like to see a Republican beat the
party." One of his first friends in Galena was lawyer John A. Rawlins,
leader of the local Democrats, who handled the store's legal affairs. If
Grant started out a Douglas man, however, he was relieved to discover that he had not satisfied the residency requirement for voter
registration, because, as fall came, he grew more undecided. "I don't
quite like the position of either party," he commented. In one instance, the newcomer did get involved, albeit indirectly, in politics.
Rawlins, alarmed at the formation of the Republican marching clubs
known as the "Wide-Awakes," sought to form a Douglas organization.
He approached Grant to help drill the company, but the retired captain refused. However, he soon found himself dropping by Wide-
Awake meetings to help out with formations and drilling. Perhaps he
was a little more of a Republican than he cared to admit.[17]

On the night of Lincoln's election, Grant somewhat reluctantly
helped host a little celebration at the general store. While others
toasted the rail-splitter's triumph, Grant curtly dismissed suggestions
that the renewed threat of secession would dissipate, saying: "The
South will fight." He remembered the strong talk in St. Louis four
years before, and he was under no illusions about whether Southerners meant what they said. As he traveled through Wisconsin and
Iowa in the winter of 1860–61, he often joined in conversations con-

cerning the future. Grant believed that there would be a war of short duration, but left no doubt as to his support for the Union. Many times he relied upon his acquaintance with Southerners to tell his fellow Northerners that, although the secessionists were possessed of "a good deal of bluster, . . . if they once get at it they'll make a strong fight. You're a good deal like them in one respect—each side underestimates the other and overestimates itself."[18]

It was a long winter. Grant, infuriated at the inactivity of President Buchanan, called him "the present granny of an executive." He could not understand secession. "It is hard to realize that a State or States should commit so suicidal an act as to secede from the Union, though from all the reports, I have no doubt but that at least five of them will do it." Upon reflection, he added, "It does seem as if just a few men have produced all the present difficulty." But, in February, he revealed his true feelings in more heated fashion. A friend entered the store to report that the seceded states had joined together, fashioned themselves the Confederacy, and elected Jefferson Davis president. Grant first shook his head in disbelief; when the visitor, a Democrat with Southern sympathies, repeated the news, Grant snapped back that Davis and his compatriots deserved hanging.[19]

On the morning of April 12, 1861, Confederate forces in Charleston, South Carolina, opened fire upon Fort Sumter. Grant's prediction had come to pass. The ensuing conflict to preserve the Union inevitably transformed both it and the life of Ulysses S. Grant forever.

1

A SOLDIER'S

DUTY

On April 15, 1861, news reached Galena of the fall of Fort Sumter. The next day, the townspeople met in the courthouse to decide what to do. Grant was there. So was John A. Rawlins, who had angrily declared, "There can be but two parties now, one of patriots and one of traitors!" Galena's mayor made a feeble plea for compromise; Republican congressman Elihu B. Washburne, sensing the need for a more vigorous response, offered resolutions to raise two companies of troops; Rawlins led the town's Democrats into the fold for war with a rousing speech. Afterward, Grant turned to his brother Orvil and quietly announced his decision to reenter the service.[1]

Two days later, Galena's citizens gathered again to raise recruits for the new army. Washburne thought it would be a good idea to have a military man, especially one of Democratic leanings, chosen as presiding officer. No sooner had the meeting been brought to order than Grant was named to the position. More than a little surprised, the ex-captain had no idea that he would be thrust forward so suddenly after years of being overlooked. "With much embarrassment and some prompting I made out to announce the object of the meeting," he remembered years later. Washburne and others offered him some relief by addressing the assemblage. Within days, Galena had enough volunteers to fill a company, and the Mexican War veteran spent the next weeks outfitting and drilling them.[2]

Grant was not easily roused by show, but he was deeply moved by the new crisis, for his allegiance to the Union was a most cherished belief. Partisan politics would have to take a back seat to the struggle to preserve the Union. "Now is the time, particularly in the border Slave states, for men to prove their love of country," he wrote to his father-in-law. "I know it is hard for men to apparently work with the Republican party but now all party distinctions should be lost sight of and every true patriot be for maintaining the integrity of the glorious old *Stars & Stripes*, the Constitution and the Union." This included himself. "Whatever may have been my political opinions before," he assured his father, "I have but one sentiment now. That is we have a Government, and laws and a flag and they must all be sustained." Echoing Rawlins, he added, "There are but two parties now, Traitors & Patriots"; he was "with the latter, and I trust, the stronger party."[3]

Although Grant had made clear in the past his opposition to what he believed to be the extreme positions on slavery advocated by some Republicans, he had no doubt as to who was responsible for the war. To him, it was evident "that in all these troubles the South have been the aggressors." Moreover, if Southerners in their calculations had counted upon Northern indifference or lack of commitment, they had made a serious error. Talk of Yankee apathy was absurd. Grant, astounded at the outpouring of patriotism, commented that "the rebels may truly quaik." If Southerners knew what they had wrought, "they would lay down their arms at once in humble submission."[4]

As for slavery, Grant realized that, with the commencement of hostilities, things would never be the same again. Southerners were risking the foundation of their society even as they defended it. "In all this I can but see the doom of Slavery," he warned his father-in-law. "The North do not want, nor will they want, to interfere with the institution. But they will refuse for all time to give it protection unless the South shall return soon to their allegiance." The disruption of the Southern economy by war would render the South vulnerable to international competition, reducing the worth of slaves "so much that they will never be worth fighting over again." Slavery would be destroyed as a consequence of prolonged conflict, becoming a casualty of events rather than the target of Union policy.[5]

But Grant did not foresee a lengthy conflict. "My own opinion is that this War will be but of short duration," he predicted. With "a few decisive victories" by the North, the "howling" Confederates would flee the field. Even then, however, he was not sure whether hostilities, no matter how quickly terminated, might not erode what the Confederate vice president Alexander H. Stephens called "the cornerstone of the Confederacy"—the peculiar institution of black servitude. "All the states will then be loyal for a generation to come, negroes will depreciate so rapidly in value that no body will want to own them and their masters will be the loudest in their declamations against the institutions in a political and economic view." Slavery would die, and "the nigger will never disturb this country again."[6]

Thus abolition was inevitable, in Grant's mind, from the moment the conflict started—not as a matter of principle but as a result of events. That it might be gradual did not disturb him, for Grant had always believed that immediate emancipation would be disruptive and possibly counterproductive. Slavery might collapse as a result of the war, but he had no desire to hasten its destruction. Abolition as a war aim would exacerbate existing differences, promote disorder, and make reunion more difficult. Indeed, he expressed some concern that slaves might take matters into their own hands and rise up in insurrection against their masters, causing a real revolution. Perhaps the forces raised to subdue the rebellion would have to be used to quell slave uprisings. He did not doubt that Northerners "would go on such a mission and with the purest of motives." But Grant did not automatically count himself among those Northerners. Once, when he heard an officer declare his willingness to join Southerners in suppressing slave revolts, Grant exploded, "I don't wish to hurt your feelings, but I must say that any officer who can make such a declaration is not far from being a traitor!"[7]

In short, to Grant the war presented a new opportunity for the country. The bickering divisiveness of party politics would be replaced by a resurgence in patriotism and selfless service, creating the kind of world in which he believed he would thrive. Moreover, the mere advent of armed conflict might well mean the end of slavery. Should the war drag on, Grant perceived that abolition could become, out of necessity, a Union war aim. But he did not consider that possibility a likely one. Indeed, he was so convinced that it would be a short war that he feared that he never would take part in it.

In light of later events, Grant's search for a command appears almost comic. At Springfield, Governor Richard Yates kept the old West Pointer around to drill men, inspect weapons, even file forms, but Grant wanted a regiment to command. He refused to engage in overt "log-rolling" or "political wave pulling" for a colonelcy, although he was aware that he stood to benefit from his acquaintance with Washburne and Yates. But he was willing to travel to Ohio to seek a regimental command or a position on the staff of newly minted Maj. Gen. George B. McClellan. Finally, on June 15, Yates put him in charge of the Seventh Congressional District Regiment (later the Twenty-first Illinois), displacing a man whose mismanagement of his recruits had nearly caused them to mutiny. (Ironically, McClellan had reviewed the regiment just that day, and pronounced himself satisfied with it—a hint of his ability for self-delusion.) Within a month, Grant was in Missouri, ready to see his first action. "I assure you my heart is in the cause I have espoused," he told his father, "and however I may have disliked party Republicanism there has never been a day that I would not have taken up arms for a Constitutional Administration."[8]

Disciplining his command was not merely a matter of preparing it for combat. Grant knew from his own experiences in the Mexican War that the conduct of soldiers made an impression upon the civilian population. Well-behaved soldiers would dispel Rebel propaganda about marauding Yankees, which in turn might make Southerners more docile under occupation and more willing for reunion. Such considerations were especially crucial in the upper South, where the population was fairly closely divided between loyalists and secessionists. Missouri, although still in the Union, was wavering, and the new colonel wanted to ensure that his men did nothing to fuel rumors of evil invaders. He kept a close eye on his soldiers, making sure that they did not disturb citizens along the line of march. Soon it appeared that he had met with some success. He told Julia that, although there existed "a terrible state of fear among the people" when his regiment arrived, within a few weeks they discovered that the soldiers "are not the desperate characters they took them for." He was convinced that "if orderly troops could be marched through this country . . . it would create a very different state of feeling from what exists now."[9]

Many Missourians, disregarding recent congressional resolutions and the pledges of Union military authorities, persisted in the belief that the Yankees aimed at abolition. "You can't convince them but what the ultimate object is to extinguish, by force, slavery," Grant complained to his father. Of course, these perceptions, misguided though they might be, only fortified the Southern will to resist by any means possible. Grant confided to Julia his concern that the war was getting out of hand. Not only were the citizens "great fools," but also they "will never rest until they bring upon themselvs all the horrors of war in its worst form. The people are inclined to carry on a guerilla Warfare that must eventuate in retaliation and when it does commence it will be hard to control." Should the conduct of hostilities transcend conventional boundaries, the war would embitter both the victor and the vanquished, making it all the more difficult to achieve a lasting peace. Moreover, to abandon notions of a limited war in favor of a people's struggle carried with it revolutionary implications. Even though both sides may have gone to war to preserve something, an escalation of conflict—whatever the result—promised to transform American society.[10]

Grant experienced Southern foolishness firsthand from an old business partner, Harry Boggs. Early in August, Grant received word that he had been promoted to brigadier general (the result of Washburne's unsolicited lobbying), and he decided to visit St. Louis, as if to show everyone that he finally had a job. There he encountered Boggs, who exploded in anger at the sight of his old real estate associate, declaring that Grant would never be welcome at his house and that the people of Illinois "were a poor misserable set of Black Republicans, Abolition paupers that had to invade their state to get something to eat." The new general was so pleased to be returning in triumph to his old town that he dismissed Boggs as "a pittiful insignificant fellow" and told him that he could not respond in anger—setting off yet another barrage of Boggs's profanity.[11]

Nor were such outbursts limited to old friends. Colonel Dent was already grumbling about his "Federal son-in-law," conveniently forgetting that his own son Fred remained in the U.S. Army. And from his Virginia relatives Grant heard an earful. His Aunt Rachel, lying sick in Virginia, gathered enough energy to dictate to his sister Clara a letter justifying secession. She had lost patience with "the harsh jargon of fanatical tirades against the institutions & people of the South." Most Yankees were "blinded by prejudice, led on by a desire for military fame, prompted by the prospect of plunder" or worse. These "Vandals of the North," this "set of Murderers," would never defeat the mighty South. As for her nephew, Rachel Tompkins told Clara Grant, "If *you* can justify your Bro. Ulysses in drawing his sword against those connected by the ties of blood, and even boast of it, you are at liberty to do so," but she could not. "And should one of those kindred be stricken down by his sword the awful judgment of God will be meted out to him, &, if not repented of, the hot thunderbolts of His wrath will blaze round his soul through eternity."[12]

Such flashes of temper, revealing the depth of Southern anger, made Grant wonder how long the conflict would last. Perhaps reconciliation would not be so easy after all. "I have changed my mind so much that I dont know what to think," he told his sister Mary. Although he still thought that the Rebels could be crushed by next April, "they are so dogged that there is no telling when they may be subdued." Stiffening resistance in Missouri lent substance to this impression. Grant soon adopted a tougher line toward secessionist sympathizers, arresting several to prevent them from relaying information, closing down a newspaper, and warning businessmen not to trade with Confederates. If Southerners were determined to wage hard war, Grant would respond in kind.[13]

Inevitably, such a struggle would affect the institution of slavery. Grant had always maintained that Northerners would not support slavery while the South continued to fight. Now he had to confront the issue of slavery in a war zone. Despite his disinclination to become involved in political questions, his actions in Missouri unavoidably carried political overtones. Whatever he did—whether he liberated slaves, left them alone, returned them to their masters, or followed Benjamin F. Butler's decision in Norfolk, Virginia, to accept refugees as "contraband of war"—was in effect a political statement, as were his policies toward Southerners restless under occupied rule. In the past, Grant had turned away from his lines both fugitive slaves and masters seeking their recovery. "We're not here to look after Negroes, but after Rebels," he explained to a black refugee seeking sanctuary. Grant's policy did not reflect his personal sentiments about slavery. One observer noted that Grant "was at heart and in expression an anti-slavery man, yet he had but little sympathy with the previous movements and opinion of the so-called ultra-Abolitionists." Grant "believed slavery to be an anomaly in a free government"; it "was subversive of the best interests of the master and the enslaved"; and it "hindered the development of the highest interests of humanity." His private sentiments and Union policy dictated that suppressing the rebellion remain the primary war aim. But the issue of fugitives would not go away. When Gen. John C. Frémont ordered Grant to take command of troops concentrating in southeast Missouri, he encountered the issue for the first time. Arriving at Cape Girardeau on August 30, Grant observed "Contrabands, in the shape of negroes," working on the fortifications. "I will make enquiries how they come here and if the fact has not been previously reported ask instructions," he informed Frémont's headquarters at St. Louis, in an effort to avoid initiating policies that interfered with slavery.[14]

Frémont did not share Grant's desire to stay out of politics; perhaps the new brigadier's recollection of his superior's political past prepared him for what was to come. On the day Grant arrived at Cape Girardeau, Frémont, tired of harassment by Confederate sympathizers, satisfied both his abolitionist beliefs and his personal ambitions by issuing a proclamation that imposed martial law on Missouri, confiscated the property of active Confederate supporters, and declared their slaves free. Col. John Cook, commanding at Cape Girardeau, asked Grant for instructions. "Protect all loyal Citizens in all their right[s]," Grant replied, "but carry out the proclamation of Genl Fremont upon all subjects known to come under it." Frémont's order was soon countermanded by Lincoln, but it had alerted Grant to the possibility that the war could assume a wider scope and thus involve him in the very political questions he wished to avoid. Lincoln's removal of Frémont several months later also reminded the new brigadier of the cost of violating established policy.[15]

Grant's decision to invade Kentucky in September 1861 provided him with an opportunity to outline his concept of the aims of the war. Through August, Kentucky had managed to preserve a precarious neutrality. Neither side had set foot in the state, although it was obvious that sooner or later Union troops would have to enter Kentucky to launch an offensive to recapture Tennessee. Frémont had sent Grant to southeast Missouri to plan for just such an operation, but Confederate forces under Leonidas Polk invaded Kentucky on September 3, conveniently relieving the Yankees of the onus of disrupting the status quo. In response, Grant advanced his troops across the Ohio River to Paducah, Kentucky, on September 6. He had decided on this move based upon information "which I am disposed to credit," he told Frémont, "although the authority is a negro man."[16]

At Paducah, Grant decided to issue his own proclamation, which, in stark contrast to Frémont's, made clear his conservative approach to the war. He had invaded Kentucky "not to injure or annoy" anyone, "but to respect the rights, and to defend and enforce the rights of all loyal citizens." The arrival of Union troops was a purely defensive move. It carried with it no political overtones. "I have nothing to do with opinions. I shall deal only with armed rebellion and its aiders and abetors." Nothing was said about slavery. Grant issued special instructions "to take special care and precaution that no harm is done to inoffensive citizens."[17]

Grant's proclamation and subsequent instructions were as much a political statement as Frémont's edict. Each was issued in states still technically loyal to the Union, and each offered different answers to the best means to achieve the goal of reunion outlined in the Johnson-Crittenden resolutions passed by Congress in July. Frémont, anxious to make a name for himself, had sought to place the war effort on advanced ground; Grant's announcement reflected his own belief that the war was one for reunion, not revolution. In contrast to Frémont, who saw his handiwork annulled by Lincoln, Grant's statement attracted some praise. Even the president reportedly liked it. But it still remained for the Lincoln administration to establish guidelines for military commanders who confronted the problem of slavery.[18]

Lincoln's decision to countermand Frémont's proclamation helped people only to understand what his policy was not. Grant was unsure of what government policy was, at least as it applied to black refugees. Within two weeks of the occupation of Paducah, blacks began entering Union lines, seeking refuge from their masters. Like Grant, Kentucky blacks knew that the presence of Union troops meant the disruption of slavery, regardless of the unwillingness of Union commanders to play abolitionist. And, if the Yankee army would not come to the blacks, they would go to it. The slaveholders followed, demanding the return of their escaped property. The secessionists among them were willing to overlook the irony that they were now asking the assistance of the very same government that they were rebelling against. Many of them had justified secession precisely because they had no faith that the government would protect slavery. Grant wired Washington for instructions. None came.[19]

Left on his own, and aware that fugitive slave legislation was still in force, Grant ordered the return of at least two slaves. Some two months later, he finally received definite guidelines on what to do. Gen. Henry W. Halleck took over for Frémont in November, with orders from McClellan to convince civilians in his command that the sole purpose of the war was to uphold "the integrity of the Union." The day after he assumed command, Halleck proceeded to carry out McClellan's wishes. General Orders No. 3, issued on November 20, 1861, closed Union lines to black fugitives. The army was not going to serve as a welcome wagon for freedom.[20]

Grant received the order with mixed feelings. To be sure, he still held fast to his belief that the sole object of the war was to restore the Union. "My inclination is to whip the rebellion into submission, preserving all constitutional rights," he told his father. But now he was willing to admit that this might not be possible. "If it cannot be whipped in any other way than through a war against slavery, let it come to that legitimately. If it is necessary that slavery should fall that the Republic may continue its existence, let slavery go." Willing to consider the possibility that slavery's demise might become a goal of Union policy instead of merely the consequence of the disruptive impact of military operations, Grant still was not ready to take that step. Aware that many Northern newspapers had seized upon Halleck's order to renew their criticism of the scope of Union war aims, Grant charged that such papers "are as great enemies to their country as if they were open and avowed secessionists." He knew that adopting such broad goals would mean that the prospects for reunion and reconciliation would give way to a bitter struggle requiring the North to conquer the entire South.[21]

Despite his reaction to press criticism of Halleck's order, Grant was not too enthusiastic about it, either. Noninterference with slavery was one thing; active support of it, especially in the face of evidence of growing Southern resistance, was another. "I do not want the Army used as negro catchers," he explained in approving the return of a fugitive to a loyal master, "but still less do I want to see it used as a cloak to cover their escape. No matter what our private views may be on this subject there are in this Department positive orders on the subject, and these orders must be obeyed." Subsequently, he remarked that he believed "that it was not the policy of the Government to ignore or in any manner interfere with the constitutional rights of loyal citizens," except in cases of military necessity.[22]

But the rights of secessionists were another matter, as Grant demonstrated two weeks later when he refused the request of a pro-Confederate slaveholder for the return of a fugitive who had sought refuge in Grant's lines. "The slave, who is used to support the Master, who supported the rebellion, is not to be restored to the Master by Military Authority," he snapped. The slaveholder might appeal to the civil authorities, but Grant felt no obligation "to feed the foe, or in any manner contribute to their comfort." This distinction was absent from Halleck's order, although it was in line with the policy set forth in confiscation legislation passed by Congress in August. Gen. Charles F. Smith echoed his superior's sentiments. "I cannot consent to act as the slave catcher myself unless it is made my duty by law," he declared. Since Grant looked up to Smith, his old commandant at West Point, such a statement could only encourage him to maintain a similar position.[23]

Grant let slip his growing antislavery convictions on other occasions. During the fall of 1861, his forces sparred with Polk's units, and the two armies collided once in a pitched battle at Belmont, Missouri. Inevitably, prisoners were taken at these clashes, and Grant met with Polk several times on a truce boat to arrange exchanges and discuss other issues. At the conclusion of one meeting, drinks were served, and Polk offered a toast: "George Washington!" No sooner had Grant tipped the glass to his lips, however, when Polk added, "The first rebel." Chagrined, Grant protested that such sharp practice was "scarcely fair" and vowed to get even. The opportunity came several weeks later, at another truce boat conference. This time Grant proposed a toast:

"Equal rights to all." Heartily assenting, Polk began to down the contents of his glass, when Grant quickly added, "White and black." A sputtering Polk admitted that Grant had achieved his object.[24]

Nor was Grant willing to tolerate actions that exceeded the bounds of conventional warfare. In January 1862, upon receiving reports that several of his pickets had been shot by civilians, he ordered that the surrounding area "should be cleaned out, for six miles around, and word given that all citizens making their appearance within those areas are liable to be shot," establishing the Civil War version of a free-fire zone. These orders restored stability. A week later, he instructed the local commander to release all civilians captured under these orders and allow all black refugees so disposed to return to their masters.[25]

In framing orders for Union advances, Grant emphasized the need to keep the goal of reconciliation in mind. The behavior of his soldiers toward civilians and their property remained a prime concern. He had prohibited foraging in Missouri because it was "apt to make open enemies where they would not otherwise exist." As 1862 opened, he instructed commanders launching probes into Kentucky to prohibit the "wanton destruction of property" and to guard against straggling. Soldiers should not be allowed to act upon their own interpretation of confiscation legislation, for abrasive behavior "makes open and armed enemies of many who, from opposite treatment would become friends or at worse non-combatants." But he was less certain about the correct policy to pursue regarding fugitive slaves. In light of Congress's refusal to renew the Johnson-Crittenden resolutions limiting war aims to reunion alone, this was understandable. Perhaps stronger measures affecting slavery were not far away. The problem of fugitives became more pressing in February 1862. Grant's army, working in tandem with a gunboat flotilla under the command of Andrew H. Foote, penetrated Tennessee along the Tennessee and Cumberland rivers and struck a brace of fortified positions that protected this gateway. Fort Henry, on the Tennessee, fell on February 6; ten days later, the Confederate garrison at Fort Donelson, having failed to break through the encircling Yankees, submitted to Grant's ultimatum for "unconditional surrender." Halleck instructed Grant to use slaves owned by secessionists to erect additional fortifications around the two forts to consolidate the Union's hold on the area. "We want laborers," Grant told Confederate general Simon Buckner, an old prewar associate in command of the men captured at Donelson. "Let the negroes work for us." Buckner, already peeved by Grant's blunt summons to surrender, had to rest satisfied when Grant allowed officers to keep their servants. Meanwhile, Grant directed division commander John A. McClernand to capture slaves to increase the available work force. At least one expedition interpreted its orders liberally, seizing "mostly old men, women and children" and destroying property. The officer had violated Halleck's order, however, and the fugitives had to be returned. Grant finally halted McClernand, explaining: "It leads to constant mistakes and embarassment to have our men run[n]ing through the country interpreting confiscation acts and only strengthens the enthusiasm against us whilst it has a demoralizing influance upon our own troops."[26]

The incident caused Grant a great deal of embarrassment. Determined to avoid any such trouble in the future, he reminded his troops that Halleck's order about returning fugitive slaves was still in force and must be observed. Union lines were flooded with slaveholders seeking to recover their slaves, proving that General Orders No. 3 continued to be a necessity. Halleck reminded officers that civil courts, not military authorities, were empowered to rule on the status of slaves. Some commanders refused to return escaped slaves to their masters; other reports suggested that, if Grant's men believed that "this war was against slavery, they would lay down their arms and go home." Fugitives disrupted military operations and sparked controversy. Keeping fugitives out of camp would keep Grant out of trouble, or so he thought.[27]

But the image of Union soldiers returning "old men, women and children" to their masters was too much for many Northerners, and newspapers attacked Grant's action. The criticism stung: "I have studiously tried to prevent the running off of negroes from all outside places as I have tried to prevent all other marauding and plundering," the exasperated commander explained to Washburne. It was not a matter of personal preference. "So long as I hold a commission in the Army I have no views of my own to carry out. Whatever may be the orders of my superiors, and law, I will execute." If Congress passed legislation "to[o] odious for me to execute," he promised to resign. He enjoined a strict observance of Halleck's order to avoid more trouble, promising to arrest any soldiers violating it. To Julia he confided that criticism of his command came from "the Abolition press."[28]

Always quick to quibble, McClernand questioned Grant's new toughness in enforcing Halleck's order. He cited the 1861 confiscation legislation passed by Congress in support of retaining fugitive slaves, "particularly if the negroes are fugitives coming into camp of their own motion." Noting that the issue "has been productive of repeated orders, and frequent correspondence," McClernand pointed out that the issues of the status of blacks and the loyalty of masters "present difficulties, which accumulate, as we proceed," and that the army "affords no competent tribunal" to settle these issues. Having made Grant aware of the obvious, McClernand was content to rest. But his letter illustrated the problems Union commanders faced in the absence of guidelines from Washington.[29]

Even when such guidelines arrived, they did not always ease Grant's mind. McClernand's letter was still a fresh memory when Grant received notification of a new War Department directive embodying congressional legislation that barred soldiers from "employing any of the forces under their respective commands for the purpose of returning fugitives." One suspects that incidents in Grant's own command had contributed to the legislation. In response, Grant pointed out the ramifications of such an order. He had heard from former U.S. Representative J. M. Quarles that Confederate enlistments had risen around Clarksville, Tennessee, because a Union colonel had taken two black slaves for his own use. The commander at Clarksville told Grant that "the return of those two negroes would do more good, & go further to cultivate a union sentiment in & about Clarksville than any other act." Grant forwarded the case, uncertain how to respond in light of the new directives, but he expressed the opinion that the blacks should be returned.[30]

Thus Grant groped for an answer to the fugitive slave question, keeping in mind that an avowed antislavery policy would embitter Southern whites and prolong the war. He no longer believed that politics and the military existed in two separate worlds. Willing to consider the possibility of abolition, Grant sheltered refugee slaves from secessionist masters and proved eager to appropriate slaves used to support the rebellion. But he would not press the issue. Believing that the rebellion was about to crumble, he set his mind on winning that last battle that would preserve the Union as it was.

As Grant realized, federal policy toward fugitive slaves was intertwined with efforts at reconciliation. Indeed, he was so eager to demonstrate the limited nature of the war effort that at Fort Donelson he punished a Union soldier who had confiscated a woman's bonnet by ordering that he be strung up by the thumbs in full view of the surrendered Confederates. Moreover, he believed that one more Union victory would end the conflict. To gain that end, his forces moved southward along the Tennessee River, stopping a few miles north of the Mississippi border. Many Tennesseans were declaring their loyalty to the Union; others were enlisting in Grant's regiments. Deserters from the Confederate army to the south reported great discontent in Rebel ranks. "With one more great success," he confided to Julia, "I do not see how the rebellion is to be sustained." Debating the question of fugitive slaves would simply disrupt the reconciliation process at a time when the end seemed so near.[31]

Whatever notions Grant held about an imminent end to the war were rudely shattered on Sunday, April 6, when Confederate columns crashed through the Union encampment around Shiloh Church, driving the bluecoats back to the banks of the Tennessee River. Grant rallied his disorganized and dazed regiments, and by nightfall he had stabilized his position. The next day, with the help of units from Don Carlos Buell's Army of the Ohio, Grant drove the Rebels away. But this, the bloodiest battle in American history up to that time, disabused Grant of the notion that peace was at hand. One does not have to get involved in the debate over the question of military surprise at Shiloh to see that Grant was astonished to find the Confederacy still very much alive and kicking. Subsequently, he also claimed that the battle changed his thinking about the conduct of the war. After Shiloh, he recalled, "I gave up all idea of saving the Union except by complete conquest." Previous policies to "protect the property of the citizens whose territory was invaded, without regard to their sentiments," went out the door, and Grant began to make war not only on Confederate armies but also on the resources that sustained the war effort.[32]

Grant's change in attitude, however, was a little slower in coming than he liked to recall in later years. In the immediate aftermath of the battle, he anticipated "a speedy move, one more fight and then easy sailing to the close of the war." The slow advance of the combined armies of Grant, Buell, and John Pope under Halleck's command quelled those hopes. Corinth, Mississippi, fell at the end of May; Grant, noting the devastation caused by the armies, believed that there would be "a vast amount of suffering" among civilians. Although he regretted such hardship, he also noted that the people "are wors[e] rebels than the soldiers who fight against us." Occupation duty presented difficult problems. At first he was uncertain about what to do. "It is hard to say what would be the most wise policy to pursue towards these people," he wrote Washburne, "but for a soldier his duties are plain. He is to obey the orders of all those placed over him and whip the enemy whenever he meets him." To Julia he was more candid. "This war could be ended at once," he said, "if the whole Southern people could express their unbiased feeling untramelled by leaders. The feeling is kept up however by crying out Abolitionest against us and this is unfortunately sustained by the acts of a very few among us." He detailed instances where Tennesseans "inclined to Union sentiments" watched as soldiers encouraged their slaves to escape. This did little to assist reconciliation.[33]

Other actions undertaken by the Confederate government portended a prolonged struggle. Within weeks of Shiloh, the Confederate Congress passed legislation establishing conscription, complementing earlier measures that authorized President Jefferson Davis to suspend the writ of habeas corpus and declare martial law. These acts suggested that the Confederacy was still full of fight, a notion already confirmed on the Shiloh battlefield. Northerners who clung to the hope that the rebellion was close to collapse should have been dissuaded.[34]

Still, as Grant took command of the District of West Tennessee in June, he expressed confidence that as soon as his district was "reduced to working order" its residents would "become loyal, or at least law-abiding." His subordinates instructed soldiers "to cultivate a conservative, friendly feeling," reminding them that Halleck's orders barring blacks from Union lines were still in effect. Such measures, intended to resuscitate loyalty, were predicated upon the supposition that Southerners needed only a little prodding to renew their allegiance to the Union. Others wondered whether Southerners were willing to come back. Dr. Edward Kittoe, a friend of both Grant and Washburne, told Washburne, "We curry favour of these secessionists, and real Union men do not fare as well as they: we are obsequious to them, we feed them, we guard their property, we humble ourselves to gain their favour, and in return we receive insult and injury." Unionists were "disgusted," and "outraged" officers and men "very naturally ask is this the way to crush this rebellion." To Kittoe the answer was obvious: "The iron gauntlet must be used more than the silken glove to crush this serpent."[35]

Dispatching detachments back and forth across a "dreary and desolated country" to stomp out guerrilla raids took up much of Grant's time. So did the feisty behavior of hostile citizens who, chafing under occupation, irritated and infuriated Union commanders more than did the greycoats. As Grant struggled to solve these problems during a time he later characterized as "the most anxious period of the war," he began to reassess his beliefs about how to conduct military operations. Perhaps it was time to stop worrying about conciliating a people who seemed irrepressible and unwilling to be conciliated, who remained so defiantly loyal to the Confederacy that they cheered on guerrilla operations. It was the restive populace and the guerrillas, not Shiloh, that toughened Grant to the notion of hard war. Southern resistance had escalated beyond conventional bounds.[36]

Once persuaded of the intensity and vibrancy of the enemy's resistance, Grant abandoned limited war with surprising speed and decisiveness. On July 1, he ordered the Memphis *Avalanche* to shut down after the paper had complained about the behavior of Union soldiers. Within days a Unionist paper, the *Bulletin*, replaced it. He countered guerrilla activities by levying assessments on the property of Confederate sympathizers to compensate for property losses sustained by his army. In addition, captured guerrillas would not be treated as prisoners of war, leaving open the possibility of execution. One Mississippian protested Grant's "infamous and fiendish proclamation . . . characteristic of your infernal policy. . . . Henceforth our motto shall be, Blood for blood, and blood for property." Tired of dealing with secessionists in Memphis, Grant ejected families of Confederate officers and officeholders. Although the order was later modified to allow such families to remain in the city upon taking a pledge not to aid Rebel operations, it outraged Confederate general Jeff Thompson, who promised revenge. In contrast, a local Unionist applauded the order: "I would suggest that all persons who *uphold*, and *preach* Secession in our midst be required to 'skedaddle' to the land of '*secession*.'"[37]

The struggle against infiltrating guerrillas intensified throughout the summer, as civilians flocked "to join the Guerrillas on their approach." Once desirous of fostering friendship, Grant was now "decidedly in favor of turning all discontented citizens within our lines out South." He reported to Halleck that "many citizens who appear to be quiet non combattants in the presence of our forces are regularly enrolled and avail themselvs of every safe opportunity of depridating upon Union men and annoying our troops." Those who would readily pledge loyalty cowered under the threat of retaliation, a very real possibility so long as Union commanders could not secure their lines. Such behavior eroded Grant's faith in a rapid end to the conflict.[38]

Grant's actions during these early July weeks stand in stark contrast to the policy proposed by McClellan, licking his wounds in the aftermath of the Seven Days Battles in Virginia. Concerned by the news that Pope, a believer in waging earnest war, had been given command of a new army assembled outside Washington, McClellan—the commander of the Army of the Potomac—urged restraint. "Neither confiscation of property, political executions of persons, territorial organization of states or forcible abolition of slavery should be contemplated for a moment," he told Lincoln. Rather, "all private property and unarmed persons should be strictly protected" and soldiers "should not be allowed to interfere with the relations of servitude." But he was out of step with the times. Congress already was debating additional confiscation legislation touching the status of slaves owned by Confederates, and Lincoln, having warned border state congressmen in vain that slavery "will be extinguished by mere friction and abrasion—by the mere incidents of war," was drafting a proclamation of emancipation. Grant was coming to accept these measures as necessary to winning the war.[39]

The scope of the war expanded as Grant conducted operations along the Tennessee-Mississippi border. At Memphis, post commander

William T. Sherman spent his time "fighting off cavalry detachments coming from the south, and waging an everlasting quarrel with planters about their negroes and fences." He told Grant, "All the people are now guerrillas." Frustrated, he predicted that "the war will soon assume a turn to extermination, not of soldiers alone, that is the least part of the trouble, but the people." Sherman was willing to meet the challenge. He ordered the burning of Randolph, Mississippi, after Confederate irregulars there had fired on unarmed steamboats.[40]

Handling the flow of refugees proved an ever-increasing burden. As Grant's brigades probed southward, blacks continued to flood into Union lines. Their sheer numbers negated any further attempts at exclusion. If whites were "sullen" at the sight of the bluecoats, Kittoe told Washburne, "the darkies seemed joyous at our presence." Grant's soldiers realized that their mere presence destroyed slavery. "Where the army of the Union goes, *there slavery ceases forever*," wrote a Wisconsin captain. "It is astonishing how soon the blacks have learned this, and they are flocking in considerable numbers already in our lines." Another officer observed, "All that came within our lines were received and put to work and supplied with clothing and subsistence. This policy was viewed by the soldiers with very general approbation."[41]

Grant moved slowly at first in responding to these new circumstances. He put blacks to work fortifying Memphis from Confederate attack, much as he had used blacks at Fort Donelson. But he remained unsure of his responsibilities in other cases. Rather than invite more criticism by acting on his own, he asked for instructions. After arresting Confederate sympathizer Francis Whitfield on July 17, 1862, Grant had to decide what to do with Whitfield's slaves, who, since they were women and children, could not be used on fortifications. Whitfield wanted the slaves sent south to relatives. Grant, preoccupied with enemy movements, asked Halleck what to do. The newly appointed general-in-chief responded that, if Grant had no use for or reason to detain the slaves, he should "let them go when they please."[42]

Halleck could have been more helpful to the befuddled Grant. On the day of Whitfield's arrest, Congress passed a second confiscation act, declaring free those slaves, owned by Confederate sympathizers, who escaped to Union lines, were captured, or were abandoned. Certainly Halleck should have been aware of this legislation, but he failed to pass policy directives down to his subordinates. Promulgation of a policy did not necessarily guarantee its immediate implementation and enforcement. Grant was not officially informed of the contents of the act for several weeks, although news of its passage quickly made its way to his command. Halleck finally instructed him to "clean out West Tennessee and North Mississippi of all organized enemies," eject civilian sympathizers, and confiscate Rebel property. "It is time that they should begin to feel the presence of war."[43]

Grant responded enthusiastically to these new guidelines. He cracked down on the activities of Confederate sympathizers and guerrillas, following Halleck's advice to "handle that class without gloves." As Sherman put it to Secretary of the Treasury Salmon P. Chase, "The Government of the United States may now safely proceed on the proper rule that all in the South are enemies of all in the North, and not only are they unfriendly, but all who can procure arms now bear them as organized regiments or as guerrillas." Grant also took steps to close down trade with the enemy, especially cotton speculators. To Chase he declared that such trade profited only "greedy" speculators and the enemy, failed to "abate [the] rancorous hostility" of Rebels, and hurt the war effort. Doubtless Grant's toughness was due to his realization that the war had taken on a new character, but he was also frustrated with his present task of holding territory while hunting down guerrillas. If he could not attack the South in battle, he would find another way to strike back.[44]

Washburne apprised Grant of the new attitudes in Washington. "This matter of guarding rebel property, of protecting secessionists and of enforcing 'order No. 3' is 'played out' in public estimation. Your order in regard to the secessionists of Memphis taking the oath or leaving" had been praised as an example of "vigorous and decided action on your part. . . . The administration has come up to what the people have long demanded—a vigorous prosecution of the war by all the means known to civilized warfare." He continued, "The negroes must now be made our auxiliaries in every possible way they can be, whether by working or fighting." He hinted that the general "who takes the most decided step in this respect will be held in the highest estimation by the loyal and true men in the country."[45]

Grant shrewdly followed Washburne's advice, freed of the responsibilities of playing slave catcher. "I have no hobby of my own with regard to the negro, either to effect his freedom or to continue his bondage," he told his father. "If Congress pass any law and the President approves, I am willing to execute it." Once his talk of duty had justified inaction; now it sanctified fighting a hard war. On August 11, his headquarters issued General Orders No. 72, establishing military guidelines to enforce the new confiscation legislation. Blacks would no longer be turned away: instead, they would be put to work. Two statements in the order, however, reflected Grant's caution as to the scope of the legislation. Unemployed blacks were still excluded from the lines, and soldiers were "positively prohibited from enticing Slaves to leave their masters."[46]

Many of Grant's soldiers were elated with the order. One Wisconsin private recorded the arrival of two fugitives who wanted to go to work for the North. They were followed within days by their master, demanding the return of his property. "We would give him just five minutes to leave camp. . . . We had the pleasure of booting him out. . . . To tell the truth we are just getting into the spirit of the war." The blacks rejoiced as well. Two days after the appearance of General Orders No. 72, the private made this prediction: "If the niggers come into camp for a week as fast as they have been coming for two days past we will soon have a waiter for every man in the Regt." Manning F. Force, commanding an Ohio regiment, was not nearly so extravagant in his hopes. He would be satisfied with forty refugees, "to do most of the working, digging, and chopping of the men."[47]

Other bluecoats were not so ecstatic, including Sherman, still commanding at Memphis. Within days of the issuance of Grant's directive, Sherman complained that although he knew Congress had passed legislation bearing on fugitive slaves he had not received any direct orders. "Masters and Mistresses so thronged my tent as to absorb my whole time, and necessity compelled me to adopt some clearly defined Rules." The next month he castigated his brother, Senator John Sherman, for causing more mischief. The beleaguered commander pointed out that while "you or Congress may command 'slaves shall be free,' . . . to make them free and see that they are not converted into thieves, idlers or worse is a difficult problem. . . . Where are they to get work? Who is to feed them, clothe them, and house them?"[48]

Grant was pleased with the new policy. "The war is evidently growing oppressive to the Southern people," he told his sister. "Their *institution*[s] are beginning to have ideas of their own and every time an expedition goes out more or less of them follow in the wake of the army and come to camp." He employed them as teamsters, cooks, and hospital attendants, but there was not enough work for all. "I don't know what is to become of these poor people in the end but it [is] weak[e]ning the enemy to take them from them."[49]

With the approach of fall, the refugee problem assumed serious dimensions. Grant's soldiers, busy repelling Confederate offensives near Corinth, found the flood of fugitives obstructing movements and causing health problems. Blacks came by the hundreds each night, "bearing their bundles on their heads and their pickaninnies under their arms." Chaplain John Eaton of the Twenty-seventh Ohio recalled that the influx of refugees resembled "the oncoming of cities": once in camp, the bedraggled blacks produced "a veritable moral chaos." There were clothing and transportation shortages. Sherman complained that "to take along and feed the negroes who flee to us for refuge," would bog down military movements. "A perfect stampede of contrabands" confronted William S. Rosecrans, who was preparing to advance against enemy positions. Rosecrans, sending the escaped slaves behind his lines to shield them from guerrillas, wondered, "But when a burden what shall be done with them then[?]"[50]

At first Grant tried to make use of the refugees. He put the men to work in the Corinth fortifications and sent the women and children to campsites east of Corinth. Some people in Chicago thought they would make excellent servants, a practice the government permitted for nearly a month, until it came under fire by electioneering Democrats pandering to racism in the Midwest. Grant then responded to the challenge by establishing refugee camps, letting blacks bring in the cotton and corn crop under his supervision. Blacks would live off the land, earn wages, and strive toward providing for themselves. Plantation owners who had remained on their property could employ the blacks at the same fixed rates paid by the government. All this would happen under the supervision of Union authorities, for Grant did not believe that blacks fresh from slavery were prepared to take on the responsibilities of freedom immediately. Rather, he sought to provide all blacks, not just able-bodied males, with some means of making the transition under the guardianship of the army.[51]

Although Grant showed no signs of having studied previous attempts to handle the refugee problem, his proposal bore some resemblance to them. In Virginia, South Carolina, and Louisiana, commanders concerned primarily with preserving order in a war zone had established programs to put blacks to work on plantations run by whites—in several cases for wages. Grant's concern about the condition and future of blacks more closely resembled that exhibited by some of the sponsors of the experiments on the Sea Islands in South Carolina and in other communities supervised by the American Missionary Association. These efforts at providing a transition between slavery and freedom were temporary expedients. It is difficult to see how Union officers could have promoted social revolution, land redistribution, and the like while waging war against a determined opponent.[52]

Grant placed Chaplain Eaton in charge of his program. Eaton was stunned when he heard about his new job. Never enamored with military brass and already holding enough responsibilities as regimental chaplain, he rode to Grant's headquarters determined to evade his new duty. The general quietly greeted him: "Oh, you are the man who has all these darkies on his shoulders." Then he set forth his ideas on the refugee problem. Congress had done little to assist the military in carrying out legislation concerning blacks, leaving it to the men in the field to offer solutions. Military necessity and "the dictates of mere humanity," as Eaton put it, had compelled Grant to act.

Eaton was impressed with Grant's proposal. The general had obviously done some thinking. The chaplain became even more intrigued as Grant went on to place his plan in broader perspective. Many whites believed that blacks would not work of their own free will. Grant disagreed. He knew that the blacks who had helped him work his Missouri farm were hard workers. Once blacks assisting the military and working on the plantations had proved that they were responsible and dispelled racist stereotypes, whites might accept the idea of blacks enlisting in the Union army. Once blacks had fought for their freedom and demonstrated again that they were responsible and hard-working, whites could begin to entertain the idea of granting citizenship, even the ballot, to them. "Never before in those early and bewildering days had I heard the problem of the future of the Negro attacked so vigorously and with such humanity combined with practical good sense," Eaton recalled.[53]

The plan reflected Grant's belief that, to achieve racial equality, white racism had to be overcome. He cared little for the rhetoric of abolitionists, arguing that racial prejudice was best countered and conquered by actual demonstrations of its falsehood. A believer in orderly change, Grant provided a plan for a controlled transition between slavery and freedom. Black slaves were simply not prepared or able to assume their position as freedmen immediately. Furthermore, in many instances their desire to exercise their freedom through rest, travel, and other activities merely confirmed white stereotypes of them as lazy and idle. Of course, the plan also provided a solution to the problems of conducting military operations while absorbing refugees. It disposed of a potential disaster and preserved order in a war zone. If it had hints of paternalism, it promised relief from the disease-ridden conditions currently confronting the freedmen, held out the prospect of progressive change, and rejected racist assumptions as it sought to disabuse them in the minds of others.

Grant took an active interest in Eaton's progress, ordering supplies and assistance whenever needed and making sure that his subordinates followed suit. This proved necessary. One newspaper correspondent recalled, "The people laughed at the experiment, and prophesied speedy and complete failure." For every soldier who encouraged the experiment, others scoffed at it. A soldier stationed at Grand Junction wrote home that the contraband that his company had commandeered "to help do the dirty work" was "mighty little help. . . . Niggers are mighty poor help as soon as they find out that they are as free as [whites]." He hoped that the war would end before the Emancipation Proclamation went into effect on New Year's Day, 1863, "in order to keep the Niggers where they belong which is in Slavery." Eaton found it difficult to find assistants, especially men "who could be kind to the Negro and just to the Negro's master"—a comment that reveals Eaton's own perspective.[54]

Perhaps the most notable aspect of Grant's solution to the refugee problem was that, for once, he acted without asking his superiors for advice. Not until four days after he had appointed Eaton did Grant tell Halleck what he was doing and ask for instructions. Halleck, too busy to be bothered by these problems, approved of Grant's policy, although he had only a vague idea of what it was.[55]

In fact, the Lincoln administration seemed more interested in taking steps that would halt Grant's plans in their tracks. On September 22, 1862, Lincoln had made public a preliminary version of the Emancipation Proclamation, promising that he would put it into force on January 1, 1863. Now he sought to take advantage of those remaining hundred days to encourage Tennesseans to reenter the Union on their own, holding out the prospect that if the Volunteer State returned to the fold it could do so with slavery intact (the proclamation applied only to areas under Confederate control). On October 21, 1862, Lincoln informed Grant and military governor Andrew Johnson of his plan, directing them to hold elections for Congress wherever they could do so. "Follow law, and forms of law as far as convenient; but at all events get the expression of the largest number of the people possible." The president hoped that Tennesseans would rejoin the Union "to avoid the unsatisfactory prospect before them."[56]

Grant, who once had held high hopes for the prospect of a speedy reunion, had by now abandoned such notions. Unionist speakers had been mobbed; the actions of Memphis's residents struck a telling blow against stories of latent Unionism. Now came reports that guerrilla bands were firing on unarmed Union steamers carrying civilians. In retaliation, Grant expelled secessionist families. Alleviating the suffering of homeless and hungry families gave him another opportunity to crack down on guerrilla activities. Convinced that those "not actively engaged in rebellion should not be allowed to suffer" amidst plenty, Grant decided that "the burden of furnishing the necessary relief . . . should fall on those, who, by act, encouragement or sympathy have caused the want now experienced." His soldiers agreed. They were tired of guarding secessionist property: one private wrote that it made his regiment "squirm like a Sarpent." He concluded that there were "few if any Union men" in the area. Another veteran later remarked that the troops complained that "they did not go South to protect Confederate property."[57]

Nevertheless, Grant was not one to question presidential policy. On December 9, 1862, he issued a proclamation to the people of West Tennessee, calling on them to hold elections for Congress. All "legal voters" as of 1860 were permitted to participate in the balloting, which would take place on Christmas Eve. Grant was more impressed with the sentiments displayed by Mississippians, who "show more signs of being subdued than any we have heretofore come across." A reporter noted that many Mississippians wanted to reenter the Union, "at whatever cost," before Lincoln's proclamation came into play.[58]

Confederate forces under Nathan Bedford Forrest and Earl Van Dorn had no intention of allowing the election to proceed. They launched an offensive that not only disrupted Grant's attempt to take Vicksburg, Mississippi, but also made it impossible to hold elections. Despite later efforts to hold elections, the scheme failed. Grant was too busy conducting military operations to take much notice of it. It was a question of priorities. Attempts at reconstruction were futile until military operations rendered the area secure. With that in mind, Grant turned his attention toward Vicksburg.

2

WAR IN

EARNEST

As 1862 gave way to 1863, Grant seemed stumped by the problem of taking Vicksburg. Sherman, stung by criticism of his repulse at Chickasaw Bluffs, urged him to withdraw to Memphis and reassess the situation. Grant disagreed, reminding Sherman of the political consequences of such a move. The Lincoln administration had suffered serious setbacks in the fall elections, especially in the Midwest. To retreat now would merely confirm charges that the war was a failure. Better, Grant argued, to accept the present situation and move on. Besides, as Sherman knew, neither he nor Grant could afford another serious repulse, for John A. McClernand was eagerly waiting to press his claims to command; some observers believed that the administration was considering just such a change. Withdrawal risked removal.[1]

So the Army of the Tennessee embarked on its most frustrating period of the war, spread out from the Tennessee-Mississippi border to the Louisiana swamps west of Vicksburg, harassed from all sides. Guerrillas proved as tough as cockroaches to stomp out. As the new year started, a frustrated Grant directed Gen. Stephen A. Hurlbut, commanding at Memphis, to transfer ten secessionist families to Confederate lines in retaliation for every enemy raid. But guerrillas were only one of the problems disrupting Grant's control of his own lines. Despite John Eaton's endeavors, the flood of refugees threatened to overwhelm Union camps. Grant sought Henry W. Halleck's guidance. 35

"Contraband question becoming serious one," he telegraphed the general-in-chief. "What will I do with surplus negroes?" One Ohio philanthropist, he reported, was willing to escort the blacks north. Once again, the proposal was abandoned as "impolitic" because it aroused the racist fears of Northern whites. Grant would have to find a place for the blacks in the South.[2]

Grant glimpsed one possible solution as he shifted his forces to the west bank of the Mississippi River opposite Vicksburg. It had long been a favorite belief of Union commanders that if the course of the river was diverted through the construction of a canal Vicksburg, stripped of its western water barrier, would be rendered vulnerable. Grant, although somewhat skeptical, was willing to try the idea himself, in part because he learned that Lincoln was intrigued by it. It made sense to please the riverboatman-turned-president at a time when Grant's political as well as military position was shaky. It would occupy his men and he could put the blacks to work. "Collect as many able bodied negro men as you can conveniently carry on your transports," he instructed a colonel, "and send them here to be employed on the canal." Even though using black laborers lessened the burden of digging trenches in the dirty swamps for white troops, Grant worried about their welfare, requesting Eaton "to make a careful observation of the conditions provided for the comfort of the Negroes engaged on the work."[3]

Yet this step was at best a stopgap measure; nothing seemed to stop the stampede of refugees. Their presence obstructed military movements and disrupted camps. On February 12, 1863, Grant ordered his soldiers to stop "enticing" blacks to enter Union camps; the freedmen should remain on their plantations and work out a labor arrangement with the planters, as suggested by the Emancipation Proclamation. He asked Washington for instructions on how to handle contrabands and explained the reasoning behind his order to Halleck. "Humanity dictates this policy. Planters have mostly deserted their plantations taking with them all their able bodied negroes and leaving the old and very young. Here they could not have shelter nor assurances of transportation when we leave." The army was simply not equipped materially or mentally to take on any more freedmen. As Grant told corps commander James B. McPherson, "the question is a troublesome one. I am not permitted to send them out of the Department, and such numbers as we have it is hard to keep them in."[4]

Antislavery advocates seized upon Grant's order as another sign of the army's insensitivity to blacks. A colonel informed Illinois senator Lyman Trumbull that there was not "one single leading Republican" among Grant's generals. At least one of Grant's subordinates lost a chance for promotion due to rumors that he was returning slaves to their masters. Chicago *Tribune* editor Joseph Medill, furious at Grant's decision to rescind a subordinate's order banning distribution of the pro-Democratic Chicago *Times*, told Elihu B. Washburne that "this dirty act . . . shows the real sentiments of Grant. He stands confessed as a copperhead and openly encourages the dissemination of secession and treason in his army." As Grant struggled through the swamps west of Vicksburg, all he needed to complete the case for his removal were stories that he was reenslaving black refugees and that he embraced treasonous newspapers.[5]

As winter turned to spring, Grant remained bogged down. Unusually high water levels obstructed the movements of his command, the canal projects collapsed due to flooding, and several offensive thrusts at Vicksburg failed. He had to struggle with cotton traders, newspaper correspondents, and personal illness. Sherman again urged him to abandon his position, return to Memphis, and launch another overland offensive. Grant demurred: he did not want to retreat now, and perhaps he knew that his military reputation could not afford it. Even as he planned his spring campaign, he could imagine Northern newspapers predicting disaster and naming replacements, and, as if to prove him right, the War Department soon sent down two observers—Charles A. Dana and Adj. Gen. Lorenzo Thomas—to find out what was going on.[6]

Dana, a former correspondent for Horace Greeley's New York *Tribune*, had been working at the War Department for a year when Edwin M. Stanton ordered him to visit Grant's headquarters. He had met Grant several times before on other missions for the government, but this one was different. Everyone knew that he was coming to dig up dirt. Deftly, Grant and his staff officers transformed a threat into an opportunity. John A. Rawlins, now Grant's chief of staff, and the inspector general, James H. Wilson, took the visitor in hand, making him feel welcome. Grant received Dana warmly and shared with him the details of his plan to take Vicksburg. Thus flattered, Dana became the staunch supporter of the commander of the Army of the Tennessee, and his dispatches to Stanton served as a shield against political criticism of the general. Not only did he befriend Grant, but also he came to share the general's suspicions about the military abilities of McClernand, whom Grant understood to be "an especial favorite of the President." Dana's reports, praising Grant and denouncing McClernand, helped to erode the latter's status at Washington. When Grant relieved McClernand from command several months later, Lincoln decided not to intervene.[7]

While Dana reported to Washington about Grant's military operations and the performance and political leanings of his generals, Thomas intended to inspect the condition of the contrabands with an eye to putting some of them to use—as soldiers. Stanton instructed Thomas to explain to Grant "the importance attached by the Government to the use of the colored population emancipated by the president's proclamation, and particularly for the organization of their labor and military strength." In the wake of the Emancipation Proclamation, the administration had decided to make war in earnest. Lincoln went so far as to claim that "the bare sight of 50,000 armed and drilled black soldiers upon the banks of the Mississippi would end the rebellion at once."[8]

Halleck—whose General Orders No. 3 in 1861 had epitomized the conservative approach toward blacks—alerted Grant to the new approach. "It is the policy of the government to withdraw from the enemy as much productive labor as possible. . . . Every slave withdrawn from the enemy, is equivalent to a white man put *hors de combat*." So far, so good, to Grant's way of thinking. But Halleck added that the government planned "to use the negroes of the South so far as practicable as a military force for the defence of forts, depots, &c." Those who "have examined the question without passion or prejudice" believed blacks could fight. These decisions probably did not surprise Grant, but Halleck's lecturing tone probably did, for the general-in-chief preached with the passion of the recently converted.[9]

Halleck then told Grant that reports had reached the War Department "that many of the officers of your command not only discourage the negroes from coming under our protection, but, by ill-treatment, force them to return to their masters." Obviously, Grant's exclusion order had not gone over well with the top brass. "This is not only bad policy in itself," Halleck continued, "but is directly opposed to the policy adopted by the government." Then the general-in-chief turned one of Grant's favorite themes on him. "Whatever may be the individual opinion of an officer in regard to the wisdom of measures adopted and announced by the government, it is the duty of every one to cheerfully and honestly endeavour to carry out the measures so adopted." Halleck directed Grant to "use your official and personal influence to remove prejudices on this subject, and to fully and thoroughly carry out the policy now adopted and ordered by the government." [10]

The new policy reflected new assumptions about the nature of the conflict. "The character of the war has very much changed within the last year," Halleck explained. "There is now no possible hope of a reconciliation with the rebels. The union party in the south is virtually destroyed. There can be no peace but that which is enforced by the sword. We must conquer the rebels, or be conquered by them." This was no news to Grant, after his tenure in West Tennessee. At last the administration had reached the same conclusion. Halleck, who in the past had been curt and unfair to Grant, had been softened by his Washington experience. Skeptical of politicians, he wanted to do what he could to keep Grant out of trouble by warning him of the new direction in policy. He closed by assuring Grant that he was writing "simply as a personal friend, and as a matter of friendly advice," which was true enough, since Thomas would be sure to note if Grant and his army did not toe the line. [11]

Grant took the hint and prepared for Thomas's arrival. To Gen. Frederick Steele, off with a division on detached duty upriver at Greenville, Mississippi, he wrote: "Rebellion has assumed that shape now that it can only terminate by the complete subjugation of the South or the overthrow of the Government." He instructed Steele to provide for the refugees already in his lines, and to "encourage all negroes, particularly middle aged males to come within our lines," with an eye toward recruiting them. Then everyone sat back to watch Thomas go to work. [12]

Grant's division commanders called their troops out on the parade ground to hear Thomas. John A. Logan's boys, with boots and rifle barrels polished for the occasion, formed in close columns surrounding an open spot where a wagon served the purpose of a speaker's platform. Someone introduced Thomas, and the "old grey haired roman nosed patriot," as one soldier described him, began to speak, explaining the government's decision to raise black regiments. The speech itself stirred little excitement, although Sherman later claimed that Thomas's assertion that he could remove anyone who opposed black enlistment was meant for him. Reports soon filtered back to Washington that Grant's generals complained about Thomas's "bad speeches." Some ears perked at the news that soldiers could apply for commissions in the black regiments. "I do not hesitate to say that all proper persons will receive commissions," the adjutant general promised. "I don't care who they are or what their present rank may be." [13]

Thomas concluded with the usual patriotic peroration, then yielded the floor to the division or corps commander. Remarks coming from someone familiar to the troops often proved more important than Thomas's address in shaping soldier reaction. Logan, for example, delivered the kind of inspiring speech that had won him renown. John McArthur told his troops that "he would always show more alacrity, in the cause when it was in consonance with his own feelings; and such he felt to be the case now." McPherson promised to muster out any officer who disagreed with enlisting blacks—but only after that officer stepped forward during formation, in front of his peers. Others proved less helpful. Sherman's lukewarm endorsement of the new policy made it clear that he was no abolitionist: "I of course always tell the soldiers we are likened to a sheriff that must execute the [law] of the Court & not go into an inquiry into the merits of the case." Thomas, pleased with Grant's support for the program, reported that "the commanding officers are perfectly willing and ready to afford every aid in carrying it out to a successful issue," quelling whatever suspicion lingered in Washington about the enthusiasm with which Grant and his generals endorsed administration policy. [14]

The reaction of the soldiers was mixed. "Great excitement in the 3rd Division over the Negro soldier question," one soldier confided to his diary. Several soldiers denounced the move; others welcomed it, albeit for diverse reasons. Many advocates of black enlistment saw not only an opportunity for blacks but also an opportunity for themselves as officers in the new regiments. "The pleasing feature is to see men who have bitterly denounced the policy of arming negroes and denounced the men who would be an officer over them bending every energy to get a commission," the diarist scribbled. "Oh consistency thou art indeed a jewel and scarcely to be found." [15]

While Thomas proceeded with his mission, Grant embarked on yet another campaign against Vicksburg. This time he was not to be denied. Crossing the Mississippi twenty-five miles downriver from the city, within three weeks Grant's army won five battles, destroyed several factories at Jackson, and laid siege to Vicksburg in one of the most brilliant campaigns of the war. As Grant's columns moved across Mississippi, some blacks swarmed into the lines while others cheered, celebrating freedom by kicking their feet in the air and rolling in the grass. But blacks also proved that they were willing to take a hand in their own emancipation. During the siege, Grant received news that the black recruits had engaged in their first battle at Milliken's Bend, some twenty miles upriver from Vicksburg. At first giving way, the blacks launched a vicious counterattack, spurred on in part by reports that Confederates were murdering blacks taken prisoner in the initial assault. Milliken's Bend proved blacks could fight; many white skeptics of black enlistment were won over when they heard accounts of the clash. Grant endorsed the report of the Union commander at the battle with the comment that although the soldiers "had but little experience in the use of fire arms" they had been "most gallant and I doubt not but with good officers they will make good troops." [16]

But, in the aftermath of the battle, stories began to surface that the Confederates had executed captured black soldiers. Adm. David D. Porter mentioned the rumors in his first report of the action, saying that the blacks turned on their opponents and "slaughtered them like sheep" when they heard the news. Less than two weeks later, Porter forwarded another letter containing an account of the hanging of a white captain and several black enlisted men captured during the battle, as well as news that a white sergeant in command of a black company had met with the same fate. Until now, Grant was unsure whether such acts had official Confederate sanction or had been perpetrated by "irresponsible persons"; but the letter made clear that Confederate general Richard Taylor had approved the measures. In contrast, Confederates captured at Milliken's Bend, although fighting under the "black flag" (no quarter), had not been killed. Grant confronted Taylor. Were the Confederates initiating "a different line of policy towards Black troops and Officers commanding them to that practiced towards White troops? If so, I can assure you that these colored troops are regularly mustered into the service of the United States." Accordingly, all Union authorities "are bound to give the same protection to these troops that they do to any other troops." He closed by expressing the hope that it was all a mistake.[17]

Taylor denied the stories, telling Grant that he would investigate the matter and promising to punish the offenders. He pointed out, however, that all black prisoners would be turned over to state authorities in accordance with Confederate policy. On July 4, the day Union troops marched into Vicksburg (the garrison's commander, John C. Pemberton, had agreed to surrender the previous day), Grant responded. Although he accepted Taylor's denial, he expressed displeasure at Confederate policy toward black POWs, commenting, "I cannot see the justice of permitting one treatment for them, and another for the white soldiers. This however is a subject I am not aware of any action having been taken upon."[18]

Again, Grant had been badly served by Halleck. The government had indeed taken a stand in General Orders No. 100, drawn up by the legal theorist Francis Lieber and issued by the War Department on April 24. Somehow, Grant never received a copy or was unaware of three paragraphs, especially Section III, Paragraph 58, which ordered the execution of one enemy prisoner for each prisoner enslaved. Nor was Grant exercising a selective memory: even Dana, Stanton's representative on the scene, had heard the stories of what had happened at Milliken's Bend yet said nothing about retaliation. That the policy went unnoticed at first was underscored when Lincoln, because of this incident and a similar one at Fort Wagner, South Carolina, issued an executive order on July 30 that promised to retaliate in kind if Confederate officials mistreated black prisoners. Lincoln's order did modify the earlier policy in one respect. If black prisoners were reenslaved, Confederate prisoners would be put to hard labor.[19]

As the paroled Confederates marched out of Vicksburg, many officers assumed that they would be able to take their body servants home. Grant quickly put a stop to that practice. "I want the negroes all to understand that they are free men." Those choosing to accompany their masters "might benefit our cause by spreading disaffection among the negroes at a distance by telling [them] that the Yankees set them all free." There remained problems associated with contraband camps that had been overlooked during the campaign, most notably their poor sanitary conditions. At least a few officers thought that the resulting illness among the freedmen confirmed the old canard that blacks were incapable of survival outside of slavery. Grant complained about two of the commissioners appointed by Thomas to oversee the plantations, although he did not list specific charges. Only Capt. Abraham Strickle gained the general's approval for being "honest and enthusiastic in the cause which he is serving," despite what Grant termed Strickle's "old theories of abolishing slavery and elevating the negro." If Grant thought the situation was bad, it was already worse: he had not yet been informed that Strickle had just died of typhoid.[20]

Grant took steps to remedy these shortcomings and to restore stability. On August 10 he issued orders establishing freedmen's camps and outlining terms for their employment by local planters. All blacks had to be either employed on a plantation or housed at the camps. Two weeks later, he sought to stop blacks from wandering through his lines by instructing his soldiers to remove all blacks not "properly employed and controlled" by the army to the contraband camps. Any blacks still meandering about would be liable to be "pressed into service." So eager was Grant to bring order to his lines and foster loyalty that he even assisted Unionist planters in securing field hands, provided the planters promised to pay good wages.[21]

Prodded by Washington, Grant also looked into complaints made by loyal planters concerning the wrongful seizure of their black field hands. He reminded one post commander that in recruiting blacks for military service slaves who belonged "to persons of known loyalty" could be recruited only "when they come and offer themselves." One plantation, owned by the Duncan family, received much attention after plantation mistress Mary Duncan protested that her rights as a loyal Unionist were being trampled and that the blacks on her plantation were free and working for wages. Unknown to Grant and other authorities, some of the Duncan blacks did not share her perception of them as contented laborers. One captain in a black regiment "noticed a great dissatisfaction among the Colored people of said plantations" because "they were poorly cared for, overworked and had but little to eat." Far from being forced to serve in the army, the blacks seemed eager to escape the plantation. Word of the investigation worked its way back to Grant, who decided to take no action in response to Mrs. Duncan's plea. By the end of the month, in fact, he tended to overlook at least some instances of black resistance. To Halleck he explained "signs of negro insurrection" north of Vicksburg as "a case of retaliation" against local whites who reportedly had whipped and shot a few blacks.[22]

Grant also punished the mistreatment of black troops by his own men. "It was pitiable to see how little people cared, even our own soldiers, whether these poor negro troops died or lived," remembered one soldier. Another noted that some soldiers had "shot several Negroes. In fact they don't think anything of shooting *them* down." Grant moved to stop such behavior. He defended Col. Isaac F. Shepard, a Massachusetts abolitionist in charge of a black regiment, who had a white soldier whipped in retaliation for the abusive behavior directed at black soldiers by white troops. "I am satisfied that the whole difficulty arose from the outrageous treatment of the Black troops by some of the white ones," he told Lorenzo Thomas, blaming white officers who failed to discipline their men. Far from viewing the new recruits as a source of trouble, he was "anxious to get as many of these negro regiments as possible," particularly to garrison the lands now under occupation as the result of the fall of Vicksburg. Pleased, Thomas wired Washington that Grant gave him "every assistance in my work."[23]

Although black soldiers had proved their ability to fight at Milliken's Bend, Grant preferred to use them to guard Union supplies and posts. He eagerly urged his subordinates to gather up as many blacks as possible, although the freedmen also came of their own accord, prompting Admiral Porter to complain to Grant that his black workers "have most all run away to join the army." As soon as the blacks were issued uniforms, however, they discovered that most frequently they were hoisting not a rifle but a shovel over their shoulder. Grant stripped the Vicksburg fortifications of white soldiers, telling Halleck: "I do not want the White men to do any work that can possibly be avoided during the hot months." Since blacks, according to the time-worn stereotype, supposedly withstood heat and humidity better than whites, they were deemed ideal for this task. Moreover, to restrict blacks to garrison duty was to reduce the risk of a repetition of the execution of black POWs—something Lincoln had already considered. "The negro troops are easier to preserve discipline among than our White troops," Grant, pleased with his new recruits, remarked, "and I doubt not will prove equally good for garrison duty. All that have been tried have fought bravely."[24]

Lincoln watched Grant approvingly. The general had sent Eaton to Washington to describe Grant's program, doubtless in part to disabuse any lingering doubts about his commitment to emancipation. Stanton, admitting that he lacked a "well defined system" to address the issues arising out of emancipation and refugees, commended Grant for taking the matter into his own hands. The president remarked that Grant's solutions closely resembled some of his own notions about the problem presented by the freedmen. "Your management of them meets present exigencies without attempting to determine impossibilities," Eaton told his general.[25]

Grant made sure that the president knew that he was a staunch supporter of administration policy. Lincoln had expressed to him the hope that the use of black troops "will soon close the contest," since their use worked simultaneously toward "weakening the enemy & strengthening us." In reply, Grant reported that he was giving "the subject of arming black troops my hearty support." Echoing the president's enthusiasm, Grant asserted that the enlistment of blacks, "with the emancipation of the negro, is the heavyest blow yet given the Confederacy." Aware that the president, in light of past reports, might still have some doubts about his position, Grant explained that regardless of his personal feelings the enlistment of blacks "is an order that I am bound to obey and do not feel that in my position I have a right to question any policy of the Government." Having issued the traditional disclaimer, he went on to assure Lincoln that "in this particular instance there is no objection however to my expressing an honest conviction. That is, by arming the negro we have added a powerful ally. They will make good soldiers and taking them from the enemy weaken him in the same proportion they strengthen us." In fact, Grant was mounting expeditions into northern Louisiana and Mississippi to secure more recruits and planned to form a "Home Guard" of black troops, under Eaton's command, to protect freedmen working the plantations along the river. Lincoln was so pleased with the letter that he cited it to defend his decision to enlist blacks.[26]

Grant took other steps to protect his rear from political opponents. Eaton was not the only visitor from Vicksburg to Washington in the month following the surrender. Rawlins made the trip in late July. Navy secretary Gideon Welles noted that Grant had "sent him here for a purpose"—specifically, to defuse the complaints of Lincoln's favorite, McClernand, who had been busy protesting his removal from command during the siege. Dana also returned to Washington and spent much time circulating among members of Congress, Stanton, and Lincoln. He urged Grant to enlist more black troops to frustrate conservatives who wished to secure the readmission of Arkansas, Louisiana, and Mississippi "with the same leaders & the same slavery with which they went out." Massachusetts senator Henry Wilson, a leading Radical, told Washburne of Dana's assurances that Grant "is in favor of destroying the cause of this civil war—of overthrowing Slavery and that his army is deeply imbued with the same feeling." This last comment was not quite true; McClernand's successor, Edward O. C. Ord, told a sympathetic Sherman that he had been "a proslavery man" until the introduction of the Kansas-Nebraska Act, "and I am not quite such a radical man now as to think we can turn all those black people loose among the whites."[27]

Grant made clear his own views to Washburne. "The people of the North need not quarrel over the institution of Slavery. What Vice President Stevens acknowledges the corner stone of the Confederacy is already knocked out. Slavery is already dead and cannot be resurrected." To maintain slavery now "would take a standing Army." Then Grant reflected on the evolution of his personal views. "I never was an Abolitionest, [n]ot even what could be called anti slavery," he admitted, "but . . . it became patent to my mind early in the rebellion that the North & South could never live at peace with each other except as one nation, and that without Slavery." With that in mind, he did not want to see the war end "until this question is forever settled."[28]

Still "anxious" for peace despite his newfound advocacy of abolition, Grant after Vicksburg evaluated anew the chances for re-

construction. He instructed officers to make sure that soldiers refrained from making "offensive remarks" as Confederate prisoners
made their way home after the surrender. Such "consideration for
their feelings," Grant reasoned, "would make them less dangerous
foes during the continuance of hostilities, and better citizens after the
war was over." Many of the greycoats remembered that gratefully and
spoke "in the highest terms" of Grant's "kindness and humanity." Perhaps, in the aftermath of the North's twin victories at Gettysburg and
Vicksburg, despondent Confederates might seek an end to the war.[29]

The behavior of some white Mississippians in the weeks after Vicksburg's fall encouraged such hopes. Newspaper reporter Sylvanus Cadwallader noted that citizens visiting headquarters "expressed their
willingness to come into the Union again on any terms." Sherman, for
one, was convinced of their sincerity. "The people are subdued, and
ask for reconstruction," he informed Grant after running off Joseph E. Johnston's troops near Jackson. "They admit the loss of the
Southern cause." Sherman elaborated in a letter the next day. "All act
as though the thing was ended." Several Mississippians, he observed,
"are actually at work & appeal for permission to build up a civil
Govt. . . . I profess to know nothing of politics but I think we have
here an admirable wedge which may be encouraged. . . . If prominent men in Miss. admit the fact of being subdued it will have a powerful effect over the South." Not everyone agreed. Perhaps whites
were simply trying to make the best they could of the situation. Cadwallader did not see that their new willingness to reenter the Union
was accompanied by any change of heart. He had "not found one
citizen who could properly be termed a Union man. . . . All are intensely pro-slavery in feeling, and curse the Yankees for 'stealing their
niggers.'"[30]

Grant was open to the possibilities of reconstruction broached by
Sherman. Having endorsed the establishment of a pro-Union paper
in Memphis, he was willing to foster loyalty in Mississippi, noting that
"the people acknowledge themselves subjugated, the southern cause
lost, and are holding meetings to devise plans for coming back into
the Union." Encouraging this process, Grant called upon Mississippians to "pursue their peaceful avocations in obedience to the laws of
the United States." He told Sherman that the behavior of his bluecoats
could play an important role in reconciliation: "Impress upon the

men the importance of going through the State in an orderly manner, abstaining from taking anything not absolutely necessary for their subsistence whilst travelling." Soldiers "should try to create as favorable an impression as possible upon the people and advise them . . . to make efforts to have law and order established within the Union." These instructions were in marked contrast to Grant's policy in northern Mississippi and Tennessee in the fall of 1862. They highlighted his view of how to conduct a war with an eye to the postwar world. So long as he believed that Southerners were anxious for reunion, he was willing to be lenient in order to foster such sentiments. When the fighting got vicious and the citizens openly displayed their hostility, he advocated harsher measures.[31]

Sherman was more concerned about the behavior of the politicians than of his own soldiers. Before long, Halleck requested his views on reconstruction policy, arguing that Lincoln might listen to "the advice of our Generals who have been in these states and know much more of their condition than gassy politicians in Congress." Sherman was sympathetic to Halleck's perspective. He, too, was convinced that politicians had bumbled their way into war, as his reply made plain. Whatever faith he had in restoring civil government in Mississippi had vanished. Restoring civil government "would simply be ridiculous." Southern Unionists were so timid that they were "afraid of shadows." It was "the young bloods," the "most dangerous set of men that this war has turned loose upon the world," who worried him: they "must all be killed or employed by us before we can hope for peace." Instead of coddling Southerners, he wanted to "make them so sick of war" that they would not consider it for centuries to come. Grant's army was "the only government needed or deserved" by them. The best way to win the peace, Sherman concluded, was to win the war first. Politicians could not be trusted with such matters. "Agitators & theorists have got us into this scrape and only practical men and fighting men can extricate us."[32]

Sherman forwarded his reply to Grant, expressing his fear that the politicians would "hasten to quit long before the 'opposed' has received that lesson which he needs. . . . Now is the time for us to pile on our blows thick and fast." Grant passed the letter on to Halleck, commenting that he did not "fully coincide" with Sherman. He thought that reconstruction should commence fairly soon, and that the administration should take advantage of the "very fine feeling . . . towards the Union" in Louisiana and Mississippi.[33]

However, Grant was less pleased with other government policies that blurred the distinction between military and civil concerns. Most notable was his long-standing complaint about the Treasury Department's attempt to restore the cotton trade. In late 1862, frustrated with swarms of speculators around his camps, he issued the misconceived "Jew" order, in which he expelled all Jews "as a class" from his command. As phrased, the order was stupid and insensitive, as Grant later admitted. Most contemporaries, however, limited their rebuke to a suggestion that, had Grant added the word "peddlers" after "Jew," everything would have been fine. By 1863, Grant, dropping the religious distinction, attacked all cotton traders. Cadwallader recalled that the general "always spoke of them as thieves." Not only were they "more damaging than the small pox," as Grant once put it, but also they were trading with the enemy. Such transactions should be halted "until the rebellion in this part of the country is entirely crushed out." Despite repeated protests to Stanton and Salmon P. Chase, however, the trade continued. "The people in the Mississippi Valley are now nearly subjugated," Grant told the treasury secretary. "Keep trade out for but a few months and I doubt not but that the work of subjugation will be so complete" that trade could then be resumed without harm. His protests were ignored. But in making them Grant revealed that he felt confident enough about his position to offer civil authorities advice on policy.[34]

In part, Grant's frustration stemmed from his impatience to move on with the war. After the capture of Vicksburg, parts of his command were sent to East Tennessee and Louisiana. His own plans to attack Mobile were shelved by Halleck after Lincoln expressed a desire to invade Texas in order to counter France's intervention in Mexico. To add injury to insult, he was laid up after his horse had thrown him while he was at New Orleans conferring with Gen. Nathaniel P. Banks. Fortunately, William S. Rosecrans came to the rescue: he lost the battle of Chickamauga to Braxton Bragg and withdrew to Chattanooga, Tennessee. At the same time, Ambrose E. Burnside marched down to occupy Knoxville, Tennessee, only to find himself unable to do much more than hold the town itself. Few Northerners trusted Burnside in a pinch after his fiasco at Fredericksburg, and Rosecrans's flight from Chickamauga lost him the confidence of the administration; rumor had it that he would evacuate Chattanooga next. It was time for Grant to take over.[35]

The Union offensive into East Tennessee was the product of political as well as military strategy. Many of the people of East Tennessee were strong Unionists, and in 1861 the majority had opposed secession; Horace Porter, soon to join Grant's staff, had observed in the summer of 1863 that the area "is just as loyal as Pennsylvania." It had long been one of Lincoln's aims to regain this region. If the military governor, Andrew Johnson, was to establish firm control of the Volunteer State, he needed to regain East Tennessee. With possession of Knoxville and Chattanooga, moreover, the only rail links remaining between Virginia and the Carolinas and the rest of the Confederacy would run through Atlanta and Columbus, Georgia, and Chattanooga would provide an ideal position from which to launch an offensive against those cities.[36]

Grant understood the political importance of East Tennessee, especially when it came to protecting Unionists. On November 5, he sought to enhance the growth of loyalty in his command (now a military division encompassing several military departments between the eastern theater and the Mississippi) by issuing orders instructing commanders to demand compensation from secessionist families in retaliation for damage done to Unionists by Rebel raiders. Several weeks later, he routed Bragg at Chattanooga, and Confederate forces under James Longstreet, after suffering a repulse at Knoxville, retreated east rather than confront Sherman's advancing force. Tennessee had been saved. And Lincoln had found his general.[37]

In the aftermath of Chattanooga, Grant began to contemplate his next move. While he mapped out military operations, he kept an eye on other problems as well. Lincoln had outlined a plan for reconstruction in his December annual message. Sherman, never reluctant to express his political opinions, deemed such planning senseless. It would protract the war "by seeming to court peace"; the Southern states "will need a pure military govt for years after resistance has ceased."[38]

Grant kept his ideas to himself. His interest in the progress of emancipation continued. Greeley's New York *Tribune* said that among Lincoln's generals no one was more committed to emancipation and the enlistment of blacks; the abolitionist New York *Independent* asserted that Grant, once a "proslavery man," was now an "unconditional emancipationist." He assisted in efforts to establish black schools in middle Tennessee and encouraged the enlistment of more blacks. However, he balked when eager recruiters sometimes conscripted blacks already at work rebuilding railroads for the army. As a gesture toward reconciliation, he allowed planters who had taken the amnesty oath to hire black workers. To General Logan he pointed out that "we want to encourage cultivation of the soil." Even though he made no move toward land redistribution and did not reject the plantation as the primary unit of production, it did not necessarily follow that he thought blacks had to work for whites. He encouraged the management by blacks of the Davis Bend plantations, once owned by Jefferson Davis and his brother Joseph, hoping the area would "become a Negro paradise." Still, his main concern was order. He did not become involved in the debate over black labor in the Mississippi Valley. While Thomas envisioned the maintenance of plantations leased to Northerners, Eaton increasingly came to consider the possibility of a tentative redistribution of land to black laborers, allowing the freedmen to work as independent farmers. Both men resisted the attempts of the Treasury Department to manage plantations, charging that treasury agents were indifferent to the fate of the freedmen. As this debate developed, however, Grant's attention was drawn elsewhere.[39]

While Grant pondered future campaigns, others were proposing that the general's next move should be to assume command of all the Union armies—or more. On December 9 the New York *Herald* reported that some congressmen were considering reviving the rank of lieutenant general and bestowing it on Grant. Washburne had already given notice that he would introduce such a bill, and Stanton had dispatched Gen. David Hunter, an army officer with well-known abolitionist leanings, to Chattanooga to check out Grant one final time. Grant viewed the proposed promotion warily. Elevation to lieutenant general might mean a transfer to the eastern theater, where he would have to fight not just Confederates but also the politicians looking over his shoulder. He told Washburne that he did not "ask or feel that I deserve anything more in the shape of honors or promotion." But he did not reject it out of hand, for he believed that perhaps Sherman or William F. Smith, who had impressed Grant at Chattanooga, might take over the Army of the Potomac, leaving him out West.[40]

Some observers suggested that the bill was not simply a military measure. The *Herald* claimed that the bill's advocates hoped that "such a high military position will switch him off the Presidential track." The *Herald*'s editor, James Gordon Bennett, wanting Grant to stay on the track for the White House, began pushing the general's name as a possible presidential candidate. Grant, argued Bennett, was the "People's Candidate," above parties and politicians. The *Herald* proclaimed that the general was "the man who knows how to tan leather, politicians and the hides of rebels." Others had mentioned the prospect of a Grant candidacy as early as the fall of Vicksburg.[41]

Talk of the presidency seemed preposterous to Grant. His reply to an Ohio Democrat concerning the presidential contest revealed either modesty or disingenuousness. "The question astonishes me," he began. "Nothing likely to happen would pain me so much as to see my name used in connection with a political office. Let us succeed in crushing the rebellion, in the shortest possible time, and I will be content with whatever credit then may be given me, feeling assured that a just public will award all that is due." The last sentence could have been penned by George B. McClellan or Salmon P. Chase, two men anxious to take the presidential oath of office on March 4, 1865. But Grant's fears of political office seemed sincere. Gen. John M. Palmer came away from a talk with Grant convinced that he had no desire for the presidency, and Rawlins reassured Washburne that Grant was "unambitious of the honor."[42]

But talk about the general's candidacy inevitably jeopardized the plans to add a third star to Grant's shoulder straps. Charles Dana and former Grant staff officer James H. Wilson, on duty in Washington, worked to squelch stories of a possible presidential run. Washburne and fellow townsman J. Russell Jones, fearing that Grant might be tempted by presidential politics, warned him of its perils. Washburne reminded the general that Lincoln had "stood like a wall of fire" in protecting Grant from his detractors after Shiloh, while those now booming his name for president "were the most bitter" in denouncing him then. Jones warned, "As things now stand, you could get the nomination of the Democracy, but could not be elected as against Lincoln."[43]

Still, the clamor continued, with the *Herald* leading the way. Grant soon made it clear that if he could not avoid hearing the noise he would not listen to it. "I am not a politician, never was, and hope never to be," he assured former Congressman Isaac N. Morris. "In your letter you say that I have it in my power to be the next President! This is the last thing in the world I desire. I would regard such a consummation as being highly unfortunate for myself if not for the country." He was happy where he was. He told Daniel Ammen, a boyhood friend and now a navy captain, that politicians led a "slavish life"; Adm. David D. Porter commented that Grant "hates politics as the devel does holy water." Grant bluntly told his father not to meddle in the current controversy.[44]

These private communications were Grant's only response to the rumors. He refused to issue a public statement denying presidential ambitions, a decision endorsed by aide Adam Badeau. "I fancy the best possible thing for the Gen. to do is to preserve the most absolute silence," he told James H. Wilson. "He cant write a line that won't be tortured into what he don't mean, by some one. If he defines his position . . . it will be thought to be a negative bid or a modest way of asking." Rawlins took the same position. Silence would soon become one of Grant's featured traits when it came to his political future.[45]

But Grant knew that Abraham Lincoln was hearing the same rumors. He had to find a way to reassure the president that he meant what he said; Lincoln, aware of George B. McClellan's dabbling in Democratic presidential politics, would doubtlessly scotch any proposal to promote another potential political rival. When one of his former subordinates, newly elected Congressman Frank Blair, inquired as to Grant's intentions, the general replied, "Everyone who knows me knows I have no political aspirations either now or for the future." It was a subject "upon which I do not like to write, talk, or think"; he hated to see his name "associated with politics either as an aspirant for office or as a partizan." Yet Grant was no fool, either. He knew that Blair was asking out of more than mere curiosity. His brother was postmaster general and the Blairs were notorious Lincoln men. Thus, when he warned Blair to "show this letter to no one unless it be the president himself," it was an ill-disguised hint that Blair should share the letter with Lincoln.[46]

Grant also made his intentions known to the president through a letter to Jones. "Nothing could induce me to think of being a presidential candidate," he flatly stated, "particularly so long as there is a possibility of having Mr. Lincoln re-elected." Sure enough, this letter was finally read by the man for whose eyes it was intended. Lincoln thanked Jones, happy that "the Presidential grub" had not been "gnawing at Grant." Reassured, the rail-splitter decided to back the lieutenant generalcy bill, now that he knew he had the support of the man he intended to name to command all the Union armies.[47]

On March 9, 1864, Abraham Lincoln handed Ulysses S. Grant his commission as lieutenant general. The next day, Grant's position as general-in-chief was formalized by orders issued through the War Department. With the new position came new responsibilities and a new theater of action. Despite Sherman's earnest entreaties to remain in the West ("For God's sake and your country's sake come out of Washington," he begged), Grant decided to make his headquarters with the Army of the Potomac in northern Virginia. The new lieutenant general believed that he could entrust Sherman with command in the West, and, in light of the record of Union commanders south of the Potomac River, he thought that perhaps he had better stay in Virginia to make sure that the easterners did not slip up again. Grant also understood, although he did not share, the awe in which the easterners beheld their opponent, Robert E. Lee. The country demanded a clash of titans; if Grant could at least nullify Lee, Sherman would take care of the rest.[48]

One of the myths of the American Civil War is that Lincoln gave Grant a free hand in planning and conducting his offensives in 1864 and 1865. Indeed, Grant, in his *Personal Memoirs*, contributed to the creation of that myth, relating accounts of his discussions with Lincoln in which the president openly avowed his disinclination to interfere. However, Lincoln did interject at certain points; moreover, political considerations often outweighed military ones. Before he came to Washington, Grant had outlined several plans of action for 1864, most notably a two-pronged offensive from Chattanooga and Mobile against Atlanta and an invasion of North Carolina from southeast Virginia, ripping up rail lines and forcing Lee to abandon Virginia or find himself isolated. As he told Halleck, the North Carolina offensive had political aims as well. Union armies would live off the land, bringing the war to the Southern people; North Carolina troops would rush to the defense of their home state or desert to return home, weakening Lee's army; and the offensive would liberate slaves in the Tar Heel State. Perhaps the presence of Union troops would fuel North Carolina's growing peace movement.[49]

Grant's plan was bold, imaginative, and achievable. It took a broad view of the eastern theater, going beyond the traditional twin concerns of Lee and Richmond. It nullified Lee's advantageous position in Virginia, where several rivers provided natural lines of defense for the Confederates. It would have promised a war of maneuver, not attrition, as Union armies repeated the Vicksburg concept in dividing the Confederacy into increasingly smaller segments. By March 1864, the North certainly had enough manpower to undertake the grand design. Perhaps the only military reservation was that Grant might have some difficulty making sure that the eastern forces would be headed by generals as capable as Sherman or McPherson.[50]

Political and psychological conditions thwarted Grant's plan, forcing him to settle for something less dramatic. Lincoln and Halleck still viewed the eastern theater in terms of Robert E. Lee, Richmond, and Washington. To them, the main objectives of the Army of the Potomac were to defeat Lee, capture Richmond, and protect Washington. They would take no chances against the Confederate leader and feared that the manpower required for Grant's North Carolina offensive, which would reduce the Army of the Potomac to mere parity with the Army of Northern Virginia, was too risky. Also, political considerations demanded that two generals with undistinguished combat records—Franz Sigel, an idol to many German immigrants, and the Democrat-turned-Republican Benjamin F. Butler—hold commands in the East, forcing Grant to find a place for them.[51]

Similar circumstances reduced Grant's planned Mobile-Chattanooga offensive to a single drive from Chattanooga to Atlanta. Lincoln wanted Banks, another political general of mediocre ability, to head an advance across Louisiana to secure the state for the Union and to threaten Texas. Supposedly Banks would scare the French in Mexico, enhance Louisiana's efforts at reconstruction under Lincoln's supervision, and capture thousands of bales of cotton to boot—and only then, with this accomplished, would he turn to Mobile. As James H. Wilson reported, "There is a somewhat feverish anxiety on the part of the Government to bring back or reorganize the state governments in the conquered territory with as little delay as possible." Banks got 10,000 of Sherman's veterans to enlarge his force for the venture. Grant, disgusted, urged that if the expedition were to take place Sherman head it. Failing that, he wanted "to have some one near Banks who can issue orders to him and see that they are obeyed." His reservations proved warranted: the Massachusetts politician bungled the whole operation, achieving nothing while wasting manpower and time. "I have been satisfied for the last nine months that to keep General Banks in command was to neutralize a large force and to support it most expensively," Grant growled upon receiving the news.[52]

Finding his hands tied by Lincoln, Grant decided to work within the constraints imposed upon him. He developed a simple plan that depended on utilizing the North's superiority in men and material through coordinated offensives designed to squeeze the life out of the Confederacy. Sherman was to defeat Joseph E. Johnston and take Atlanta while Meade, Butler, and Sigel, under Grant's supervision, would drive Lee back to Richmond, if not defeat him outright, pinning the Confederate commander against his capital. Immediate success on the battlefield was essential to inspire a war-weary North. Indeed, the campaign had to score some major successes before the fall presidential contest, lest a restive Northern public, frustrated by the length of the war, decide to reject Lincoln's bid for reelection.

This plan of campaign was shaped primarily by concerns of manpower and politics. For his plan to work, Grant had to do all he could to increase his margin of manpower over Lee. Halting prisoner exchanges, increasing enlistments through conscription, limiting the impact of the losses due to the expiration of the terms of service of the three-year regiments raised in 1861, using black troops, and responding to reports of the mistreatment of black prisoners of war were all military decisions with political consequences. Were such a campaign to take place in a vacuum devoid of political considerations, Grant would eventually overwhelm his opponent. But wearing the Rebels away was not enough: the timetable set by the electoral process pressured Grant to seek success as soon as possible. The price of an early decision would be heavy casualties costly both in terms of human life and political support. Moreover, to retain incompetent generals in command to appease political constituencies could only prolong the campaign, hinder opportunities to achieve a quick victory, and increase the toll in human life. Thus, decisions made for political rather than military reasons would ultimately damage the prospects for victory by hindering military operations. The interplay of these varied considerations proved that Grant was fighting a political war after all, for political and military concerns were inextricably mixed.

The Confederacy held several advantages in such a campaign. Battlefield triumphs were not necessary to gain victory. Understanding that the ultimate fate of the Southern bid for independence lay in the hands of Northern voters, Confederate generals needed only to blunt Yankee thrusts, hold on to a few major cities, inflict severe casualties, and perhaps launch a few minor counteroffensives designed to distract Grant and to promote anxiety in the Northern public. To frustrate Grant was to defeat Lincoln and thus win the war through a negotiated peace acceded to by a war-weary North. Grant was well aware of the strategic dilemmas presented to him. His great accomplishment was to meet this challenge and to devise a plan for victory that would overcome the handicaps placed on him.

One component to Grant's plan was the raising of more black regiments. The additional manpower thus gained would free battle-hardened soldiers from occupation chores; eventually, blacks could also be employed in offensive combat operations. By now Grant's advocacy of enlisting blacks was well known. While recuperating from his New Orleans injury, he had told a young officer that, although he had opposed the idea in 1862, he now supported it. He urged the officer to seek command of a black regiment, remarking that if he was in the same situation he would probably do the same thing. One officer noted, "He is a soldier and of course regards Negroes at their value as *military* materials. . . . He esteems *men* black or white as too valuable to be wasted." In advising Augustus Chetlain to take over the recruitment of blacks in Tennessee and Kentucky, Grant told him, "I believe the colored man will make a good soldier. He has been accustomed all his life to lean on the white man, and if a good officer is

placed over him, he will learn readily and make a good soldier."
Knowing that Daniel Butterfield professed Radical beliefs, Grant
toyed with the idea of putting him in command of a corps of black
troops. At a time when he could say little else that was positive about
Banks, Grant at least gave him credit for his actions in raising black
troops, although he told General Hunter that they needed better organization and equipment before they could be counted on for more
than garrison duty. Nor would he tolerate dissent from this policy.
After assuming command of all the armies, he ordered the arrest of
a Kentucky cavalry colonel for speaking against black enlistment.[53]

Before long, Grant once again confronted the issue of Confederate
treatment of black prisoners. Reports had reached Washington of the
storming of Fort Pillow by Confederate troops under the command
of Nathan Bedford Forrest on April 12. Most of the soldiers in the
fort were black; accounts of the battle claimed that the Confederates
continued to shoot black soldiers even after the fort commander had
capitulated. Upon reading Sherman's telegram reporting that some
300 blacks were massacred, Grant immediately replied, "If our men
have been murdered after capture retaliation must be resorted to
promptly." Neither Sherman nor the administration shared Grant's
sentiments. Years later, Sherman, admitting that Forrest's men "acted
like a set of barbarians," still held Forrest blameless and claimed that
the only reason that any troops were at Fort Pillow was to "encourage
the enlistment of blacks as soldiers, which," he added disparagingly,
"was a favorite political policy at that day." Lincoln and his cabinet
also decided against retaliation; Secretary Welles called such a policy
"barbarous" and "inhuman." Such attitudes, openly at variance with
previous administration declarations, rendered retaliation useless.[54]

Fort Pillow doubtlessly contributed to Grant's support of the administration's controversial decision to halt the exchange of prisoners. Indeed, he became the policy's staunchest defender. Already disturbed
by irregularities in the Confederate conduct of prisoner exchanges
(most notably, releasing from parole prisoners taken at Vicksburg in
order to press them into service), Grant decided that no more Confederate prisoners would be released until enough Union prisoners
held in the South were set free to meet the balance of some 30,000
owed to the North. Furthermore, Grant insisted that black prisoners
should be treated no differently than their white counterparts, con-

trary to the Confederate practice of reenslavement. If the Confederates refused to accede to these conditions, then Grant refused to participate in further exchanges. Besides, as Grant and Stanton pointed out, the exchange system benefited a Confederacy in dire need of manpower. Exchanged Rebels, back in butternut ranks, would prolong the war and increase Union casualties.[55]

In taking this step, Grant was well aware of its political cost. Anguished Northerners, knowing how Union prisoners in Andersonville and Libby Prison suffered, would find such a policy hard to sustain in the best of conditions. Should Grant's combined offensives fail to crack Confederate resistance, the cessation of exchanges might prove too much of a political liability for the administration. And the general-in-chief, already aware of the human cost of war on the battlefield and in the hospital, now had to assume the awful responsibility for the suffering of imprisoned bluecoats. But it was a necessary price to pay. "It is hard on our men held in Southern prisons not to exchange them," Grant commented, "but it is humanity to those left in our ranks to fight our battles." In August he reaffirmed his position to Secretary of State William H. Seward: "We have got to fight until the Military power of the South is exhausted and if we release or exchange prisoners captured it simply becomes a War of extermination."[56]

Certainly military operations during the spring of 1864 did much to reduce the Confederacy's chances of outright victory, although the cost was high in terms of human life. In the first week of May, Grant moved across Lee's right flank, forded the Rapidan River, and plunged the Army of the Potomac into a mass of tangled undergrowth known as "the Wilderness." There, his army collided with Lee's Army of Northern Virginia; the two antagonists fought to a bloody stalemate. Undeterred, Grant assured Lincoln that there would be no turning back, advanced around Lee's right once more, and headed south toward Spotsylvania Court House, site of another ten days of fierce battle. The pattern of stalemate and advance continued until Grant faced Lee just east of Richmond; a last chance to break Confederate lines through a frontal assault was repulsed with heavy casualties at Cold Harbor on June 3.[57]

Grant was forced to engage in such bloody battles due to the failure of Sigel and Butler to execute their roles in the combined offensive.

Sigel's advance in the Shenandoah Valley proved abortive. Butler, who was supposed to threaten and perhaps take Richmond, stabbing Lee in the rear, did not seriously threaten either it or the valuable rail junction of Petersburg. Grant's last flanking movement, a dash south across the James River toward Petersburg, nearly succeeded, but indecisiveness and hesitation among Union corps commanders frittered away a sure victory. He then settled down to laying siege to Richmond and Petersburg, pinning Lee to the defense of those cities. Meanwhile, Sherman and Johnston had engaged in a similar, if less costly, campaign; by July Sherman's veterans were on the outskirts of Atlanta.[58]

It had become a war of sieges. More men were needed if Union armies were to take Richmond and Atlanta. Military men, including Lee, could see that Union success was just a matter of time and patience, but both were increasingly in short supply. Lincoln successfully withstood Radical challenges for the Republican nomination, but the future was uncertain. Long casualty lists discouraged a Northern electorate hungry for a sensational victory and unconvinced of the eventual success of Grant's grand offensive. Should victory—the kind of victory that led to torchlight parades, illuminations, and 100-gun salutes—continue to elude Grant and his subordinates, it would be hard going for Lincoln in the fall.[59]

To win that sort of victory, Grant needed more men. One source was the draft. Grant had said little about conscription before 1864 and maintained his silence through the first months of the campaign. But the combined impact of heavy casualties and expired enlistments proved a serious drain on Union numbers. Grant urged the administration to issue new calls for troops, although he knew that such a request would incur political costs. "The greater number of men we have the shorter and less sanguinary will be the war," he advised Lincoln, who anticipated Grant's request by issuing a call for 500,000 men in July. The news disturbed those Northerners already haunted by the countless men lying dead in the red Virginia clay. Stanton, aware that Republican politicians wanted to delay the draft until after the 1864 elections, suggested that Grant compose a telegram—intended for publication—outlining the reasons for immediate action. The general complied. "We ought to have the whole number of men called for by the President in the shortest possible time," he argued. "Prompt action in filling our Armies will have more effect upon the enemy than a victory over them" and would prove wrong those Southerners who pointed to dwindling enlistments and resistance to the draft as signs of decaying public support in the North for the war. If Northerners demonstrated that they still possessed the will to fight, he continued, Confederate soldiers would grow discouraged and desert. Having hammered Lee's army for months and pinned the Confederates against Richmond, Grant believed that he had broken his foe's ability to launch a major offensive. But Union victory was inevitable only if the Northern people continued to support the war effort.[60]

One source of manpower remained the black soldiers. At the beginning of the Wilderness campaign, Grant had assigned a division of black troops to Burnside's Ninth Corps. Led by Edward Ferrero, the division spent its first months on duty guarding the army's extensive supply train as Grant and Lee marched and fought. Once the two armies reached the outskirts of Petersburg, however, black troops from both the Army of the Potomac and Butler's Army of the James were used in a combat role. Although the initial attempt to take Petersburg by storm in the middle of June failed, corps commander Smith commended the blacks' bravery and announced that they had proven themselves the equal of white troops under fire. Given the large casualty lists generated during the previous six weeks of combat, it was now nearly a necessity to put blacks in the front line, and Grant did not hesitate to ask for black regiments to reinforce him from other fronts.[61]

Indeed, Ferrero's men were supposed to play a key role in a surprise assault to take Petersburg. By July the trenches of the opposing sides were so close to each other that the members of the Forty-eighth Pennsylvania Infantry, miners by trade, conceived the idea of digging a tunnel underneath the Confederate entrenchments, loading it with explosives, and literally blowing a hole in the enemy line. Grant, who had endorsed the use of such tactics at Vicksburg, approved the plan. Burnside hit upon the idea of using black soldiers in the initial assault force. The attack was set for the early morning of July 30.[62]

George G. Meade, the commander of the Army of the Potomac, was skeptical of the plan. Nevertheless, he prepared to carry it into effect. One infantry corps and the cavalry under Philip H. Sheridan would swing north and hit Lee's left above Richmond; if the Yankees could not sever one of Lee's railroad arteries, at least they could draw enough men away from Burnside's front. Lee met the maneuver in force, whereupon Grant turned to the second half of the plan, featuring Burnside's mine. The black soldiers, who had been practicing assault tactics for weeks, were ecstatic. At last they would escape guard duty and see combat. When they heard the news, one private began singing, "We looks like men of war a-marching on, we looks like men er war," and within moments the whole camp chimed in.[63]

Less than twenty-four hours before the attack, however, Meade balked. The hero of Gettysburg had no faith in the fighting abilities of black soldiers, believing that employing them as a spearhead would mean useless slaughter. Having tangled with the Joint Committee on the Conduct of the War about Gettysburg, and aware that he was not the darling of the Radical members of the committee, he now feared that they would accuse him of ordering the sacrifice of blacks. Though Burnside grumbled, Meade took the issue to Grant, who endorsed the change in plan.[64]

What followed was a series of blunders for which Grant was ultimately responsible. Unable to use Ferrero's division, Burnside let his other three division commanders draw lots to decide which unit would lead the attack. Fortune smiled on the Confederacy, for the commander chosen to lead the assault, James H. Ledlie, was not only incompetent but also liked to fortify himself before battle with alcohol. Told that Ledlie was to lead the assault, Grant, although aware of his shortcomings, did nothing. The mine itself was a success, blowing a sizable hole in the Confederate defenses; but, instead of using the resulting crater as an avenue through which troops would pass to Petersburg and roll up the Confederate line on each side, Ledlie's men—and eventually the remainder of Burnside's corps—merely crowded into it. Once the Confederates recovered from the initial shock, they surrounded the crater, making the position untenable, and the troops were withdrawn after sustaining terrible losses.[65]

"So fair an opportunity will probably never occur again for carrying fortifications," Grant told Meade. But he had no one but himself to blame. Distrusting Burnside, aware that Meade lacked enthusiasm for the plan, and alert to Ledlie's ineptitude, Grant inexplicably failed to intervene and take control. His support of Meade's decision not to use the black division, although explained as a political decision, left him open to charges that he was unwilling to employ black troops as an assault force under any circumstances, despite his praise of their behavior in the initial thrust at Petersburg in June. Later, Grant testified that if Ferrero's men had been used the assault would have succeeded. Despite all the effort to protect the black soldiers, they were not only engaged but also mishandled, resulting in significant casualties. Opinions differed as to their performance. Horace Porter noted that the blacks "rushed gallantly into the crater," but one of Meade's staff officers said that "the troops would not go up with any spirit at all." Another staff officer thought that "the blacks seem to have done as well as whites—which is faint praise." Fifth Corps artillery commander Charles Wainwright spoke to one of the colonels of the black regiments. "He says that his men behaved admirably in the excitement of the first onset, but soon lost heart; also that every man who was hit yelled and groaned most hideously, which tended to demoralize the others. As both the traits are natural to the negro character, I have no doubt of his correctness."[66]

On the day after the failure at the Crater, Grant met Lincoln at army headquarters at City Point. The president was concerned with the presence in the Shenandoah Valley of Confederate troops under the command of Jubal Early, who had led his command to the outskirts of Washington in mid-July before veering toward Pennsylvania. Lee had decided to throw a scare into Washington once more. It was an election year, and Lincoln worried not only about the Democratic opposition but also about the disgruntled Radicals in his own party, who wished to replace him with someone more to their liking. The long casualty lists of the spring campaign had added to his political burdens.

Lincoln's problems impinged upon Grant's ability to choose capable commanders. Fearing the political consequences, the administration was less than enthusiastic about a proposal to remove Butler from field command, forcing Grant to drop the idea. Indeed, no sooner had rumors surfaced about Butler's removal than Radical leaders Benjamin F. Wade and Zachariah Chandler had hurried down to the Massachusetts general's headquarters, as if to remind Grant of the stakes involved. Now several of Lincoln's advisers were suggesting that he bring McClellan out of retirement, perhaps to head the forces opposing Early. Lincoln told Grant what was going on, so that the general could keep the political situation in mind as he planned future operations.[67]

As Lincoln returned to Washington, Grant decided to put not McClellan but Sheridan in charge of the forces confronting Early. This time he would make sure that Lee would never again use the Shenandoah Valley to divert Union offensives. Once Early was driven out of the valley, Grant instructed Sheridan, "nothing should be left to invite the enemy to return." Whatever provisions, forage, or stock Sheridan could not use himself should be destroyed; protesting citizens would be told "that so long as an army can subsist among them recurrences of these raids must be expected, and we are determined to stop them at all hazards." If Grant could not increase his manpower, at least he could cripple the Confederacy's ability to feed its own soldiers, as well as deprive Lee of the use of the valley as a staging area for thrusts against Washington and the North. Within six weeks, Sheridan had driven Early from Maryland and fulfilled the general-in-chief's desire to turn the fertile valley into "a barren waste."[68]

By this time, Grant's strategy of depleting Confederate manpower and resources while maximizing his own was beginning to bear fruit. In late August, Lee remarked that it would prove difficult to break Grant's hold on Richmond and Petersburg, especially now that Early's offensive had failed to ease the pressure. Unless he could find a way to augment his forces, Lee believed that "the consequences may be disastrous." Grant agreed. "All we want now to insure an early restoration of the Union is a determined unity of sentiment North," he assured Washburne. "The rebels have now in their ranks that last man. . . . A man lost by them cannot be replaced. They have robbed the cradle and the grave equally to get their present force." Confederate hopes now rested upon "a divided North," especially if it resulted in the election of a Democratic president. The defeat of the administration would not bring peace. Southerners "would demand the restoration of their slaves already freed . . . indemnity for losses sustained, and . . . pay or restoration of every slave escaping to the North." True peace demanded a Republican victory; Washburne, aware that this letter represented as good an endorsement of the administration as he was going to get from Grant, made it available as campaign literature.[69]

If Lincoln's reelection was essential to military victory, military victories were essential to Lincoln's reelection. The Northern population simply did not have the patience to wait for a slow but sure victory. Fortunately, Grant's combined offensives finally began to score the kind of successes essential to restore civilian morale. On September 2, after a siege lasting nearly two months, Sherman entered Atlanta. The news came as a shock to the Democratic party, which had just nominated McClellan on a platform that essentially declared the war a failure. Nearly three weeks later, Sheridan thrashed Early in a series of battles near Winchester.[70]

Now it was Grant's turn. In the last week of September, he launched an offensive against Lee's lines east of Richmond, capturing several forts. Although he failed to capture the city, he tightened the noose around Lee's neck. Black troops played a key role in the offensive, suffering severe losses. During the battle, Grant visited one black brigade. "As soon as Grant was known to be approaching," an officer later recalled, "every man was on his feet & quiet, breathless quiet, prevailed. A cheer could never express what we felt."[71]

Grant repaid the tribute in his own way. More than 100 men in the brigade had been captured. When Lee inquired about the possibility of exchanging prisoners just after the battle, Grant explicitly limited the exchange to men captured during the last engagement, then reminded Lee that many of the Rebels' prisoners were black: "I would ask if you propose delivering these men the same as White soldiers." Lee tried to finesse the issue: he was willing "to include all captured soldiers of the U.S. of whatever nation [or] Colour under my control," but he stated that "negroes belonging to our citizens are not Considered Subjects of exchange & were not included in my proposition." Rejecting Lee's reasoning, Grant argued that "the Government is bound to secure to all persons received into her Armies the rights due to soldiers" and refused to exchange any prisoners.[72]

Doubtless Grant expected the affair to turn out this way. After all, resuming prisoner exchanges would thwart his objective of depleting Confederate manpower. In fact, Lee had just asked the Davis administration to do something to increase his numbers, warning that otherwise "it will be very difficult for us to maintain ourselves." Maybe, with an election approaching, Grant would bow to pressure from the home front and relent on his no-exchange policy. Skillfully, Grant turned the tables on his opponent. By expressly restricting the exchange to prisoners captured during the recent offensive, he shifted the focus of attention to the problem of black soldiers. Lee's response reminded everyone that the Confederacy was created to defend slavery, something Northern voters might keep in mind.[73]

Two weeks later, Grant discovered that Lee was determined to continue the controversy over the status of black prisoners. Rebel deserters had told Butler that the Confederates were employing black POWs as laborers on fortifications within the range of Union fire. Butler immediately forwarded the information to Grant, informing his commander that he planned to retaliate by using Confederate prisoners to erect and improve his entrenchments. Grant approved of Butler's action, dispatched prisoners for employment on Butler's lines, and confronted Lee once more.[74]

Lee backed down, withdrawing the black prisoners from the front while asserting that it had been an administrative mix-up. However, he staunchly defended the action, claiming that the prisoners were not put to work under enemy fire, and treated Grant to a lengthy defense of the reenslavement of black soldiers once they were identified as fugitives. Willing to concede that free blacks should be exchanged, Lee still held that former slaves, "like other recaptured private property," would be returned to their masters. While he awaited Grant's response, he made plans to retaliate. He built a pen, fifteen yards square, in front of the artillery shelling Dutch Gap. One hundred Union prisoners would be placed in the pen. Should Butler try to open fire on the Rebel position, he would risk killing these men. It was up to Grant to resolve the problem.[75]

Grant refused to consider the merits of Lee's argument. He told his counterpart that it was "my duty to protect all persons received into the Army of the United States, regardless of color or Nationality." Hence, all Federal soldiers captured should be treated as prisoners of war. Any deviation from this rule would force Grant to retaliate. "I have nothing to do with the discussion of the slavery question," he replied in dismissing Lee's effort at justifying Confederate policy. Since Lee had removed the prisoners, Grant would do likewise. The Union commander was proving to be as stubborn on this issue as he was on the battlefield. He was successful in both areas, for that night he ordered a 100-gun salute in celebration of Sheridan's victory at Cedar Creek.[76]

Sheridan's triumph was the latest in a series of Union successes that assured Lincoln's reelection. Grant did what he could to contribute to that result, sending troops to New York to guard the polls and furloughing Delaware regiments when Stanton informed him that "the vote of the State will depend on them." He warned his subordinates to be prepared for an enemy attack designed to disrupt voting in the field. On the morning after election day, he informed Washington of the results, which showed Lincoln majorities in the regiments of every state. He celebrated the president's reelection as a "double victory," since no riots or violence attended the event.[77]

As Grant knew, Lincoln's victory was much more than that. It reaffirmed the North's desire to see the war through, confirming that certain results of the war—including emancipation—were irreversible. Of course, Grant had much to do with Lincoln's triumph. The fruition of his coordinated offensive at Atlanta and in the Shenandoah Valley, along with the nullification of Lee as an offensive force, reassured Northerners that the end was finally in sight. From now on, the war would be conducted not only to defeat the enemy but also with an eye to the shape of the peace to follow.

By November 1864, the general who once protested that he would keep his opinions about politics to himself had made it plain that he did possess opinions and that he was no longer reluctant to express or to act upon them. Politics were fundamental to the 1864 campaign, and Grant, struggling under severe handicaps, had overcome them to assure Lincoln's reelection. Moreover, in his attitude toward the treatment of black prisoners of war, Grant revealed a grasp of the political aims of the conflict. He would have something to say about the form peace should take, even as he concentrated his energies on securing that peace through victory. He was discovering firsthand Clausewitz's maxim that war was politics by other means. Within a year, he would discover that the lines between the two endeavors were very blurred indeed.

3

SWORD

AND

OLIVE

BRANCH

With the government safely in Republican hands for the next four years, Grant turned to planning the moves that would close out the war. In fact, he and Sherman had already mapped out the first step. Sherman, frustrated at countering Confederate attempts to cut his line of communications with Chattanooga, had been prodding Grant to let him replicate the Vicksburg campaign on a larger scale. He proposed that he leave sufficient force to keep John Bell Hood's army in check and take the remainder of his army, some 60,000 strong, across the Georgia countryside, with Savannah or Charleston as his ultimate destination. Supply lines would become irrelevant, for Sherman planned to live off the land and bring the war home to the South. Such an operation would prove to white Southerners that their government could no longer provide them with protection from the invader. Sherman's objective would be not the defeat of an army but of Confederate morale and matériel; he would strike down the will as well as the means to carry on the rebellion. Subjugation would lead to submission. "This may not be War," he told Grant, "but rather Statesmanship"—an odd comment coming from a man who abjured politics, yet appropriate for one who was now prepared to undertake a campaign that had at least as much political as military importance. After some discussion, Grant approved Sherman's plan. Within a week of Lincoln's victory at the polls, Sherman commenced what would become known as "The March to the Sea."[1]

Grant and Sherman, two men who claimed to have nothing to do with politics, were now answering political questions with the sword. Moreover, peace was now becoming a proper subject for them to consider. Joshua Hill, a Georgia Unionist, called upon Sherman after Atlanta's fall. Perhaps Georgia's governor, Joseph E. Brown, who was skeptical of the Confederacy's chances for success, might be persuaded to withdraw his state from the war effort. Sherman jumped at the idea, proposing to "spare the State" by confining his lines of march to the main roads and paying for all food and forage taken if Brown complied. Moreover, he expressed a willingness to meet with Confederate vice president Alexander H. Stephens to talk over possible peace terms. Lincoln discovered what Sherman was up to and decided to see what the general could do before intervening. Sherman, taking this as approval, bragged that if such an agreement was reached "it would be a magnificent stroke of policy."[2]

Grant encouraged Sherman's endeavors but was concerned about Lincoln's interest in the proceedings. Like Sherman, Grant mistrusted politicians and remembered the confusion he had witnessed as a result of civilian policy along the Mississippi. Perhaps he believed that Lincoln had allowed these situations to fester, but he did not want to address the president directly on a political question—that might seem insubordinate and would smack too much of George B. McClellan. Instead, he expressed to Edwin M. Stanton his hope that Lincoln would "not attempt to doctor up a state government in Georgia by the appointment of citizens in any capacity whatever. Leave Sherman to treat on all questions in his own way the President reserving his power to approve or disapprove of his action." Grant complained that the behavior of treasury agents in the Mississippi Valley and the impact of "a very bad civil policy in Louisianna" had "conciderably protracted" the war and alienated many white Southerners. Ever cautious, he reminded Stanton that these were his "private views."[3]

The commanding general had hopes that Sherman's mission would succeed. "If this is done," he wrote Julia, "it will be the end of rebellion, or so nearly so that the rebelling will be by one portion of the South against the other." Eventually, the plan fell through: Brown rejected the proposal and Stephens confessed that he was not empowered to treat for peace. But the incident revealed that the North's two most important commanders were willing to become involved in negotiations transcending their purely military duties in order to secure peace; and it revealed their distrust of the ability of politicians, even Lincoln, to handle such issues satisfactorily. That Grant was willing to act upon such an enlarged perception of his responsibilities was confirmed in several seemingly separate incidents during the winter of 1864–65.[4]

In Virginia, Governor Francis Pierpoint had been trying for years to restore civil rule to Norfolk, only to be frustrated by Benjamin F. Butler. Grant, none too happy with Butler, had sided with Pierpoint, and the two discussed the issue with Lincoln several weeks after the election. But Grant would have to wait for Butler to err before acting. His patience soon paid off. In late December, Grant dispatched an expedition—drawn from Butler's troops—to take Fort Fisher, North Carolina, which guarded Wilmington, the last major Confederate port. Butler, who had insisted on commanding the invasion force in person, decided on Christmas Day to abandon the project. Grant was furious. Aware that this time there was no election in the offing, he secured Butler's removal, citing not only his military incompetence but also reports of maladministration. Rumors had it that some of the goods coming out of Norfolk went to feed Confederate troops, and that the proceeds accrued to certain investors sanctioned by Butler. Grant put a stop to such traffic by halting trade along the Atlantic Coast. Butler's removal also paved the way for Pierpoint to proceed with his plans. Thus the man who once had declared that he was above politics and civil policy had obtained the removal of a politically important subordinate while working toward the reestablishment of civil rule in the Old Dominion.[5]

Other plans were even more far-reaching. In November Grant met with J. J. Giers, an Alabama Unionist with connections to the Confederate state government, who thought that Alabamians had had enough of war. Grant sent him back to find out whether what had failed in Georgia might succeed somewhere else. Contacting several Confederate commanders in Alabama, Giers reported that a staff officer "frankly admitted to me that the affairs of the Confederacy were in a hopeless condition, and that the people were anxious to know the best terms which could be given to Alabama in case of an immediate popular movement for reconstruction." Unfortunately, that was about all that came of the mission. Before long, James H. Wilson's troopers swept through the state, rendering such discussions academic.[6]

Grant explored similar opportunities in Texas. Both he and Gen. Lew Wallace had heard of Francis P. Blair, Sr.'s, plan for peace based on an armistice and followed by a joint invasion of Mexico to drive out the French regime under Maximilian. Blair, whom Lincoln had allowed to visit Richmond to present his plan to Jefferson Davis, stopped off at Grant's headquarters during his trip and apparently discussed his idea with the general, who heartily approved of any measure to eject Maximilian. Moreover, Grant was concerned by reports that a California Confederate, Dr. William Gwin, was organizing a refuge for Rebels in Mexico. It seemed much more important now than in the previous spring, when Grant had protested Nathaniel P. Banks's ill-fated campaign, to consider Mexican affairs as part of the war. Although Blair's proposal soon faded from consideration, Wallace, with Grant's approval, discussed a possible peace agreement with several Rebel commanders along the Rio Grande and went so far as to draft an agreement that went far beyond mere surrender. He proposed to promise the Confederates "a full release from and against actions, prosecutions, liabilities, and legal proceedings of every kind" and added that both civil and military officials who took the oath of allegiance would "be regarded as citizens of that Government, invested as such with all the rights, privileges, and immunities now enjoyed."[7]

As with the Giers mission, Wallace's plan fell through. In retrospect, what appears most interesting about these two operations is Grant's low profile. Very little evidence of his participation survives, and neither Grant nor his most prominent chroniclers mention these endeavors. But what little evidence there is reveals that Grant was already thinking about ending the war and was willing to explore alternatives other than pitched battles to achieve that end.

As 1865 opened, Grant knew that the war was drawing to a close. Sherman's march across Georgia had confounded the Confederacy, destroying property and devastating morale—as evidenced in increased desertion from Lee's army. Now, with Savannah in his hip pocket, Sherman prepared to advance across the Carolinas toward Virginia. George H. Thomas, after much hesitation, had demolished Hood's counteroffensive at Nashville, ending the last significant Confederate threat in the West. Even apparent failures became successes, for less than two weeks after Butler's removal Fort Fisher fell. Meanwhile, Lee remained pinned in his trenches around Richmond and Petersburg. Each day, dozens of Rebels slipped away and set out for home. It seemed only a matter of time before the war ended.[8]

Yet all was not well for Grant. In fact, some twenty years later he characterized these weeks of waiting as "one of the most anxious periods of my experience." He was afraid that Lee, aware of the hopelessness of remaining in his entrenchments, would try to escape under cover of darkness and make his way south to join Joseph Johnston's forces in North Carolina. Pursuit might be difficult, for the roads were in bad shape and Philip H. Sheridan's cavalry was still in the Shenandoah Valley. Even worse, Lee and his men could head for the hills and inaugurate a guerrilla war, a fearsome specter to Grant, who remembered all too well his experiences in Tennessee and Mississippi. His harsh orders to Sheridan to lay waste to the Shenandoah Valley and to execute John S. Mosby's men reflected a rage born of frustration. Guerrilla war created disorder and confusion, transforming the way men waged war and influencing the way they made peace. Military victory would be difficult to achieve and would be costly. A peace based upon reconciliation would be nearly impossible.[9]

Grant recognized an opportunity to avoid such a possibility and to end the war without further bloodshed when he was informed that three prominent Confederate officials were waiting on the picket line at Petersburg. These "peace commissioners from the so-called Confederate States," as Grant called them, wanted to see Lincoln personally. As the three men waited between the lines, one Union officer observed "that the *bone of contention* between the two armies . . . came with them in the shape of a black man carrying a valise." Grant welcomed the three commissioners—Vice President Alexander H. Stephens, Assistant Secretary of War John A. Campbell, and R. M. T. Hunter—to his headquarters and settled them on a steamer anchored off City Point. Then he telegraphed Washington, apprised Lincoln of the situation, and asked for instructions.[10]

Stanton wanted nothing to do with the commissioners. He sent Maj. Thomas Eckert down to City Point to talk to the three Rebel officials, with instructions to find out what they wanted. If the Confederates were willing to accept reunion and the end of slavery, Eckert could send them on to Fort Monroe and negotiations could commence; otherwise, they might as well return to Richmond. Meanwhile, Grant was instructed to keep the pressure on Lee as if nothing was happening. When Grant tried to join Eckert's discussion with the commissioners, he was rebuffed by the major, who suggested that peace was none of his business.[11]

At first it looked as if the mission would be short-lived. Stephens spoke of a peace settlement between two countries, which meant an end to all further discussion. But Grant intervened. He talked to Stephens and Hunter, found their "desire sincere to restore peace and union," and believed that they were in fact willing to discard the pretense of a peace treaty. Stephens noted that Grant, too, seemed anxious for peace and impatient with Eckert. But that was not all on the general's mind. In December he had told one of his subordinates that an armistice would deplete Confederate ranks as surely as another battle, and at far less cost in human lives. If a truce was declared, Grant asserted, half of Lee's army would desert within six weeks.[12]

Grant's handling of the opportunity presented by the commissioners' visit suggested that he had the finesse required for political success. He did nothing overtly out of line for a military commander, remaining silent when the commissioners prodded him to declare his own opinion. At the same time, however, he urged them to come up with a statement of intent that would circumvent the differences over phrasing, allowing Lincoln to talk to them without recognizing the legitimacy of the Confederacy. The commissioners complied, composing a note declaring their willingness to consider any settlement "not inconsistent with the essential principles of self government and popular rights upon which our institutions are founded," a sufficiently vague basis for negotiations.[13]

An unhappy Eckert once more told Grant to stay out of politics. Miffed at a mere major telling him what to do, Grant outmaneuvered his nemesis, telegraphing Stanton that it was his opinion that Lincoln should meet the envoys and relaying his belief that they were willing to talk about reunion if given the chance. "I have not felt myself at liberty to express even views of my own or to account for my reticency," he assured Stanton, but added, "I fear now their going back without any expression from any one in authority will have a bad influence." Grant knew Lincoln would see the telegram; the next morning the president sent word that he would meet Stephens, Hunter, and Campbell at Hampton Roads, offshore Fort Monroe. Grant, anticipating the answer, had made preparations to transport the Confederates to the conference site. He ran to the commissioners' boat, waving the telegram, and sent them on their way to meet Lincoln.[14]

The result was anticlimactic. Stephens and company were not willing to give in on the basic issue of Confederate sovereignty, despite Lincoln's willingness to make emancipation as painless as possible. To Grant's disappointment, the Confederates returned to Richmond. Later, Julia Grant asked Lincoln what had happened. When the president revealed his conditions, she was surprised that the commissioners did not accept terms "most liberal." The war would have to go on a bit longer, although the incident had given Grant some idea of Lincoln's thoughts about the terms of a settlement.[15]

Grant was already thinking about peace during the winter of 1864–65. "Every thing looks to me to be very favorable for a speedy termination of the war," he confided to a friend. "The people of the South are ready for it if they can get clear of their leaders." Meanwhile, he continued to do all he could to subvert the Confederacy by any available means. Hearing that the old Mississippi Unionist Henry S. Foote sought clemency in order to persuade Southerners to abandon the Davis government, Grant approved. Yet the desire to appear the simple soldier above politics remained. "I do not profess to be a judge of the best civil policy to pursue to restore peace and the integrity of the Union," he told Secretary William H. Seward, "my duty being to apply force to accomplish this end." Seward, who had been at Hampton Roads, knew better. Perhaps memories of Zachary Taylor, the Mexican War hero whom Seward had helped elevate to the presidency, resurfaced. Taylor had liked to talk in such terms. Perhaps Grant had learned more from "Old Rough and Ready" than merely a certain casual approach to the wearing of the uniform.[16]

Throughout February, Grant continued to extend his lines westward, always with the goal of stretching Lee's army to the breaking point and severing Petersburg from the rest of the Confederacy. And not much of the Confederacy was left. Sherman's forces entered Columbia, South Carolina, on February 17; Wilmington fell five days later. Lee (now formally in command of all the Confederate armies), James Longstreet, and the other generals holed up in Richmond knew that the end was near. There were two options left. The Army of Northern Virginia could abandon the Confederate capital, either to join forces with Johnston or to head for the Blue Ridge Mountains in order to engage in a hit-and-run guerrilla war, or the Confederates could open peace negotiations.[17]

Sensing that Lee remained undecided over what to do, Longstreet took advantage of a February 25 meeting with Union commander Edward O. C. Ord, Butler's replacement as head of the Army of the James, to suggest that perhaps the two generals-in-chief ought to shift from the battlefield to the negotiating table. Ord, an advocate of negotiation, had witnessed Grant's willingness to promote the Hampton Roads conference; he had no doubt that his superior would welcome the chance to meet Lee face-to-face. Moreover, he believed that politicians North and South were unable to negotiate a peace settlement. Northerners could not make the mistake of recognizing the existence of the Confederacy, and Southern politicians would be placed in the difficult position of discussing the dissolution of the very government they represented. Only the generals could make peace. Indeed, Ord wanted to make it something of a special occasion, suggesting that perhaps Mrs. Longstreet and Mrs. Grant, childhood friends from St. Louis, might want to have a little chat. According to Ord, Julia Grant could enter Richmond long before her husband did—and to return a social call![18]

Back at Richmond, Lee, Davis, and other Confederate officials met to discuss the conversation between Ord and Longstreet. Secretary of

War John C. Breckinridge was especially captivated by the roles assigned to Mrs. Longstreet and Mrs. Grant: Louise Longstreet, living in Lynchburg, was told to come to Richmond. More important, Davis assented to the proposal. On February 28, Ord and Longstreet met again, ostensibly to discuss the exchange of "political prisoners," but in reality to iron out details. Ord claimed that Grant "had the authority" to meet Lee and discuss a peace settlement. Longstreet relayed the message to his chief. "If I have not misunderstood General Ord's conversation," he reported, "General Grant will agree to take the matter up without requiring any principle as a basis further than the general principle of desiring to make peace upon terms which are equally honorable to both sides."[19]

On March 2, Lee wrote Grant that he was willing to enter negotiations for "the possibility of arriving at a satisfactory adjustment of the present unhappy difficulties by means of a military convention." Leaving "nothing untried which may put an end to the calamities of war," Lee expressed his willingness to meet his counterpart "at such convenient time and place as you may designate." It was now up to General Grant.[20]

Grant was aware that Ord had been talking to Longstreet, but he was not sure how serious was the offer to negotiate. One afternoon he called Julia over and explained the proposed encounter with Louise Longstreet. "Oh! How enchanting, how thrilling!" she responded. "Oh, Ulys, I may go, may I not?" Grant smiled; then, when Julia persisted, he replied, "No, you must not. It is simply absurd. The men have fought this war and the men will finish it." Lee's letter, however, was another matter. Grant's response suggests that Ord had been engaging in wishful thinking when he indicated to Longstreet that Grant was both willing and able to engage in a peace conference. Instead of replying to Lee's request, he forwarded the text of the message to Washington, along with a request for instructions.[21]

Lincoln received Grant's dispatch at the Capitol, where he was considering bills passed during the last moments of the Thirty-eighth Congress. Among those with him was Stanton. At first Lincoln warmed to the idea of a conference, expressing his desire to extend "the most lenient and generous terms to a defeated foe." Stanton sternly reminded the president that it was Lincoln's responsibility, not Grant's, to set forth peace terms. Lincoln pondered this and then concurred.

To City Point went a dispatch written by Lincoln but signed by Stanton: "The President directs me to say to you that he wishes you to have no conference with General Lee, unless it be for the capitulation of General Lee's army, or on some minor, and purely military, matter. He instructs me to say that you are not to decide, discuss or confer upon any political question." Lincoln would not submit other issues to "military conferences or conventions. Meanwhile you are to press to the utmost your military advantages." In another telegram, Stanton criticized Ord's actions.[22]

Smarting at this apparent rebuke, Grant shot off a reply that made clear that he understood he had no authority to treat on matters of peace. Furious, he was tempted to remind Stanton that "peace must Come some day" but upon reflection crossed out those words. Doubtless the sharp edge to Grant's retort was due to his impression that Stanton, not Lincoln, had written the dispatch. At the same time, Grant told Lee that he had no authority to enter upon such negotiations and excused Ord's actions by suggesting that his comments were misinterpreted (although it seems that it was Ord who was at fault). Probably Grant was a little disappointed that he had not been given a chance to try to work something out. But he realized that, meeting or no meeting, the war was drawing to a close—if he could make sure that Lee's legions could not make it to the mountains. The day after he sent off his letter to Lee, he heard that Sheridan had smashed Jubal Early's tattered remnants near Charlottesville; within a week, the cavalryman was on the way to Petersburg to help wrap things up.[23]

As he was making preparations for the spring campaign, Grant must have thought about the possibility of a struggle culminating in the surrender of a large portion of Lee's army. He had just been chastened regarding peace terms; perhaps it was time to find out exactly what Lincoln's thoughts on peace were. Julia, reading accounts of the president's haggard appearance, thought it would be a good idea if the Lincolns came to City Point for a visit. The president's son Robert, now a captain serving as a volunteer aide on Grant's staff, seconded Mrs. Grant's proposal, and Grant extended an invitation on March 20, which Lincoln immediately accepted. But this was not to be a purely social occasion. Three days later, Sherman, headquartered at Goldsboro, North Carolina, expressed his desire to "run up to see you for a day or two" to plan the final moves.[24]

Lincoln arrived on the evening of March 24; Sherman appeared three days later and, with Grant, visited the president aboard the *River Queen*, anchored off City Point. Sherman regaled his listeners with stories of his marches through Georgia and the Carolinas. The next day, the three men, along with Adm. David D. Porter, met once again in the steamer's stateroom. This time the topic was war—and peace. Lincoln had been concerned that the hard-fighting Grant and Sherman were "not very solicitous to close hostilities" and that they would "exact hard terms." He asked whether the conflict could be ended without another major battle. Both Grant and Sherman doubted it. Then Sherman raised several questions. Was Lincoln ready for the end of the war? How would he treat the Rebel soldiers? What about the Rebel leaders? In response, Lincoln made clear that he favored a lenient peace, that all he wanted was reunion and emancipation. Those two terms being met, Lincoln "was almost ready to sign his name to a blank piece of paper and permit them to fill out the balance of the terms." Sherman later wrote that Lincoln was even willing to recognize the existing Confederate state governments "until Congress could provide others."[25]

Grant said very little during the conference. Perhaps Lincoln and he had already reached a meeting of the minds on the general outline of the surrender terms. He was familiar with Lincoln's desire to "let 'em up easy." "Let them once surrender," the president remarked during his City Point visit, "and reach their homes, they won't take up arms again. . . . Let them have their horses to plow with. . . . Give them the most liberal and honorable terms." Grant, as his aides could testify, was always a good listener.[26]

But first things first. Talk of terms was well and good, but Lee still had to be brought to the point of surrender. As Sherman steamed back to rejoin his troops, Grant turned to the task of finishing off the enemy in his front. With Lincoln peering over his shoulder, he mapped out a plan of attack.

Grant's 1865 spring offensive originally had two objectives. Sheridan was to sever Lee's supply lines running west from Richmond and Petersburg along the Southside and Danville railroads and to block any attempt Lee might make to unite with Johnston. Meanwhile,

George G. Meade and Ord would try to turn Lee's right flank in an effort to force the Confederates out of their entrenchments. As Grant told his father, "I think [we] will be able to wind up matters around Richmond."[27]

Lee had already presented proof that the end was near. On March 25, the morning after Lincoln arrived at City Point, Lee launched a last strike at Grant's lines at Fort Stedman. The assault proved a miserable failure; Lincoln termed it "a little rumpus." During the next several days, as Grant, Sherman, and Lincoln conferred over peace, Union soldiers began to move into position. On March 29, Grant and Lincoln parted, and the general went to the front. At last, after months of waiting in the muddy trenches, the army would be on the move once more—perhaps for the last time. "I feel now like ending the matter," Grant told Sheridan as he sent him around Lee's right.[28]

A steady downpour slowed the movement for several hours, but by the evening of March 30 Sheridan was ready "to strike out tomorrow and go to smashing things." He did so in the next forty-eight hours, and the Confederate lines at Five Forks collapsed under the blow. Grant seized upon the opportunity afforded by Sheridan's triumph to order an assault all along the line. On April 2 Petersburg fell; Richmond followed a day later. Fittingly, elements of the all-black Twenty-fifth Corps, a unit created by Grant during the past winter, were the first Union units to enter the Confederate citadel.[29]

There was little time to celebrate. Richmond and Petersburg were valuable so long as Lee had to protect them, but the Confederate leader, having evacuated both cities, was now heading west. Grant was not sure where his opponent intended to go. Perhaps Lee would try to link up with Johnston in North Carolina; maybe he would seek cover in the Blue Ridge Mountains. Either move would prolong the war. Grant was already considering how best to pursue Lee when he rode into Petersburg to meet once more with Lincoln. The president was ecstatic at the fall of Petersburg. "Do you know, general," he said upon meeting Grant, "I had a sort of sneaking idea for some days that you intended to do something like this." He then reiterated his desire for a lenient peace, mentioned again his preference for "the most liberal and honorable terms," and spoke about the "civil complications" that would result from Confederate defeat. As the two men engaged in discussion, Petersburg blacks, slaves only yesterday, crowded around and watched. After talking with the president, Grant took his leave and rode off to rejoin the pursuit.[30]

Grant's initial movements were designed to discourage Lee from joining Johnston. When he discovered that Lee had arranged for rations to be sent to Farmville, not Danville, he concluded that Lee had abandoned any notion of heading toward North Carolina. Now Grant had to make sure that Lee did not make it to the mountains, and so he directed his columns to head off the Rebels. Nor was the Army of Northern Virginia moving with its accustomed verve. Lee later complained that troop movements "were not marked by the boldness and decision which formerly characterized them. . . . This condition, I think, was produced by the state of feeling in the country, and the communications received by the men from their homes, urging their return and the abandonment of the field." Opportunity beckoned to the bluecoats. "If we press on," Sheridan declared, "we will no doubt get the whole army." Pushing to the front, Grant reminded Meade that "we did not want to follow the enemy; we wanted to get ahead of him," and he watched as Sheridan shredded Lee's rear guard at Sayler's Creek outside of Farmville on April 6.[31]

At this point, Grant's thoughts began to turn toward surrender. Sheridan had forwarded to him a letter from one of Lee's aides describing Confederate demoralization. Captured Confederate corps commander Richard S. Ewell (one of Grant's old army friends) thought further fighting pointless, and that "for every man that was killed after this in the war somebody is responsible, and it would be but very little better than murder." Lincoln was eager for the end. Notifying Grant of his meetings with Campbell concerning the possible convening of the Virginia legislature to take the Old Dominion out of the war, the president reminded his general that such plans should not "delay, hinder, or interfere with you in your work" but plainly hinted that the sooner the war was over, the better. When the cocky Sheridan, effusive over his triumph at Sayler's Creek, announced, "If the thing is pressed I think Lee will surrender," Lincoln urged Grant, "Let the thing be pressed."[32]

The Confederates already felt pressed enough. The Army of Northern Virginia was unraveling as it staggered westward. The disaster at Sayler's Creek compounded already desperate circumstances. If Grant could see this, he reasoned, certainly Lee could, too. It was time to bring things to a close. On the evening of April 7, Grant contemplated his next move on the front porch of a Farmville farmhouse. Cheering soldiers marched by, and "delighted" blacks crowded up "in huge numbers" to see their liberator. Awaiting orders with Grant were Ord and Gen. John Gibbon, commanding the Twenty-fourth Corps. Grant at last looked up at them and quietly said, "I have a great mind to summon Lee to surrender." In a moment, with paper and pen in hand, he did just that. "The result of the last week must convince you of the hopelessness of further resistance," he began; then, re-membering last June, when pointless squabbling in the aftermath of Cold Harbor had delayed his attempts to call a truce to remove the wounded and that most of them had died, Grant informed his oppo-nent that he regarded it "as my duty to shift from myself, the respon-sibility of any further effusion of blood" by asking Lee to surrender. The dispatch was sent off, and Grant sat back to wait in a room that Lee had occupied the previous night.[33]

Over seven hours later, Grant had Lee's reply. It revealed that Lee was as cagey about peace as he was about war. No, the Confederate commander did not think that further resistance was hopeless; but, because he too wanted "to avoid useless effusion of blood," he asked to hear Grant's terms. Grant slept on this. In the morning, he re-sponded, making sure to restrict himself to strictly military considera-tions. "*Peace* being my great desire there is but one condition I would insist upon, namely: that the men and officers surrendered shall be disqualified for taking up arms again, against the Government of the United States, until properly exchanged." Expressing his willingness to meet Lee to arrange terms of surrender, Grant, aware that Lee's pride had gotten in the way of previous attempts at negotiation, added that subordinates from both armies could work out the details, sparing Lee a personal confrontation with Grant.[34]

April 8 was a painful day for Grant. Suffering from a migraine headache (perhaps a sign of the pressure he was under), he could not stop to rest, for he had to follow his columns closely. It was a tired and fatigued general who crossed the Virginia countryside on horse-back in pursuit of Lee. That evening he sought relief, bathing his feet in hot water and applying mustard plasters. As if the horseback ride had not added enough backbeat to the pounding in his head, he un-fortunately stopped for the night at a farmhouse equipped with a piano. Grant did not much fancy music at the best of times, and it was tough enough to worry about Lee without his staff officers trying their hand at the keyboard. Finally someone stopped the noise. But Grant was in such pain that he could not sleep, anxious as he was about Lee's reply to his morning message.[35]

When Lee's response arrived late that night, Grant grew more depressed. "To be frank," Lee wrote, "I do not think the emergency has arisen to call for the surrender of this army." Instead, "as the restoration of peace should be the sole object of all, I desired to know whether your proposals would lead to that end." This was more gamesmanship. Obviously, Grant saw Lee's surrender as the necessary prelude to peace, but Lee did not want to admit it. Somehow, he wanted to have peace without having to surrender first. He declined to meet Grant to discuss surrender terms, but he would be willing, "as far as your proposal may affect the Confederate States forces under my command, and tend to the restoration of peace," to engage Grant in a discussion on the next day.[36]

Grant was not pleased with Lee's letter. In later years, he would recall his disappointment with the Confederate leader. "Lee does not appear well in that correspondence," he noted. The Virginian was still striving for a settlement in the spirit of his March effort, but by now he should have been aware that Grant was not empowered by Lincoln to do likewise. Chief of Staff John A. Rawlins expressed his displeasure more vehemently. "He now wants to entrap us into making a treaty of peace. . . . No Sir! No Sir. Why it is a positive insult; and an attempt in an underhanded way, to change the whole terms of the correspondence." Grant replied that Lee was just trying to save face, but Rawlins continued to fume. "'He don't think the emergency has arisen!' That's cool, but another falsehood. That emergency has been staring him in the face for forty-eight hours. If he hasn't seen it yet, we will soon bring it to his comprehension. He has to surrender. He shall surrender. By the eternal, it shall be surrender, and nothing else."[37]

Grant quietly concluded, "It looks as if Lee still means to fight," and he returned to his struggle to gain some sleep. The effort proved fruitless; at four in the morning Horace Porter found him pacing back and forth outside. Trying to find the silver lining, Porter remarked that Grant's headaches usually preceded successes, where-

upon Grant responded that getting rid of the headache would be sufficient. At dawn he went over to Meade's headquarters, drank some
coffee, and composed a response to Lee's message.[38]

Grant began by reminding Lee that he could not negotiate a peace
settlement and repeated that he was "equally anxious for peace with
yourself," in an attempt to stop the one-upsmanship from continuing.
Then he entered upon the heart of the matter. "The terms upon
which peace can be had are well understood. By the South laying
down their arms they will hasten that most desirable event, save thousands of human lives, and hundreds of millions of property not yet
destroyed." He expressed his hope that the two generals could bring
an end to the fighting "without the loss of another life." Once more,
he placed the responsibility on Lee's shoulders. There was no mistaking Grant's message. Lee could no longer play games or stall for time.
Sheridan had already seen to that. His troopers had occupied Appomattox Station, seizing Lee's last rations, and two infantry corps were
on the way to head off the Rebel columns approaching Appomattox
Court House. Sheridan was confident that "we will perhaps finish the
job in the morning" and, reading Grant's mind, added that Lee probably would not surrender "unless compelled to do so."[39]

April 9 was Palm Sunday. Grant and his staff mounted up once
more to join Sheridan. The general was not in great shape. His head
still ached, and his boots and trousers were splattered with red Virginia clay as the entourage made its way across the countryside. One
of Grant's aides turned to see a horseman charging toward the group,
waving his hat and shouting. It was one of Sheridan's staff officers,
delivering another dispatch from Lee. Rawlins accepted the message,
tore open the envelope, and read the letter. Without comment, he
passed it along to Grant. The general read it "mechanically," as an
observer noted, then told Rawlins to read it to the group. It was Lee's
offer to meet Grant to discuss the surrender of the Army of Northern
Virginia.[40]

"A blank silence fell on everybody for a minute," wrote newspaper
correspondent Sylvanus Cadwallader. One staff member attempted to
lead the group in cheers but met with a feeble response. Only after
they had recovered from the stunning news did they engage in "a
little jollification." Grant sat down to compose a reply, telling Lee he
would move as quickly as possible to meet him. As staff officer Orville

Babcock galloped off to deliver the letter, Porter asked Grant how he felt; Grant replied that the headache was gone.[41]

Early that afternoon, after making sure that neither Meade nor Sheridan launched assaults against Lee's lines, Grant and his staff rode up to Wilmer McLean's farmhouse, located less than 100 yards west of the county courthouse. Inside were Lee, aide Charles Marshall, and Babcock. Lee had donned a new dress uniform, complete with sash and jeweled sword, for the occasion; he "behaved with great dignity and courtesy but no cordiality," observed Adam Badeau. Grant wore a private's blouse, his shoulder straps alone indicating his rank. His boots and trousers were caked with clay. He had been so determined to catch Lee that he had outdistanced his headquarters baggage, and he saw no need to delay this meeting simply to spruce up.[42]

At first Grant, a bit subdued, did not quite know how to begin. He spent several minutes chatting with Lee about their experiences in Mexico, probably to give both of them an opportunity to gather their thoughts. At last the two men got down to business. In response to Lee's inquiries, Grant stated that he intended to parole both the officers and men of his army and would send them home. An obviously relieved Lee accepted these terms, and Grant commenced to reduce them to writing. "When I put my pen to the paper I did not know the first word that I should make use of in writing the terms," he recalled twenty years later. "I only knew what was in my mind, and I wished to express it clearly, so that there could be no mistaking it." Two additional considerations came to mind. "Let them have their horses to plow with," said Lincoln; perhaps this prompted Grant to exclude the officers' horses from the property to be turned over to the Union army. Glancing at Lee's sword, he decided that it would be "an unnecessary humiliation" for the officers to surrender their side arms. Lee would not have to hand Grant that beautiful sword.[43]

Having done this, Grant added one more sentence. It did much to shape the peace to follow. "This done each officer and man will be allowed to return to their homes not to be disturbed by United States Authority so long as they observe their parole and the laws in force where they may reside." This was politics with a vengeance. Grant, executing a fait accompli, made sure that there would be no future reprisals or treason trials. He may have been sure that Lincoln would endorse such an agreement, but he made it at his own discretion.[44]

Lee was pleased with the finished product, commenting that it would have "a happy effect upon his army." Still, there was one question. Lee's soldiers owned most of the animals used by the Army of Northern Virginia. Could they, too, take these animals home with them? At first Grant demurred. Then, observing Lee's dejection, he remarked that, since the war was near its close and the men would need the animals "to put in a crop to carry themselves and their families through the next winter," he would instruct his officers "to let all the men who claim to own a horse or mule take the animals home with them to work their little farms." Lee brightened, responding, "This will have the best possible effect on the men. It will be very gratifying and will do much toward conciliating our people." The terms were copied, Lee composed a letter of acceptance, and, after Grant agreed to send Lee some rations to feed his men, the interview was over. The Confederate commander walked down the stairs, mounted his horse, Traveller, and rode away toward his army. Grant, on McLean's porch, slowly raised his hat in salute, an act followed by his staff. Only after the Union commander and his staff left the house to return to headquarters did Porter remind Grant that perhaps he should notify Washington of the day's events. The dispatch was short and straightforward: "General Lee surrendered the Army of Northern Virginia this afternoon on terms proposed by myself. The accompanying additional correspondence will show the conditions fully."[45]

The news of the surrender preceded the mounted group of officers. The celebrating had already started by the time Grant returned to his tent. Meade's staff officers were busy waving Confederate paper money; soldiers "shouted, screamed, yelled, threw up their hats and hopped madly up and down"; Meade, who had been too sick to attend the surrender itself, was "galloping around and waving his hat with the best of them!" Bands played and cannons fired. To Grant's ears, this was just noise that could only make the surrendered feel worse. Staff officers were dispatched to various commands with orders to stop the firing. As Grant put it, "The war is over. The Rebels are our countrymen again."[46]

4

THE
WORD OF
GENERAL
GRANT

      Soldiers and officers of both sides slept well for the first time in weeks on the night of April 9 in the fields surrounding Appomattox Court House. A steady rain awakened them the following morning. While commissioners appointed by Grant and Lee met to work out the details of the surrender, including the stacking of arms, the transfer of property, and a formal ceremony (Grant had insisted that the Confederates could not merely drop their rifles and walk away), the two commanding generals met on horseback east of the courthouse between the picket lines of the two armies. Lee freely admitted that for all practical purposes the war was over. He had seen the end result for some time—in fact, he remarked that if Grant had accepted his proposal to negotiate in March the war might have ended a month sooner. Such a meeting would have excluded politicians from the process, which was fine with Lee. Like Grant and Sherman, the Virginian blamed politicians and extremists for bringing on the conflict. Now the fighting would fizzle out, and Lee expressed the hope "that everything would now be done to restore harmony and conciliate the people of the South." Even the fact of emancipation "would be no hinderance to the restoring of relations."[1]

Seizing on Lee's comment, Grant suggested that perhaps the Confederate commander could perform another service to prevent further bloodshed. "I asked him," he later recalled, "to use his influence with the people of the South—an influence which was supreme—to bring the war to an end." Such advice, Grant thought, "would be followed with alacrity." But Lee, who had just mentioned the opportunity missed the previous month, now shrank from talk of surrendering all of the remaining Confederates in the field. He claimed that he would have to confer with Jefferson Davis first. When Grant urged him to do so, he replied that such an act would be beyond what he conceived to be his duties as a soldier. This last comment was puzzling, for Lee had not always felt that way. In March he had been ready to discuss the possibility of peace negotiations with Davis; in ten days, he would advise Davis to sue for peace. As the commanding general of Confederate forces, Lee was empowered to agree to a general surrender. But this he would not do at this time.[2]

The conversation shifted to other topics. Lee asked Grant to provide his soldiers with some evidence of their status as paroled prisoners and reaffirmed his understanding with Grant that his men would be allowed to take their horses home with them. Finally, it appears that Grant and Lee worked out an arrangement to provide the defeated Rebels with transportation home. After nearly an hour, the two generals returned to their lines.[3]

By this time, the Confederates were aware of Grant's generous terms, and they were both surprised and pleased. "Judging from their hearty confessions of generous and liberal treatment by us," noted a newspaperman, "one would conclude they expected to have been chained together as felons to grace the triumphant march of our victorious general." Edward P. Alexander, Lee's artillery chief, concluded that "the exceedingly liberal treatment" contained in the terms "could only be ascribed to a policy of conciliation deliberately entered upon." Alexander later commented that Grant's demeanor indicated "a great & broad & generous mind. For all time it will be a good thing for the whole United States, that of all the Federal generals it fell to Grant to receive the surrender of Lee." The clause allowing soldiers to keep their horses was especially popular. Apparently, the terms had their desired effect: Elihu B. Washburne, who had arrived at Appomattox Court House just after the surrender, observed that the

Confederate officers he talked to displayed "a much better spirit than I had anticipated." One Union officer commented that most of his former foes "say that if the government will only show the same spirit of kindness, and goodwill that the army has, all will soon be all right, and a real peace again extend over all the land."[4]

Grant had an opportunity to sample this attitude firsthand before he left Appomattox. After he concluded his discussion with Lee, he and several staff officers rode over to McLean's house once more. Soon James Longstreet, Henry Heth, and Cadmus Wilcox—all pre-war friends—appeared, as did John B. Gordon, George E. Pickett, and some other officers. Gordon commented on Grant's "modest demeanor," adding, "There was nothing in the expression of his face or in his language or general bearing which indicated exultation at the great victory he had won." Indeed, Grant seemed to want to talk about anything except the war itself, recalling incidents dating back to their service in Mexico. He was especially glad to see "Pete" Longstreet, and took his friend by the arm in greeting. "Pete," he said, "let's have another game of brag to recall the old days." This was the sort of reunion Grant wanted, with men he could understand, away from the politicians. Several of the visitors expressed concern about their futures. Would the government confiscate their property? Would they be tried for treason? Judging from his later comments, although Grant made no assurances about confiscation, he promised to protect those who surrendered from prosecution for treason. Moreover, he was impressed by what he had seen and heard. "If advantage is taken of the present feeling in the South," he telegraphed Edwin M. Stanton that evening, "I am greatly in hopes an early peace can be secured."[5]

Grant left Appomattox on the afternoon of April 10, declining to witness the formal surrender ceremony two days later. He wanted to get back to Washington as soon as possible, not only to wind down the war program but also to oversee the final movements over the rest of the South. Reaching City Point on April 11, he placed Edward O. C. Ord in charge of Richmond with instructions to do what he could to restore peace and good feeling among the city's inhabitants. (Ord took this directive literally, at least in relation to Richmond's white inhabitants. His first action was to order the transfer of the black Twenty-fifth Corps out of the city, suggesting that he equated reconciliation with honoring racial prejudice.) Despite the pleadings of staff officers and his wife, Grant refused to visit Richmond, arguing that his presence "might lead to demonstrations which would only wound the feelings of the residents, and we ought not to do anything at such a time which would add to their sorrow." His gesture was recognized and appreciated by so staunch a Rebel as Edward A. Pollard, who noted that Grant "spared everything that might wound the feeling or imply the humiliation of a vanquished foe."[6]

The next day, the general's party departed for Washington, arriving on the morning of April 13. Grant conferred with Stanton on putting an end to recruiting and on reducing orders for munitions and supplies, but he was more interested in meeting Lincoln. The president was delighted with the terms Grant had given Lee, exclaiming, "Good! . . . All right! . . . Exactly the thing!" Indeed, Grant's terms embodied Lincoln's spirit of magnanimity, achieving what the president wanted—a solid foundation for reconciliation. John Gibbon, who supervised the formal surrender of the Army of Northern Virginia on April 12, confirmed this impression in a telegram to Grant on the same day, adding "that by announcing at once terms and a liberal merciful policy on the part of the Government we can once more have a happy united Country. I believe all reasoning men on both sides recognize the fact that slavery is dead."[7]

It is customary to recall that the North greeted news of Grant's terms to Lee with unrestrained enthusiasm and approval. Such was not the case. True, some newspapers applauded the terms. Grant's "noble spirit," according to one Washington journal, "says, *submission is restoration, amnesty, and peace.*" The New York *Times* argued that, although the surrender was primarily a military question, "the supplementary political task of completing a general measure of pacification, is already simplified to a degree beyond all public anticipation." The conservative New York *Herald*, whose correspondent Sylvanus Cadwallader was a favorite among some members of Grant's staff, was especially pleased. "By sending these soldiers home on parole Grant has provided for the immediate demoralization and dispersion of the rebel forces under Johnston . . . and has opened a way, broad and plain, for the reconstruction of the Union. Great as is Grant the general, he is equally matched by Grant the statesman and the diplomatist." The lenient terms did not disturb the *Herald*. "We apprehend no danger from a pardon to the rebel leaders, political or military. . . . Refuse them the honors of martyrdom," offered a *Herald* editorial. The New York *Times* agreed that "the immense influence of Lee throughout the South will make his efforts in the direction of pacification of the very highest importance."[8]

But not everyone was overjoyed with the substance of Grant's terms. "With a second reading of the matter came the American desire for details," editorialized the *Times*, "and to many the details were a cause of dissatisfaction. . . . It was very evident that a large number of our citizens would have been better satisfied if Grant had not allowed Lee and his men their parole." Noting the "very liberal character" of the terms, the Washington *Star* reported that "a large number of officers, together with thousands of the men of this army, express their dissatisfaction." A New York *Tribune* correspondent claimed that the terms "are regarded with disgust and unqualified indignation by large numbers of the most sensible, loyal and influential citizens in this region." Ralph Waldo Emerson growled, "General Grant's terms certainly look a little too easy, as foreclosing any action hereafter to convict Lee of treason." George G. Meade commented that "the Radicals are down on Grant for the terms he granted Lee." The new vice president, Andrew Johnson, rushed to the White House to protest. For all the celebration, there still lurked a feeling of vengeance, held in check only by the knowledge that Lincoln would stand by Grant's terms.[9]

On April 14, Grant attended a cabinet meeting. Discussion soon turned to reconstruction policy, with topics ranging from reopening trade with the South to the status of Francis Pierpoint's provisional government in Virginia. Stanton read drafts of two proclamations outlining one way to proceed with bringing the seceded states back into their normal relation to the Union. With Lee's army disbanded, there remained no reason to work with the Virginia legislators, and so Lincoln had abandoned that idea. But the president professed himself not ready to decide just yet what to do, instructed Stanton to submit copies of the proposal to every member, and then adjourned the meeting. As the cabinet members filed out of the room, Lincoln drew Grant aside. Mrs. Lincoln had made plans for the Lincolns and the Grants to attend Ford's Theater that night. Already the newspapers were publicizing the event. Would the Grants go?[10]

Grant declined the invitation. He had not seen his family in several weeks; Julia and he had planned to take a train to Burlington, New Jersey, where admirers had recently presented him with a new house—which, among other things, was away from Washington and its political intrigue. He also had no stomach for another encounter with Mrs. Lincoln and her infamous temper, rooted in her jealous nature. At City Point, the First Lady had offended Mrs. Grant several times by suggesting that Julia could not wait to move into the White House. Just the previous evening, Grant had suffered Mrs. Lincoln's spite. The president had asked the general to accompany the First Lady on a tour of the illuminations around the city. Unfortunately, Mrs. Lincoln grew resentful when she noticed that the crowds lining the streets were cheering for the general and not the president or his wife. A night at the theater was sure to produce the same results. Moreover, during the cabinet meeting, he had received a message from Julia. Disturbed by the behavior of several strange men who observed her eating lunch, she wanted to leave Washington as soon as possible. Secretly relieved, Grant explained his wife's determination, and Lincoln, all too aware of the consequences of offending one's wife, accepted the result. That afternoon the Grants boarded the train for home.[11]

The train made its way to Philadelphia without incident, and the Grants debarked to get something to eat. Several excited messengers sought out the general and thrust telegrams into his hands. Grant turned pale as he read the dispatches. Lincoln had been shot at the theater. He was dying. Secretary of State William H. Seward, already suffering from injuries received in a carriage accident, had also been attacked in his bed by a knife-wielding assailant. Rumor had it that Vice President Johnson and Grant himself were also targeted for assassination—Julia later believed that the strangers who had observed her at lunch included John Wilkes Booth. A stoic Grant reviewed the messages. "Not a muscle of his face quivered or a line gave an indication of what he must have felt at that great crisis," one courier recalled. After making sure that Julia and Jesse were safe in Burlington, a deeply disturbed Grant returned to Washington.[12]

In later years, Grant referred to April 14 as "the darkest day in my life." Just when peace seemed assured, it appeared as if assassination had replaced war as the order of the day, possibly portending the terrorist and guerrilla conflict Grant had feared. He had great confidence in Lincoln's ability to manage the process of reconstruction, and he knew that the president would consult closely with him on the proper course to follow. "I knew his goodness of heart, his generosity, his yielding disposition, his desire to have everybody happy," he later recalled, remembering "above all his desire to see all the people of the United States enter again upon the full privileges of citizenship with equality among all." Filled "with the gloomiest apprehension," he told Julia that Lincoln's death was "an irreparable loss to the South, which now needs so much both his tenderness and magnanimity." When Julia mentioned that Andrew Johnson would become president, Grant replied that "for some reason, I dread the change."[13]

Grant's uneasiness was understandable on grounds of policy and personality. Johnson had earned a reputation as an advocate of a harsh peace, and Grant later recalled that the Tennessean's vehement denunciation of Confederates presaged a policy that "would be such as to repel, and make them unwilling citizens," widening the gap between North and South. As if to reaffirm his fears, Johnson had visited Lincoln earlier that day, and some reports of their meeting claimed that the vice president had expressed his displeasure with Grant's Appomattox agreement. "I felt that reconstruction had been set back, no telling how far," the general remembered years later. Grant had established a close working relationship with Lincoln, and the two men had become good friends. Now he would have to cooperate with Johnson, whom he had encountered infrequently when Johnson was military governor of Tennessee.[14]

First, however, Grant had to make sure that the violence at Ford's Theater was not part of a larger plot to subvert the government. Hastily he sent word to Ord, commanding at Richmond, to arrest John A. Campbell and others "who have not yet taken the oath of Allegiance" as well as "all paroled officers. . . . Extreme rigor will have to be observed whilst assassination remains the order of the day with the rebels." Removed from the scene of the chaos, Ord realized that Grant's order made little sense. He reminded Grant that Lee and his staff were among the paroled officers in Richmond and, if they were arrested, "I think the rebellion here would be reopened." Campbell,

still pursuing Lincoln's now-abandoned overtures to the Virginia legislature, had asked permission to go to Washington, which suggested
that he was not part of any conspiracy. Grant decided to rescind the
order, although he left it as a suggestion should Ord need to take such
drastic steps.[15]

By the morning of April 16, Grant appeared to reject the notion
that Lincoln's assassination was part of a widespread Confederate conspiracy. Richard Ewell, quartered with other high-ranking Rebels at
Fort Warren, Massachusetts, reported to Grant that he was shocked
"by the occurrence of this appalling crime, and by the seeming ten-
dency in the public mind to connect the South and Southern men
with it." At the same time, Grant realized that there would be no more
efforts to use the existing Confederate state governments to aid the
reconstruction process. Meanwhile, he assisted in preparations for the
late president's funeral. In the past, he had often ordered black regiments out on review for Lincoln, knowing how much interest the
president took in their welfare. Now he asked Ord to send a black
regiment to Washington for the ceremonies, a fitting symbol of Lincoln's legacy. On April 19 the general-in-chief attended the funeral
service in the White House. He stood, alone, at the head of the cata-
falque, and newspaper correspondent Noah Brooks remarked that
the general "was often moved to tears."[16]

Of course, the best way to remember Lincoln was to secure the
peace that the late president had so ardently desired. But this was not
going to be easy. Grant knew that not all Radical Republicans were
torn by grief over Lincoln's assassination. Several of them welcomed
Johnson's elevation to the presidency as an opportunity to impose a
harsher peace. Grant, aware that the passions of the time had moved
even him to momentary extremism and vengeance, had good reason
to believe that these men might seek to overturn the settlement
achieved at Appomattox. He had already clashed with the Radicals,
first over an inquiry concerning the Battle of the Crater, then again
in the aftermath of Benjamin F. Butler's removal in January. Butler
had not taken dismissal quietly, growling about butchery and the no-
exchange policy for prisoners. Radical members of the Committee on
the Conduct of the War, who had left Grant alone for much of the
war, were infuriated by the removal of their favorite in the field. They
launched an investigation touching on several aspects of Grant's gen-

eralship in order to vindicate their fallen idol. "This is the beginning of a war on Grant," Meade, still smarting from his own brushes with the committee, grumbled.[17]

Grant had handled the interrogations, one at City Point and the other in Washington, in stride. But he was aware that committee members were still out to discredit him. In fact, a delegation had made plans to visit Fort Fisher and had reached Richmond before discovering that Lee had surrendered. Doubtless their vessel crossed paths with Grant's as the general returned to Washington. Now these same men, already disgruntled about Grant's terms, apparently had a friend in the White House—indeed, a close friend, for the new president had been one of the original members of the Committee on the Conduct of the War. Upon hearing of the fall of Richmond, Johnson had greeted a crowd by outlining how he would treat with Rebels. "I would arrest them; I would try them; I would convict them; and I would hang them," he declared. Then he uttered what was to become a recurring reprise in the weeks to come: "Treason must be made odious and traitors must be punished and impoverished." The day after Johnson took the presidential oath of office, Benjamin Wade, the Radical senator from Ohio, and a delegation visited the new chief executive at his temporary office in the Treasury Department. "Johnson, we have faith in you," Wade exclaimed. "By the gods, there will be no trouble now in running the government." Just a few days before, the Marquis Adolphe de Chambrun, in the United States to embark upon a legal career, observed that "every where the words peace, pardon, and clemency can be heard"; now, he noted, "Vengeance on the rebel leaders is the universal cry heard from one end of the country to the other."[18]

But Grant soon had cause for hope. After conferring with Johnson, he concluded that maybe he could work with the Tennessean. Newspapers reported that the president and the general were in full agreement on the proper course to pursue. "I have every reason to hope that in our new President we will find a man disposed and capable of conducting the government in its old channel," Grant told a St. Louis associate. "If so we may look for a speedy peace." He was satisfied that "the country has nothing to fear from his [Johnson's] administration." Besides, it was "unpatriotic at this time for professed lovers of this country to express doubts of the capacity and integrity of our Chief Magistrate." Duty demanded that Grant cooperate with Johnson.[19]

The first test of the new relationship occurred the day the train carrying Lincoln's coffin left for Springfield. A drained Grant returned to his headquarters to await the latest news from North Carolina. Several days earlier, Sherman had telegraphed him that Joseph Johnston, having been informed of Lee's surrender, was now willing to open negotiations with his opponent. Sherman had assured Grant that he would offer Johnston the same terms Grant had given Lee and would "be careful not to complicate any points of civil policy." Grant was pleased with the news, but he also noticed that Sherman described meetings with William A. Graham, William W. Holden, and other North Carolina Unionists—encounters that could not fail to be political in content. Still, Grant seemed gratified that "malice toward none, and charity for all" seemed to be the guiding force behind negotiations. Severe measures would not produce a lasting peace, he told Orville H. Browning. The policy outlined at Appomattox "was the true one," needing only to be complemented by a similar civil policy. Reconstruction would collapse if it "excluded more than half of the people of the South from participation."[20]

Grant's optimism about Sherman proved short-lived. On April 21, Maj. Henry Hitchcock, one of Sherman's aides, arrived, carrying a proposed agreement with Johnston and a cover letter. Grant read the latter first. Sherman explained that his proposal, if adopted, "will produce peace from the Potomac to the Rio Grande." Moreover, he said, "the point to which I attach the most importance, is that the dispersion and disbandment of these armies is done in such a manner as to prevent their breaking up into guerrilla bands." Grant approved these aims. To end guerrilla operations in the Shenandoah Valley, he had offered John S. Mosby and his men the same terms extended to Lee at Appomattox. He told Winfield Scott Hancock, however, that if the Confederate partisan leader did not surrender immediately he should "hunt him and his men down. . . . Guerrillas . . . will not be entitled to quarter."[21]

But, when Grant read Sherman's proposed settlement, he realized that his trusted subordinate had ranged far beyond the sphere of his competency in addressing civil as well as military questions. Under

Sherman's agreement, Confederate state officials and legislators, once they took the oath of allegiance, would be restored to power, pushing aside established provisional governments until the Supreme Court ruled which one was legitimate. Within weeks the civil courts would be in full operation, and most Southerners would resume their full civil and political rights. Having heard Lincoln's musings about what he would do to commence reconstruction, Sherman had taken it upon himself to enact what he believed to be Lincoln's plan. The fact of emancipation was conspicuous by its absence; indeed, in restoring to Southerners their "rights of person and property," one could argue that the agreement reinstated slavery.[22]

Grant was shocked. Only days before, Sherman had assured him that he would offer Johnston the same "magnanimous and liberal" terms Grant had given Lee. The general-in-chief could not believe that Sherman, far from avoiding issues of civil policy as he had promised, had plunged right into the maelstrom of the peace process. Failing to find Stanton at the War Department, Grant hurriedly scribbled a note to the war secretary, remarking that Sherman's dispatches "are of such importance that I think immediate action should be taken on them." The president and cabinet should convene immediately.[23]

Grant hoped that by acting quickly to quash Sherman's agreement he could protect his subordinate from serious repercussions. Surely he knew that if the terms were made public at a time when sorrow over Lincoln's assassination was mixed with feelings of vengeance against the South, they would only incite further heated debate. However, as Grant feared, neither Stanton nor Johnson were exactly cool-headed men. Cabinet members assembled at Johnson's temporary residence that evening to hear Grant read Sherman's proposal. Everyone immediately agreed that the terms should be rejected, but Stanton, Attorney General James Speed, and the president went on to denounce Sherman's actions as smacking of treason.[24]

This was too much for Grant. Sherman's terms were unacceptable and improper, but he was no traitor. At worst, he had broadly construed Lincoln's lenient sentiments expressed on the *River Queen*—a meeting at which neither Stanton nor Johnson had been present. Sherman had little idea of Northern reaction to the news of Lincoln's assassination, although he was concerned that his troops might react by reopening hostilities. At a time when chaos threatened in the form of assassination as well as guerrilla war, it was understandable that Sherman would take steps to create a lasting peace and reconciliation and to restore order. With these thoughts in mind, Grant defended his subordinate against the rash accusations of others, engaging in a little heated discussion himself. He volunteered to notify Sherman personally that the agreement had been rejected, partly to forestall a blunt rebuke that would serve only to embarrass and infuriate Sherman. He could placate his irritable subordinate, bring him up-to-date on the new political environment in Washington, and oversee new negotiations. Johnson agreed. Within several hours, Grant, Hitchcock, and several staff officers were on their way to North Carolina. As he prepared to depart, Grant, still smoldering over attacks upon Sherman's loyalty, exclaimed, "It is infamous—infamous! After four years of such service as Sherman has done—that he should be used like this!"[25]

Before he left, Grant sat down to write a letter telling Julia that he would not be able to return home for several days. It was obvious, however, that not only was he bothered by the events of the past hours, but also that he felt an increased sense of responsibility to make sure that what had been won in war was not now lost through miscalculation and malice. "I find my duties, anxieties, and the necessity for having all my wits about me increasing instead of diminishing. I have a Herculean task to perform and shall endeavor to do it, not to please any one, but for the interests of our great country that is now beginning to loom far above all other countries, modern or ancient." In an awkward way, Grant was trying to link together his life, the outcome of the war, and the destiny of the Republic. Somehow he had to make sure that the fruits of victory ennobled the nation. "That Nation, united, will have a strength that will enable it to dictate to all others, *conform to justice and right*. Power I think can go no further. The moment conscience leaves, physical strength will avail nothing, in the long run." It was up to Grant to protect that conscience.[26]

On his way down to Sherman's headquarters, Grant stopped off at Fort Monroe to telegraph Henry W. Halleck, now commanding at Richmond, to set in motion Philip H. Sheridan with his cavalry and some infantry. Should Johnston not submit to a new surrender agreement, Grant wanted to make sure that the Confederates would be surrounded and finished off. There could be no route left open for escape. With this objective achieved, he continued down to North Carolina, debarking at New Bern, where a surgeon noted that the general "had been dreadfully seasick and he looked sad and careworn." On April 24, Major Hitchcock entered Sherman's headquarters near Raleigh. Sherman and his staff looked up. "Well, major, do you bring peace or war?," someone asked. Hitchcock promptly replied, "I brought back General Grant." [27]

Sherman was not surprised when Grant told him that his agreement had been disapproved. While Grant was making his way to Raleigh, Sherman had read the reaction of the Northern press to Lincoln's assassination, and he had informed Johnston that it was unlikely that their agreement would find favor in light of recent events. He was upset, however, when Grant showed him a copy of the March 3 telegram from Lincoln and Stanton to Grant instructing the general to confine himself to military negotiations. This was the first Sherman had known of the dispatch, and he remarked that had he been aware of it he never would have concluded such an agreement. Instead, he had been guided not only by the discussions aboard the *River Queen* but also by the story that Lincoln had planned to let the Virginia legislature meet. No one was quite sure if Lincoln's comments during his meeting with Grant and Sherman in late March had modified the import of the March 3 telegram, since Grant's Appomattox terms had blurred the line between civil and military negotiations. Grant, in an effort to calm the excitable war secretary, tried to convey this impression to Stanton, remarking that Sherman's action was guided "entirely by what he thought was precedents authorized by the President." Sherman notified Johnston that the terms had been rejected and that hostilities would resume in forty-eight hours. He called on his opponent to surrender on the same terms Grant had offered Lee. [28]

Aware that it was futile to continue fighting, Johnston assented to Sherman's proposition, and on April 26 the two men signed a document identical in substance to the Appomattox agreement. After approving the agreement, Grant began to make his way back to Washington. He had been deeply impressed by what he had seen at Raleigh. "The people are anxious to see peace restored," he wrote

Julia from Sherman's headquarters. "The suffering that must exist in the South the next year, even with the war ending now, will be beyond conception. People who talk now of further retalliation and punishment, except of the political leaders, either do not conceive of the suffering endured already or they are heartless and unfeeling." To a newspaper reporter, he described Southerners as "unfortunate, a desolated race" and added that "he would treat the masses of the South with kindness and humanity especially in view of the fact that they had been forced to obey their own desperate leaders." In early May, he concluded, "Management is all that is now wanted to secure complete peace."[29]

First, however, Grant had to manage a conflict that arose between Sherman and Stanton from the war secretary's actions after the April 21 cabinet meeting. The next day, Gideon Welles had noted approvingly that Grant had gone to Raleigh to confer with Sherman. Within hours, however, Welles began hearing rumors reflecting adversely on Sherman's motives. Since Massachusetts senator and renowned Radical Charles Sumner, an associate of Stanton, was one of Welles's informants, the navy secretary concluded that his colleague in the War Department was up to something. The next day, Stanton's account of the affair appeared in the morning papers. The war secretary not only rebuked Sherman for making such an agreement, but also insinuated that Sherman had succumbed to Confederate influences and might even have taken steps to aid Jefferson Davis's escape attempt. This hysteria proved contagious: Attorney General Speed went so far as to wonder out loud what would happen if Sherman should actually put Grant under arrest. Halleck compounded the problem by suggesting that Sherman's movements would allow Davis to evade capture and escape with gold from the Confederate treasury.[30]

Sherman's predictable outrage was justified. Reminding Grant that it was unfair "to withhold from me the plans and policy of Government (if any there be), and expect me to guess at them," he argued that Stanton's insinuations of insubordination and treason were calculated to invite "the dogs of the press to be let loose upon me"—a fate worse than death to Sherman. "I envy not the task of 'reconstruction,'" he concluded, "and am delighted that the Secretary of War had relieved me of it." Over the next several weeks, the debate raged in the press as Sherman engaged in a fiery correspondence with both Stanton and Halleck, with Grant in the middle.[31]

In Grant's eyes, both Stanton and Sherman had erred, and their fractious natures had exacerbated an already difficult situation. Sherman's telegram to Stanton announcing Grant's arrival at Raleigh had been a sign of what was to come. In it, Sherman had admitted his "folly in embracing in a military convention any civil matters" but added that "such is the nature of our situation that they seem inextricably united." Fair enough. But Sherman then added that Stanton himself had hinted that a quick peace might require "a little bending to policy" and that he believed that the new administration "has made a mistake." In such an essay, Grant discerned that Sherman was indeed involved in politics when it came to framing the terms of peace and was not above needlessly offending Stanton to press his point. But Stanton was no better. Later that day, the war secretary informed Grant that Sherman's proposal "meets with universal disapprobation. No one class or shade of opinion approves it. . . . The hope of the country is that you may repair the misfortune occasioned by Sherman's negotiations."[32]

Behind this clash of temperamental personalities lay signs of the emergence of a significant policy problem for peacemakers. Military and civil concerns were indeed intertwined, as Sherman had asserted. Moreover, it was clear that soldiers like Sherman and civilians like Stanton had different beliefs on the course reconstruction should take. Sherman believed that behind Stanton's action was a desire to gain "the vast patronage of the military Governorships of the South, and the votes of negro[es]" to satisfy his political ambitions. Sherman adamantly opposed black suffrage, agreeing with John M. Schofield that "prompt and wise action" was necessary "to prevent the negro from becoming a huge elephant on our hands." Grant would find it difficult to harmonize the views of his most trusted subordinate and his immediate civilian superior.[33]

Moreover, it was apparent that Grant was going to have to play a major role in postwar reconstruction, in large part because the army would have to administer many aspects of whatever policy was adopted. Sherman, Sheridan, and other soldiers looked to Grant to protect their interests and to present their views; Johnson, Stanton, and other politicians also leaned on him for support, to the point where some of the president's advisers were concerned that the Tennessean relied all too much on Grant's opinion. Grant knew he had an immense responsibility to ensure that what was achieved at Appomattox and Durham's Station was not frittered away in fractious political debate.

During May, Grant attended cabinet discussions on reconstruction policy. He preferred to speak only when his opinion was requested, making clear that his major concern was "to see something done to restore civil governments in those states" as soon as possible. "I did not want all chaos left there, and no form of civil government whatever," he recalled two years later. However, Grant expected that any action undertaken by Johnson would be only a temporary expedient. Congress would have the last say. In the interim, he told Sheridan, it would probably be best to divide the South into several military districts and supervise events "until Congress took action about restoring them to the Union." There should be no elections or renewal of political activity. The resulting quiet "would give the Southern people confidence, and encourage them to go to work, instead of distracting them with politics." Grant was more specific when Johnson discussed with him a draft of an amnesty proclamation; Grant argued that Confederate generals, by virtue of their rank alone, should not be excluded from the general terms of the amnesty, and for some time he questioned the exclusion of Southerners owning $20,000 worth of property. Radical Henry Winter Davis questioned Johnson's reliance on Grant, "of whom he seemed not exactly to stand in awe of but anxious to conciliate rather than resolved to command."[34]

Grant's anxiety to secure some sort of plan, however temporary, for the restoration of civil government was prompted in part by the concerns voiced by his subordinates. He informed Gen. Frederick Steele that there was no need for the Alabama legislature to meet since no one recognized the legitimacy of the body or its acts during the war. Schofield, left to run affairs in North Carolina, submitted to Grant a plan calling for the appointment of a provisional governor, the election by white voters who had taken the amnesty oath of delegates to a state constitutional convention, and the framing of a constitution in harmony with the results of the war, including emancipation and the repudiation of secession. Grant understood Schofield's frustration but counseled patience. "Until a uniform policy is adopted for reestablishing civil government in the rebellious States, the military authorities can do nothing but keep the peace." Agreeing with Schofield that something had to be done, Grant forwarded the plan to Johnson and Stanton, who appeared pleased with the suggestions. Still, in the absence of definite policy, Grant was unable to send instructions to anyone.[35]

The general-in-chief also had to contend with the behavior of the occupation forces and the racial attitudes of their commanders. In Virginia, Halleck and Ord complained of the behavior of the black soldiers in the Twenty-fifth Corps. Grant had already consented to the corps' transfer to Petersburg, but now Ord and Halleck launched a campaign to oust it from the state. They asserted that the black soldiers were ill-disciplined and offended the white community. Ord told Grant that several cases of "atrocious rape" had occurred, a product of the soldiers' "want of discipline and good officers." To prevent the emigration of blacks to Richmond, a labor system had to be organized in the countryside. In mid-May, Gen. George L. Hartsuff reported that Petersburg whites had complained that black soldiers had destroyed buildings and participated "in the exciting of the colored people to acts of outrage against the persons and property of white citizens. . . . Colored soldiers are represented as having straggled about, advising Negroes not to work on the farms, where they are employed, and had been told by the soldiers, that if they had not arms to use against their former masters, that they 'the Soldiers' would furnish them."[36]

These reports did not go unchallenged. In reply, officers of the Twenty-fifth Corps charged that Ord was a racist, jealous of the corps' accomplishments during the last week of the war, and overly concerned with appeasing white Southerners. "The behavior of my entire corps during the last month has been most excellent," corps commander Godfrey Weitzel protested to Grant in a report that Ord weakly endorsed.[37]

The debate over the use of black troops in the postwar South epitomized the basic dilemma facing Grant and others who sought to reconcile moderation toward white Southerners with the recognition that blacks had to be accorded at least civil equality. Grant thought highly of the performance of black troops during the war. "For guard duty and picket duty, on the march and in an assault," he said, "I consider the negro troops surpassed by no soldiers in the world, and equalled by very few." But this was not at issue. Whatever the behavior of black soldiers, it was obvious that their mere presence inhibited genuine reconciliation. Southern whites were irritated, indeed shamed, that their former slaves were now armed guards overseeing them. Black privates encouraged other blacks to stand up for their rights—an act many white Southerners claimed was akin to insurrection—and even offered protection for such assertions of freedom. With white soldiers impatiently pressing to be mustered out, black units were often the only ones available for occupation duty. To insist that black regiments remain was to invite conflict and to foster hostility; to remove them was to bow to racism and to concede that efforts to secure black civil equality were doomed. That many commanders endorsed charges of misbehavior without first investigating the alleged incidents suggested that at least some commanders shared the racist assumptions of the complainants. In this cross fire of assertion and counterassertion, it was often difficult for Grant to discover exactly what had happened.[38]

In the case of the Twenty-fifth Corps, Grant decided that its removal to the Texas-Mexico border would serve several purposes. Not only would it reduce interracial friction, but also it would provide additional strength for possible operations against the French-supported regime of Maximilian in Mexico, which Grant eagerly anticipated. To him, the French intervention was as much a part of the war as was the Confederate rebellion—for it, too, tested the viability of the United States. In May Grant ordered Sheridan to take command of the forces, including the Twenty-fifth Corps, assembling along the Rio Grande, explaining that "our success in putting down secession would never be complete until the French and Austrian invaders were compelled to quit the territory of our sister republic." Grant believed that the black troops might decide upon leaving the army to emigrate to Mexico, where, as Mexican representative Matías Romero observed, "the Negro race is not the victim of prejudice." That most of the black soldiers involved in the transfer were angry to be sent far away from their homes in Maryland and Virginia, and that

Richmond and Petersburg blacks had lost a friend, was overlooked by the general. In this instance, Grant, although aware of the prejudice existing against blacks, seemed more concerned with pacifying white Southerners to secure peace.[39]

On May 23 and 24, Grant, President Johnson, cabinet members, and other civil and military officials presided over a grand review of many of the units of Meade's and Sherman's armies. Five days later, Johnson formally commenced the reconstruction process by issuing two proclamations. One contained Johnson's amnesty policy, complete with oath of allegiance and a list of "excepted classes," including generals, West Point graduates, and men who had resigned army commissions to join the Confederacy. Despite Grant's objections, the clauses excluding both Confederate generals and individuals possessing $20,000 in taxable property were retained. The other proclamation outlined a plan by which North Carolina could be restored to the Union. In many respects it resembled Schofield's proposal as well as Lincoln's previous policy, with its appointment of a provisional governor and a call for a constitutional convention chosen by voters who had taken the amnesty oath and met the suffrage requirements of the prewar constitution—meaning no black suffrage. Military commanders were instructed to "aid and assist" the provisional governors and were admonished against "hindering, impeding, or discouraging the loyal people from the organization of a State government." In the following months, Johnson issued similar proclamations covering the other states that were not already operating under governments established during the Lincoln administration.[40]

The president had not followed all of Grant's advice, but the general, according to Adam Badeau, "has every reason to be satisfied with the support that Johnson gives him." On June 7 Grant attended a New York rally at Cooper Union—arranged by New York War Democrats—to endorse Johnson's policy. Although he was perfectly willing to show his support for the president, he expressed no opinion about the recent proclamations. The New York World, a leading Democratic organ that would have been happy to record Grant's presence as indicative of his position, instead stressed the nonpolitical nature of Grant's reception. "In honoring General Grant," it asserted, "our people feel that they are honoring all that is best in themselves. . . . They endorse no political theory in this frank homage; they serve no political ambition in paying it." Indeed, Grant received such an enthusiastic reception that he nearly defeated the purpose of the meeting. The crowd interrupted Daniel S. Dickinson's speech celebrating Johnson with cheers for Grant. Finally, the general left the hall, allowing Dickinson and the generals John A. Logan and Frank Blair to continue extolling the chief executive. In light of later events, the resolutions presented at this meeting take on especial interest: they included a call to enfranchise black soldiers and an endorsement of impartial suffrage. Perhaps no one was quite sure of Johnson's ultimate intentions, since neither measure had been included in the North Carolina proclamation.[41]

With Johnson having made public his policy, everyone waited for signs of Southern reaction. Grant had kept a careful eye on conditions in the South since Appomattox, looking for evidence of returning loyalty. From Richmond, Halleck kept Grant apprised of conditions in the former Confederate capital. "The rebel feeling in Va. is utterly dead and with proper management can never be revived," he relayed at the end of April. (In Halleck's mind, "proper management" included the removal of black troops.) One reason for the quiet, as Grant's brother-in-law Fred noted, was the "starving multitude" in the city seeking relief. Such reports did not rouse sympathy in every Yankee heart. One of Butler's cronies, Gen. John W. Turner, reported so much generosity to Rebels that "we don't quite understand what we have been fighting for."[42]

Halleck thought that the best way to further Southern submission was to display lenience toward Robert E. Lee. By early May, it was rumored that the Confederate commander was considering petitioning the president for pardon. "Should he do this," Halleck told Grant, "the whole population with few exceptions will follow his example." On the same day, Meade visited Lee at his Richmond home to urge his former foe to take the oath of allegiance. Lee replied that, though he had no objection to taking the oath, he preferred to wait for word of Johnson's reconstruction policy before acting.[43]

Grant enthusiastically approved of conciliating the Confederate hero. "Although it will meet with opposition in the North to allow Lee the benefit of Amnesty," he told Halleck, "I think it would have the best possible effect towards restoring good feeling and peace in the South to have him come in. All the people except a few political leaders [in the] South will accept what ever he does as right and will be guided to a great extent by his example." Such an act would further the cause of peace and reconciliation by demonstrating that vengeance was not a part of the reconstruction process.[44]

But many Northerners did not share Grant's sentiments. Some papers called upon the government to try Lee for treason. The New York *Times* argued that "the terms granted to General Lee and his army cannot in the slightest degree affect their future responsibility to the civil authorities. Time only and the calm judgment of the American people will show what punishment is to be meted out to them." Butler, eager to gain revenge for his removal by Grant, sought to curry favor with President Johnson by fueling the chief executive's announced desire to punish traitors. He told the president that the Appomattox agreement "was a purely military convention, and referred to military terms only." Furthermore, he said, "As soon as these men cease to be prisoners of war, all supposed obligation to them will cease." Grant, he insisted, "had no authority to grant amnesty or pardon." An opinion issued in late April by Attorney General Speed narrowly defined the rights of Confederates who claimed residence in states that had not formally seceded, which led observers to claim that "the terms of the capitulation were strictly military." The distinguished legal theorist Francis Lieber took the same ground, although he wavered on the topic of Lee's vulnerability to a treason indictment.[45]

As if in response to this desire for revenge, federal judge John C. Underwood convened a grand jury at the end of May in Norfolk. Calling for Lee and other Confederate leaders to be indicted for treason, Underwood characterized the Appomattox agreement as "a mere military arrangement" that had "no influence upon civil rights or the status of the persons involved." The grand jury, following Underwood's bidding, indicted Lee and a score of other prominent Confederates in early June. Coming on the heels of Johnson's May 29 proclamation outlining his amnesty policy, the news prompted Lee to ask for a pardon, not only to protect himself but also to set an example for others.[46]

Before submitting his application for pardon, Lee sought to find out how Grant would receive it. He contacted Ord, who was still at Richmond, and Senator Reverdy Johnson of Maryland, to make inquiries. Ord dispatched Gen. Rufus Ingalls to visit Grant. Speaking on behalf of Grant, who was still in New York, John A. Rawlins assured Ingalls that Grant would "cheerfully advise the President to grant it." Several of the president's associates also told Ingalls that the chief executive would approve Lee's request. Adam Badeau advised Senator Johnson that Grant would stand by his terms and approve Lee's application, although the commanding general believed that Lee should apply for pardon soon. Thus assured, on June 13 Lee forwarded his application for presidential pardon to Grant, asking whether the Appomattox terms protected him from Underwood's proceedings.[47]

Grant returned to Washington to find Lee's letter waiting for him. He endorsed both documents, urging that Lee be pardoned, defending the sanctity of the Appomattox terms, and asking the president to "quash" Underwood's actions. "Good faith as well as true policy dictates that we should observe the conditions of that convention," he argued, adding that the terms "met with the hearty approval of the President at the time, and of the people generally." On June 16, as Grant prepared to leave for the White House with the documents in hand, Badeau sat down to write to James H. Wilson. Not only did Grant believe that the terms Lee accepted precluded any treason trials, but also the president, according to Badeau, "is not at all vengeful or bitter towards the high officers of the late rebel army." Indeed, the president's only desire was "to let in the rank and file first." Both Johnson and Grant, continued Badeau, would follow "a merciful policy . . . despite what you may see in Radical papers to the contrary. Neither of them favors negro suffrage, at least any interference by the general government in the matter."[48]

Badeau may have correctly described his superior's attitude on the subject, but, as Grant soon found out, Andrew Johnson had different ideas. Earlier that month, a Virginian seeking a pardon for George Pickett came away from the White House disappointed. Apparently Johnson "thought he would hold some of their principal leaders in suspense for some time." The president presented the same case to Grant, arguing that Lee and other Rebel leaders had to face punishment. The general dissented. Johnson "might do as he pleased about civil rights, confiscation of property, and so on," but the terms at Appomattox had to be honored. Not only would legal proceedings prosecuting Lee for treason disrupt and possibly destroy the prospects for reconciliation, Grant insisted, but also they represented a breach of faith on the part of the government. To obtain Lee's surrender, Grant had to promise to forbid reprisals—otherwise, Lee's army would have dissolved into bands of outlaws and guerrillas, perpetuating the conflict. Furthermore, Lincoln approved Grant's terms (albeit after the fact), and Johnson himself had endorsed them when he had ordered Grant to offer the same terms to Johnston. The president persisted, in part because he had accepted Butler's argument that the parole extended to Lee and his men applied only so long as they were prisoners of war. "When can these men be tried?" he asked. "Never," replied Grant, "unless they violate their paroles."[49]

Both Grant and Johnson were stubborn men who held tightly to their convictions of right and wrong. Johnson wanted traitors to be punished; Grant believed that both his personal honor and that of the nation would be shattered if Johnson broke the pledge made at Appomattox. Finally, Grant played his last, most powerful card. He threatened to resign his commission if Johnson did not relent and honor the surrender terms. At once Johnson realized that without Grant's support his administration would be in serious trouble. Unwilling to take on the hero of the war, he backed down. On June 20 Attorney General Speed told U.S. District Attorney Lucius Chandler to drop the proceedings. Grant thereupon wrote Lee, assuring the Confederate commander that he was safe and that Grant would protect him.[50]

That same day, Grant sat down to compose his official report describing military operations during the closing year of the war. He was not thinking of the past and victories won, however, but of the need to secure the benefits of those victories in peace. For the past two months, he had tried to balance leniency with his desire to smother the rebellion, rejecting both Johnson's desire for vengeance and Sherman's excessive generosity. Renowned as a warrior, all he wanted now was peace and cooperation in rebuilding a nation that would realize Lincoln's desire "to see all the people of the United States enter again upon the full privileges of citizenship with equality among all." What was needed now was statesmanship and compromise for the greater good, not further chaos and disruption.[51]

With such thoughts in mind, he prepared a report that said as much about peacemaking as it did about warmaking. "Lee's great influence throughout the whole South caused his example to be followed," resulting in "peace and quiet." If the Confederate leader had known at Appomattox that he would be tried for treason, "the surrender never would have taken place." Even though Grant advocated leniency toward the Confederacy's military leaders, he called for punishment of its political leaders, men "guilty of the most heinous offenses known to our laws. Let them reap the fruit of their offenses." Implicit in such a statement was Grant's belief that politicians were responsible for the war; in this sense he was still the Grant of 1861, who had called for the hanging of Jefferson Davis. He now feared that the same selfish bickering and maneuvering that had sparked the conflict would thwart the success of the peacemaking process. Calling for unity among Northern politicians as they embarked on the work of reconstruction, he observed that the soldiers had "learned moderation and forgiveness"; could not the politicians do the same? He pointed out that "those professedly loyal throughout the great conflict" were now "so differing in opinion as to what should be done in the great work of reconstruction as to endanger peace among friends. . . . Would it not be well for all to learn to yield enough of their individual views to the will of the majority to preserve a long and happy peace?"[52]

Then the general looked at what he had written. He felt uneasy about expressing such sentiments in an official report. After all, he had said that military men should keep out of politics, yet here he was, violating his own maxim. Reluctantly, he decided to restrict himself to military matters: the passages quoted above were omitted in his final report. He was not yet ready to become explicitly involved in the politics of reconstruction. He would soon find out that he had little choice.

5

FROM

CONCILIATION

TO

PROTECTION

By the end of the spring of 1865, all remaining Confederate forces had laid down their arms. Nevertheless, the U.S. Army's job was not over. It had to remain in the South on occupation duty until civil governments were reestablished and the insurrection was formally declared at an end. Grant's subordinates attended to their new responsibilities with mixed feelings. They tried to maintain order, relieve suffering, and assist the Freedmen's Bureau (although some commanders obstructed rather than supported Bureau operations). At times they clashed with civil officers, especially the provisional governors appointed by Johnson. In New Orleans, Philip H. Sheridan found it "hard to enforce martial law after war has ceased and a form . . . of civil government is in existence." Even so, he assured President Johnson, "we can well afford to be lenient," even in the face of Southerners' "impotent ill-feeling." Since "it is so hard by any species of legislation to correct this feeling, magnanimity is the safest and most manly course." Others were even more optimistic. George H. Thomas believed that "judicious management" would allow military authorities to restore "perfect order" in Tennessee, Alabama, and Georgia with "but little trouble." From North Carolina, John M.

Schofield wrote Grant that "the presence of troops seems almost unnecessary."[1]

William T. Sherman, still smarting over the rough handling of his April peace proposal, looked to events to vindicate his approach to reconciliation. "I am well satisfied at the course things are taking," he told his brother John in September. "No matter what change we may desire in the feelings and thoughts of people South, we cannot accomplish it by force. Nor can we afford to maintain there an army large enough to hold them in subjugation." Lest his senator brother concern himself with reports of renewed Southern resistance, Sherman quickly dismissed such notions. "You hardly yet realize how completely the country has been devastated, and how completely humbled the man of the South is." Two months later, he noted with more than a touch of satisfaction, "You observe that Mr. Johnson is drifting toward my terms to Johnston. He cannot help it, for there is no other solution." Echoing Sherman, George G. Meade advocated reconciliation "as the policy most likely to effect a speedy reunion." If a vindictive policy was to be pursued, "We shall have to shed almost as much blood as has already been shed."[2]

The first priority of most army officers on occupation duty was stability. Whether serving in the Freedmen's Bureau or commanding detachments of soldiers, order was uppermost in their minds. Both the unwillingness of blacks to make contracts for their labor on white-owned plantations and farms and the insolent and sometimes violent behavior of whites disrupted that order. Another potential source of instability was the promise of some Radical Republicans to initiate a social revolution in the South featuring the enfranchisement of the freedmen and the distribution of confiscated lands to allow blacks to establish small farms. Believing that blacks were not ready to assume the full responsibilities of freedom, that any effort to transform the Southern economy and society would only thwart reconciliation, and that Republican policy was motivated primarily by partisan concerns, few commanders endorsed these plans. So long as Southern whites readily accepted the verdict of Appomattox, commanders were more supportive of economic recovery and political restoration as essential to order.

Ulysses S. Grant took little part in the restoration process during the summer of 1865. This was surprising in the light of the importance he placed on establishing the conditions for a lasting peace. Instead, the general, tired of politics and looking for some rest after years of pressure, escaped the confines of the nation's capital and toured throughout the North. Crowds received him everywhere; he was showered with gifts; at Galena he was presented with a house; and at nearly all stops he refused to utter more than a sentence of thanks, adding to his reputation as a sphinx. When he thought about national affairs, his mind drifted to the Texas-Mexico border, where federal troops were massed, ready to cross the border to support Mexican resistance to French occupation. Grant wanted to fight this war in part to field an army composed of Union and Confederate veterans. One way to facilitate reunion might be to reforge the bonds of brotherhood in the furnace of combat against a common foe. In his mind, the Civil War was not completely over until the French were ejected from Mexico. Reporters seemed more interested in uncovering his musings on this topic than in delving into his opinions on Reconstruction.[3]

Grant's traveling took him away from the capital, preventing him from participating in discussions about the role of the military in the occupied South. When he did speak, he endorsed a policy of recovery, restoration, and reconciliation and looked to an early end to military occupation of the South. "It is time that military arrests and military commissions were at an end," he told one commander in ordering the release of a Kentucky minister arrested under martial law. "We are now at peace, and if any citizen commits any political offense he should be taken before the civil courts and there tried for his crime." He transmitted the same advice to other subordinates. "As a rule," he wrote Sheridan, "I am opposed to the military taking the law into their own hands." It was also time to stop punishing Southerners merely for fighting on the Confederate side. When Johnson refused to pardon one of John S. Mosby's men, Grant objected, commenting "that there had been suffering enough." He worked hard to secure pardons for several Confederate generals, including James Longstreet, and intervened on behalf of the imprisoned Alexander H. Stephens and Clement C. Clay. There seemed to be little harshness now in the man who once waged relentless war.[4]

The general-in-chief also found himself once more defending the parole provisions of the Appomattox terms. Alfred E. Jackson, a former Confederate brigadier, had surrendered to Union authorities upon hearing of Lee's capitulation. Returning home to Jonesborough, Tennessee, he discovered that a federal district court in Knoxville had indicted him for treason. Grant was furious to find out that the paroles issued at Appomattox were still not being honored. "Good faith required that he should protect those who surrendered from prosecution and punishment," Orville Browning reported Grant as saying, "and he intended to do it." Indictments should cease; confiscation of property should stop. How else could the Rebels become "our countrymen again"?[5]

So optimistic was the general about "the peaceful condition of the South" that he pushed hard to demobilize the army as quickly as possible. He told Edwin M. Stanton that "submission was perfect" throughout the region and that the number of soldiers left "to secure order and protect the freedmen in the liberty conferred upon them" had been reduced, "as continued quiet and good order have justified it." Still, Grant was ready to recommend a continued military presence, however small, to guard against "the possibility of future local disturbances arising from ill feeling left by the war or the unsettled questions between the white and black races at the south." Some of his subordinates were more cautious about predicting an end to occupation. Meade, who had toured the Atlantic seaboard in the summer of 1865, told Grant that the presence of the military was essential to preserve order, protect blacks, and prevent interracial clashes until "the passage of such laws by the respective states as would guarantee to Freedmen the essential civil rights."[6]

Grant's emphasis on conciliation was evident in his stance toward black troops, the Freedmen's Bureau, and black suffrage. By the summer of 1865, complaints about black troops had multiplied, and at the end of August Grant requested the War Department to muster out all black regiments raised in the North. To him, the truth of the charges was irrelevant; the mere presence of black troops was destabilizing and inhibited reconciliation, which justified their removal. However, he retained in service black regiments organized in the South, enabling him to control the behavior of part of the Southern black population by keeping it in uniform. Many of these units continued on occupation duty. Other regiments were sent to the frontier, where Grant was confident that they would render good service; after their discharge, the black veterans might also "furnish labor hereafter for our railroads and mining interests." Had these troops been discharged immediately, they might have compounded the chaotic social situation or responded to white provocation with violence. One way to prevent such confrontations was to prohibit black troops from keeping their weapons after muster out, a privilege accorded to white troops. To Grant, the best way to reduce interracial friction, no matter the cause, was to control black behavior, for to place additional restraints on whites would antagonize them, prolonging sectional divisiveness. He seemed less sensitive to protecting blacks from whites than to protecting whites from themselves.[7]

The Freedmen's Bureau presented similar problems. Grant did not embrace demands for massive redistribution of property through confiscation, but he favored some sort of federal agency to assist Southern blacks in the transition from slavery to freedom, modeled on John Eaton's refugee relief efforts in Tennessee and Mississippi. While he assisted Bureau head Oliver O. Howard's efforts to staff his organization, he also punished alleged misbehavior by Bureau officials. In August he received reports that Gen. Edward A. Wild, supervising Bureau operations in Georgia, was terrorizing white citizens in his excessive zeal to carry out his business. Grant, objecting to Wild's "prejudice in favor of color," called for his removal and suggested that staff officer Cyrus B. Comstock tour the region to observe conditions and make recommendations to Howard. To Grant's mind, the Bureau was supposed to act as a mediator and harmonizer between the races as well as a guardian for the freedmen, not as an advocate for social upheaval and revolution, which could only perpetuate hostility.[8]

The general-in-chief also opposed immediate enfranchisement of Southern blacks, fearing that such a step would only aggravate social disorder and interracial friction. Senator James R. Doolittle of Wisconsin told a Milwaukee crowd that Grant believed that "a considerable portion of the troubles between the whites and the blacks that had already occurred, was in consequence of this unwise attempt to force negro suffrage in those states." It was Grant's opinion "that if the Federal government were to attempt to do it and to enforce it, it would undoubtedly produce war between the two races there." The search for a stable social order was foremost in Grant's mind; he did not base his argument against black suffrage on grounds of racial inferiority. The previous June, the Chicago *Tribune* reported that the general thought that "it is too soon to declare that the loyal blacks in the South shall not be allowed to vote," in part for practical reasons. Eventually, should problems persist in the South, policymakers "may have to choose between keeping a standing army . . . or . . . enfranchising the blacks, and thereby enabling them to support the white loyalists." But, for the present, Grant believed that until blacks became literate, they needed protection more than they needed the ballot.[9]

The theme of conciliation was also evident in Grant's relations with white Southerners. Several Southern papers praised him for his "delicacy of feeling" and his "generous and respectful consideration" for the defeated. He rejected a proposal to place a painting of Lee's surrender in the Capitol's rotunda, arguing that it would remind Southerners of their defeat. Prominent leaders made clear to him their acceptance of the results of the war. Henry A. Wise, who as governor of Virginia in 1859 had approved of the execution of John Brown, went so far as to tell Grant that he applauded emancipation and would work "to make it beneficent to both races and a blessing especially to our country." The spirit of submission was surprising. As Adam Badeau noted, "People have been vanquished before, but some of the vanquished have refused to get on their knees. Now the scramble is who shall get down first and lowest." Such incidents reinforced Grant's belief that true reconciliation and justice for the freedman was only a matter of time. He did what he could to help Southern whites, especially Confederate officers, get back on their feet. George Pickett was astounded when Grant offered to assist him meet the costs of rebuilding his house. When Henry Heth opened an express company, Grant sent his encouragement. Such an enterprise, employing veterans from both sides, would "restore what is now wanted above everything else in this country—harmony and friendship between the two sections." Unable to attend a meeting devoted to relief efforts, Grant made his views known in a letter. "However we may have differed from our Southern brethren in the events of the past four years we have now become one people and with but one interest," he wrote, pledging his support for whatever "is calculated to increase the friendship and brotherly feeling between the two sections of our Country." [10]

In all of this, Grant displayed a somewhat naive optimism about the regeneracy of Southern loyalty. Slow to appreciate the resiliency of white resistance to change, he overlooked reports of antiblack violence, rationalizing that it was to be expected during the process of readjustment. Not until later did he come to realize that such behavior revealed deep-seated and durable white racism. Although his attitude during the summer and fall of 1865 should not be mistaken for indifference, apathy, or an endorsement of racist attitudes, it does suggest that he was willing to tolerate much to reestablish sectional harmony. Absent from Washington during much of the summer, he failed to pay sufficient attention to the problems of military occupation, and many crucial decisions were made without his participation. Mistaken in believing that racism and recalcitrance were short-lived, Grant would soon come to realize his error.

Reports in the Northern press during the summer and fall of 1865 of interracial friction, violence, and unrepentant ex-Confederates unwilling to concede the consequences of defeat suggested that the emergence of true "brotherly feeling" was some time off. Under the provisional governments established through a series of presidential proclamations in the spring and summer of 1865, conventions revising state constitutions convened; in several instances, resolutions abolishing slavery, nullifying secession ordinances, and repudiating the Confederate war debt passed only after heated debate. State legislatures had enacted a series of laws, collectively labeled Black Codes, designed to reduce blacks to a state of second-class citizenship not all that far removed from slavery.

Andrew Johnson knew that such behavior threatened to endanger his policy of an easy peace. Unlike Grant, he accepted reports of racial violence as part of the inevitable process of reducing blacks to second-class citizens (if, indeed, they were to be citizens at all), but he realized that many Northerners were growing concerned over stories of Southern outrages. The president had inadvertently added to the body of information about unsettled Southern conditions in July, when he had sent Carl Schurz south to observe the postwar situation; the German Radical's letters made it clear that many Southern whites still harbored deep resentments against the conquering Yankees and that blacks were victims of violence and fraud. Such a picture augured ill for the success of the administration's policy when Congress reconvened in December, so Johnson looked to negate it. Ignoring Schurz was impossible, for the public was aware of his journey through newspaper reports, and Senator Charles Sumner of Massachusetts, a renowned Radical, was prepared to call on the president to release Schurz's final report.[11]

One idea had especial appeal to Johnson. He would use Grant to counter Schurz by asking the general to examine Southern conditions firsthand. The general's well-known desire for a lenient settlement was sure to produce a report that would contradict Schurz's criticisms. Badeau first mentioned the possibility in October, telling Elihu B. Washburne, "This is a matter of duty, the President having requested it."[12]

In making this request, Johnson exploited the general's obedience to civil superiors. He also sought to take advantage of a growing rapprochement between them. In the months following the confrontation over Lee, the president and the general had developed a working relationship. Grant, relieved that Johnson's desire to hang traitors had abated, viewed the president as moderate, reasonable, and flexible. Johnson's public statements, implying some concern about Southern behavior and a willingness to contemplate the idea of limited black suffrage for those who were literate or who had borne arms, reinforced this impression, as did the widely held belief that the president's program was an experiment awaiting final congressional approval. Whatever his reservations about the specifics of the Tennessean's policy, Grant thought that by appeasing the president and opposing extremist demands for revenge he could play a major role in building the peace. He did not share others' fears that Johnson was already halfway into the Rebel camp—he remembered his experience in resisting the president's desire to put Lee on trial. Cooperating with Johnson on reconstruction could also enhance his chances of winning acceptance for his Mexico policy and for wresting control of the army from the meddling and officious Stanton. He shared with others his "implicit faith" in the Tennessean, asserting that the president "will 'follow the people.'" Washburne thought the two men were "in perfect accord and it is vastly important to the country it should continue so."[13]

Although he wished to preserve harmony with the president, Grant initially responded coolly to the idea of a Southern trip. Problems and friction were to be expected during a period of readjustment. To report on Southern conditions as they were might provoke extreme reactions, disrupting a process that required patience. Time, he maintained, would heal all wounds. Yet to refuse the request would be to offend the president and to ruin his efforts to influence him. On November 22, Grant told Comstock that he still had not made up his mind about the trip. Comstock opined that "he had better go so that he might be able to speak decidedly on questions of reconstruction." Grant remained undecided for several days, however, until Johnson pressed him to go. On November 27, along with staff officers Comstock, Badeau, and Orville Babcock, Grant departed Washington and commenced his fact-finding tour.[14]

Arriving at Richmond that afternoon, Grant and his staff watched blacks parade by torchlight that night. Aware that Congress was about to convene, Grant told one reporter that he believed that those Southern congressmen-elect who could take the test oath—pledging past as well as future loyalty—should be admitted to their seats. Then, as there would be plenty of opportunities to visit Virginia from nearby Washington, the group continued on to North Carolina the next day. At Raleigh, the state legislature interrupted its deliberations on the Thirteenth Amendment to welcome him. Many North Carolinians visited the general to offer their opinions; even an ailing William W. Holden, the provisional governor, conferred with him. "There seems to be the best of feeling existing," Grant concluded, "and nothing but the greatest desire expressed, by both original Secessionists and Unionists, to act in such a way as to secure admittence back and to please the general Government." Meanwhile, Comstock investigated the black labor situation. The freedmen, he learned, would work for Northerners who had emigrated to the South to establish plantations. "They distrust their old masters who are rarely able or willing to pay them weekly or monthly," he reported. Many blacks, holding firm to the belief that they would receive land on New Year's Day, 1866, "in spite of efforts to set them right, . . . will not make contracts" for the coming year. "Whites fear negro uprisings—both sides wish troops to remain," he concluded.[15]

Reporters caught up with Grant at Wilmington the next day. He was "dressed in the plainest civilian clothes" and was wearing "a black felt hat." The party boarded a segregated train and discussed what they had seen as they bounced along the recently laid rails. After a stop in Florence, South Carolina, the group continued down to Charleston, and a restless Grant went to smoke a cigar in the car reserved for blacks. A reporter noted that the general's "views regarding matters of political import were expressed with the utmost frankness and simplicity" but neglected to discuss what those views were.[16]

Arriving in Charleston on the morning of December 1, Grant was greeted by Gen. Daniel E. Sickles. The two men engaged in a long discussion about the need for reconciliation. But others were not so sure that Southern whites would be receptive to such overtures. Comstock reported that conditions were worse than they were in Raleigh. "Feeling of citizens apparently bad," he jotted down in his diary. Gen. Charles Howard, brother of the head of the Freedmen's Bureau and an advocate of black rights, told Comstock that relations between whites and blacks were tense, "the negroes having no trust in the whites & the latter fearing an uprising." There were other signs of Southern recalcitrance. "As we rode through the city I saw several who called themselves ladies make faces at the Yankee officers with us," Comstock observed. "It is useless to say they are only women— they express openly what their husbands & brothers feel but do not show."[17]

Whites and blacks vied for Grant's favor at Charleston. Blacks crowded the streets outside Sickles's house to welcome Grant on the evening of his arrival. The next day, whites dined with him and presented their case. Newly elected governor James L. Orr, William Aiken, and other prominent South Carolina politicians were eager to ingratiate themselves. At breakfast, Aiken, claiming "to have always been a union man," lobbied to have his rice plantation restored. Grant directed Sickles to investigate Aiken's claim and, if it was true, to restore the plantation, if "without prejudice to the negroes" who had established small farms on the land in accordance with orders issued by Sherman the previous January. Doctor Albert G. Mackay and Judge Andrew G. Magrath joined Orr, Aiken, and Grant and his staff at dinner. Magrath had just been released from Fort Pulaski, and Comstock commented that "the imprisonment has apparently done him good," for the judge "admits & accepts all the results of the war & is perfectly willing to make the most of the present situation." Grant came away from Charleston expressing "great pleasure and satisfaction at the general good feeling, spirit and disposition which he had observed along his route, evinced by the Southern people toward the government, and their cheerful adaptation to the new order of affairs." [18]

Few Northern visitors to Charleston could leave without also visiting the Sea Islands to observe the black colony established there during the war. Grant proved no exception. On December 3, he traveled to Hilton Head, where, "in his civilian dress and smoking the traditional cigar," he reviewed a black regiment and made a brief inspection of the colony before continuing on his way to Savannah. Arriving there on the morning of December 4, Grant and his party were greeted by another throng of cheering blacks. "Gen. Grant is in town today, God Bless him!" celebrated one. "He's next of kin to Uncle Lincoln who took the wings of morning and went straight up to Glory!" Anxious to downplay news of Southern loyalty, the Savannah *Republican* reported that the general's visit was "an event, but a very tame one. . . . There was not the slightest enthusiasm manifested at the arrival, except by the few Northern merchants and the colored population." Grant was still in civilian clothes, "and his movements," according to another paper, "were marked by that plain and unostentatious manner which has become his most familiar characteristic." [19]

That evening, after a day filled with more interviews, Grant watched a fireworks display and attended the theater. News of his presence had leaked out, and some two-thirds of the ticket holders demanded their money back. Unionists quickly gobbled up the tickets and packed the house. What did the general think of this evidence of Southern intransigence? "Oh, nothing at all," he told a reporter. "The close of the war being so recent, a natural soreness is to be expected on the part of certain individuals but it will soon pass away." Besides, he added, "my faith in the future rests on the soldier element of the South. I feel assured that those who did the fighting may be depended upon to restore tranquility." The general believed that many white Southerners were willing to do their part in restoring the

Union. "People all seem pleasant . . . at least towards me," he wrote
Julia. Southerners appeared ready "to enter faithfully upon a course
to restore harmony between the sections."[20]

The next day, Grant continued into the interior. Again, the entourage bumped along the railroads, and an observer noted that by now
"they seemed to think it was great fun: they said they were riding on
Sherman's *hairpins*." Along for the ride from Savannah to Augusta
was the former Confederate general John B. Gordon. Comstock
noted that, although at one time Gordon was "very bitter," he now
seemed "entirely 'reconstructed,' and thinks the war will prove a blessing to the south." The Confederate beseeched Grant to remove
black troops from Georgia to avert the catastrophe of race war. Although Grant dismissed Gordon's fears, the Confederate general later
claimed that he had agreed to withdraw the black units. Gordon's prediction of bloodshed proved accurate—only it was black blood that
was shed. Hardly had Grant passed through Augusta when a city po-
liceman murdered a black private. Infuriated, black soldiers patrolled
the streets with "bayonets and loaded muskets," disarming whites.[21]

Grant slipped into Atlanta so quietly that few knew he had been
in town. One newspaper commented that the general "travels very
quietly, refuses all public receptions, and demonstrations of every
kind—an evidence of a great man, in these days of snobbery and
boot-licking." He conferred with Gen. James H. Wilson, a former staff
officer. Wilson later recalled that Grant professed that Lincoln's death
was "an irreparable blow to the orderly and conservative reconstruction of the Southern states." Grant had belittled "the judgment and
statesmanship of Andrew Johnson," but he also "distrusted the sena-
torial group with which Stanton was associated." Grant's own views,
according to Wilson, were "not only thoroughly conservative, but
thoroughly kind" toward Southerners, and he hoped "that all classes
would frankly accept the situation and devote themselves unselfishly
to the restoration of friendly relations" between the sections.[22]

By now the trip was beginning to tell on Grant. Sick and exhausted,
he thought it time to return to Washington, especially since Congress
had already been in session several days. After a night in Knoxville,
he headed back toward Virginia. Stopping at Jonesborough, Tennessee, for dinner, he found himself surrounded by townspeople wishing
to shake his hand. One old Confederate pushed his way through the

throng, telling those who would listen, "I fought that man pretty hard, but I would like to see him." Overhearing the remark, Grant replied, "That does not keep you from being a good citizen; I had as soon see you as anybody."[23]

Grant arrived in Washington on December 11. Three days later, Johnson, along with Secretary of the Navy Gideon Welles, greeted him at the White House. The Southern people, Grant reported, were "more loyal and better-disposed than he expected to find them, and that every consideration calls for the early reestablishment of the Union." Welles, finding Grant's views "sensible, patriotic, and wise," urged the general to compose a written report of his findings and share his views with members of Congress. Johnson seconded this proposal. Both men believed that Grant was in full accord with their position, though he had simply said that the situation was better than he had expected. Still, these views contradicted Schurz's gloomy picture. Since Sumner had already called for Schurz's report, the president could now pair it with Grant's impressions. He was certain that the public would believe Grant, not Schurz.[24]

Sumner got wind of Johnson's plan the next day, when he visited Welles. Grant, the cabinet member told him, "had found the people disposed to acquiesce and become good citizens" and thought that "those who had been most earnest and active" for the Confederacy "were the most frank and thorough in their conversion." Sumner was furious. What about the opinions of Chief Justice Salmon P. Chase, an ally of the Radical cause, who had returned from a visit along the Atlantic seaboard in May convinced that black suffrage was an essential component of reconstruction? Welles responded that Grant's opinions were worth more. They reflected "practical common sense" from someone without apparent political ambitions, he said, while the chief justice was prone to propound unrealistic theories in his endless quest for political advancement.[25]

On December 19, the day after the ratification of the Thirteenth Amendment, Johnson submitted Grant's and Schurz's reports to the Senate. The president asserted that the Southern states had acted with "more willingness and greater promptitude than under the circumstances could reasonably have been anticipated" in commencing the work of reconstruction. Not only had they abolished slavery, but also they were in the process of passing legislation concerning the "rights and privileges" of freedmen "essential to their comfort, protection, and security." That these Black Codes might discriminate against blacks was of little concern to him. Acknowledging the existence of some disorder, Johnson dismissed it as "local in character, not frequent in occurrence," and sure to evaporate with the full restoration of civil rule. Implicitly enlisting Grant in support of his views, the president went on to say that information "recently derived from the most reliable authority" had convinced him that "sectional animosity is surely and rapidly merging itself into a spirit of nationality" that would soon evolve into "a harmonious restoration."[26]

Grant's report was then read to the Senate. The general believed that "the mass of thinking men of the south accept the present situation of affairs in good faith." This was a fairly noncommittal statement, especially in light of his next observation that Southerners, after four years of war, were not yet ready "to yield that ready obedience to civil authority" characteristic of Americans. Both whites and blacks required a continued military presence to preserve order. This was a change from his previous statements looking toward the end of military occupation. He added that the troops stationed in the interior should be white. Freedmen, "imbued with the idea that the property of his late master should, by right, belong to him," flocked to the camps of black troops—many of whom, Grant claimed, encouraged indolence. He wanted to remove black regiments to avoid trouble arising in clashes between blacks and whites, overlooking the possibility that freedmen flocked to these posts in search of protection.[27]

Turning to restoration, Grant asserted that whites seemed anxious for a rapid "return to self-government" and wanted to know how to accomplish this goal. Undoubtedly this was true, yet Grant went on to suggest that what was really needed was "a greater commingling, at this time, between the citizens of the two sections, and particularly of those intrusted with the law-making power." This was subtle yet shrewd. In effect, Grant was asking members of Congress to see for themselves what was going on in the South. Such interaction might soften the hard edges between the two sections.[28]

To the Freedmen's Bureau, Grant gave a mixed review. He had long been aware of the misbehavior of some Bureau agents, especially in their contributions to the rumors of land redistribution. In some cases, Grant concluded, such advice had encouraged blacks to believe that they "had the right to live without care or provision for the future," which led to "idleness and accumulation in camps, towns, and cities." These observations merely summarized the findings of other observers, including Schurz. Despite these reservations, Grant continued to believe that "in some form the Freedmen's Bureau is an absolute necessity until civil law is established and enforced, securing to the freedmen their rights and full protection." This was an acknowledgment that blacks were the victims of violence and fraud. Certainly he recognized that racism persisted: "It cannot be expected that the opinions held by men at the south for years can be changed in a day, and therefore the freedmen require, for a few years, not only laws to protect them, but the fostering care of those who will give them good counsel, and on whom they can rely." In pursuit of that goal, Grant requested that the Bureau be put under his control.[29]

Doubtless Grant's ambivalence toward the freedmen reflected in part where and when he had traveled. White Southerners had been talking for months of a "Christmas uprising" by blacks eager to seize land; many blacks continued to believe that the government would indeed give them "forty acres and a mule" and were understandably reluctant to negotiate labor contracts for the following year while they held onto that hope. Moreover, despite Grant's support for the formation of black regiments during the war, reports he had received suggested a lack of discipline among them. He did not succumb to the view of blacks as innately lazy and worthless, instead attributing their behavior to bad advice. He did not overlook white behavior, either, in suggesting that blacks still required protection and advice. The transition from slavery to freedom would be gradual, requiring the supervision of the federal government.[30]

On the whole, Grant's report seemed a balanced review of the situation, acknowledging that serious problems existed among both blacks and whites. Crucial to perceptions of the general's observations, however, was the fact that Johnson volunteered the report. Many assumed that Grant embraced the president's policy, including Charles Sumner. The clerk had hardly finished reading Grant's report when Sumner demanded that Schurz's lengthy missive be read. When his fellow senators demurred, Sumner charged that Johnson and, by implication, Grant had presented a "whitewashing message" of Southern conditions. Schurz's report, Sumner claimed, was "accurate, authentic, and most authoritative"; Grant's visit was "hasty." Over the next several days, the Massachusetts senator continued his rampage. As Welles noted, "Senator Sumner by his impetuous violence will contribute to put things right beyond any man. The president's message and General Grant's letter seem to have made him demented."[31]

One French correspondent, Georges Clemenceau, noted that Johnson had used Grant's message "as a prop." He, too, thought that Grant's report supported Johnson's position and noted that it suggested that blacks were not ready to exercise the rights and privileges of citizenship. William T. Sherman, also back from an inspection tour through the South, told Grant that his observations "confirm yours literally," which, in light of Sherman's differences with Grant over blacks, suggests that he had skimmed over some sections as well. Discussing the trio of reports submitted by Grant, Schurz, and Oliver O. Howard, the *Army and Navy Journal* described all three as "very interesting and instructive. . . . The only trouble is these tidings do not all agree." Grant appeared "very well satisfied," Howard came across as "less confident," and Schurz thought the situation "mixed, and rather bad."[32]

Most newspapers commended Grant's report. The general's "practical, common-sense view of the whole subject" was refreshing, thought the Springfield *Republican*. The Southern press was especially pleased. Praising Grant's "great good sense and generous feelings," the Mobile *Register* expressed its opinion that he "fought in sincerity and in earnest for the preservation of the 'Union'—not as a pretext for ulterior views, not as an excuse for slaughter, plunder, confiscation and subjugation." The general's report "has produced a marvellous effect," recorded a Nashville paper, adding that "great confidence is reposed in Gen. Grant's judgment." The New York *Times* added that the general's comments about the Freedmen's Bureau were "surely practical statesmanship." (They also produced results, for Oliver O. Howard called the attention of Bureau officers to Grant's report.) The Democratic New York *World*, in noting Sumner's response, stated, "Never were the MAN and the FANATIC more sharply brought face to face than here." Grant, who "has never trod the crooked ways of politics," had demonstrated again proof of his "solidity of judgment and strength of character. . . . The people will never stop to weigh the crotchets of such men as Carl Shurz and Carl [*sic*] Sumner against the good sense of General Grant."[33]

But Radicals grumbled. Massachusetts politico Francis W. Bird, mastermind of the Bay State's Radical clique, bemoaned Grant's "utter lack of statesmanship." A North Carolina carpetbagger told Thaddeus Stevens that Grant "cannot find out the real Sentiments of the Southern people in a flying visit through the South." Another Stevens correspondent dismissed as "ridiculous" the idea that Grant's impressions, based as they were on such a brief visit, could be seriously entertained. "And that he could be induced to make a report, simply for the purpose of giving the weight of his name to the President's policy, amazes me." Such a decision showed "that a very good general may have very little sense about questions of Policy, & principles of Government." The New York *Tribune* preferred Schurz's findings. One Chicago correspondent noted that some of Grant's friends were perplexed by the tone of the report and worried that the general was "throwing himself into the arms of the secessionists."[34]

Grant's observations about race relations also came under fire. William S. Robinson, the Radical correspondent for the Springfield *Republican*, assailed his conclusions. "Did he ask any of the negroes how they liked the situation? No; they are not 'thinking men'. . . . But no matter for Gen. Grant's opinions. They are made for order and are good for nothing." Other journals, including Robinson's own paper, rejected these charges. The Boston *Advertiser*, responding to similar attacks on Grant, replied that "nothing is further from his intentions than a surrender of the negroes to their former master. . . . He proposes that the government . . . shall stand as the guardian of those whom it has freed, until it sees them firmly established in the rights of citizenship." But no one who read both reports could doubt that Schurz was far more strident than Grant on the issue of protecting the freedmen.[35]

Andrew Johnson may have called Grant's letter a ringing endorsement of his policy, shaping public perception of the document, but a close reading of the report belies this impression. Nor should Grant's fervent desire for conciliation be mistaken for a willingness to extend unconditional clemency. Actually, the tour and its aftermath marked the emergence of a counterpoise in Grant's thinking; he began to emphasize justice for the freedmen and loyal whites as an essential part of the peace settlement. Noting the unwillingness of many white Southerners to demonstrate a "ready obedience to authority," he thought that blacks required protection and guidance until white racism and its consequences were eradicated. He still shared the president's hopes for an early reconciliation between the sections, but his concern about the status of blacks and white Unionists was growing. Partly for that reason, he now proposed to tour the lower South, ranging west toward New Orleans and Texas.[36]

Johnson had hoped that Grant's letter would neutralize Schurz's negative findings, but the German's account of violence against blacks—backed up by supporting documents that bluntly and graphically described maimed, mutilated, and murdered freedmen—was hard to ignore. Moreover, Grant was one of the people who read Schurz's voluminous report most carefully. A week after Johnson released the two reports, Grant was persuaded that the issue of violence against blacks required further investigation and directed his commanders in the South to report "all known outrages . . . committed by White people against the blacks, and the reverse," with an eye toward making the results known to Congress. It was a sign of Grant's growing awareness and concern about antiblack violence.[37]

Grant moved in step with Republican senator Lyman Trumbull, who was busy preparing a brace of bills designed to protect Southern blacks. The first extended the life of the Freedmen's Bureau and expanded its powers. Although the bill made some provision for land sales to freedmen, Trumbull's major concern was to overcome the combined impact of the Black Codes and a civil judiciary disposed by prejudice to deny blacks equal justice. If, "in consequence of any State or local law, ordinance, police or other regulation, custom, or prejudice, any of the civil rights or immunities belonging to white persons . . . are refused or denied" to blacks, or if blacks "are subjected to any other or different punishment, pains, or penalties" than whites for committing the same crimes, military courts could intervene to assure color-blind justice. Having erected this stopgap measure, Trumbull then moved to make the change permanent in his proposed civil rights bill, which defined citizenship and civil rights, outlawed denial of these rights, ensured equal protection and punishment under law, and empowered federal authorities to enforce the legislation.[38]

By January 11, when Trumbull's bills were reported out of committee, Grant had heard from his commanders. Their reports convinced him that blacks desperately needed protection. To Schurz, he confessed to feeling "very bad about his thoughtless move" in submitting his report, regretting his overly optimistic portrayal of Southern conditions. Nor were blacks the only people requiring federal protection. Union officers, soldiers, and veterans were being prosecuted by Southern state authorities for acts committed under orders during the war. In light of these circumstances, he told Johnson that "for the present, and until there is full security for equitably maintaining the right[s] and safety of all classes of citizens in the states lately in rebellion, I would not recommend the withdrawal of United States Troops." He advised against forming a state militia in Alabama, convinced that it would be used against freedmen and Unionists.[39]

Against this background, Grant issued General Orders No. 3 on January 12, 1866. It directed commanders in the South to protect military personnel, Freedmen's Bureau agents, and loyalists from civil prosecution for acts committed under military authority and extended the same protection to blacks "charged with offenses for which white persons are not prosecuted or punished in the same manner and degree." Grant would use the military to protect the rights that Trumbull sought to secure through his legislation. Senators immediately noticed that Grant's public priorities had changed in the last month from reconciliation to protection. Democrat Thomas A. Hendricks cited Grant's December report to support his claim that an enlargement of the Freedmen's Bureau would provoke "discord and strife" in the South. Trumbull replied that Grant, in an order that "contains many of the provisions of the bill under consideration," demonstrated the need for both the Bureau and a continued military presence in the South.[40]

General Orders No. 3 did not always accomplish its objective. In Mississippi, department commander Thomas J. Wood and Freedmen's Bureau assistant commissioner Samuel Thomas debated its meaning. Thomas finally gave in, announcing that the Bureau would "recognize the civil authority of the state to the fullest extent," and that federal officials should seek the voluntary cooperation of civil authorities. Bureau officials in Florida, urged on by Oliver O. Howard, moved to reverse several provisions of the Black Codes concerning corporal punishment and the right to bear arms but left untouched discriminatory legislation on labor contracts and vagrancy. In other areas, enforcement was more swift and sure. Georgia's governor, Charles Jenkins, discovered that military officers would not allow him or his officials to enforce discriminatory sections of the state code. In Virginia, Gen. Alfred H. Terry cited the order to halt the enforcement of a vagrancy law, even though the law was not discriminatory on its face, because he judged that its impact would affect blacks far more than whites.[41]

To Grant, however, General Orders No. 3 was merely a first step. He had planned to take a second trip through Louisiana, Mississippi, and Texas to find out more about Southern conditions, but events required his presence in Washington. Important legislation concerning the organization of the postwar army was under consideration, and Grant found himself feuding with Stanton over their respective spheres of authority. Instead, he sent Comstock and Ely S. Parker. In New Orleans, Comstock met with Philip H. Sheridan and Edward R. S. Canby. Sheridan believed "that if Northerners are protected by martial law & the presence of troops that in a short time all questions will be settled without trouble." If troops were withdrawn, however, Sheridan and Canby agreed that Northerners "could get no justice from the courts." Canby, who felt that Southern whites' behavior had deteriorated since Appomattox, also warned that blacks "would be far worse off than before the war" if the bluecoats left. Gen. Absalom Baird urged that troops remain lest a race war erupt in their absence. When Gen. Andrew A. Humphreys confidently reported that he found even the planters along the Mississippi "ready & willing to do what is desired," Comstock noted in his diary his belief that that favorable impression was due to planters' awareness that they would need Humphreys's support later, when they asked for aid to repair the river levees.[42]

Comstock concluded that Unionists agreed unanimously that "troops and martial law must be retained here until the labor system and northern men who have come here become firmly established." Southerners still adhered to the Confederate faith, an impression reinforced by a conversation between Comstock and "two unconstructed rebs. Rather bitter, nominally admitting results of war, but one I believe would have liked to have lynched me" because Comstock thought "the negro must be treated like the white man." His observations, relayed to Grant though a series of letters to John A. Rawlins, reinforced Grant's increasing skepticism about Southern loyalty. So did Parker's observations. "Time alone will change the long settled convictions of the Southerner into the necessity of granting to the negro all the rights demanded for him by the General Government," he concluded, "and I fear that until that event takes place the presence of troops in the South will be an absolute necessity." To Parker, the Freedmen's Bureau and occupation forces were necessary "to guard against an unjust oppression of the negro." Florida freedmen also pleaded for protection, asking Grant to "not allow us to be Stript of Every Defence in the World."[43]

Concern about maintaining order in the South led Grant to advocate the retention of an occupation force. When the Mississippi legislature petitioned Johnson to withdraw federal troops, the president forwarded the request to Grant for comment. The commanding general, denying that civil authorities were "amply sufficient to fairly and justly execute the laws among all her citizens and to perpetuate their loyalty," replied that troops should remain in place. When news reached Washington that Georgians were upset with the continued presence of black soldiers and were threatening violence, Grant, although noting that he had issued orders "for the withdrawel of Colored troops from the interior of the Southern states to avoid unnecessary irritation and the demoralization of labor," would not cave in to ultimatums. "It is our duty to avoid giving unnecessary annoyance," he told George H. Thomas, "but it is a greater duty to protect troops acting under Military Authority, and also all loyally disposed persons in the Southern states." Future troop transfers should not endanger "the rights of loyal Whites and Freedmen." Anybody "resisting the authority of the United States must be arrested and held for trial for their offense." The commanding general's emphasis had shifted from reconciliation to protection.[44]

The hostility of Southern papers toward army personnel and other Northerners also irritated Grant. Knowing that the press played a powerful role in shaping public opinion, he charged that malignant editorials did "more to hinder the work of reconstruction, by keeping alive the spirit of hatred between the two sections, than all the politicians in the land put together." Thus, when he heard that the Richmond *Examiner* had chastised Southern women for attending a ball held by General Terry, he first telegraphed Terry for a copy of the article in question and then, furious at "the dangerously inflammatory course" of the paper, ordered him to take possession of its offices. Editor H. Rives Pollard immediately headed to Washington to talk to Grant and Johnson. The general stood by his order. "The course of the *Examiner*," he informed Johnson, "has been such as to foster and increase the ill-feeling toward the Government of the United States by the discontented portion of the Southern people." He believed "it to be for the best interests of the whole people, North and South, . . . to suppress such utterances." Finally, he reminded the president that his actions were legal: "The power certainly does exist when martial law prevails, and will be exercised."[45]

The president disagreed, even though Grant later grumbled that the original order had been approved by Johnson. Pollard won a reprieve when he promised that in the future the *Examiner* "shall be devoted to the support of the Union, the Constitution, and the laws, and . . . will continue heartily to support the President's policy." Johnson was won over by such assurances, and Grant received a "request" from the White House to allow Pollard to resume publication. Overruled, Grant instructed Terry to reopen the *Examiner*'s offices "upon the express condition that in future it will not pursue a course inimical to the Government," and that it would assist "the cultivation of friendly relations between the people of these states." He added that the *Examiner* should in its editorials and excerpts from other papers "give support[,] countenance and friendship to acts and expressions of loyalty to the Union and its supporters." At the same time, he ordered commanders to forward copies of newspapers that "contain sentiments of disloyalty and hostility to the Government in any of its branches."[46]

The incident awakened Grant to the idea that perhaps he and Johnson were following different paths toward reunion. The president had been more than willing to assert that he and the general were as one on reconstruction policy if it served his interests; the *Examiner* affair hinted that he was perfectly willing to desert the alliance if it suited him. Grant could recall when he had to restrain Johnson's desire to try Lee for treason. Now, just as Grant was growing more skeptical of the chances for a rapid reconciliation, Johnson seemed willing to overlook Southern transgressions in his haste to wrap up the restoration process. Pollard had pledged to support Johnson's policy; Grant's order, issued the same day, warned against expressions of "hostility to the Government in any of its branches," including Congress. Perhaps government policy and the president's policy were no longer one and the same in Grant's mind.

Further confirmation of this notion arrived on the same day that Grant told Terry to let Pollard resume publication. As Grant and Johnson debated the merits of the *Examiner*'s editorial perspective, the Freedmen's Bureau bill awaited Johnson's signature. Reportedly, Grant "heartily" approved the bill, although he had reiterated his preference that Bureau agents should be army officers. As if to remind Johnson of the purpose of the bill, Grant forwarded a summary of the reports he had received from several of his subordinates in response to his inquiry concerning interracial crimes, demonstrating that blacks needed protection. But Johnson ignored Grant's advice. On February 19, he vetoed the bill; the Senate failed to override it by a handful of votes. Three days later, responding to serenaders outside the White House, Johnson proclaimed that the real traitors to the Union were the Radicals, not the Confederates.[47]

That the president appeared determined to offend Republicans was almost understandable, for he had weathered some rather caustic criticism. Less understandable was his disregard of Grant's advice. The general was still steering a middle course, advocating the seating in Congress of those Southern members-elect "who are loyal, and who are elected by loyal constituents, and can take a test oath." In an effort to reduce racial violence and unnecessary inflammation of Southern sensibilities, he approved Terry's decision to prohibit Richmond blacks from celebrating the first anniversary of the fall of the city—a prohibition not heeded by freedmen excited at the opportunity to celebrate their emancipation. But Johnson was unwilling to compromise. Once more, he needlessly irritated Grant by questioning the protection afforded Confederates by the Appomattox agreement; Grant had to demand the release of Bradley T. Johnson, a former Confederate general imprisoned in Baltimore. When Attorney General James Speed questioned the scope of the Appomattox terms, Grant snapped. "I will be drawn and quartered before they shall be violated." It seemed as if the president was bent on losing support as quickly as possible.[48]

Nor was Johnson done yet. On March 27, he vetoed the Civil Rights bill, shocking moderate Republicans, many of whom were led to believe that he would sign it. On April 2, he struck yet another blow, issuing a proclamation that declared the "insurrection" at an end except in Texas. The proclamation cast doubt on the continued legitimacy of martial law throughout the South; his statement in the winding preamble that military occupation, martial law, and military tribunals "ought not . . . to be sanctioned or allowed" in time of peace suggests that he possessed previous knowledge of the Court's impending preliminary ruling in *Ex parte Milligan*, which appeared to strike down the use of military courts in peacetime.[49]

This proved too much. On April 6, the Senate, by a vote of thirty-three to fifteen, overrode the president's veto of the Civil Rights bill. That night, the Grants held a reception that foreshadowed the struggle between Republicans and Johnson for Grant's support. As Welles put it, those in attendance presented "not only a numerous but a miscellaneous company of contradictions." Several Republicans, including Thaddeus Stevens and Lyman Trumbull, arrived in the hope that their presence would be interpreted as a sign of Grant's support for their opposition to Johnson's actions. When they walked in the door, however, they were surprised to see the president and his two daughters greeting some guests while Montgomery Blair and Alexander H. Stephens milled around the living room. Thaddeus Stevens, chortled Welles, "was taken aback and showed himself discomfited," and Trumbull "betrayed surprise." Alexander H. Stephens noted that Johnson's presence was noteworthy in itself, since presidents usually did not practice "going out into society." He perceptively observed that "General Grant and the President seemed a little awkward, or not at ease, in the characters they were acting; both seemed to be out of their element." Other guests murmured that someone, perhaps Mrs. Grant, had erred, and Welles reported "expressions of vexation that there was such a strange attendance here." Congressman Rutherford B. Hayes came away with a different impression, observing that Stevens "shook hands cordially with Andy. . . . It was the happiest gathering I have seen. Andy looked and behaved very well indeed."[50]

Three days later—on the first anniversary of Appomattox—the House overrode Johnson's veto of the Civil Rights bill. The same day, the War Department instructed subordinates that, despite the president's proclamation, martial law was still in force in the occupied South, although it could only be employed after recourse to civil authority had failed. Both steps suggested that the insurrection had not so much ended as entered a new phase in which federal intervention was needed to secure the safety and rights of blacks and white Unionists. In such circumstances, it was critical to know exactly where Grant stood. Politicians began to speculate about the general's future. Senator John Sherman thought it "evident that Grant has some political aspirations and can, if he wishes it, easily attain the Presidency." Former Confederate general Richard Taylor drew the opposite conclusion from a conversation with the general: "He declared his ignorance of and distaste for politics and politicians," Taylor recalled later, "with which and whom he intended to have nothing to do. . . . He expressed a desire for the speedy restoration of good feeling between the sections, and an intention to advance it in all proper ways." For Grant, the problem was to discover the proper way.[51]

6

WALKING A

POLITICAL

TIGHTROPE

Johnson's proclamation declaring an end to insurrection throughout most of the South left Grant and his generals uncertain of the scope of military authority in the occupied region. Requests for clarification flooded the telegraph office at the War Department. Finally, on April 9, Grant and Edwin M. Stanton, with Johnson's approval, notified commanders that although they had to defer to civil authority whenever possible they were still authorized to impose martial law or to use the Freedmen's Bureau court system to provide justice if civil courts did not meet their obligations. These instructions overturned the prevailing interpretation many politicians and Southerners gave to Johnson's proclamation, but they also conceded that military action was to be used only when civil authorities failed to enforce the law.[1]

These initial interpretations reassured Grant, but they were followed by new challenges to military authority. On May 1, Johnson directed Stanton to issue General Orders No. 26 in order to clarify his policy. Noting that "some military commanders are embarrassed by doubts" about the impact of the April proclamation "upon trials by military courts-martial and military offenses," Johnson offered the following clarification: "Hereafter, whenever offenses committed by civilians are to be tried where civil tribunals are in existence which can try them, their cases are not authorized to be, and will not be, brought before military courts-martial or commissions, but will be committed to the proper civil authorities." Obviously, the key phrase open to interpretation was "which can try them": much depended on one's definition of "can." Grant advised a subordinate several days later that although he believed that General Orders No. 3 remained in force, military authorities could no longer protect blacks from unjust treatment by removing their trials to military courts. At best, commanders could halt civil actions against Union soldiers for acts done under orders and protect freedmen from the enforcement of the Black Codes.[2] Two weeks later, Supreme Court Associate Justice Samuel Nelson added to the confusion with his decision *In re Egan.* Freeing a man imprisoned by federal authorities on charges of murdering a young black at Lexington, South Carolina, Nelson declared that "the moment the rebellion was suppressed" and civil government had been organized, civil rule resumed. Had the rebellion been suppressed? Had legitimate civil governments been reestablished? These questions, implicitly answered in the affirmative by Nelson, were precisely the ones at issue.[3]

The possible consequences of prematurely reestablishing civil rule were vividly illustrated at Memphis, Tennessee, on May 1—the same day General Orders No. 26 was issued. For months, black soldiers and their families stationed at Fort Pickering, along with other blacks who had flocked to Memphis during and after the war, had encountered resistance from the Irish immigrant population on the south side of the city, who resented the competition for jobs from the freedmen. The black soldiers in the area were not always well disciplined, either, occasionally committing robberies and provocatively brandishing their weapons. Crime, overcrowding, unemployment, and, of course, racism made Memphis an accident waiting to happen. And happen it did on May 1. After several days of minor clashes between blacks and whites, a mob of white citizens and policemen descended on south Memphis and, encouraged by several municipal officials, attacked the blacks. Some forty-six blacks and only two whites died in the subsequent riot; up to eighty people were wounded; five black women were raped; and black churches, schools, and houses were burned.[4]

After some delay, Gen. George Stoneman finally intervened on May 2, ordering all armed bodies to disband. Ten days later, he filed his report with Grant, outlining the mutual antagonism at the root of the dispute and promising further investigation. Congress decided to take a look as well. Elihu B. Washburne headed the House committee investigating the Memphis riots. Grant waited for reports from his subordinates before passing final judgment on the incident. When he finally forwarded the documentation to Stanton, however, he made it clear where he stood. He termed the riot a "massacre": the rioters had engaged in "murder, arson, rape, and robbery, in which the victims were all helpless and unresisting negroes." The blacks sought protection from the meager federal force in the area, which was "inadequate for putting down the riot speedily."[5]

Yet the riot at Memphis was merely the most sensational example of violence in the South that spring. It overshadowed another riot at Norfolk in late April. By mid-May Grant had concluded that peace was still far off. "A small Military force is required in all the states heretofore in rebellion," he notified Stanton; it would be required "for some time to come. . . . The difference of sentiment engendered by the great war . . . will make the presence of a Military force necessary to give a feeling of security to the people." Still, Grant was willing to consider the possibilities of excess on both sides. On the same day that he wrote to Stanton about retaining troops in the South, he expressed concern about the activities of Freedmen's Bureau agents in North Carolina.[6]

In a newspaper interview, Grant revealed his growing dissatisfaction with the temper of the South. "There were some parts of the country where our armies had never trod, . . . which needed to feel the blighting effects of war" to gain a sense "of the enormity of their crime and the necessity of a thorough repentance," he remarked. "I find that those parts of the South which have not felt the war . . . are much less disposed to accept the situation in good faith than those portions which have been literally overrun by fire and sword." Southern whites had become more defiant. "A year ago," he observed, "they were willing to do anything; now they regard themselves as masters of the situation." Even Robert E. Lee was "behaving very badly" by "setting an example of forced acquiescence so grudging and pernicious in its effects as to be hardly realized." Troops must remain in the South, he concluded, to preserve the peace and to protect the freedmen. "Of course there is some bitterness of feeling among all the classes, but I am satisfied it would soon die out if their leading men had not somehow got the idea that treason after all was not very bad, and that the 'Southern cause,' as they phrase it, will yet triumph, not in war, but in politics."[7]

One incident illustrates how Washington authorities responded to reports of violence. On June 28, Mrs. L. E. Potts of Paris, Texas, wrote to President Johnson about antiblack violence: "I wish that my poor pen could tell you of their persecutions here. . . . It is not considered [a] crime here to kill a negro." Something had to be done to protect blacks. "I wish that we could have a few soldiers here for a while, just to let these rebels know that they have been whipped." Johnson referred the letter to Oliver O. Howard, who shuffled it to Grant on July 2. Four days later, on July 6, Grant instructed Philip H. Sheridan "to furnish, upon applications of agents of the Freedmen's Bureau, such assistance as the means at his command will permit, either for the protection of refugees, freedmen, and Union men, or to enforce punishment for crimes." It seemed that there was no end in sight either to the violence or to the failure of local civil authorities to offer protection and punish crime.[8]

Potts's plea for federal protection of blacks was only one sign of the need to respond to increasing Southern violence. The day after Howard forwarded Potts's letter to army headquarters, he notified Grant that reports of violence against freedmen and Freedmen's Bureau agents were multiplying, in part because of the failure of Southern civil courts to arrest, prosecute, and convict offenders. Howard suggested that military commanders step in to make the arrests. Grant agreed and issued General Orders No. 44, instructing army commanders to arrest civilians for crimes whenever civil authorities failed or were unable to act. In line with Johnson's General Orders No. 26, these new orders made no provision for trying those arrested. Commanders were simply to detain suspects "in military confinement until such time as a proper judicial tribunal may be ready and willing to try them."[9]

The first test of the order came the next day, when Grant transmitted to Stanton evidence regarding the Memphis riot and a suggestion that the army arrest and hold the instigators of the riot until the civil courts took action. Stanton forwarded the request to Johnson, who asked Attorney General James Speed for an opinion. Speed replied a week later that the military's authority ceased when it put down the riot. Since the courts were open in Tennessee, it was up to local officials to take action. After all, Tennessee was on the verge of ratifying the Fourteenth Amendment and gaining readmission to Congress; surely this suggested the restoration of civil rule. In August, when George H. Thomas reported that the rioters had been identified and requested instructions, Grant, hamstrung by Speed's ruling, told Stanton: "I do not feel authorized to order the arrest of the Memphis rioters but I think it ought to be done with a strong hand to show that where the civil authorities fail to notice crime of this sort there is a power that will do so." Seeing the threat to General Orders No. 44, Grant decided to treat Speed's opinion as applying only to that specific case, leaving his order in force elsewhere. From this point on, he would not automatically seek presidential sanction for his actions but would act increasingly on his own.[10]

Before long, other military commanders were employing Grant's new directive to protect Southern blacks. George G. Meade, commanding the Division of the Atlantic, approved Alfred H. Terry's decision to arrest two people accused of murdering blacks in areas where the justices of the peace were too intimidated to take action. When the local courts served Terry with a writ of habeas corpus, Meade directed him to produce the prisoners and then telegraphed Grant: "I think it best to test the question whether the civil authorities of Virginia will or will not respect General Orders No. 44." In Florida, Gen. John G. Foster assured Sheridan that both General Orders Nos. 3 and 44 "will be strictly enforced." But one week after General Orders No. 44 was issued, Johnson retaliated, authorizing release from imprisonment for those sentenced by military courts and tribunals who had already served at least six months. This could not fail to weaken the legitimacy of military tribunals in the eyes of many Southerners. As Thomas informed Grant, "The people of the States lately in rebellion are each day growing more and more insolent and threatening in their demeanor, as they find themselves relieved from punishment by military authorities."[11]

While Grant and the army struggled to protect Southern blacks and Unionists, Congress debated over how to guarantee such protection. Johnson's willingness to use executive proclamations, orders, and vetoes, plus the vulnerability of legislation to later repeal, forced Republicans to turn to the amendment process to establish minimal terms for reconstruction that would be at least somewhat insulated from executive and Southern civil obstruction. The Black Codes, the waffling of Southern state legislatures over the Confederate war debt, the selection of former Confederate generals and high civil officials as members-elect to Congress, and the possibility of increased Southern representation in Congress haunted Republicans. Their answer was the Fourteenth Amendment, passed by Congress on June 13. By defining blacks as citizens, protecting due process, and assuring all citizens equal protection under law, Section One of the proposed amendment would nullify the Black Codes and override the insidious behavior of Southern civil courts. Although the other sections of the amendment—outlining representation, officeholding, and war debts—were the cause of much political controversy at the time, it was Section One that most affected Grant and the army.[12]

Grant immediately—and inadvertently—was drawn into the struggle over the ratification of the new amendment. In Tennessee, Johnson's old political enemy, William "Parson" Brownlow, pushed for a quick ratification of the amendment. Aware of Brownlow's intentions, several members of the state legislature absented themselves from the state capital in order to prevent a quorum. Brownlow asked Thomas to use federal troops to arrest the absent legislators. Thomas wired Grant for instructions, and Grant forwarded the telegram to the War Department—where it sat for several days. By the time Stanton brought the telegram to the attention of the president, Brownlow had employed state officials to arrest the absent members and, having secured a quorum through force, watched with satisfaction as the amendment was ratified on July 19. Gideon Welles and Johnson, who mistakenly assumed that Thomas had acceded to Brownlow's request, wondered why the telegram had taken so long to work its way up in the bureaucracy and suspected that either Grant or Stanton was to blame for the delay.[13]

While awaiting ratification of the amendment, Congress sought to buttress the ability of the army and of the Freedmen's Bureau to protect Southern blacks. Johnson's April proclamation encouraged speculation that he would soon announce the end of hostilities, which would give the Bureau but a year to conclude its business under the act of March 3, 1865. The February veto of Lyman Trumbull's bill, which would have extended its life and expanded its powers, had been sustained; now it was time to try again. A new bill, introduced in mid-May by Massachusetts congressman Thomas D. Eliot after consultation with Trumbull and others, did not include the broad plans for land confiscation and redistribution promised in Trumbull's bill, but it did authorize the president to "extend military protection and have military jurisdiction" over cases involving blacks' civil rights in each of the late insurrectionary states until civil government had been fully restored *and* that state's representatives had been seated in Congress. This ensured that Congress as well as the president would be the judge of when a final settlement had been reached. On July 16, three days after he had issued his order releasing from military confinement those who had served a minimum of six months, Johnson vetoed the bill. His message straddled the question of whether peace had indeed been restored; more outrageous was his assertion that Southern civil courts offered ample protection for the freedmen. Congress immediately overrode the veto. A week later, it seated Tennessee's representatives, following the state's ratification of the Fourteenth Amendment.[14]

Angry and frustrated over the course pursued by Congress, Johnson countered by trying to associate Grant with his policy and working to win his support. The president appointed the general's eldest son, Fred, to West Point and nominated old Jesse to be postmaster at Covington, Kentucky. The heaviest competition for the general's favor came through Johnson's effort to create the rank of General of the Army—with the understanding that Grant would fill the post. Republicans supported the measure because of their suspicion of Johnson. "If the President," Senator Justin Morrill commented, "should undertake to carry out the copperhead programme of reorganizing as the next Congress representatives from the South and their Northern allies—they having a majority—it would be important to have a man directly in command of the army of no doubtful tendencies. In this point Grant (though not the greatest man) is the safest man." Even Thaddeus Stevens, no friend of Grant, supported the bill and, amidst the laughter of his colleagues, announced that he was "willing to promote General Grant, not only to the office of full general, but also to a higher office whenever the happy moment shall arrive." Johnson signed it on July 25, 1866, and Grant added a star to his shoulder straps.[15]

At least one of Grant's former staff officers was already looking forward to that "happy moment." Even though the next presidential election was more than two years away, James H. Wilson was already making plans to run his former chief for the office. At first he advised Adam Badeau to keep Grant out of the political morass; soon, however, he became more concerned about the possible influence of those around the general. "I have noticed an inclination now and then since the termination of the war, on the part of Rawlins and others to commit the General to a certain set of political tendencies." This could not be permitted. Grant had to steer clear of Johnson and conservatism. "It is his duty and that of those about him," Wilson insisted, "to keep him from putting into writing—or practice[—]any principle of politics which he may not abandon without injury to himself." But Wilson approved of newspaper reports that Grant "has expressed his decided preference for the Congressional Reconstruction policy," adding, "for *he ought* to feel that way if any man should." Other staff officers kept a low profile. As Badeau put it, "It is desirable, especially at this juncture, that we should not be represented as politicians, or partisans."[16]

Radicals and Southern conservatives alike maneuvered for position around the hero of Appomattox. Georgia's Herschel V. Johnson warned Alexander H. Stephens to do nothing to push Grant "into the arms of the Black Republicans," for Grant "certainly loves us as much as Johnson does." Joseph E. Brown, for one, wished to embrace the general even more tightly: "The Southern people owe a debt of gratitude to General Grant for the firmness with which he stood by the terms of the capitulation; the liberality which has characterized his whole conduct since that time; and the many acts of kindness which he has performed for Southern men in adversity and distress."[17]

In contrast, some Radicals looked to Grant with hope after the release of General Orders No. 44. "His recent order does not sound like the orders from the White House," stated the *Independent*. "No man knows better than the President that Gen. Grant is anxious, that he is disappointed with the President's course." Moderate Republicans spoke with more confidence. John A. Logan, aware of Grant's support for the congressional program, expressed his faith. "The call of Grant on Congress to send more troops to all the southern states to protect the wrights [sic] of all loyal men . . . had secured the confidence of the Country intensly on Gen. Grant," proclaimed one New Yorker. For most, however, determining Grant's sympathies remained a game of wait and see.[18]

At the end of July, Grant gave an interview to an Annapolis reporter. He had just refused to permit military intervention in the Maryland civil courts despite protests that they were not offering blacks equal protection under law. The general "spoke very happily concerning the conditions and prospects of the freedmen, pronouncing his belief that time will bring with it the full fruition of their newly acquired liberty; and arguing that while anxious they should obtain all their rights as freemen, any unnecessary interference by the military with the civil authorities would not only tend to embitter the whites against the government, but delay the consummation of that harmony between the races so much to be desired. . . . He understands that so great a work as the securing of perfect justice to an entire race lately enslaved cannot be brought about in a day." But, by the time these words appeared in print, and in light of the events at New Orleans on July 30, 1866, Grant might have wondered whether in fact he had been too optimistic. What happened there that day helped convince him that perhaps he should not be so reluctant when it came to military intervention and protection.[19]

In July Grant and Sheridan had turned their attention from Southern affairs to Mexico. Rebel successes south of the border were followed by rumors that the French might delay their departure in order to stabilize Maximilian's position. Sheridan, hoping that at last he might have an opportunity to pitch into the French, decided that it was time to pay a visit to the Rio Grande. He left New Orleans, however, just as Louisiana Radicals claimed that they would reconvene the 1864 constitutional convention and were gathering in the city to frame a new state constitution that would provide for black suffrage. This meeting promised trouble and, possibly, bloodshed. Grant, occupied with legislative wrangling over the army appropriations bill, trusted Sheridan's judgment and let him leave Gen. Absalom Baird in charge of the Crescent City. Baird refused to use troops to prevent the meeting, much to local Democrats' dismay, and stationed detachments throughout the city to preserve the peace. Unfortunately, he thought that the Radicals would convene at the Mechanics' Institute at 6:00 P.M. on July 30; instead, the meeting opened at noon, with no troops in sight. Parading blacks and whites clashed outside the convention hall. Local police intervened, emptying their pistols into the throng of blacks and joining the whites in an assault on the institute itself. By the time Baird's soldiers arrived on the scene three hours later, the riot was over. Thirty-four blacks and three white Unionists were dead, with over one hundred people, most of them black, injured. Only one white rioter had died.[20]

Two days later—two days too late—Sheridan returned to the city, proclaimed martial law, and began to investigate what had happened. At first he was inclined to parcel blame out to both the Radicals (whom he described as "political agitators and revolutionary men") and local officials who had used the police to attack the crowd "in a manner so unnecessary & atrocious as to compel me to say that it was murder." Upon further investigation, however, Sheridan began to discern that the Democrats had been looking for a collision. The more he found out, he told Grant, "the more revolting it becomes. It was no riot, it was an absolute massacre by the police which was not excelled in murderous cruelty by that of Fort Pillow." The next day, he called for the removal of Mayor John Munroe and Governor J. Madison Wells, both renowned troublemakers.[21]

Grant endorsed Sheridan's actions. Johnson's supporters, however, were less pleased. Gideon Welles criticized Sheridan's "judgment and administrative ability" and suspected that the "impulsive" general's telegrams were dictated by Republicans. Evidently the president agreed. When he released Sheridan's initial dispatch to the press, he did some editing of his own, omitting sections critical of the Democrats involved but leaving in the sentences attacking the Radicals. Sheridan exploded when he learned of Johnson's selective editing. Grant, who knew that Johnson was responsible for the publication of the dispatches, reassured his subordinate that "the purity of your motives will never be impeached by the public no matter what capital the politicians may attempt to make of garbled or partial publication."[22]

In subsequent weeks, Grant found much to ponder in what had happened at New Orleans. Always blind to Sheridan's shortcomings, he excused the general's absence from the city. He was more concerned with the actions of Stanton and Johnson. Neither man had kept him informed of Baird's dispatches (nor did Baird communicate with Grant, for that matter); indeed, no one knew for several weeks that Baird had telegraphed Stanton for instructions on the eve of the riot. Since Stanton failed to show Baird's communication to Johnson or Grant in time to send instructions, it was obvious that Johnson was not the only person playing politics with the military. That Johnson chose to issue orders to Baird through civil officials was at least unusual. True, Baird might have moved with more alacrity to prevent violence, but his actions were guided by a desire to maintain neutrality in an ostensibly political conflict. Finally, the publication of a selectively edited dispatch suggested that Johnson was not above using a tragic incident to partisan advantage. Neither the president nor the war secretary could be totally trusted. Grant would have to become more actively involved in administering reconstruction; it was obvious from what had happened at New Orleans that peace was not at hand.

Or so Grant thought. Andrew Johnson, however, believed that the Radicals and blacks in Louisiana were responsible for what had happened in New Orleans. He set to work on a proclamation that would announce the end of hostilities, once and for all, and prepare the way for the army's withdrawal from the South. On August 20, 1866, Johnson declared the insurrection at an end in Texas—which had been omitted from the April proclamation. He also proclaimed "that peace, order, tranquility, and civil authority" existed throughout the nation. Once again, Johnson remained vague on several crucial points. Unlike the April proclamation, the August proclamation's preamble mentioned that the suspension of the writ of habeas corpus would "continue throughout the duration of the rebellion," or until the proclamation suspending the writ had been modified or revoked; yet Johnson failed explicitly to restore the writ, as he had done for Kentucky the previous December.[23]

Observers wondered about the status of military authority in light of this latest presidential pronouncement. A draft stated that all orders concerning the Freedmen's Bureau and "all military orders now existing for the purpose of sustaining the civil authority of the Federal Government . . . are not affected by this proclamation, and the same will remain in force until hereafter specifically revoked, or countermanded," but these words did not appear in the final proclamation. It was now a matter of debate as to whether General Orders Nos. 3 and 44 were still in effect. Sheridan certainly thought they were, although to buttress that belief he engaged in a bit of hairsplitting: he declared that Johnson's proclamation "has never been officially promulgated" and that the orders had not been rescinded. "If civil authorities are to be looked to for justice," he added, "I fear that the condition of affairs will become alarming." Grant, unwilling to accept such deception, immediately informed Sheridan that he construed Johnson's August 20 proclamation as nullifying both General Orders Nos. 3 and 44 and reminded him that "the duty of the military is to encourage the enforcement of the civil law and order to the fullest extent."[24]

The general's retreat extended to questions of property confiscation as well. Grant had said very little about the issue of confiscating the property of Confederates and redistributing it to blacks and others, claiming that such questions were outside his purview. Yet he had intervened in Florida to protect black and white Unionist landholders who had purchased property from federal tax officials when the former owners tried to repossess their property through the state courts. In the aftermath of the August proclamation, Grant backed away from this position, allowing the state courts to impose their will on the hapless blacks and white Unionists.[25]

By August 1866, Johnson had done much to frustrate Grant's efforts to pacify the South, protect the freedmen, and maintain order. Indeed, his encouragement of white Southerners seemed designed to foster further intransigence. It would be up to the Northern electorate in the fall of 1866 to pass judgment on the president's policy. Should it endorse his course, Grant would have to abandon much of his policy under the weight of presidential directives. If the Republican party triumphed, Johnson might bow to political reality; otherwise, Grant would have to look to Congress to bolster his hand.

Disturbed about Johnson's course, Grant became even more disgruntled when the president tried to make it appear that the general endorsed administration policy. During the summer of 1866, Johnson and his supporters had decided to create a political movement, independent of the major political parties, designed to foster support for the administration and its head. Styled the National Union Movement, this smorgasbord of Democrats, conservative Republicans, and white Southerners met in Philadelphia in August. Movement leaders James R. Doolittle and Orville H. Browning returned to Washington on the evening of August 17, "fresh from the convention and overflowing with their success and the achievements of that assemblage," noted Gideon Welles. With the navy secretary in tow, they visited the White House and informed Johnson that a committee would transmit the resolutions of the convention to him the next day. Perhaps the cabinet and Grant could attend the ceremony? Johnson agreed. Here was a chance to tie Grant to his policy, at least in the eyes of the public.[26]

The next day, a message from the White House arrived at army headquarters, requesting Grant's presence at the afternoon reception. Reluctant to comply, Grant viewed the invitation as a polite summons, leaving him little alternative. Walking to the White House, he sought Johnson out to excuse himself from the ceremony, only to encounter the president just as the proceedings were about to commence in the East Room. The crowd began to applaud, cutting off any chance for Grant to beat a hasty retreat. Flustered, he soon found himself at Johnson's right side, listening to Reverdy Johnson proclaim the virtues of the incumbent, followed by three cheers for the president and three more for himself. Returning to headquarters "full of indignation at the device by which he had been entrapped," he grumbled to his staff about Johnson's trickery. His disgust grew when he read the account of the affair by New York *Times* correspondent Benjamin C. Truman, a supporter of Johnson, who said that Grant's "manner and looks" obviously meant that he endorsed the proceedings. Two days later, the president issued his Texas proclamation—adding injury to insult.[27]

Having taken this trick, Johnson shrewdly moved to associate Grant with his policy still further by securing the general's presence on a speaking tour through the North. Although the announced purpose of the trip was to dedicate a memorial to Stephen A. Douglas, Johnson planned to use it to campaign on behalf of his policy and to bolster the chances of the National Union Movement's success in the fall congressional elections. Grant looked for some way to evade Johnson's design, but the president compelled the general's acquiescence by approving Grant's recommendations for army promotions. Once again, Johnson had outmaneuvered Grant, and the general was among the dignitaries who accompanied the president on what would become known as the "Swing around the Circle."[28]

The trip began uneventfully. Only when Grant drove a four-in-hand through Central Park did he attract attention. But, as the tour moved west through New York and Ohio, things took an ugly turn. Rattled by hecklers planted in the audience by Radicals, Johnson often lost his composure and reverted to his stump-speaking style. Unfortunately, what worked in Tennessee did not go over well in the national press. Accounts of Johnson's speeches suggested to many readers that the president was mentally disturbed, intoxicated, or both.

Inevitably, Grant's name was invoked in these exchanges. At several stops, Johnson attempted to speak only to find his words smothered by cries of "Grant! Grant!" Nettled, Johnson once revealed his secret fears when he exploded, "We are not here in the characters of candidates running for office against each other!" For his part, Grant tried to remain silent, quietly puffing away on his cigar while the president spoke. At one stop, Grant rebuked William H. Seward when the latter pointed to Grant's presence as indicating his support of Johnson, declaring, "No man has the right or authority to commit me on that or any other political question." At another stop, he told Welles that he did not care to be introduced to crowds by Copperhead Democrats such as Congressman John Hogan of Missouri.[29]

At first Grant did not mind being seen with Johnson. "Of course he saw, as did all others, the partisan intentions of the Radicals," reported Welles, "but he did not, so far as I could perceive, permit it to move him from his propriety." John A. Rawlins observed that, though the general "was at first quite fidgety," he "has finally grown quite tranquil and seems to enjoy himself very much." At one point, he even reportedly made light of his situation. After Johnson and Seward delivered lengthy addresses at a hotel in Niagara, New York, Grant told the crowd in one of his rare public statements, "I have had a long nap since I have been here." However, as Johnson increasingly lost control of his tongue, the general began to disassociate himself from the entourage, rarely speaking to Johnson and avoiding the presidential car. Indeed, the general "could scarcely be induced to appear on the platform with Mr. Johnson," recalled New York *Herald* correspondent Sylvanus Cadwallader, another Johnson supporter. "He was morbidly anxious to not be identified with the administration and its measures."[30]

"I am getting very tired of this expedition and of hearing political speeches," Grant wrote to Julia at the end of August. Several days later, at Buffalo (or Cleveland, depending on the account), the pressure got to him. Several observers, including Cadwallader, claimed that Grant, "in a drunken stupor," had to be laid down in a baggage car. The general certainly disappeared from public view for a few days, but a letter to Julia at the time argues against the incapacitation suggested by the *Herald* correspondent. Grant, however, was definitely bothered at what was going on. "Perhaps on no other occasion," close friend Daniel Ammen recalled, "have I seen General Grant so discomposed."[31]

Grant tried to maintain his impartiality in public. He told a reporter near Chicago that his presence on the train did not imply that he supported Johnson, he objected to the use of the army as "a party machine," and he did not "consider the Army a place for a politician." But he would not insult Johnson, either. At Indianapolis, he rebuked an unruly crowd: "Gentlemen, I am ashamed of you. Go home and be ashamed of yourselves." Arriving ahead of Johnson at Cincinnati, he admonished another demonstration put on by his admirers. "I am no politician," he told them. "The President of the United States is my superior officer, and I am under his command. . . . I consider this merely a political demonstration for a selfish and political object, and all such I disapprove of." Only the careful listener might have noted that Grant omitted any mention of Johnson's policy. Duty required obedience, not endorsement.[32]

Others on the train were aware of the struggle to gain Grant's support. Mexican minister Matías Romero noted that Seward and Johnson were making an effort to "publicize that General Grant supports the president's policy. This has greatly mortified the General who holds the maxim that soldiers ought not mix themselves in politics." But Johnson soon grew annoyed when crowds chanted Grant's name. Such adulation for the general, Romero remarked, caused "some jealousy and rivalry between friends of the two." Once, when Grant and

Adm. David G. Farragut retreated to the other end of the car to quell the noise so Johnson could speak, the crowd followed the two war heroes.[33]

Even Grant's staff officers got into the act. Rawlins still adhered to Johnson's policies. "I am now more than ever glad that the General concluded to accompany the President," he told his wife, "for it will do Grant good, whatever may be his aspirations for the future, and fix him in the confidence of Mr. Johnson." The chief of staff did what he could to further this impression, granting an interview to correspondent Truman in which Rawlins affirmed his support for Johnson. Yet Rawlins had to admit that Grant remained silent about the issues of the day. "I tell you, Truman, Grant never talks politics," he asserted. "He is no politician; and if he entertains any political opinions whatever, I am not aware of the fact. It is decidedly ludicrous to see first one side claim him, and then the other."[34]

Wilson took a contrary view. He was working with Orville E. Babcock and Horace Porter to enlist Grant into Radical ranks. "All the good influence which can be exerted should be exerted to keep the General true to his principles," he wrote Babcock. "You can see what a terrible effort Johnson has been making to commit him to 'my policy.'" Hearkening to the battlefield, Wilson added, "If the General wavers now—it will be as fatal to himself and the country, as hesitation or indecision would have been in the Wilderness!" But Grant made it clear that he was not going to involve himself in the political debate. As Badeau put it in a letter declining an invitation for Grant to attend a soldiers' and sailors' convention, "It is contrary to his habit and to his convictions of duty to attend political meetings of any character whatsoever." When William S. Hillyer declared that Grant was a supporter of Johnson's policy, Grant fired off a letter to his former aide, cracking down on such talk. Nobody, he snapped, "is authorized to speak for me in political matters."[35]

Grant needed only to look at the consequences of Johnson's oratory to confirm his predilection for silence. "The President has no business to be talking in this way," he complained to Ammen. "I wouldn't have started on this trip if I had expected any thing of the kind." In correspondence, he unburdened himself to Julia. "I never have been so tired of anything before, as I have been with the political stump speeches of Mr. Johnson," he confided. "I look upon them as a National disgrace." He warned Julia to keep his letter confidential, "for so long as Mr. Johnson is President I must respect him as such, and it is in the country's interest that I should also have his confidence." To his brother Orvil the general was even more blunt, declaring, "I am disgusted with this trip. I am disgusted at hearing a man make speeches on the way to his own funeral."[36]

Grant was indeed disgusted with Johnson. He was tired of the president's attempts to manipulate him in support of administration policy. He was also disappointed that Johnson, with his verbal mudslinging, continued to treat reconstruction policy as a partisan issue. Obviously, the president did not see that the behavior of white Southerners demanded a change in administration policy. Instead, he clung even more stubbornly to his original ideas, giving moderate Republicans little choice but to work with the Radicals in formulating an alternative. Once, Grant had hoped that Johnson would follow in Lincoln's footsteps in seeking the high ground of statesmanship and ruling with a firm but forgiving hand. But this was not to be. Between the president's reactionary course and the emboldened Radicals, those—like Grant—who sought middle ground soon discovered that it was giving way under their feet.

Grant also could not avoid noticing the public reaction to his own presence. As Wilson put it, "The recent trip out West ought to leave him no doubt as to the relative respect entertained for him & the President." Moreover, the trip had an impact upon the minds of several of Grant's staff officers who had been inclined to support Johnson. "Porter writes me that the 'Swing around the Circle' completely cured Rawlins of his sympathy," Wilson confided to Washburne, "and that he is *now* for the amendments. Rather late in the day, but better than not at all." Badeau, too, had come around.[37]

In many ways, the trip highlighted the difficult position in which Grant found himself. It was obvious from his orders and correspondence that he disagreed with Johnson's approach to reconstruction. Private letters and conversations revealed his growing contempt for the chief executive. But duty demanded that he maintain the proper relationship with his superior. Johnson, of course, aware that the war hero's popularity far outweighed his own, had taken advantage of this sense of obligation time and again to make it appear as if he had Grant's support. As a result, Grant had to weather a great deal of criticism from Johnson's opponents, who failed to understand his position.

Concerned Republicans viewed Grant's presence on the tour with apprehension. Many wrote to Washburne, who was widely regarded as being privy to Grant's true leanings. "Many of our friends are afraid that Grant will fall into and give countenance to the Johnson-Copperhead Party," read one letter to the Illinois congressman. "If the people get an idea that Grant is with the President it will do us great injury." Another anxiously asked, "Is Gen. Grant in sympathy now with the nefarious policy of the President?" Stanton, who had wisely avoided joining the Chicago excursion, noted that Johnson had been making "persistent efforts to capture Grant" for over a year. Although the war secretary believed "that the head of the armies cannot ultimately be corrupted," he worried that Grant's daily visits to the White House and his presence "on a deplorable joust with Mr. Johnson" boded ill.[38]

Others pointed to Grant's presence on the trip to Chicago as proof of the general's support for the president's policy. Radical congressman James H. Ashley claimed that Johnson and Grant "suck through the same quill." Wendell Phillips charged that Grant "occupied the most humiliating position of any man on the continent"; in response to rumors about the general's presidential prospects, Phillips predicted that Grant would be "content to be the unassuming tool of men about him." One of Benjamin F. Butler's Wisconsin correspondents agreed. "His pretended neutrality at such a crisis as this," while giving "his influence" to "the odious Johnsonian policey is truly despicable. . . . Now it is well said silence gives consent—& silence at such a time is more [than] mere assent."[39]

Butler seized on such information to discredit his old commander. "Our Republican friends have relied upon Grant in case of a collision with the President that he should disobey the orders of the President and stand boldly for the right and the laws," he told Horace Greeley, Radical editor of the New York *Tribune*. Yet the weak-willed general "feels obliged to obey the orders of his Commander in Chief so strictly that he will not even refuse an invitation to be *Hawked* about the country as an appendage to the President's tail." This was not the mark of a reliable Republican. "Can Grant be trusted to disobey positive orders of his Chief when the hour of Peril comes[?] Shall we not be leaning on a broken reed?" Greeley's paper could help answer the question, Butler continued. "Smoke Grant out so that we may know where he is upon the great questions of the day."[40]

Johnson's campaign trip failed to prevent a Republican victory in the fall elections. Newspapers speculated whether the president would accept the verdict of the people. The day after the Republicans triumphed at the polls in Pennsylvania, a Philadelphia paper reported that Johnson had submitted a list of inquiries to Attorney General Henry Stanbery aimed at determining the legitimacy of the Thirty-ninth Congress. The column revived rumors that the president was contemplating recognition of a Congress made up of Southern representatives and cooperative Northern Democrats—in effect, committing a coup d'état. Administration officials immediately denied the story, but Grant feared that the spurious missive might contain a kernel of truth: Johnson had posed just such a situation—hypothetically, of course—to Grant in conversation. Prodded by the president for his response, Grant replied, "The army will support the Congress as it is now and disperse the other."[41]

The president's reaction to a Republican victory caused Grant great concern. He confided to Sheridan that Johnson "becomes more violent with the opposition he meets with until now but few people who were loyal to the Government during the rebellion seem to have any influence with him." Johnson listened only to those people who were willing to join him "in a crusade against Congress" and its Southern policy; Grant feared "that we are fast approaching the point where he will want to declare the body itself illegal, unconstitutional and revolutionary." Such a scenario, although unlikely, did not seem impossible to Grant. Indeed, for several weeks, he had made preparations to ensure that in case of crisis "no armed headway can be made against the *Union*." Quietly, he ordered the removal of federal arms and munitions from arsenals located in the South, dispatched Cyrus B. Comstock to Tennessee to ferret out the truth behind rumors of "secret Military organizations," and instructed Sheridan to prevent the Texas legislature from calling out that state's militia.[42]

Nor were Grant's fears about Johnson's possible actions in the event of an electoral crisis unfounded. He needed only to look at events in

Maryland, where Democratic governor Thomas Swann was trying to sweep the Republicans from power with the aid of a new voter registration law that opened the polls to thousands of ex-Rebels. Baltimore Republicans had successfully resisted Swann's attempt to apply the registration law to a municipal election in October, which led to a Republican victory. Swann then announced his intention to remove the Republican registrars, and the police commissioners who protected them, before the November state election. Both Democrats and Republicans professed peaceful intentions but took actions that promised violence. Republicans held "Boys in Blue" meetings to plan their next move. Swann, bereft of state militia, denounced such organizations as "illegal and revolutionary combinations" and turned to Johnson for help.[43]

Andrew Johnson wanted to do what he could to help Swann. Of course, one way to assist his ally would be to send federal soldiers to Baltimore to maintain order during the November election—an idea endorsed by Francis P. Blair, Sr., still advising the president from his roost on Lafayette Square. But such a move would depend on the cooperation of the general-in-chief, and Johnson was none too confident that Grant would follow such orders. The president thought he knew someone who would. The previous February, William T. Sherman had assured Johnson of his support for the president's policy. Perhaps he could be trusted to do Johnson's bidding. To replace Grant outright with Sherman would be impossible, in light of Sherman's legendary loyalty to his chief. Rather, Grant would have to be removed from Washington on some pretense, allowing Sherman, as second-in-command, to take over temporarily.[44]

Fortunately for Johnson, the current situation in Mexico provided him with just such an opportunity to get Grant out of Washington. After months of patient negotiation, Napoléon III, preoccupied by events in Europe, had finally agreed to Secretary Seward's demands that he abandon Maximilian's regime. At last, the republican forces of Benito Juarez were on the verge of victory. In anticipation of Maximilian's collapse, Johnson had named an old crony, Lewis A. Campbell, minister to Mexico. Grant had always taken an interest in Mexico's struggle for independence; why not order him to accompany Campbell to the Rio Grande, if not into Mexico itself? Such an escort would certainly lend prestige to Campbell's mission. And, with

Grant out of the way, Sherman would presumably do Johnson's bidding. "It would indeed have been a Machiavellian triumph to have got rid of Grant at that juncture in affairs at home and at the same time forced him to carry out Seward's policy in Mexico," Badeau later observed.[45]

On October 17, Johnson began to implement his plan. Calling Grant to the White House, he broached the subject of the Mexican mission. Grant, unaware of the president's ulterior motives, agreed to accompany Campbell. Nor did the commanding general offer any objection to Johnson's request that Sherman be ordered to Washington for several days. But the president then clumsily revealed his motive. Showing Grant the letter Sherman had written the previous February, Johnson inquired whether Grant thought Sherman would object to its publication. Grant, his suspicions aroused, answered that military men "did not like expressions of theirs which are calculated to array them on one or the other side of antagonistic political parties to be brought before the public." Such a remark checked Johnson, and the letter remained private.[46]

Grant's suspicions intensified within a day, when he read newspaper reports of Stanton's impending resignation. Of especial interest to the general was speculation that Sherman would be named Stanton's successor, "as he harmonizes with President Johnson in his policy of restoring the Southern States to their practical relations to the Union." Grant immediately wrote to Sherman describing the present situation. "I will not venture in a letter to say all I think about the matter," he told Sherman, suggesting that something was afoot. Engaging in some politics of his own, Grant invited Sherman to stay with him if he came to Washington, thus ensuring that he would be able to keep an eye on his comrade.[47]

Two days later, Grant, complying with Johnson's request, ordered Sherman to report to army headquarters. The supposedly apolitical Sherman asserted that he was "not aware that I have ever on paper expressed any opinion of this seeming conflict between Congress and the President," although both the letter to Johnson and his correspondence with his senator brother suggested otherwise. John Sherman warned his brother to stay out of politics, predicting that the administration was doomed to suffer a major defeat in the fall. But William T. Sherman had no intention of accepting the War Department portfolio. "The military ought to keep out of quasi-political offices," he told Grant. Grumbling that "this is some plan to get Grant out of the way," Sherman departed for Washington on October 23.[48]

Up to this point, Grant had made no connection between the Mexican mission, events in Maryland, and Sherman's arrival. But, by October 21, he had. On that day, he withdrew his offer to go to Mexico, claiming that it was "a diplomatic service for which I am not fitted either by education or taste." Reports of violence in Hagerstown, where Democrats had forcefully broken up a Republican meeting, may have contributed to his change of mind. Johnson persisted, hoping to impose on Grant's sense of duty once more. On October 23, Grant arrived at the White House and encountered Governor Swann and the president in conference. Swann, citing the potential of violence, asked for federal soldiers to be sent to Baltimore. Grant was alarmed by Johnson's inclination to honor the governor's request, especially in light of the president's reluctance to provide federal protection for blacks and white loyalists in the South. But no definite commitment was made. After Swann left, the president and the general made their way to the cabinet meeting. The first order of business was Mexico. Johnson, in blatant disregard of Grant's wishes, inquired of Seward whether Grant's instructions for the mission to Mexico had been prepared. But, if the president hoped that the general would succumb under the gaze of the cabinet ministers, he reckoned without his quarry. Startled, Grant reminded Johnson that he did not wish to accompany Campbell. Furious, the president, attempting to compel Grant's obedience, asked Attorney General Stanbery if there was any reason why Grant should not obey a presidential order—thus abandoning any notion of a request. Grant, cutting Stanbery off in midsentence, stood up and declared that although he was subject to Johnson's orders in his military capacity this was a diplomatic mission, leaving him free to decline the request. Lest Johnson think that there was room for negotiation, Grant firmly concluded: "No power on earth can compel me to it." Johnson backed down, and the meeting moved on to other topics. Grant promised to look into affairs at Baltimore by contacting the commander on the scene, Gen. Edward R. S. Canby.[49]

Fuming, Grant returned to headquarters, where he complained to his staff that the Mexico mission was "a scheme to get him out of the way in case of trouble here between Congress & the Presdt." Johnson's sharp questioning of Grant's refusal sounded like a man willing to do anything to gain compliance. After all, had diplomatic concerns alone been at issue, there would have been no need for Sherman's attendance at Washington—army headquarters had been located outside of Washington before in peacetime, under Winfield Scott. Later that day, Grant wrote Washburne that he would be unable to attend Babcock's wedding in Galena. "I cannot fully explain to you the reason but it will not do for me to leave Washington before the elections." Stanton, for one, was certain that the Mexico trip was "only the forerunner of the efforts to get Grant out of the way."[50]

Grant continued his counterattack the next day. He had received Canby's report about affairs at Baltimore. Pointing out that the police commissioners could be removed easily under existing procedures should they violate the election laws, Canby concluded that Swann's effort to remove them was "an effort to secure political power" by allowing ex-Rebels who did not meet suffrage qualifications to vote. Grant forwarded this report to Johnson, adding that he saw no reason to supply Swann with federal troops, at least not until the riot predicted by the governor materialized. Federal intervention, he argued, would "produce the very result intended to be averted," by exciting opposition and disorder; "military interference would be interpreted as giving aid to one of the factions no matter how pure the intentions or how guarded and just the instructions." So that Johnson could not mistake his position, Grant concluded his letter in strong language. He hoped that he would never be called upon "to send troops into a state *in full relations with the General Government,* on the eve of an election, to preserve the peace."[51]

This was disingenuous, for Grant had just sanctioned the use of federal soldiers in Missouri to keep the peace during voter registration—at the request, ironically, of conservatives in the state. He simply did not trust Johnson or Swann. Indeed, had he wanted to, he could have justified intervention in Maryland to preserve the peace against Democratic violence. Maryland Republicans portrayed Swann's policy as portending "another civil commotion, with its accompanying horrors and probable loss of life." Swann, unable to obtain troops from Johnson, decided to investigate the conduct of the police commissioners in what amounted to a show trial; on November 1, he dismissed the commissioners, naming as replacements two local Democrats. This decision, coming as it did days before the election, intensified tensions in Baltimore. Johnson remained inclined to send at least some troops to Baltimore and, in stiffly worded missives, made repeated inquiries of Grant and Stanton about the availability of forces in the area. Both the war secretary and the general-in-chief had to wonder about the president's willingness to use force in Maryland after having been adverse to federal intervention in the disloyal South.[52]

Sherman arrived in Washington on the evening of October 25. Grant escorted him back to his house, where after dinner they discussed the situation. Grant made it clear that Johnson wished to use Sherman, as Sherman put it, "on the supposition that I would be more friendly to him than Grant." Grant told Sherman "that he had thought the matter over, would disobey the order, and stand the consequences." Two days later, Grant once more declined Johnson's "request" to go to Mexico, offering a series of excuses.[53]

Nor would Sherman help the president. He turned down Johnson's offer of Stanton's post as well as command of the army in Grant's absence. After advising Johnson that Grant would not go to Mexico under any conditions, Sherman volunteered to go. When Johnson hesitated, Sherman reminded him that any quarrel with Grant would prove to be costly to the administration; the president then gave way to Sherman's suggestion. "Both Grant and I desire to keep plainly and strictly to our duty in the Army, and not to be construed as partisans," Sherman told his brother after the substitution was made. "Neither the President nor Congress ought to ask of us of the Army to manifest any favor or disfavor to any political measures. We are naturally desirous for harmonious action—for peace and civility." Doubtless Sherman also wanted to avoid any conflict with Grant.[54]

Johnson accepted Sherman's advice reluctantly, for he was convinced that Grant sympathized with the Republican cause. The general's chief-of-staff was similarly disgusted with Grant's behavior. Rawlins told cabinet member Browning that he was "heartily and entirely with the President" but was "annoyed, indeed provoked at Grant's reticence." Grant, Rawlins believed, "is thoroughly conservative, but . . . not a politician or statesman." He blamed the Radicals, who, he believed, "are anxious to use him as a candidate for the Presi-

dency to promote their own ends, and he is a little unsettled about it."
This bitterness reflected the growing distance between Grant and
Rawlins, who, despite his earlier wavering, held fast to his own conservative notions. A newspaper report connected the president's distrust of the general with the next presidential election. When Grant
complained that Johnson was failing to heed his advice on appointments, the story went, the president pointed to Grant's repeated declarations of disinterest in the White House and pledged to "grant you
any favor in my power to bestow" if Grant would promise not to run.
Grant responded that he was not a candidate. "But," he added, "suppose the people insist on making me one, what can I do? And besides,
Mrs. Grant has been recently looking at the White House, and thinks
she can run that establishment quite as well as it is run now. And you
know, Mr. President, that these women will do pretty much as they
please. And Mrs. Grant would decidedly object to my giving any such
promise." Johnson looked understandably puzzled, unsure whether
Grant was jesting or threatening. Such stories only added to his suspicions that Grant was unreliable.[55]

Grant, with Sherman's assistance, had succeeded in resisting the
president's efforts to remove him from Washington just in time, for
affairs in Maryland demanded closer attention. Afraid that Johnson
would be only too happy to supply Swann with troops, Grant decided
that he had to become involved. On November 1, he went to Baltimore to mediate between the police commissioners and Swann. Comstock, who accompanied the general, thought that his boss "did not
urge the old commissioners & their friends quite so strongly as he
ought" to offer "no resistance to force." He advised Swann's appointees to seek recourse through the legal process. Swann seemed to want
as judges of election "men who will not scrutinize too closely the right
of disfranchised rebels to vote. . . . He may bring on a terrible riot &
civil war." Both sides assured Grant that they would not be the first to
resort to violence. Nevertheless, no sooner had Grant left than Swann
telegraphed Johnson to inquire whether soldiers would be sent.[56]

Swann's decision to remove the police commissioners, made the day
of Grant's visit, promised to worsen the situation. At a cabinet meeting
on November 2, Grant reported that he thought it "very probable"
that there would be violence in Baltimore as the result of Swann's
decision. Johnson, excited, announced that Washington itself was not

safe "from insurrection and violence," but Grant did not respond. Reports drifted out of the meeting that the two men "had very harsh words about it." Johnson declared that, "should an insurrection take place, the Government should be prepared to meet and promptly put it down." He instructed Stanton "to call General Grant's attention to the subject, leaving to his own discretion and judgment the measures of preparation and precaution that should be adopted." A disappointed Browning (who had joined the cabinet as interior secretary) concluded that Grant "is very obviously leaning to Radicalism and inclined to throw the blame on the Administration party. . . . He also says that the friends of the Administration in Maryland are anxious, and trying to force the radicals into firing upon the U.S. flag, but that they will not do it." To Browning, it was clear "that all his sympathies are with the radicals."[57]

Grant, convinced that Swann wanted to provoke a conflict, intervened once more. In a meeting with Swann, Johnson, Attorney General Stanbery, and Stanton on November 4, Grant offered to return to Baltimore to mediate the dispute, in part because Johnson again was considering military intervention and the declaration of martial law. That night, Grant met with Baltimore Republicans; the next day, he conferred with Swann's supporters and then met with both sides. To reporters he made it known that he was not in Baltimore "in his official capacity, but as a citizen, desirous of preserving the peace of the city and willing to use his influence in compromising the difficulty." Grant was willing, if necessary, to use more than his influence. He directed six companies of infantry, who were aboard steamers ready to depart from New York to join their commands in the South, to stop at Fort McHenry and remain until the election was over. Swann's supporters kept Johnson informed of Grant's actions by telegraph, bemoaning that "both Canby & Grant sympathise with & will support Radical interests."[58]

Nevertheless, Grant, Swann, and the Radicals appeared to work out a compromise in which Republicans and Democrats each posted judges of elections at each polling place to judge the qualifications of voters. Grant left satisfied that a settlement had been achieved, only to discover that the agreement had broken down within hours amidst charges of bad faith from both sides. But his presence had effectually prevented violence, for on November 6 the elections passed off peacefully. The Democrats claimed victory. A pleased Swann labeled Grant and Canby "honorable peacemakers." Republicans also commended Grant. "The firmness of the Union men of Baltimore backed by *Gen'l Grant* & *Sec Stanton* has thrown the whole thing on the rebels," one observer concluded. As to Johnson, "Genl Grant is a block in his way, & without any doubt he had much rather have Lee in his place."[59]

President Johnson sent Swann a congratulatory telegram on the results in Maryland, but he had little else to be happy about. Republicans achieved an overwhelming victory in the congressional elections, securing a large enough majority not only to pass legislation but also to override possible vetoes. But Johnson's behavior remained a source of great concern to Grant. The general was disturbed by the president's reluctance to stop Southern violence, a stance reaffirmed when Johnson ordered Sheridan not to arrest individuals indicted in the New Orleans riot under General Orders No. 44.[60]

Grant had always prized the concept of duty. He had often spoken in terms of duty during the war, using it as a justification and sometimes as a rationalization for his policy decisions. Johnson's actions brought two concepts of duty into conflict. Grant's duty to his superior officer was a clearly defined legal duty, reinforced by years of training to obey orders. But there was also Grant's obligation to those who had sacrificed much, if not all, during four years of war. Was that sacrifice in vain? Johnson had denigrated Reconstruction by making it into a partisan issue; in pursuit of political success, he seemed willing to subvert the national government; he seemed blind and insensitive to the persecution of blacks, white Unionists, and army personnel in the South. The president's open espousal of the Southern perspective and his willingness to involve Grant in political intrigue repelled the general. Johnson seemed shameless in his pursuit of political advantage.

If Grant was unsure of the trend of events, his father sensed them with an eye to the future. During the fall campaign, Jesse spoke at an anti-Johnson meeting in Cincinnati. "For myself," he declared, "I don't think these men whose hands are reeking with the blood of their fellow citizens ought to be entrusted any further with the affairs of the Government." Yet it seemed that Andrew Johnson was about to do exactly what Jesse was warning against.[61]

7

HARDLY

A PARTY

MATTER

Ulysses S. Grant had always prided himself on doing his duty, regardless of personal preference, and on remaining above partisan politics. To be sure, at times he had stretched these axioms in his approach to wartime reconstruction, but he had always sought to rationalize his actions by explaining them in the context of these tenets. Now, in the aftermath of Republican victories in the election of 1866, he reformulated his understanding of those two guiding principles. Having lost respect for Andrew Johnson, he redefined his sense of duty as obedience to the office of the president, not support of the person occupying it—a far cry from the days of his close working relationship with Lincoln. At the same time, he began to assert himself in the arena of legislative policy-making and implementation to secure peace and justice throughout the South. In so doing, Grant insisted that he was engaging in an effort to reunite the country rather than becoming immersed in partisan squabbles. Never had the general "felt so anxious about the country as at this time." It was his duty to protect the fruits of Northern victory.[1]

The Republican triumph at the polls convinced Grant that the public favored a more rigorous reconstruction policy. He refused Johnson's request to provide arms for the state militias of the Southern states "in advance of their full restoration and the admission of their

representatives to Congress," making public what he had done secretly the previous month. To Edwin M. Stanton, the general made it
clear that the military orders he had issued that had been nullified by
Johnson's proclamations were still essential: "The provisions of the
Civil Rights Bill cannot be enforced properly without the aid of Order
No. 44 or a similar one." The orders had not been revoked, "nor has
my construction of the effect of the President's Proclamations upon
these orders been officially announced to any but Gen. Sheridan's
command." Obviously, Andrew Johnson was not the only one in
Washington who could practice strict constructionism skillfully, for
Grant's explanation was artful, even disingenuous.[2]

Reports from military commanders in the South confirmed Grant's
belief that provisions for protection remained inadequate. Philip H.
Sheridan believed "that the trial of a white man for the murder of a
freedman in Texas would be a farce," while Daniel E. Sickles concluded that in South Carolina "a freedman has little security for life,
limb, or property, apart from the presence and protection of a garrison of United States Troops." Such reports made a mockery of the
president's assertion that peace had been restored. In his official report to Stanton, Grant deemed it "necessary to keep a Military force
in all the lately rebellious states to insure the execution of law, and to
protect life and property against the acts of those who, as yet, will
acknowledge no law but force." It was obvious to Grant that much
work remained to be done. "I shall not be able to leave Washington
this winter," he informed his old friend Daniel Ammen. "Affairs have
taken such a turn as to make this course necessary. I cannot explain
in a letter."[3]

At first Grant hoped that both white Southerners and President
Johnson would heed the results of the fall elections. The overwhelming Republican victory might convince Southerners that the Northern
public, contrary to the president's oft-expressed belief, did not support the administration's policy. Rid of such illusions, perhaps they
would come to terms with Congress, accept the Fourteenth Amendment, and cease harassing, attacking, and murdering freedmen and
white Unionists. Perhaps Johnson would also come to his senses and
drop his opposition to the Fourteenth Amendment. Grant advised
the president to pursue such a course and remarked that, although
Johnson did not exactly concur, the suggestion "did not bring out

the strong opposition he sometimes shows to views not agreeing with his own." These early hopes proved futile, however, as the president openly encouraged Southern state legislatures to reject the amendment.[4]

Failing to influence Johnson, Grant courted prominent Southerners in an effort to reach a settlement. In the aftermath of the fall elections, several leading Southerners, including Richard Taylor, Joseph E. Brown, and James L. Orr, visited the general in Washington. He warned them that if they did not accept the amendment Congress would enact harsher legislation. He advised them to negotiate with the Republican congressional leadership and not the Democratic minority, since it would be the Republicans who would frame future policy. Several important Republicans in Congress had expressed what Grant termed "the most generous views as to what would be done" if the Fourteenth Amendment was ratified. He concluded that he "would like exceedingly" to see at least one state ratify the amendment, "to enable us to see the exact course that would be pursued. I believe it would much modify the demands that may be made, if there is delay." He hinted that improved conditions at the South would result in the withdrawal of many of the troops currently stationed there, freeing them for frontier duty.[5]

As 1867 opened, a delegation from Arkansas visited Washington. In conferences with the president, William H. Seward, congressional Republicans, and others, the Arkansans attempted to assess the political environment in Washington and to find out whether the state would be readmitted to the Union upon ratification of the Fourteenth Amendment. The example of Tennessee suggested such a possibility, although Radicals, flushed with victory in the aftermath of the 1866 elections, denied the precedent. Grant welcomed the opportunity to meet with the delegation, advising them "to go home and adopt the Constitutional Amendment immediately, and after they had done that to pass a bill giving suffrage to all persons without regard to color." He reiterated his belief that Congress would offer readmission to any state that ratified the amendment. Secretary of the Treasury Hugh McCulloch told Gideon Welles "that General Grant urged upon them to adopt the Amendment—said the North was in favor—that they had decided for it in the late election; that if not adopted Congress would impose harder terms." Welles, terming such talk "nonsense," concluded that the general "has been led astray" by Stanton and Elihu B. Washburne.[6]

But Grant had not been "led astray." Rather, he believed that the rejection of the Fourteenth Amendment by the Southern states would justify demands for more extreme measures, which would engender yet more bitterness. He argued this position passionately, "showing a warmth of feeling at the time that was more conspicuous because of his inexcitability during the war." The general, Adam Badeau observed, "seemed to have a keener personal interest, an unwillingness to lose what had been secured at so much cost." Grant had always worried about the impact of political intrigues upon the peace process; he was astonished that Johnson, who prided himself on being a representative of the people, would cast aside the popular mandate of 1866 and side with the very people he had once denounced as traitors. It was becoming obvious that the president's policies, although often cloaked in terms of constitutional process, endangered the Constitution's aims of ensuring order, justice, liberty, obedience to law, and national supremacy. None of these goals were being served by Johnson's approach to Reconstruction.[7]

Grant also encouraged his subordinates to build support for the amendment. He directed Sheridan to meet with Taylor, adding that Taylor accepted the fact that "those who were victorious in war will not only dictate the conditions of peace but . . . have the right to do so." Sheridan needed little prodding, but the conservative Edward O. C. Ord was another matter. Grant dispatched Horace Porter to Arkansas with a letter outlining his belief "that if one single Southern State should adopt" the amendment "Congress would establish a precedent that would induce all the others" to follow suit. Southerners had to realize that the North, through Congress, had "the power to fix the terms of political reconstruction. I have nothing to say of the merits of the terms propose[d]," he added, but delay "may cause further demands. . . . It is scarcely within the range of possibility that less will be accepted." Urging Ord to consult with civil officials, Grant sidestepped any reservations his subordinate might have about political involvement. "It is not proper that officers of the Army should take part in political matters," he acknowledged. "But this is hardly to be classed as a party matter. It is one of National importance. All parties agree to the fact that we ought to be united. . . . It ought to be seen that no way will succeed unless agreed to by Congress." Since Grant was well aware that Ord sympathized with Johnson's approach to Reconstruction, his message was as much for Ord himself as for Arkansas's civil authorities.[8]

Accepting the Fourteenth Amendment meant accepting the possibility of black suffrage. Despite his earlier reservations about how prepared blacks were to exercise the right to vote, Grant, like many Republican moderates, now saw no alternative but to give blacks the means to protect themselves at the ballot box. "I never could have believed that I should favor giving negroes the right to vote," he explained, "but that seems to me the only solution of our difficulties." To friends he expressed his belief that "the ballot was the only real means the freedmen had for defending their lives, property, and rights." He urged his views on his Southern visitors, pointing out that if they did not accept black suffrage under the terms of the amendment Congress might well impose it as a necessary condition.[9]

Grant was also convinced that something more needed to be done to protect Southern blacks. The Memphis and New Orleans riots, bloody as they were, overshadowed the incessant violence in other areas of the South. In response, Grant advocated continuing military occupation "to insure the execution of law, and to protect life and property against the acts of those who, as yet, will acknowledge no law but force." General Orders Nos. 3 and 44 had been issued with that end in mind. But now the Supreme Court seemed to be challenging the very foundation of the military's efforts to secure justice for all. On December 17, 1866, it released its decision in Ex parte Milligan. Speaking for the majority, Justice David Davis declared, "Martial law can never exist when the courts are open, and in the proper and unobstructed exercise of their jurisdiction. It is also confined to the locality of actual war." Grant and others, of course, would have pointed out that, although such courts might be open in the South, questions remained as to "the proper and unobstructed exercise of their jurisdiction." Nor was it clear yet exactly what constituted the end of the war, Johnson's peace proclamations to the contrary; as Grant and others pointed out, the events of 1861 to 1865 were not envisioned by the framers of the Constitution back in 1787.

Left unclear by the decision was the issue of whether military courts and commissions established by congressional, as well as executive, directives were in jeopardy. Chief Justice Salmon P. Chase's opinion suggested otherwise. As Chase pointed out, the justices and courts of Indiana involved in *Milligan* may have been loyal to the government, but this was not necessarily the case in the South: "In times of rebellion and civil war it may often happen, indeed, that judges and marshals will be in active sympathy with the rebels, and the courts their most efficient allies." Grant would have suggested that this remained the case.[10]

Although *Milligan* may have caused Grant some concern, of considerably more importance to him was Andrew Johnson's response to the ruling. In October the president had overruled Oliver O. Howard's attempt to establish military commissions under Section Fourteen of the Freedmen's Bureau Act of 1866; now he could strike at Grant's directives as well. In November 1866, Dr. James L. Watson of Rockbridge County, Virginia—a white man—had shot and killed William Medley—a black man—in retaliation for a carriage accident the previous day involving Medley and Dr. Watson's wife and daughter. The local court discharged Watson even though he confessed to the crime, whereupon Gen. John M. Schofield arrested him on December 4 and prepared to try him by military commission. Not only did Schofield believe that Watson's release signaled the lack of local legal protection for blacks, but also he wished to test the legality of the Freedmen's Bureau Act of 1866 and of Grant's General Orders No. 44, which, he asserted, authorized military intervention. Certainly the Watson case seemed a model example of the failure of Southern civil courts to protect blacks. On December 19, Schofield refused to comply with a writ of habeas corpus issued by Richmond's Circuit Court and served by one of Johnson's correspondents, James Lyons. But, on December 21, Johnson intervened and, following Attorney General Henry Stanbery's advice, dissolved the military commission, citing *Milligan* as justification.[11]

Johnson's decision promised to overthrow the entire administration of justice by the military to protect blacks and white Unionists from the capricious actions of Southern civil courts. Military commissions and Bureau courts alike were now forbidden by presidential action. Howard directed his subordinates to discontinue the use of military commissions as allowed under Section Fourteen of the Freedmen's Bureau Act of 1866. Johnson's decision justified Stanton's fears that

Milligan struck "at the roots of the Freedmen's Bureau law, and as leading directly to its entire abrogation, as well as other legislation looking to the protection of loyal men, white and black, by the Federal government, from the persecution of the disloyal and rebellious, whose bogus State power is thus confirmed to them."[12]

The president's decision also fueled Southern intransigence. At times, the behavior of white Southerners became so atrocious that it tested one's credulity. Grant told visitors about a North Carolina judge who, "having discovered in the statute-book of the State a clause that no man who had been flogged should afterwards exercise civil rights, has recently set himself to flog as many of the negroes in his district as he can bring under the lash, in order to disqualify them for citizens in case Congress shall give them votes." This was just the sort of behavior that suggested that Southern whites were their own worst enemies.[13]

Sheridan was convinced that the spirit of the Confederacy continued to reign in Louisiana. "The condition of Freedmen and Union men in remote parts of the State is truly horrible," he told Grant at the beginning of 1867. "The Government is denounced; the Freedmen are shot and Union men are persecuted, if they have the temerity to express their opinion." Furthermore, Sheridan had doubts that he could quell such disturbances with the forces at his disposal. The soldiers "have so little power that they are effective only in the moral effect which their presence has." Such comments reinforced Grant's conviction that something had to be done to protect blacks and white Unionists. The information he had received was testimony to "the powerlessness of the military in the present state of affairs to afford them protection." Martial law was the best solution. He told Stanton that it "would give security, or comparatively so, to all classes of citizens, without regard to race, color, or political opinions." Although the necessity for it "is to be deplored," its use should be limited, leaving "all local authorities and civil tribunals free and unobstructed, until they prove their inefficiency or unwillingness to perform their duties." Nevertheless, it was needed. Perhaps one state could be chosen as an example, "as a warning to all."[14]

Certainly there was enough evidence to document the continuing pattern of violence, intimidation, and harassment. When the Senate requested the president to transmit information regarding violations of the 1866 Civil Rights Act, Grant asked Howard to list all "authenticated cases of murder and other violence" that had been reported to the Freedmen's Bureau. "My object in this is to make a report showing the courts in the states excluded from Congress afford no security to life or property . . . and to recommend that martial law be declared over such districts as do not afford the proper protection." On February 8, Grant forwarded similar information to Stanton, who presented it, along with Howard's extensive list, in a cabinet meeting the following week. Welles, ever ready to dismiss news that contradicted his beliefs, characterized Howard's findings as "an omnium-gatherum of newspaper gossip" and "vague, infinite party scandal." It must, he concluded, have something to do with politics. The next day, in discussing the matter with the president, Welles was unable to accept Grant's concerns as sincere and worried that Grant had been brainwashed by Stanton and the Radicals. Johnson shared his friend's doubts, and, "but for the rain," would have sent for Grant, "to know how far he really was involved in the matter." In their obsession to uncover Radical conspiracies, Johnson and Welles overlooked the possibility that it was the actions of white Southerners and of the president himself that had made Grant "strongly but unmistakably prejudiced."[15]

Although angered and disappointed by Southern behavior, Grant was also displeased with Northern self-righteousness over the issue of black suffrage. He noted that many Republicans who demanded that the South accept black enfranchisement refrained from pressing the issue in their home states. When Johnson vetoed a bill enfranchising blacks in the District of Columbia, Grant remarked in a cabinet meeting that he "thought it very contemptible business" for congressmen representing states where blacks were barred from the polls "to give them suffrage in this District." Whether this sign of disapproval meant that he opposed black suffrage was another question. Certainly both Welles and Orville H. Browning thought so. Others contradicted such claims. The abolitionist New York *Independent* claimed that "if he had been President he would have signed the bill, and he has said so since the veto-message came in." Subsequently, Grant told a group of Republican congressmen that, although "impartial suffrage" was inevitable, he would still make allowances for white Southerners' prejudice. Besides, he added, "I confess it does seem a little hard that we should enforce equal suffrage upon the South while we lack the moral courage to enforce it at home."[16]

Welles observed Grant closely during these winter weeks and concluded that he did not understand constitutional government. Other Johnson supporters also were concerned about where the general stood on the important issues of the day. Alexander Randall, Johnson's postmaster general, dismissed talk of a possible Grant presidential candidacy, for "a year hence Grant's opinions would be a matter of no sort of consequence one way or the other" because the general's habitual recourse to the shot glass would seal his fate.[17]

Tired of speculation about his political position, Grant unburdened himself to Sherman. Johnson and his cronies were working to align him with administration policy. Republicans also claimed him as one of their own. "No matter how close I keep my tongue each tries to interpret from the little let drop, that I am with them." This tug-of-war so exasperated Grant that he concluded, "I wish our troubles were settled on any basis."[18]

Southern rejection of the Fourteenth Amendment forced Grant's hand. Efforts at compromise had failed. Southern whites remained defiant, and Johnson's inflexibility only stiffened their resolve. Even Sherman complained that "outrages on negroes and Union Men appear to increase. It is alleged that the better people don't lend their help to stop it, as they say it is none of their business." Some Southerners saw the mistake. Brown and other Southerners, visiting Grant's headquarters in February, admitted in the aftermath of rejection "that nothing would be accepted by the North but universal suffrage."[19]

Having failed to persuade white Southerners to accept the Fourteenth Amendment, Grant now advocated new legislation to buttress military rule in the occupied South and to establish procedures for the full readmission to the Union of the ten remaining states. Little Jesse Grant later recalled, "Always father seemed in consultation with some one, Senators and Congressmen more in evidence than army men. When he was at home the stream of callers was unbroken, often until late at night." The visitors were there to discuss proposals under consideration by Congress to establish anew the military governance of the conquered South. They were not the only ones interested in Grant's opinions. As an English visitor noted, "At the present time, when the President and the Congress are defying one another, and are at open rupture, . . . the General in Chief becomes a very interesting person."[20]

These conferences served to reassure many Republicans of Grant's support for more radical measures. Still, many were concerned about the steadfastness of Grant's subordinates. This was no idle fear: Sickles, renowned as a Radical, came up from the Carolinas and informed Browning that "the Freedmen's Bureau had filled the Southern states with petty tyrants, knaves and robbers"; perhaps it would be best, he thought, if the South was left to its own devices. With friends like these, Republican plans for reconstruction faced an uphill battle. George H. Thomas, Thomas J. Wood, Sickles, and the redoubtable Sheridan all visited Washington to testify about conditions in the South. Grant's aide Cyrus B. Comstock came away from a conversation with Thomas and Wood convinced that "they are all radical, as far as the South is concerned." Rutherford B. Hayes, a Republican congressman from Ohio, assured the home folks that "Grant, Thomas, and Sheridan are now known to be all right."[21]

Such meetings went beyond mere advice, at least in Grant's case. The general-in-chief took an active role in the framing of reconstruction legislation. Most important was legislation outlining the process whereby Southerners could frame new state constitutions and elect civil governments under military supervision. Grant conferred with Senator John Sherman, who headed a Senate committee charged with reconciling various proposals. He suggested that a House bill that authorized him to name the commanders of the military districts be changed so as to allow the president to make that choice. News of Grant's support for the legislation was leaked to the press. "General Grant speaks openly in favor of the Reconstruction bill," reported the *Independent*. "He remarked to a friend, a day or two since, that all his generals at the South were radical in their opinions, though, when first sent down, they were eminently conservative." This was quite a change from "Ulysses the Silent," as Grant had come to be known by some. "For once, at least, there is no doubt whatever of the General's position. He has spoken in all places, where he could do so with propriety, in support of the bill."[22]

Another bill suggested that congressional Republicans viewed Grant's personal presence in Washington as essential to the proper administration of reconstruction policy. By now it had become a matter of common knowledge that Johnson had tried to get Grant out of the way the past October. A concerned Stanton met with Radical congressman George S. Boutwell to draw up legislation to protect the general-in-chief. Grant welcomed the bill, in part because it established in law the chain of command he had argued for since Appomattox. During the war, Lincoln and Grant had enjoyed a close working relationship, and Stanton had served in an integral but nevertheless supporting role. With the advent of peace, however, Stanton attempted to wrest control of the general staff and military bureaus from Grant. The commanding general had protested against this arrangement to both Johnson and Stanton. He demanded that the adjutant general's office be brought under his control and insisted that "the general-in-chief [not the secretary of war] stands between the President and the army in all official matters."[23]

Section Two of the Army Appropriations Act of 1867 protected Grant from both Stanton and Johnson, reinforcing the commanding general's control of the army. It established Grant's headquarters at Washington; stated that he could not be "removed, suspended, or relieved from command, or assigned to duty elsewhere" without his consent or the previous approval of the Senate; and directed that "all orders and instructions" issued by the president or the secretary of war "shall be issued through the General of the Army." Officials disobeying the last clause were guilty of a misdemeanor (an impeachable offense), and army officers could be subject to imprisonment for violating the act. This section guaranteed that no one could circumvent Grant's control over the army, including Johnson, Stanton, or anyone Johnson wished to put in Stanton's place. Another provision in the act prohibited the organization of Southern state militias. Grant welcomed this legislative buttress to his previous orders, for he feared that Southern governors would use the militia as a police force to intimidate freedmen and Unionists.[24]

By the last half of February, Congress had produced several important pieces of legislation. The Reconstruction Act (soon to be known as the First Reconstruction Act) divided the ten Southern states still not represented in Congress into five districts, each to be headed by a major general appointed, as was Grant's wish, by the president. The existing civil governments were declared provisional and subordinate to the military. To restore civil government, each state had to hold a constitutional convention. Delegates to these conventions were to be elected by all eligible adult male voters, including blacks, but excluding those individuals—who also could neither serve in the convention nor vote on the resulting state constitution—disqualified from holding office under the terms of the Fourteenth Amendment. The new state constitutions had to eliminate race as a barrier to voting. Once a state had ratified its new constitution and the Fourteenth Amendment, Congress would admit its representatives to their seats.[25]

Nor was this the only legislative accomplishment of the session. The Army Appropriations Act passed, as did legislation validating retroactively all the actions of the president or his subordinates, including military officers, regarding the use of military commissions to try offenses related to the rebellion. Explicitly aimed at *Ex parte Milligan*, it resembled Congress's action in the summer of 1861, when it sanctioned steps taken by Lincoln in the aftermath of the firing on Fort Sumter. Now army officers could breathe easier, freed from the possibility of civil suits brought by white Southerners for acts done under martial law or judgments rendered by military commissions. Also noteworthy was a third piece of legislation, the Tenure of Office Act, which required Senate approval of the president's decision to remove any official who had been appointed with the advice and consent of the Senate, including cabinet officers. Although this act stopped Johnson from removing Republican officeholders at will, it was unclear whether Stanton, widely recognized as Johnson's chief foe in the cabinet, was protected by its provisions.[26]

The Tenure of Office Act would come to play a large role in Grant's life, but he did not pay much attention to it at the time. More important were the Army Appropriations Act and the Reconstruction Act. The former reinforced Grant's control of the army and offered protection against Johnson. The latter promised to restore order to the South. By allowing military commanders to establish military commissions, the bill repaired the damage done by *Milligan*. The bill also reflected Grant's belief that the terms for readmission had to be specified. Although he agreed with Thaddeus Stevens and others that the Southern states had reverted to territorial status, he had little patience for detailed constitutional argument and even less for measures that would prolong the uncertainty and deepen the antagonisms of the past year. He remained silent concerning the issues of confiscation and redistribution, regarding the issues of protection and civil equality as far more essential and fundamental. Moreover, Grant's support of the legislation was widely known, as was his endorsement, however belated, of black suffrage. Since the majority of white Southerners showed no sign of granting blacks and Unionists equal protection under the law and a minority remained violently hostile to such a possibility, Grant abandoned his previous reservations about enfranchising blacks and accepted it as just and necessary. As Comstock noted, "The General is getting more and more Radical."[27]

It was obvious to most observers that the commanding general was not the president's pawn. To Grant, Johnson was no Lincoln, and the general who once deemed it his duty to support the president now reassessed exactly what duty meant. With the collapse of compromise solutions, Grant, worried over the impact of executive policy on the army and the reconstruction process, turned to Congress for support. Congress was both the source of the popular will and the framer of the laws that defined proper responsibilities and restrained actions —including those of the chief executive. Embracing this new source of authority even as he shaped its mandates, Grant moved further away from Johnson while maintaining an essential facade of cooperation in an effort to induce the president to refrain from obstructing the reconstruction process.

To no one's surprise, Johnson on March 2 vetoed both the Reconstruction Act and the Tenure of Office Act. Attorney General Stanbery and Jeremiah S. Black, who had done what he could to obstruct the military in the courts, cooperated on preparing a draft of the Reconstruction Act veto; Seward, assisted by none other than Stanton, worked on the Tenure of Office Act veto. Johnson reluctantly signed the Army Appropriations Act, although he protested the sections regarding Grant's headquarters and the Southern militia as not germane to an appropriations bill.[28]

Johnson's vetoes were overridden the day they were issued. In a rare display of triumph, Grant told Washburne that Johnson's message explaining his veto of the Reconstruction Act was "one of the most ridiculous veto messages that ever emanated from any President." Quickly recovering his mask of objectivity, he added, "Do not show what I have said on political matters to anyone. It is not proper that a subordinate should criticize the acts of his superiors in a public manner." After all, Grant still wished to maintain some influence over Johnson, especially when it came to the president's selection of officers to head the new military districts. One of Johnson's favorites immediately removed himself from consideration: William T. Sherman informed Grant that he did not want to be assigned to a district command, especially the one including Louisiana and Texas.[29]

Grant had made sure that the president and not he was entrusted with the responsibility to select the district commanders. This did not mean that he proposed to abdicate his responsibility to advise Johnson about appropriate appointees. Welles had tried to impress his chief on "the importance of selecting the right men" but soon despaired when he heard that Johnson had turned to the commanding general for advice. On March 11, the selections were announced. John M. Schofield would head the First District, which encompassed Virginia; Daniel E. Sickles was put in charge of the Second District, comprised of the Carolinas; John Pope took over the Third District, including Alabama, Georgia, and Florida (after George H. Thomas declined the command); Edward O. C. Ord would supervise affairs in the Fourth District, consisting of Mississippi and Arkansas; and Grant, heeding Sherman's request, convinced Johnson to leave Philip H. Sheridan in charge of the Fifth District, formed by Louisiana and Texas.

Immediately, observers searched for the political significance of the appointments. "General Grant has borne himself under all influences as well as could be expected," Welles sighed in relief, "yet I think he has been to some extent affected and has been swayed by Radical influence." True, Sheridan, Pope, and Sickles all inclined to moderate if not Radical Republicanism; Schofield, although he had privately expressed serious reservations about the congressional policy, could be relied upon to protect blacks; only Ord could be considered a conservative. But the selections were based as much upon convenience and prior experience as upon conviction. All of the generals, except Pope, already had established headquarters in the districts they had been named to command. Thus there was minimal change in the status quo. Indeed, Grant, in offering to replace Sheridan with Sherman, had sought to placate Johnson, and Pope's appointment came only after Thomas, once another presidential favorite, had asked to be extricated from the tangle of Reconstruction.[30]

It did not take long for recalcitrant white Southerners to find loopholes in legislation that had been the result of haste, compromise, and in some cases deliberate ambiguity. Although the Reconstruction Act had outlined the process whereby Southerners could reinstitute civil government and congressional representation, it had failed to specify how the process would commence. Many white Southerners, lacking the compulsion to act, sat back and waited, content with a policy of masterly inactivity. Congress moved to remedy the problem. On March 23, it passed over Johnson's veto a second Reconstruction Act, specifying procedures for registration, voting, apportionment of delegates, and other matters related to the calling of the convention. With the Second Reconstruction Act in place, the work of reconstituting Southern state governments could begin.[31]

As March drew to a close, Grant looked "forward with a good deal of confidence to a final settlement" under the new legislation and hoped that the worst was over. He allowed himself to daydream about the possibility of spending some time in Missouri to raise "some fine horses," his consuming passion. Not even an attack by the Radical spokesman Wendell Phillips disturbed him. "I never feel annoyed at anything he has to say. Phillips is one of the class of men whose enmity is better than his friendship," he told Isaac N. Morris. "I think reconstruction is now in a fair way of being finally and favorably consummated, unless obstacles are thrown in the way from the North. I hope for the best however." To maintain the peace, he and Stanton visited the Capitol to urge the legislators to remain in session and watch over the president. Surely Johnson would not accept defeat so easily. Congressional Republicans ignored the request, however, and on March 30 adjourned until July 3. Until then, it would be up to Grant and Stanton to confront Johnson alone.[32]

8

GRANT

VERSUS

JOHNSON

By the spring of 1867, Ulysses S. Grant had come out for the congressional plan of reconstruction and was ready to supervise the process of rebuilding Southern state governments. As he prepared to counter Southern resistance to Reconstruction, he kept a watchful eye on Andrew Johnson, anticipating that the president would do what he could to obstruct the implementation of the congressional plan. What would happen politically in the Southern states was dependent in large part on the outcome of the struggle at Washington.

"Everything is getting on well here under the Congressional Reconstruction Bill," Grant observed in April, "and all will be well if administration and copperhead influence do not defeat the objects of that measure." Although Johnson had left the district commanders alone, there had been grumbling about Philip H. Sheridan's removal of several civil officials in New Orleans. These rumblings portended possible future trouble, forcing Grant to put aside plans for a European excursion. "I am not egotistical enough to suppose that my duties cannot be performed by others just as well as myself," he told Elihu B. Washburne, "but Congress has made it my duty to perform certain offices, and whilst there is an antagonism between the executive and legislative branches of the Government, I feel the same obligation to 177 stand at my post that I did whilst there were rebel armies in the field to contend with."[1]

The general-in-chief's hopes for an end to political controversy proved short-lived. No sooner had the Reconstruction Acts become law than they were challenged in the U.S. Supreme Court by state officials from Mississippi and Georgia. Mississippi's suit, which sought an injunction to stop Johnson from administering the acts, was tossed out on the grounds that the Court could not stop the president from performing his constitutional responsibility to execute the law. Any charge of unconstitutionality, the Court directed, should be made against the legislation itself. But there were other ways to test the acts' constitutionality. Georgia's governor, Charles Jenkins, petitioned the Court to issue an injunction against Edwin M. Stanton and Grant, circumventing the Court's objection in *Mississippi v. Johnson* concerning infringements upon presidential power. Jenkins argued that the Reconstruction Acts, by setting aside Georgia's 1865 constitution, promised to inflict irreparable damage and injury to the state. This plea was rejected by the Court, which dismissed the case for want of jurisdiction. Other means of challenging the constitutionality of the legislation were still to be tested, but for now the process could commence unimpaired by legal obstacles.[2]

Before John Pope headed south to take command of the Third Military District, Grant conferred with him at Washington about the framing of Southern state constitutions in accordance with the Reconstruction Acts. Aware that many whites would resist the enfranchisement of blacks, Grant advised the adoption of property or literacy requirements similar to those in the North. He knew that racial prejudice would take time to erode and that an insistence on immediate equality might well result in a backlash that would only make things worse. Should the Southern constitutional conventions do their best to meet the requirements laid down by Congress and demonstrate a sincere desire to reach an agreement with the North, he promised to work for their readmission. To Grant, the delegates' intentions and the spirit in which they undertook their labors was as important as the result. "What he desires, above all things," Pope told one Georgian, "is a supreme effort on the part of your people to bring about that harmony which should exist between the states."[3]

Grant's advice reflected his belief in the gradualism of momentous social change. Attitudes could not be revolutionized overnight; years of prejudice could not be wiped away by legislative enactment alone. Yet the general also made clear that his understanding of white sensitivities did not mean that he would forgive continued intransigence. If he was willing to admit that change would take some time, he nevertheless insisted that change must happen. To support conciliation and compromise did not mean to shy away from confrontation.

The Second Reconstruction Act outlined the procedure under which the military supervised the restoration of civil government in the ten remaining ex-Confederate states. After registering voters, the district commander would order an election to decide whether to hold a convention and to select delegates to such a convention: this presented the possibility that voters would select delegates to a convention that might not meet. Several classes of persons who had aided the rebellion were prohibited from registering to vote or serving as delegates. Anyone presenting himself before the registration boards had to swear that he never had held office under the Confederate regime or never had violated any previous oath taken to support the Constitution by engaging in rebellion. In addition, the acts authorized the district commanders to arrest uncooperative state authorities.

The broad and general wording of the legislation was deceptively simple, for it left unanswered several key questions. Which Confederate officeholders were barred from voting? Did local clerks, postmasters, and the like fall under the definition of "executive or judicial" offices excluded from registration? Could registration boards refuse to register anyone who committed perjury by taking the oath? How were military authorities supposed to stop interference by state officials left over from the abortive Johnson governments? Could the district commanders remove or suspend recalcitrant civil officials? These questions were susceptible to various answers, depending on one's interpretation of the poorly drafted legislation. Yet the answers would go far to determine which Southerners would frame new state constitutions. The haste involved in passing bills and reaching compromises had produced acts that offered ripe targets for Johnson and Attorney General Henry Stanbery. Within weeks, the number of queries submitted by the military commanders asking for clarification or interpretation of the law were so numerous that Stanbery, at Johnson's direction, began to draw up a document outlining the proper course to follow. When the two men pledged to execute the law in *Mississippi v. Johnson*, they did not add that they would also try to emasculate it.

Both district commanders and their subordinates attended to matters other than preparing for elections. When rioters in Mobile attacked Republican congressman William D. Kelley, Pope removed the mayor and the chief of police, and Grant notified other commanders to take precautionary measures against future outbreaks. Sheridan ordered the desegregation of New Orleans streetcars. Gen. Charles Griffin, supervising Sheridan's efforts in Texas, made sure that blacks were eligible for jury duty, a step soon taken by other commanders. Daniel E. Sickles issued extensive orders altering the civil and criminal code of the Carolinas. Several commanders virtually repeated General Orders Nos. 3 and 44 in their early directives, as when John M. Schofield promised military protection "in cases where the civil authorities may fail, from whatever cause, to give such protection, and to insure the prompt suppression of insurrection, disorder, and violence." Liquor manufacture, road repair, education—these and other diverse topics were often subject to military orders. News of these measures were forwarded to army headquarters in Washington for Grant's information. The general-in-chief lent assistance and advice, commending some orders implementing the legislation and suggesting changes or expressing disagreement in other cases.[4]

Controversy surrounded Sheridan's actions in the Fifth District, comprised of Louisiana and Texas. Sheridan warned that individual officeholders who impeded or delayed the process of reorganization were subject to removal. It did not take long for him to identify these people, and on March 27 he removed New Orleans's mayor, attorney general, and Judge Edward Abell, all of whom had played a major role in precipitating the riot of the previous July. Some conservatives were outraged at what they considered to be Sheridan's high-handed behavior and called for his removal, but Grant applauded his subordinate's action. "It is just the thing, and merits the universal approbation of the loyal people at least," he reassured Sheridan. "I have no doubt but that it will also meet with like approval from the *reconstructed*."[5]

Pope also employed the threat of removal, directing state officials to restrict themselves to their duties and to avoid abusing their positions to argue against compliance with the Reconstruction Acts. He contemplated removing Governor Jenkins for delivering speeches in Washington that urged Georgians to refuse to acquiesce in the process, but Grant discouraged him. Grant thought that, if removal became necessary, Jenkins should be brought before a military commission, a recourse specifically mentioned in the Reconstruction Acts. Nevertheless, the commanding general observed that Jenkins's behavior "demonstrated . . . how possible it is for a discontented civil officer of the unreconstructed States to defeat the laws of Congress," unless district commanders were expressly clothed with the power to remove civil authorities.[6]

To Grant, the power of removing obstructionist civil officials was essential to the success of the new legislation. "There is nothing clearer to my mind," he declared, "than that Congress intended to give District Commanders entire control over the civil government of these districts." But, principles aside, the pragmatic Grant suggested a more cautious course. He confided to Sheridan that "there is a decided hostility to the whole Congressional policy of reconstruction, at the 'White House,' and a disposition to remove you from the command you now have." The district commander should refrain from making further removals until Stanbery issued his opinion on the Reconstruction Acts. He hinted, however, that ultimately such an opinion would carry little weight, for "the law contemplates that district commanders shall be their own judges of the meanings of its provisions."[7]

Grant interpreted his own role in implementing the legislation as an advisory one. "My views are that District Commanders are responsible for the faithful execution of the Reconstruction Act of Congress, and that in civil matters I cannot give them an order," he told Pope. "I can give them my views, however, for what they are worth, and above all, I can advise them of views and opinions here which may serve to put them on their guard" against Johnson's machinations. Grant suggested that civil officials, instead of being removed, be suspended and tried by military commissions. Regarding registration, Grant was more blunt. "Go on giving your own interpretation to the law" in the absence of Stanbery's opinion, he instructed Sheridan. He believed that the procedures outlined by the law were clear but added that perhaps registration boards should keep a separate list of persons whose eligibility to register was disputed. Even though these opinions were often presented as advice, Badeau later noted that the district commanders "without exception took his advice as orders."[8]

Stanbery's opinion on voter registration and disfranchisement was published on May 27. As expected, it severely curtailed the grounds for disfranchising Southern whites. Johnson released the opinion to the newspapers but did not communicate it to the district commanders, which left its applicability in question. The president was more forceful when it came to removals. Once again, Sheridan's actions raised the issue. Both the Louisiana legislature and Governor J. Madison Wells had appointed a board of commissioners to supervise the construction and repair of levees along the Mississippi. Rather than sanction either slate, Sheridan decided to appoint the board himself. Wells protested, and Johnson ordered the reinstatement of the board appointed by Wells. The general complied but immediately reasserted his authority by replacing Wells with Radical Benjamin F. Flanders. Gideon Welles characterized Sheridan's actions as "arbitrary and despotic," but Grant enthusiastically endorsed them. "I shall do all I can to sustain you in it," he told Sheridan. "You have acted boldly and with good judgment, and will be sustained by public opinion."[9]

Not everyone was as pleased with Sheridan. Stanbery commenced the drafting of a more elaborate opinion, this time covering all of the powers and duties of the district commanders. The cabinet deliberated for a week over the result. Stanton was pitted against Johnson and the rest of his advisers. Although Stanton lost most of the battles, he (and thus Grant) gained an important victory when it was decided not to make the interpretation binding on the district commanders. In an unlikely turn of events, Welles supported this move, arguing that Johnson should rest content with transmitting Stanbery's interpretation "as the opinion of the law officer of the Government and leave the generals to carry on their respective governments." For Johnson to issue it in the form of an executive order would "give his sanction to the law."[10]

Those curious as to Grant's opinion on the ongoing controversy over reconstruction legislation paid avid attention to a speech delivered by his trusted chief-of-staff, John A. Rawlins, on June 21 at Galena. Implicitly repudiating his earlier support of the president, he reaffirmed the constitutionality and necessity of the Reconstruction Acts; to those who might refer to *Ex parte Milligan* or other Supreme Court decisions bearing on military commissions, he replied that such decisions "do not seek to deny the validity of military tribunals in States or districts where all civil tribunals were suspended or destroyed by actual war, or where, resultant from that war, the civil tribunals had ceased to protect society by the punishment of offenders against it." Proclaiming his support for black suffrage, he urged Northern states to act "the part of wisdom, as well as justice," by erasing the barrier of color to voting in their own states. These propositions were intended to reassure Radicals; Rawlins's opposition to attempts to circumscribe the power of the Supreme Court and his promise that the military commanders would do all in their power "to facilitate the complete restoration of civil authority" sought to satisfy moderates and conservatives.[11]

Coming from someone who once pronounced himself "a Johnson man," Rawlins's speech was a surprise. James H. Wilson pronounced it "quite a reconstruction for him." But Grant obviously had a pretty good idea of what Rawlins was going to say. The man who had urged members of the military to abstain from political discussions was now tacitly sanctioning just such an effort. Of course, Grant could argue (and doubtless did) that Rawlins's speech spoke of political institutions and not political parties, that it did no more than outline what had happened during the past several months, and that in any case Reconstruction should be above partisan bickering. To Grant, the last point was no mere rationalization, yet the fact that it had been Rawlins and not Grant who had delivered the address suggested that the commanding general preferred to let others do the talking for him. As the Springfield, Illinois, *State Journal* put it, "Gen. Grant's position in the army and his close association with the government have not rendered it suitable or proper for him to be blatant in expressing his views on questions of mere partisan politics; but he does not conceal the fact that those sympathies are all with the Republican party."[12]

As Rawlins spoke, Stanbery's opinion was being transmitted southward. As expected, it narrowly defined the powers of the district commanders, despite Sickles's fear that advocates of resistance and reaction would be encouraged. Commanders lacked the power to remove civil officials, were subordinate in every respect to the president, and were not to interfere with civil courts apart from criminal cases—a slap at Sheridan and Sickles. Registration boards had no authority to question the veracity of someone taking the oath. The opinion was an effort to stop congressional reconstruction in its tracks. Sheridan, one of those who had initially requested an advisory opinion, complained that it opened "a broad macadamized road for perjury and fraud to travel on." The opinion inspired unrepentant white Southerners. Within days, Sheridan noted "a defiant opposition to all Acts of the Military Commanders, by impeding and rendering helpless the civil officers acting under his appointment." It was of some relief to the hero of Cedar Creek when Johnson backed down from his original intention to frame orders to the military commanders embodying Stanbery's opinion.[13]

Sheridan's critical comments, which appeared immediately in the public press, peeved administration supporters. Welles characterized Sheridan's comments as "impudent and disrespectful if not disobedient." Nor was this the first time that Sheridan had been tactless in his communications to Grant. The previous week, he had complained about Johnson's repeated requests to extend the registration period. "This state will come in as a Union State if the president will let me alone," he assured Grant. Of course, if Sheridan terminated registration, he would—by closing the books before the new guidelines could be applied—effectively circumvent Stanbery's purpose of relaxing registration requirements. Grant, probably wishing that "Little Phil" would exercise a little restraint, urged him to comply with Johnson's wishes. "It will silence all charges of attempting to defeat the Atty Genl's construction of the reconstruction acts." Grant added, however, that Sheridan should delay issuing such instructions for as long as possible: "In the meantime Congress may give an interpretation of their own acts differing possibly from the one given by the Atty Gen'l."[14]

While Grant waited for Congress to convene in early July, he took full advantage of the leeway afforded by the fact that Stanbery's opinion was not binding. Informing Ord that he disagreed with the opinion's statement that registration boards should register anyone who took the oath—even in the face of evidence that perjury had been committed—Grant reaffirmed his belief that "in my opinion the Atty

Genl or myself can no more than give our opinion as to the meaning of the law; neither can enforce their views against the judgment of those made responsible for the faithful execution of the law, the District Commanders." To queries from Sheridan and Pope, Grant responded more succinctly. "Enforce your own construction of the Military Bill until ordered to do otherwise. The opinion of the Attorney General has not been distributed to district commanders in language or manner entitling it to the force of an order." His next comment was rather disingenuous: "Nor can I suppose that the President intended it to have such force." As Badeau later put it, "The situation was approaching mutiny on one side, or else treason on the other."[15]

The debate over registration, disfranchisement, and removal overshadowed other questions of substance. Pope noted that simply overseeing the drafting of new constitutions was not enough. "These politicians are wily and sagacious. They will make no laws which are not equal on their face to all men. It is in the execution of these laws, which seem to bear equally on all, that wrong will be done, and a condition of things produced which bears no resemblance to free government except in name." Southerners had been attentive to the letter of the law for years, he observed, and would exploit every loophole possible. "There are acts which cannot be reached by the General Government, and yet which quietly and silently render justice impossible, and establish discrimination against classes or color odious and unbearable." In the interim, Grant did what he could to prevent the realization of this prediction. When word reached Washington that Gen. Alvan C. Gillem, head of the Freedmen's Bureau in Mississippi (and one of Johnson's favorites), was taking the side of employers in labor disputes with blacks, Grant called for an investigation. Likewise, he instructed Ord to appoint judges who would "administer justice impartially to all irrespective of race and former political status." Grant also endorsed the efforts of his commanders to secure the presence of blacks on juries as one means to ensure equality before the law.[16]

Congress reconvened on July 3 to draft legislation that would overturn Stanbery's opinion. Stanton assisted in framing the bill and furnished Congress with copies of the communications between the district commanders and Grant. Not only did this action support the case for an additional Reconstruction Act to reaffirm the powers of the military commanders jeopardized by Stanbery's opinions, but also it made public Grant's support of Congress.[17]

On July 13, Congress passed the Third Reconstruction Act, designed to close the loopholes exposed by Stanbery's narrow interpretation of the scope of the previous acts. The civil governments set up under Johnson's plan were explicitly declared "not legal," yet they were continued on a provisional basis, subject to the consent of Congress and its agents, the district commanders. The district commanders could suspend or remove civil officials and appoint replacements. Grant was empowered to approve or disapprove these decisions and could remove or suspend civil officials and appoint replacements on his own. Registration boards could refuse to register persons who had perjured themselves by swearing the oath specified by the Second Reconstruction Act; the act defined broadly the officeholders excluded from registration and election as delegates. Having crippled Stanbery's extant opinions, Congress took care to preclude future action by the attorney general by declaring that district commanders and registration boards would not be bound "by any opinion of any civil officer of the United States." Furthermore, it directed that the clauses of the Reconstruction Acts "be construed liberally, to the end that all the intents thereof may be fully and perfectly carried out."[18]

At first glance, this legislation seemed to repair the defects of the first two acts. However, Congress and Stanton—the bill's major drafter—were so obsessed with overturning Stanbery's interpretation of previous legislation that they overlooked other weaknesses in the congressional program. Grant, chastened by experience, now pushed for measures protecting the district commanders from removal by the president. Congress failed to heed this advice, leaving the president with a powerful weapon. Nor were the commanding general's duties as clearly defined as they should have been. Newspaper commentary on the bill suggested that Congress intended to place Grant in charge of all aspects of Reconstruction. However, the drafters of the bill were focused on Stanbery's opinion and concentrated on remedying the clauses concerning removals; the final bill neglected to endow Grant with total authority over all stages of the reconstruction process and merely gave him oversight authority on appointments and removals of civil officials. These shortcomings would soon haunt the bill's drafters, who ought to have been alerted by previous events to Johnson's ability and dogged determination to ferret out the weak points of any legislation. Nor did Congress follow Grant's advice to stay in session to prevent the president from hindering the execution of the acts according to Congress's intentions.[19]

While the new bill sat on Johnson's desk, Republicans took advantage of an investigation by the House Judiciary Committee—which ostensibly was looking into grounds upon which to impeach Johnson—to interrogate Grant about Reconstruction. Appearing before the committee, he answered questions about pardon and amnesty during the months after Appomattox, defended his terms to Lee, and recalled Johnson's first steps toward establishing a Southern policy. Of particular interest to the Republican members of the committee was Grant's response to questions concerning rumors that Johnson intended to recognize as the legitimate Congress Northern Democrats and the senators and representatives elected by the Southern states, not the existing body dominated by Republicans. Though the general did not express an opinion on whether Johnson ever seriously entertained such a notion, he made it clear that the president had speculated about it. On the whole, his testimony satisfied the Republicans that he could be trusted, and in private conferences he assured them that he endorsed black suffrage wholeheartedly.[20]

On July 19, Johnson vetoed Congress's latest handiwork; the veto was promptly overridden. Grant told Stanton that, as soon as he received a copy of the new legislation, he would "make such orders as seem to me necessary to carry out the provisions of the bill and direct that they be shown to you before being issued." Then he left sweltering Washington for the cool breezes of the seaside resort of Long Branch, New Jersey. "By vesting supreme authority in Gen. Grant, Congress has removed the source of many fears," the New York *Times* enthused. "The North will no longer be in doubt as to the fidelity with which the law will be applied." Americans had "unlimited faith in his devotion to the principles which have been consecrated by the war." A week later, the *Times* returned to this theme. "The responsibility, the fidelity, the sagacity of Gen. Grant," it editorialized, "constitute the only guarantee vouchsafed to us for the adequate enforcement of the conditions dictated by Congress in the spirit in which they were conceived."[21]

But there was no rest for the general. No sooner had he arrived in Long Branch than George H. Thomas reported trouble in Memphis on the eve of a local election. Stanton, afraid of another riot, urged Grant to go to Nashville and take matters in hand, in part because in the past Thomas had proved unwilling to act without first checking with Washington. Such delays could be costly. Grant believed that his presence was unnecessary but, worried that Thomas might wait "until people are killed and the riot beyond control before interfering," gave Thomas explicit instructions that suggested his previous frustration with Thomas's hesitancy. "Go to Memphis in person and remain there until after election," he directed. "Let it be felt that where the military is law must prevail and the guilty be punished. Do not wait for a riot to take place but use the military vigorously to prevent one commencing." In subsequent days, Grant and Stanton dispatched arms and troops to Tennessee to assist Governor William Brownlow. These preventive measures were effective, and the election passed off peacefully.[22]

Watching this telegraphic activity, Welles told Johnson "that Grant had, unconsciously perhaps, very much changed his views within a year," perhaps under the influence of Stanton and the Radicals. Johnson noted that the previous November Grant had spoken of his extreme reluctance to send troops into a state "in full relations with the general government on the eve of an election to preserve peace," yet that was just what he was doing now. Perhaps Grant was not a simple soldier after all.[23]

The vacation at Long Branch did little to relieve Grant's anxiety. "Every day that I am absent from Washington," he confided to Stanton, "I see something in the papers, or hear something that makes me feel that I should be there." Questions concerning the administration of the new law, Thomas's concern about affairs in Tennessee, rumors that the president was once more contemplating the removal of Sheridan—all were on his mind, leaving little time for relaxation. If necessary, he would return to Washington. "Things might so easily have been different now and given repose to the country and consequently rest to all interested in administering the laws," he sighed in anticipation of more directives from the White House.[24]

Grant's concern was justified. Only days after the Third Recon-struction Act became law, Johnson stirred murmurs at a cabinet meet-ing when he inquired whether he could remove the district com-manders. It was hard to believe that he did not already know the answer to that question since he had just issued a veto message con-cerning the legislation, which reflected an examination of its provi-sions. In the aftermath of the Third Reconstruction Act, removal of those commanders who adhered to Radical tenets would be the best way to obstruct Congress's intentions.[25]

The most logical target was Sheridan. In July the hero of Cedar Creek discovered that Johnson had sent two trusted subordinates, James B. Steedman and Lovell Rousseau, to New Orleans to gather evidence to justify his removal. As expected, they filed reports critical of Sheridan but did so through the military telegraph service, which furnished Sheridan with copies of the messages. Sheridan told Grant that Steedman "was loud in advocating your claims for Presidential honors . . . seeking to get an expression of opinion on that subject from me, but he did not succeed"; Rousseau was "engaged in dirty business for one of his rank in the Army." The president was willing to create turmoil in the officer corps to get his way; Grant must have wondered what was next.[26]

Although Sheridan believed that his "get tough" policy was suc-ceeding in Louisiana, the upsurge of violence in Texas disturbed him, and he held Governor James Throckmorton responsible. Once again, thoughts of exercising the removal power danced through Little Phil's head. For nearly a year, he had suspected the governor of exagger-ating the threat of frontier warfare to justify the raising of a state militia. On July 30, with Grant's approval, Sheridan deposed Throck-morton; within a week, he replaced twenty-two members of the New Orleans city council, the city treasurer, and the chief of police, as well as several local officials elsewhere in Louisiana. That such actions would only further inflame Johnson seemed of little concern to Sher-idan, whose behavior was approaching the point of recklessness.[27]

This final series of removals proved to be Sheridan's undoing. When the news reached Washington, Johnson thought once more of transferring him. From Louisiana, conservative R. King Cutler wired the White House that Sheridan's ouster "will not only be a God-send to the good people of Louisiana and Texas, but to all honest men of this republic." Rousseau had already forwarded the same advice. At the same time, Johnson was exasperated with Stanton and talked of replacing him with Grant on an ad interim basis. At first glance, this move seemed senseless; Grant, a staunch supporter of congressional reconstruction, had endorsed Sheridan's actions, although he had advised him to move with caution. Perhaps the president concurred in Welles's belief that Grant was merely a puppet, susceptible to outside influences, and that by replacing Stanton with Grant he could not only exclude Stanton from the ranks of the puppeteers but also enhance his own influence over the general. Tying Grant to the administration would not hurt Johnson, and it might injure Grant's popularity with the Republican party, removing him as a possible presidential candidate. With Grant gone, the Republicans might well nominate a renowned Radical after all, which in turn could increase Johnson's appeal as the Democratic candidate in 1868.[28]

To Johnson's surprise, Grant, in an August 1 meeting at the White House, argued against the president's proposal to depose both Sheridan and Stanton. He hedged against outright rejection of the offer of office, however, fearing that, should he decline, the president would turn to someone else more like-minded. Rather, he told Johnson that he would not "shrink from the performance of any public duty that may be imposed upon me," conveniently forgetting that he had done just that the previous October in turning down the Mexican mission.[29]

But Grant preferred things as they were. After returning to headquarters, he decided to repeat his objections to Johnson in a letter. Stanton, he asserted, was protected by the Tenure of Office Act. "The meaning of the law may be explained away by an astute lawyer, but common sense and the views of loyal people will give it the effect intended by its framers." Sheridan "has had difficulties to contend with which no other district commander has encountered." Speaking "as a friend desiring peace and quiet," Grant warned "that it is [in] my opinion more than the loyal people of the country . . . will quietly submit to, to see the very men of all others whom they have expressed confidence in removed."[30]

For the moment, Johnson delayed acting, although the cabinet continued to discuss Sheridan's possible removal. At a second meeting with Johnson on August 3, Grant once more expressed his reluctance about taking over for Stanton. Afterward, the president conferred with Welles. "Grant is going over," Welles remarked. Johnson, agree-ing, announced that he "intended to bring this matter to a conclusion in a few days. But the president did not make this public, telling re-porters that he would be "surprised to find out" that Grant opposed "what I have been attempting to do."[31]

On August 5, Johnson called on Stanton to resign. The secretary refused the request. For a week, no one was quite sure how the deadlock would be resolved. Finally, Johnson approached Grant once more. This time the result was different. During "a pleasant inter-view," the two arrived at "a mutual understanding." Grant informed the president that, although they disagreed on the Fourteenth Amendment and Congress's reconstruction legislation, there was no personal friction between them. At the conclusion of the meeting, Grant agreed to accept the War Department portfolio with the com-ment, "I will, of course, obey orders."[32]

Why did Grant change his mind? After all, he was not ordered to take Stanton's position, and even if he had been he had already re-fused to obey an order to take a civil post during the Mexico imbro-glio. Probably he believed that his earlier refusal to supplant Stanton had put an end to the matter, not anticipating that Johnson would move ahead regardless of his advice. Perhaps he thought that Stanton would accede to Johnson's request for his resignation, however unwise he thought such a request would be, and was surprised by Stanton's decision to stand fast. Now, with the confrontation having occurred, new considerations attracted Grant's attention. There had been ru-mors that Johnson was looking around for someone else to take the job, perhaps Sheridan's foe Steedman, and in fact the president had inquired of Montgomery Blair about the availability of his brother, Frank Blair. Since Stanton could not be saved in any case, Grant chose to stave off possible disaster by accepting Johnson's offer, "mainly from the conviction that if I do not accept, some objectional man would be appointed." "I think it most important that someone should be there who cannot be used," he explained to Julia.[33]

That night, Grant stopped by Stanton's house to inform him of his decision. The secretary was not happy, nor was Grant happy with his reaction. The next day, Grant formally transmitted Johnson's notifi-cation to Stanton and expressed "my appreciation of the zeal, patrio-tism, firmness and ability with which you have ever discharged the duty of Sec. of War." However, Grant struck out even more positive phrases about "the duties thus imposed upon me" and "the regret I now feel" at Stanton's suspension. Stanton's bitterness showed through in his reply, which impressed Grant as stiff and touchy. However much the general and the secretary had stood together during the past year, Stanton's behavior reminded Grant how difficult he could be. As he told Julia, Stanton was "very offensive" to Johnson; he "would have gone and on a double-quick long ago if I had been President"—a comment that hinted at Grant's own troubles with the irascible secretary.[34]

"Grant is not at all displeased with his position," Welles smugly noted as the general appeared at his first cabinet meeting as secretary of war. "On the contrary there is self-satisfaction very obvious." Orville H. Browning scoffed at Grant's "rather ridiculous arrogance" and mocked the general's willingness "to deliver his crude opinions upon all subjects, and especially upon legal questions." Sour comments by members of the cabinet aside, other administration supporters cheered the change. One army officer visiting Grant's headquarters judged "from the papers that the Johnston [sic] people are trying to make it appear that Genl Grant is in the same boat with them." Nor did Johnson's cronies shed tears over Stanton's removal. "There is an unusual glee here over it," Montgomery Blair reported, "and the best of the joke is that the blow was given by General Grant." Meeting the Grants a few days later, Blair concluded, "Dont think either of them are sorry for Stanton a great deal."[35]

Grant's acceptance of the War Department portfolio gave rise to much adverse comment by Radicals. The *Independent* concluded that the general "appears to have become a cat's paw for the President." Carl Schurz commented that Grant had taken "the only step which could prevent him from becoming president. He has allowed himself to be imposed upon and placed in a false position. Everything depends on how he is going to get out of it." Other Radicals crossed their fingers and hoped for the best. Almost in a panic, George S. Boutwell implored Grant "to adhere rigidly under all circumstances, to the plan of reconstruction prescribed by Congress, and to avoid, especially, all commitments to or complications in any antagonistic schemes." Henry D. Cooke came away from a talk with the general convinced that "he was actuated by good motive in taking the place," and he credited him with "patriotic courage in taking it, at the risk of *misconstruction.* . . . I have no doubt that Grant's object was to prevent a *general sweep* of the Military Reconstruction District Commanders, and the substitution of *obstructionists.*" The historian John Lothrop Motley was amused by the flurry of speculation. "I suspect the time is fast approaching when Ulysses must cease to do the 'dumb, inarticulate man of genius' business."[36]

Sheridan's fate was the first test of the new Grant-Johnson relationship. When Johnson took no immediate steps to remove Sheridan, Grant optimistically concluded that the crisis was over, at least for the moment. Nevertheless, he advised Sheridan to be ready for anything and urged him to issue his orders concerning the state election as soon as possible, so that in case of his replacement his successor's hands would be tied.[37]

Grant's hopes proved illusory. On August 17, Johnson prepared orders relieving Sheridan from his position, replacing him with Thomas. Before issuing his orders, he asked Grant's opinion. He did not anticipate the lengthy, impassioned answer that followed. Speaking "in the name of a patriotic people who have sacrificed hundreds of thousands of loyal lives, and thousands of millions of treasure to preserve the integrity and union of this country," Grant insisted that "it is unmistakably the expressed wish of this country that General Sheridan should not be removed from his present command." In a nation "where the will of the people is the law of the land," he begged "that their voice may be heard" and Sheridan retained. To remove him now would "only be interpreted as an effort to defeat the laws of Congress" and would "embolden" the "unreconstructed element" of the South. Such clumsy and stilted rhetoric was characteristic of Grant's writing when he was highly wrought up. It presented an easy target for Johnson, who rebutted the general's arguments in a cool, dispassionate, and lawyerly response. Chiding Grant, he reminded him that the Constitution, not the will of the people, was the law of the land; characterized Sheridan's conduct as that of a tyrant; and concluded that it was his, not Grant's, responsibility "to take care that the laws be faithfully executed." The order stood. "Sheridan is relieved!," Horace Porter exclaimed to his wife. "We are dreadfully sorry[.] The General had a hard fight for him, but no go."[38]

As the Sheridan crisis reached its climax, Welles sized up his new cabinet colleague. In an effort to uncover Grant's leanings, he engaged the general in conversation after one cabinet meeting. Grant expressed dismay at "these changes that are going on, striking down men who have been faithful through the War." Welles shrugged this off to probe into the general's theory of the Constitution, only to discover that Grant, betraying his Whig roots, believed that Congress's will ought to be heeded. This differed from Welles's preference for a Jacksonian model of executive supremacy; and, so, Grant must be wrong. "It pained me to see how little he understood of the fundamental principles of our government, and of the Constitution itself." Grant, tired of Welles's Socratic interrogation, finally fired back with a salvo of his own. He recalled that on the eve of the war then Senator Johnson had remarked that those who talked the most about the Constitution seemed the most intent on destroying it. The exasperated Welles abandoned his self-appointed task of enlightenment, later concluding that the general "is a political ignoramus."[39]

The navy secretary retreated to his well-worn notion of Grant the puppet and the dupe. "General Grant is clearly afflicted with the Presidential disease, and it warps his judgment. . . . Obviously he has been tampered with and flattered by the Radicals, who are using him and his name for their selfish and partisan purposes." He hurried over to Johnson to reveal his apprehensions "that Grant was a little farther astray than I had apprehended." Then it was across Lafayette Square to Blair House, where Welles pleaded with Montgomery Blair "to see Grant, talk with him, get others who are right-minded to talk with him also, and write him." Perhaps the general could still be saved for Johnson.[40]

Grant was too busy defending the district commanders to pay much attention to Welles. With Sheridan on the way out, Johnson next fingered Sickles for extinction. The commander of the Second Military District had superseded major portions of the civil and criminal code of South Carolina and stayed judgments calling for imprisonment or confiscation of property in payment for private debts contracted during the war. Such liberal and broad interpretations of his authority naturally drew criticism from the Johnson administration, and Stanbery had singled him out for acting outside the bounds of the Reconstruction Acts. But, when Sickles attempted to enforce his stay order against the federal district court, he went too far. Grant suspended the order and demanded an explanation. Sickles explained that he believed that the court's rulings would favor ex-Rebels. Thus persuaded, Grant lifted the suspension on the day that Sheridan was removed.[41]

On August 23, the cabinet met to discuss the Sickles case. Assistant Attorney General J. M. Binkley charged that Sickles was attempting to subvert the supremacy of civil rule and dismissed Sickles's claim that the district court intended to rule on the constitutionality of the Reconstruction Acts. Grant, claiming that Sickles should be allowed to explain his action, added that to strike down the acts of the district commanders would diminish their authority and encourage continued resistance to the law. Furthermore, he stated that Congress had empowered him (and, implicitly, not the president) with ultimate authority to oversee the implementation of the Reconstruction Acts and that he intended to see the law executed. This did not go over well with Welles and, more importantly, with Johnson, who for the moment refused to challenge Grant's assertion of power. Whatever hopes he had entertained for winning over the commanding general had been smashed.[42]

Alerting Sickles to the opposition of the president and his cabinet to the order, Grant advised him to modify it to exclude U.S. courts from its scope. "My own views always have been that the military should be subordinate to Civil authorities as far as is consistent with safety," he explained; thus, such interference as proposed by Sickles was unjustified "unless such Courts were acting clearly in a way to defeat the Acts of Congress for the reconstruction of the 'Rebel states.'" He called on Sickles to furnish him with information on the background of the order so that he could present "the other side" of the question. About to lose Sheridan, Grant was going to do all he could to save Sickles.[43]

The ensuing conflict between Grant and Johnson was rooted in their contrasting interpretations of the Third Reconstruction Act. Grant believed that the act made him, as general-in-chief, responsible for all aspects of its administration. This reading relied not only upon the specific provisions of the act, but also upon the broad powers confirmed by the final section, which held that the three Reconstruction Acts "shall be construed liberally, to the end that all the intents thereof may be fully and perfectly carried out." Chief among those intentions, according to Grant, was to place him in control of the process. Johnson was looking for some basis upon which to influence the actions of the district commanders in the wake of the negation of Stanbery's opinion; he took a narrow view of the legislation, claiming correctly that Grant's authority, according to the letter of the law, extended only to the suspension, removal, and appointment of civil officials and registration board members. Otherwise, the district commanders were on their own, for they would not be bound "by an opinion of any civil officer of the United States," whether that be the attorney general, the president, or the secretary of war. Ironically, this was exactly the position taken by Grant before Stanbery issued his opinion. Once Johnson had adopted this interpretation, he realized that the best way to ensure an administration of military reconstruction according to conservative principles was to remove the Radical commanders, replace them with officers of more conservative sympathies, and then insist that they were independent. Thus Johnson seized upon the vague wording of hastily drafted legislation to support his position, while a frustrated Grant was left to wonder why Congress had not explicitly translated into law its intentions to give him complete control.[44]

Grant's defense of Sickles's action, his protests against Sheridan's removal, and his insistence that he possessed ultimate authority under the Reconstruction Acts alarmed Welles, who shared his fears with the president. Johnson remained unconvinced that Grant was unfaithful, but Welles needed no further evidence to conclude that the "simpleminded" Grant had "fallen into the hands of Radical rogues." The navy secretary had given up on the general. "He is an insincere man, I fear, very ambitious, has low cunning, and is unreliable, perhaps untruthful."[45]

Events provided Grant with one last slim opportunity to save Sheridan. Thomas, alarmed by the prospect of becoming a district commander, bridled at replacing Sheridan and privately informed Grant of that fact. But this would not do for Johnson; so, to get out of the transfer, Thomas telegraphed that he was ill, and an army physician testified that Thomas suffered from a liver ailment. Grant showed Johnson the report, and the president put his orders on hold. But Johnson soon found someone else to replace Sheridan. Winfield Scott Hancock was available and, given his Democratic credentials, might well be a distinct improvement over Thomas. In fact, he had been Johnson's first choice. Possessing a distinguished combat record with the Army of the Potomac, Hancock's loyalty to the Union could not be questioned. On August 26, Johnson ordered Hancock to assume Sheridan's position. Sheridan replaced Hancock at the head of the Department of the Missouri. Thomas would remain at his post.[46]

At the same time, the president took care to reject Grant's broad interpretation of his powers under the Reconstruction Acts. When Grant framed the original order replacing Sheridan with Thomas, he announced that Thomas "will continue to execute all orders he may find in force" in Sheridan's command, unless Grant directed otherwise. Thus he protected Sheridan's measures while asserting once more his oversight authority. Johnson countered this effort to hamstring Hancock by stating that Hancock "will, when necessary to a faithful execution of the laws, exercise any and all powers conferred by acts of Congress upon district commanders, and any and all authority pertaining to officers in command of military departments." This embodied Johnson's new notion, now that he had a sympathetic man at the head of the Fifth Military District, that the district commanders were the sole interpreters of their authority.[47]

Grant was dismayed by Johnson's decision. His initial intent had been to retain Sheridan in command, using Thomas's complaints about his health to frustrate Johnson's desire to remove the cavalryman. Now the president had outflanked him. Immediately upon receiving Johnson's order, Grant prepared a reply designed to protect Sheridan. Thomas, he argued, had not yet acknowledged receiving Johnson's original order. Why not wait for Thomas's formal reply? Besides, with the prevalence of yellow fever in New Orleans, Grant believed that, unless there were "very grave public reasons, no officer should be sent to Louisiana now." But Grant did not stop here. Once more, he asserted that the Third Reconstruction Act "throws much of the responsibility of executing faithfully the reconstruction laws of Congress on the General of the Army." Having approved Sheridan's actions, he insisted "on instructing his successor to carry out those orders so far as I am authorized to do so by Acts of Congress." Johnson's meddling might well prove counterproductive, he warned. "Will not further opposition necessarily result in more stringent measures against the South?"[48]

The next day, at a cabinet meeting, Grant tried one last time to avoid the inevitable. He alleged that Hancock was indispensable where he was and that, since both Thomas and Sheridan's second-in-command—Charles Griffin—were ailing, any shift at this moment would be ill-timed. This was mere subterfuge; the previous day, Grant had not described Griffin as sick but as "absolutely incompetent by law" to replace Sheridan until Hancock arrived. Why not wait until Thomas recovered from his illness, then follow the original plan? He reiterated that the law placed the execution of the Reconstruction Acts in his hands, and that it was his duty to see them executed. Johnson, "very cool and calm, and deliberate in his reply," rejected this last-gasp attempt to prolong Sheridan's tenure as the head of the Fifth Military District. Hancock would go to New Orleans. Sickles fell next, as a subdued Grant agreed to his replacement by Edward R. S. Canby, who, if no conservative, was also no Radical.[49]

Grant, upset with his failure to stop Johnson from removing Sheridan and Sickles, decided it was time to separate himself from the administration. He remarked that, "while it was proper he should discharge the duties of the office of secretary of war, he preferred not to be mixed up in political questions." In the future, he would excuse himself from discussions not related to his department. When Johnson replied that "that was at his own option," Grant rose and left. That afternoon, the new orders went out. Johnson had won his point. The wording employed by Grant in the Thomas order—about successors continuing to enforce the decisions of their predecessors —was omitted, leaving Hancock free to reverse Sheridan's directives.[50]

Unfortunately for Grant, Johnson had not yet received the general's letter of August 26 outlining his interpretation of the Third Reconstruction Act. He did receive the letter after the cabinet meeting, and it reopened the dispute that had just been settled. Grant backed down, withdrawing the letter after a meeting with the president during which Johnson once more shredded the general's argument. Obviously, Grant was out of his element when it came to lawyer-like reasoning; Welles judged him "somewhat pig-headed, having evidently been inspired with certain notions by the Radicals, without resources or the intelligence necessary to carry him through." Or so it seemed.[51]

"Gen. Grant is evidently in a dangerous position," noted the *Independent*. "He cannot remain long in the War Department without offending the President or his Republican friends." Chicago *Tribune* editor Joseph Medill chastised Grant for failing to sustain Sheridan and Stanton. Grant's silence was injuring his image. "Why in the name of manhood do you not let the people know what your political opinions are?" demanded one New Jerseyite. Nor was anyone exactly sure where Grant stood any more. "That he does not approve of the President's conduct is clear enough," continued the *Independent*. "The President himself knows it; but, on the other hand, he is not a Radical. . . . He seems to strike for the 'golden mean' between President and Congress." Grant informed several visiting Republicans, "It is not my business to go about the country making political speeches; but when it is in the line of my duty to express my opinion upon Reconstruction, I shall do so freely, as I have done in the past." Perhaps that moment had come, hinted the Philadelphia *Daily Bulletin*. "Solomon said that 'there is a time to keep silence and a time to speak.' Gen. Grant's time would seem to have arrived." [52]

Apparently, Grant agreed. He decided to make public his dispute with Johnson by releasing to the press his August 17 letter protesting Sheridan's removal. "Every word is golden," proclaimed the *Army and Navy Journal*. One New Yorker reported that the letter "has had a wonderful effect & our friends are jubilant." The letter, announced one paper, placed "Grant before the country in his true light as the earnest and reliable adherent of the Congressional policy of Reconstruction and as the determined opponent of the reactionary policy upon which Johnson has been bent." Another paper rejoiced, "General Grant is a Radical all over," dedicated to a thorough reconstruction. "President Johnson has found out that General Grant has not been so pliant a tool in his hand as he supposed," cheered John Binney, a New York newsman and Republican adviser. But it was left to Wendell Phillips and other Radical commentators to note that, for all Grant's sound and fury, Johnson had still gotten his way. [53]

But Grant was not through yet. Johnson had conceded that Grant had the authority to supervise the appointment or removal of civil officials. Aware that Hancock would do what he could to overturn Sheridan's directives, Grant forbade the reinstatement of removed officials, thwarting Johnson's intent. "This order is in bad taste and bad spirit," Welles wailed. "General Grant is more intensely partisan than I was aware, or than he himself supposes." [54]

Johnson retaliated, immediately issuing a proclamation that enjoined obedience to the Constitution and that specifically denounced Sickles's actions in the Carolinas against the federal courts. There seemed no need for such a proclamation, since Sickles's removal had already been announced, unless it was to badger military authorities. Implicit in such a declaration was the notion that the whole scheme of congressional reconstruction was unconstitutional. Four days later, Johnson expanded the scope of his previous amnesty proclamation, striking out several categories of exceptions from his May 1865 proclamation. He asserted yet again in another rambling preamble that Southerners were obeying the laws, that "large standing armies, military occupation, martial law military tribunals, and the suspension of the privilege of the writ of *habeas corpus*" could not be justified in time of peace, and that "a retaliatory or vindictive policy" hindered reconciliation, recovery, and prosperity.[55]

These statements served only to antagonize Republicans and encourage intransigent white Southerners. At least one reporter wondered whether there was more to Johnson's actions than just an intent to annoy Republicans. Georges Clemenceau, after a careful examination of the proclamation, argued that the president's real intent was to allow for the registration of those people pardoned. If the Tennessean pursued this course of action, Grant might resist, and a serious crisis could ensue. Once more, Radicals talked of impeachment; Johnson pulled back from insisting on the registration of all who had received executive pardon, but only after suggesting that this result could be achieved through a court test.[56]

Such rumors only increased the tension around Washington. Stories appeared that Grant and Johnson had exchanged harsh words. Visiting Washington, Henry D. Cooke, brother of financier Jay Cooke, concluded that Grant was the right man in the right place. "He is true and firm in his purposes," he told his brother, "and will do all the law will allow him to do to thwart the president's attempts to practically annul the reconstruction acts of Congress." But the general "was in a difficult position, and it is important for the country that he should not break with the President, or abandon his position at the head of the War Department." Grant told Henry Cooke that he would not be surprised at anything Johnson might do. It was imperative to keep an eye on the president, lest he prove to be even more wily an opponent than even Robert E. Lee. If war was politics by other means, Washington politics was increasingly resembling war by other means.[57]

As fall came, Grant expressed concern over the prolonged military supervision of Southern civil affairs. "I am exceeding anxious to see reconstruction effected and military rule put an end to," he told Ord. "Politicians should be perfectly satisfied with the temperate manner with which the military have used authority thus far; but if there is a necessity for continuing it too long, there is a great danger of a reaction against the army. The best way, I think, to secure a speedy termination of military rule, is to execute all the laws of Congress in the spirit in which they were conceived, firmly but without passion." Until this happened, however, Grant would be willing to use force or the threat of force where appropriate—as an incident in Tennessee demonstrated.[58]

At issue was registering voters for a municipal election in Nashville. As in the Baltimore crisis the previous year, both the conservative mayor of Nashville and the Radical governor Brownlow recognized different sets of election judges, who would rule on the eligibility of voters. At issue was whether blacks would be allowed to vote: the mayor, insisting that the election was to be held under the city's charter, said no; Brownlow, arguing that state suffrage requirements applied to local elections as well, pressed the blacks' right to participate. Thomas, afraid as usual to act on his own, wired Grant for instructions. "The military can not set up to be the judge as to which set of election judges have the right to control," Grant advised, "but must confine their action to preventing or putting down hostile mobs." The military's mission was not to take sides "but to prevent conflict." But such instructions posed a problem, as Thomas pointed out. Brownlow had decided to suspend the city election, while the mayor insisted on it being held. "A collision is inevitable. If I command the peace, my action will be a practical decision against State authority & against the franchise law." This information caused Grant to clarify his instructions to ensure the proper result. "Nothing," he wired Thomas, "is clearer . . . than that the military can not be made use of to defeat the executive of a State in enforcing the laws of the State." When Thomas showed this telegram to the mayor and announced that he would support Brownlow, the mayor backed down.[59]

Grant's action infuriated Johnson. The general had kept to himself during this crisis, and, by the time it was brought up at a cabinet meeting, the election had taken place. Welles fumed that Tennessee Radicals "will not regard the rights of Nashville if they conflict with the negro." At the same time, stories began to appear about a renewed effort to impeach the president. What made these rumors distinctive was the proposal that Johnson should be suspended from office pending trial. Johnson, of course, would resist this. What would Grant do? The president decided to send once more for Sherman. Perhaps he could talk some sense into Grant, or, better yet, perhaps he would replace Grant in the War Department.[60]

Welles, always searching for the dark side, doubted that the "erratic and uncertain" Sherman would defy Grant. Henry Cooke believed that if Sherman took over the War Department it would be with Grant's approval. They were right. When Sherman arrived, he made it clear to Johnson that he was not interested in a cabinet post and that he would not be used against Grant. "The President don't comprehend Grant," Sherman concluded, "and tho' there is no breach it is manifest there is not a cordial understanding."[61]

Although Sherman tried to reassure Johnson and his cabinet members that Grant, regardless of his political sympathies, would stop any effort to oust the president, few believed him. Johnson was convinced that the general had embraced the Radicals. Browning agreed, labeling Grant "a radical of strong passions and prejudices" who would "obey Congress instead of the President in the event of a conflict." Despite his harsh characterizations of Grant in the past, Welles was still willing to concede that the commanding general was "at heart honest, patriotic, and desirous of doing right." Calling upon Johnson to abandon using Sherman as an intermediary, Welles advised that it was time to have "a frank and unreserved interview with Grant" to find out where he stood. Sherman pressed the same advice on the president.[62]

At first, Johnson hesitated, failing to raise the issue at a cabinet meeting. This was a missed opportunity, for Grant, having been briefed by his house guest, Sherman, "was prepared to give him an

answer that would have relieved him at once." On the next day, however, Johnson visited the War Department, and Grant assured him
that he would resist any attempt "to depose or arrest him" prior to
the conclusion of an impeachment trial. Grant made his position clear
to other Republicans, including Boutwell, one of the prime advocates
of impeachment. At about this time (perhaps at this meeting), Grant
also promised Johnson that, should the Senate reinstate Stanton when
it convened in December, he would either hold on to the office, forcing a court test of the Tenure of Office Act, or vacate it in time for
Johnson to appoint somebody else.[63]

During the fall, Grant also informed Republicans and Johnson supporters alike that he did not support proposals to impeach the president. He had little use for the attempts by Benjamin F. Butler and
others to scrape up charges against Johnson, including a persistent
effort to implicate Johnson in the assassination plot against Lincoln.
Although Montgomery Blair joked that the general "would be against
any thing Butler is for," others were reassured by this information.[64]

Grant's pledges to Johnson were sincere, but they were also shrewd;
by winning Johnson's confidence, he avoided being replaced in the
War Department, thus keeping it out of hands hostile to congressional
reconstruction. As the *Army and Navy Journal* put it, to resign would
constitute "an evasion of duty." This seemed all the more important
in light of the rumors of coup d'état circulating throughout Washington. Most suspicious was the behavior of Governor Thomas Swann of
Maryland, Grant's old adversary from the Baltimore crisis, who was
busy forming a state militia. Before long, the size of this militia gave
rise to speculation that Swann might employ it on Johnson's behalf,
especially after Swann attempted to arm it with cannon. Denying
Swann's request, Grant commented, "I have a mind to write to the
Governor of Maryland and notify him that I am fully aware of what
is going on, and intend to keep my eye upon it." During the next
several months, he did just that, receiving periodic reports on the
militia. Johnson, afraid that the Radicals themselves were plotting a
coup, inquired whether Washington blacks had formed two regiments and were busy drilling. Tired of Johnson's negrophobia, Grant
replied: "In addition to military organization here reported, I understand there are four companies of white military in the district raised

by the authority of the Government." The sarcastic response hit home, for the president complained that the dispatch "showed an unkind feeling."[65]

Such exchanges suggested that there existed nothing more than a temporary truce between Johnson and Grant. Sheridan announced that Grant "is radical to the core," even more so than the deposed district commander himself. But these political differences, important as they were, were increasingly overshadowed by another question. Once, in a conversation with Grant, Johnson had alluded to it when he stated that he was not a candidate for another term. Grant replied that he had no intention of seeking the office, either. Neither man trusted the other's ambition. The pull of presidential politics and reconstruction policy together would stretch the relationship to the breaking point on the eve of the 1868 election, in part because events in 1867 made it nearly inevitable that the general would seek the president's job.[66]

9

THE
PRESIDENTIAL
QUESTION

Ever since his battlefield triumphs had brought his name to the attention of the American public, Ulysses S. Grant had been considered as a possible candidate for president. The question became a most pressing one in 1867, as politicians of both parties closely scrutinized his actions, weighing the possibility of the general's candidacy in the 1868 presidential election. "It is now becoming extremely important to know precisely what Grant wants in connection with the Presidency," John Sherman noted in August. "If he has really made up his mind that he would like to hold the office, he can have it. Popular opinion is all in his favor. His position is the rare one of having his office within his easy reach, and yet it is clear that his interest is against his acceptance. The moment he is nominated, he at once becomes the victim of abuse; and even his great services will not shield him." Gideon Welles, as if out to prove the Ohio senator's point about abuse, thought the idea of Grant as president preposterous: "He has not studied nor made himself familiar with our Constitution . . . but has permitted himself to be flattered, seduced and led astray by bad men."[1]

The debate over Grant's political ambitions had been going on for some time. Back in 1864, Grant had stifled a boomlet pushing him for the presidency. Ever since Appomattox, however, a Grant candidacy had been discussed by everybody but the prospective candidate.

"All that I can say to discourage the idea of my ever being a candidate for an office I do say," he told William T. Sherman. In 1867 the question assumed new importance. Both moderate and Radical Republicans viewed that year's state elections as a test of the strength of Radicalism. Voters would be able to endorse or repudiate Congress's plan of reconstruction; they would also accept or reject proposals made by some Radicals to expand the boundaries of political and social change. Although some Radicals continued to advocate property confiscation, redistribution of land to the freedmen, and free public education, they also began to talk about racially nondiscriminatory suffrage requirements in all the states, North and South. Such far-reaching reforms threatened to disrupt efforts to build a biracial Republican party in the South, a process dependent in part upon conciliating at least some white Southern moderates. They also challenged persistent Northern racism. As revealed in the defeat of a series of constitutional referendums that would have enfranchised blacks in several Northern states, a majority of the Northern electorate, including a minority of the Republican party, was unwilling to open the doors to racial equality at home.[2]

The outcome of the election would also influence the party's choice of its standard-bearer for the 1868 presidential contest. Most Radical Republicans leaned toward one of two Ohioans—Chief Justice Salmon P. Chase, who had been the leader of an abortive dump-Lincoln movement in 1864, and Senator Benjamin F. Wade, president pro tempore of the Senate. Sentiment for Chase was strongest among the abolitionist wing of the Republican party. George W. Julian and Charles Sumner made clear their preference for the chief justice in conversations during the fall of 1867. Financier Jay Cooke and his brother Henry embraced a Chase candidacy, in part because of Chase's views on financial issues, as did John Sherman. Others echoed Chase supporter James A. Hamilton, who told the chief justice that the Republican triumph in the congressional elections of 1866 proved that the party "was so strong that there was no excuse for taking a candidate who was most *expedient* . . . as for instance Genl. Grant." Even Richard Yates, who had given Grant his first command as a colonel in 1861, preferred Chase.[3]

Moderate Republicans looked askance at both Chase and Wade. The chief justice's abolitionist background and unqualified support for black suffrage labeled him an extremist. Others distrusted his seemingly inordinate desire for self-promotion, agreeing with Abraham Lincoln's description of his treasury secretary as "a man of unbounded ambition . . . working all his life to become President." Wade's chief liability was his advocacy of currency inflation, an issue that threatened to divide the party. Moreover, many moderates realized that the secret to the party's success in the 1866 elections was not the popularity of its reconstruction program—its position at that time was still only partly defined—but the intense dissatisfaction over Johnson's policy and behavior.[4]

Such concerns reflected the coalition nature of the party's origins. In their opposition to the slave power and slavery extension, Republicans had always papered over differences concerning race and economics. The war had radicalized the party to a certain extent on slavery and race, but old divisions surfaced again after the war. Deep fissures remained within the party on the pace and extent of social revolution. The commitment to black equality had never been a broad one, as suggested by the original Republican legislative proposals. As during the war, it had been primarily Southern resistance that, more than anything else, expanded the scope and extent of change, as Republicans adopted more extreme measures to overcome Rebel recalcitrance. Nevertheless, moderates had refrained from adopting the extreme positions of Thaddeus Stevens and Sumner, whose programs promised to transform Southern society economically and politically. Even those moderates who agreed with the ultimate goal of racial equality often disagreed with Radicals on how best and how fast to attain that goal. And party members found themselves in disagreement over postwar economic policy, which loomed as a potentially major issue in the years to come. To nominate Chase or Wade would be to force Republicans to define party positions on racial and financial issues, areas in which the party remained divided and electoral victory would be far more difficult to secure.

But there was no moderate with a sufficient national following to contest either Wade or Chase for the nomination. Handicapped by the lack of a compelling alternative within the ranks of the party proper, they looked elsewhere for a candidate who could gain majority support—and found in Ulysses S. Grant the solution to their problems. Grant's popularity and reputation would allow Republicans

once more to define themselves in terms of what they were against
—the resurgence of Southern power and the revitalization of the
Confederate spirit—in order to maintain party unity and to galvanize
an electoral majority. As the general had taken no stand on the outstanding economic issues of the day, that possibly divisive area could
be avoided. Moreover, Grant's image as an apolitical soldier-statesman
who stood for peace, stability, and order was tailor-made for a time
when Americans were showing signs of looking for a respite from
years of crisis and clamoring politicians.

Radicals were suspicious of Grant, and rightly so. Many, including
Stevens, Julian, and George S. Boutwell, had opposed the creation of
the rank of lieutenant general for him in 1864 because they doubted
his commitment to emancipation. Some recalled Sumner's character-
ization of Grant's 1865 report on the South as a "whitewashing" document. Commenting on the speculation about Grant's presidential
prospects, the Massachusetts senator opined that "we are left in har-
rowing uncertainty with regard to his opinions. Who can say that, as
President, he would give to the freedmen, during the coming years,
and through the processes of reconstruction, that kindly and sympathetic support which they need?" Chase's lieutenant, William P.
Mellen, reported that even some Union veterans lacked "confidence
in his principles and feelings toward colored loyalists, and think he
has too much faith in and sympathy for rebels." Grant's acceptance of
the War Department portfolio in August, coming nearly a year after
his attendance on the "Swing around the Circle" fiasco, seemed to
provide ample confirmation of Radicals' fears. The commanding general "well deserves unmitigated condemnation," one fumed, because
he "has so often danced to the tune of Andy Johnson."[5]

Among the most vociferous opponents of a Grant candidacy was
Wendell Phillips. In a series of widely publicized speeches, the fiery
abolitionist denounced Grant, pointing to his December 1865 report
to Johnson as proof of his conservatism and holding him responsible
for the bloodletting at Memphis and New Orleans. The general was
not obliged to take Edwin M. Stanton's position; surely, his presence
in the war office had been of little protection to Philip H. Sheridan
and Daniel E. Sickles. Had Grant stood firm against the president,
Phillips asserted, Johnson would have been driven from office. Instead, the general did nothing. "Grant is the staff which holds up

the traitor President. Without him Johnson could neither stand nor walk." Even when Grant's opposition to the removals of Stanton and Sheridan became public, Phillips was unimpressed, commenting that the general had "blundered" and characterizing him as "a weed caught in the Presidential maelstrom." The Massachusetts abolitionist went so far as to say that he preferred a Democratic victory in 1868 to Grant's triumph. Phillips's supporters seconded their leader's opposition. At the May 1867 meeting of the American Anti-Slavery Society, Thomas Wentworth Higginson argued that Union veterans were disenchanted with the hero of Appomattox's lukewarm attitude toward blacks. Heeding Higginson's remarks, the convention passed a resolution warning the American people of the dangers of "heedless hero-worship."[6]

Horace Greeley's New York *Tribune* also believed that the Republicans could do better than Grant. The party's candidate "must represent and embody Republican principles, and be neither afraid nor ashamed to avow his faith in them and his willingness to stand or fall by them"—a barb aimed at the general's silence as to his partisan position. The American people "are not in the mood for any grab-bag experiments." Greeley and his editorial writer Whitelaw Reid, a Chase supporter, bashed Grant whenever they could, attacking "hero-worship," ridiculing the general's supporters, and pointing to his acceptance of the War Department position as evidence of his support for Johnson.[7]

Some Radicals, like Wade and Benjamin F. Butler, opposed Grant's candidacy for more personal reasons. Wade had declared his support for Chase but nursed presidential ambitions of his own. Although he had been aware of Grant's disputes with Johnson and of the general's support for congressional reconstruction, he chose not to make his knowledge public and claimed instead that Grant's supposed reticence masked his conservatism. Butler's opposition dated back to January 1865, when Grant removed him from command following his botched assault on Fort Fisher, North Carolina. Humiliating as that was, it was topped by Grant's description of Butler's failed campaign against Richmond in 1864. A markedly inferior Confederate force had not only halted Butler's half-hearted lunge toward the Rebel capital but also had contained him in a defensive position that Grant, in his final report, likened to being "in a bottle strongly corked." Embarrassed and outraged, Butler broke off all relations with Grant and set out to destroy him. He characterized Grant's refusal to exchange prisoners freely as needlessly cruel, revived rumors about Grant's intoxication, and employed detectives in an effort to prove that Grant was "a drunkard, after fast horses, women and whores." Grant, he announced, was "a man without a head or a heart, indifferent to human suffering and impotent to govern."[8]

Even the rumblings about impeaching the president were connected to speculation about the Republican nomination. During 1867, several Radicals had gone beyond mere mutterings to entertain seriously the prospect of removing Johnson through impeachment as the best way to gain control of the reconstruction process. Sincere fears about rumors that Johnson might attempt a military coup and anger with his encouragement of Southern white intransigence at the expense of the freedmen took their place alongside ridiculous accusations, supported only by manufactured evidence corruptly obtained, that Johnson was somehow involved in Lincoln's assassination. Yet more was at stake than ejecting Johnson, for if the Radicals gained uncontested control of patronage and other government favors, they could do much to deny Grant the party's nomination in 1868. It was no accident that among the staunchest opponents of impeachment was Elihu B. Washburne. As one of Chase's associates later explained, "The impeachment programme had . . . two motives; the first and most important was, of course, to get Andrew Johnson out of the presidency, and the second and hardly less important was, to keep General Grant from getting in."[9]

To be sure, some Radicals endorsed Grant. Henry Wilson characterized Grant and the military district commanders as "radical, earnest Republicans, every one of them." He noted that Grant "has been more anxious during the last twelve months about the conditions of affairs than he ever was during the war." The veteran abolitionist newspaper editor Oliver Johnson informed William Lloyd Garrison that he had been "assured by Senator Wilson and others" that Grant "is in thorough sympathy with Congress in all that pertains to reconstruction and that he loathes and hates the whole Copperhead party."[10]

At the forefront of the Grant movement were moderate Republicans, most of whom would have concurred in the endorsement of the New York *Times*:

> The next Administration will find the business of Reconstruction accomplished, so far as laws and enactments can do it. What will be needed then will be the restoration,—or rather the inspiration,—of mutual faith and good feeling, of common sentiments, motives and principles of action between the different sections of the Union. The North will need a man in whose devotion to the principles that have been established by the war . . . they can have a firm and abiding faith. And the South will want a man in whose justice and magnanimity they can find security against relentless persecution, and the protracted infliction of ruinous punishment for past offenses.[11]

Moderate Republicans endorsed Grant's approach to Reconstruction as sound and sensible. They viewed Radical programs of land redistribution and social change in the South with skepticism, and they were aware that a majority of the Northern electorate was not enthused about making blacks equal participants in American society. Removing legal obstacles to black equality, especially in the South, was one thing; undertaking social revolution was another. Cherishing both the rule of law and the maintenance of social order, they looked to Grant as the embodiment of those principles.

Some moderates masked their support of the general under the guise of a "no-party" movement. Charles F. Adams, Jr., believed that Grant's support "is rising so rapidly and is so universal that I think he will probably be elected, North and South, by acclamation." The general, Adams thought, could "cause a general revolt in both the Republican and Democratic parties against the party leaders," thereby attracting William Pitt Fessenden, John A. Andrew, William M. Evarts, and other respectable moderates. Some Southern papers echoed these themes, finding Grant not only bipartisan but bisectional. The Richmond *Dispatch* declared that "upon him the whole nation, North and South, may unite with more harmony than any prominent man yet named, who stands the remotest chance of being elected."[12]

Most prominent among moderate supporters of a Grant candidacy was the general's old friend Washburne. The congressman had eagerly contemplated a Grant candidacy since 1865. Most people curious about the general's political plans tapped Washburne for information; he remained silent as to Grant's political ambitions but assured Republicans publicly and privately of Grant's support for congressional reconstruction and black suffrage, telling voters that Grant "believed there is no protection or safety to the colored people and the loyal white people in the rebel States except through impartial suffrage." [13]

Conservatives also embraced a possible Grant candidacy. Pennsylvania's Andrew Curtin, a longtime foe of Radicalism, supported the general. So did Thurlow Weed, the crafty New York politico who, despite his fading power and influence, still irritated Radicals. The New York *Herald* spoke approvingly of Grant's candidacy. To Radicals like Greeley, such supporters alone were enough to taint the Grant movement. "All that is fishy and mercenary in the Republican ranks," he scrawled to Zachariah Chandler, "combines with everything Copperhead to escort Grant as the man destined to curb Radicalism and restore conservatives to power." [14]

A movement among some Democratic leaders justified Radical fears. In the aftermath of setbacks in the 1866 election, several Democratic politicos, mostly from New York, toyed with the idea of running Grant on their ticket. Manton Marble, editor of the New York *World*, and August Belmont, chairman of the Democratic National Committee, had worked together to engineer George B. McClellan's nomination in 1864. Now, another general loomed as a possible choice for the Democracy. Some survivors of Johnson's National Union Movement—including Senators James R. Doolittle and Reverdy Johnson, as well as New York *Herald* editor James Gordon Bennett, who had been pushing Grant for years—also found the idea intriguing. Marble and Belmont were convinced that the inflationary financial theories of Democratic senator George H. Pendleton of Ohio were harmful to eastern financial interests. The Pendleton Plan, which called for the repayment of federal bonds in greenbacks, threatened to divide the party along inflationist/deflationist lines. Like their counterparts among the moderate Republicans, they perceived that a Grant candidacy would take the focus off economic issues. More importantly, it would purge the party of the taint of treason and copperheadism. The general's moderation on the suffrage issue complemented Marble's and Belmont's willingness to drop their opposition to black suffrage.[15]

Such Democrats hoped "that Grant may be saved to the cause of conservatism, and patriotism, and constitutional liberty." Montgomery Blair, once Lincoln's postmaster general and now a firm Johnson supporter, also saw Grant as the savior of the Democratic party. He planned to assist Grant much as his father, Francis P. Blair, Sr., had served Andrew Jackson. Frank Blair advised his brother not to pursue the general. "I perceive that you and my father concur in the opinion that Grant will ultimately come to us. This is not my idea. I think he has succeeded or will succeed in disgusting both parties." Frank Blair suspected something far more sinister—the creation of a military despotism. The commanding general's "ambition has been more deeply touched than by the mere hope of the Presidency." He need not have resorted to such fantastic explanations. Although Grant maintained friendships with some Democrats, such as Oregon senator James Nesmith, it was highly improbable that he would ever consent to head the ticket of a party that included Copperheads like John Hogan, who had infuriated him during the "Swing around the Circle," and Clement Vallandigham. Democrats such as these were traitors; only those Democrats who supported the war were tolerable. "It is an insult," he declared, "to ask any Northern man to support a candidate whose anxiety that the Flag should have thirty-six, and not twenty stars, did not come to him until after Lee's surrender."[16]

No one had engaged in more speculation about the general's possible candidacy than the current and former members of his staff. James H. Wilson, Horace Porter, Cyrus B. Comstock, Adam Badeau, William S. Hillyer, Orville E. Babcock, and John A. Rawlins all took an early interest in Grant's presidential prospects. Wilson, Porter, and, to a lesser extent, Comstock had been trying to detach Grant from Johnson for some time, but Hillyer portrayed Grant as an ally of the administration. Rawlins and Badeau, who had supported Johnson during the early days of his administration, had wavered during 1866 and by 1867 showed signs of falling into line behind Wilson and Porter. Only Babcock remained fairly quiet. "I am one of those who hope Genl Grant will not be President," he told Washburne. "I look upon it as a great misfortune to him." Grant was probably aware of these divisions and discussions but apparently took no part in them. Nor, to the disgruntlement of Rawlins and others, did he welcome their political advice.[17]

Grant also kept Washburne in the dark concerning his political ambitions. Judging from the congressman's incoming correspondence, many politicians and editors viewed him as Grant's chief political adviser and, in some sense, his patron. Yet, although Grant kept in close touch with Washburne, often revealing in private correspondence his personal responses to political events, he said nothing about his presidential prospects. Washburne was familiar with Grant's attitude toward Reconstruction but was not sure where the general stood when it came to the presidential question.[18]

Grant's greatest confidant when it came to his political future may have been William T. Sherman. To his old comrade, he revealed his distaste for the political maneuverings within the Johnson administration and Congress. Cabinet service had eroded whatever remained of his naive belief that government was conducted by disinterested public servants. "All the romance of feeling that men in high places are above personal considerations and act only from motives of pure patriotism, and for the general good of the public, has been destroyed," he told Sherman in September 1867. "An inside view proves, too truly, very much the reverse." Sherman shared Grant's distaste for politics. "I am determined not to be drawn into politics let what may follow," he told his wife in September 1867, "and to avoid such a result I would even resign and try something else again." He believed that his wartime comrade wanted nothing to do with the presidency: "I think that if Grant can avoid the nomination he will." To his brother in the Senate, he reported that Grant "never has said a word that looks like wanting the office of President." But it was to his father-in-law, Thomas Ewing, Sr., that Sherman gave the most detailed analysis of Grant's position:

He does not want to be President, told me that 50 millions of dollars would not compensate him therefor, but that events might force him [in] spite of inclination—just such events as would "compel him to throw himself into a breach." If the Republicans can find a good nominee he will be content. He is not an extremist at all, but his many good officers at the South force him to the conclusion that there is necessary there some strong power to protect the negroes & union men against legal oppression, or the acts of badly disposed Ex-Rebels. He is frank and friendly to all well disposed men South. He is very reticent, wisely so to strangers, but open and frank with me and others he knows well.

Sherman concluded that the matter might be out of Grant's hands. "I think all sides will try to have Grant as a candidate without pledge or party, to give them another four years in which to wire-work for ultimate political power. Grant would simply allow the laws to take their course and would only use force or the Army when violence was attempted." Other wartime comrades, notably Sheridan, viewed the prospect of Grant's presidency more eagerly, and Little Phil urged his commander "to again lend yourself to secure the Union and development of the country."[19]

Grant was uncomfortable under this intense—and immense—scrutiny. "He still disclaimed any partisan bias," recalled Badeau, "and was unwilling to be called either Republican or Democrat." He supported moderate congressional Republicans in their efforts to reconstruct the South, although such support was not a function of partisan affiliation but arose "because he believed that the acts of the President had made their course the only one practicable." Indeed, the commanding general "saw not a little in the conduct of Congress and individual members of the Republican party which he did not commend." Badeau noticed nothing "that betrayed any political aspiration or indicated the faintest ambition to succeed Johnson in the Presidency." Grant told another staff officer that he did not want to live in the White House, for it would "drag him into the storms and excitement of politics." When friends spoke about the possibility in his presence, "he put it away and was evidently annoyed"; comments by strangers about the subject angered him, and the inquirers received "very mortifying and unexpected rebuffs." He refused to discuss the topic with Rawlins and dismissed it in conversation with his wife.[20]

In denying any interest in the presidency, Grant was not playing coy. He despised the partisan maneuvering and crass opportunism characteristic of politics, possibly because they reminded him of his father's sharp business methods. Always sensitive to criticism, he knew that to let himself be drawn into a political contest was to put his reputation at risk. Nor could the presidency add to the glory and fame he had won on the battlefield; indeed, it might tarnish it. The accolades and cheers he received everywhere he went would be interrupted by boos, jeers, and bickering. Lincoln and Johnson had come in for more than their share of vicious attacks, and Grant did not want to share their fate. Politicians led "a most slavish life," he had said in 1864, and nothing had happened since then to change his mind. Moreover, having struggled to make ends meet since 1854, he was not about to abandon permanent economic security. Becoming president would mean giving up his commission for a temporary post that, even should he win reelection, would leave him fifty-four years old and unemployed on March 5, 1877. Put simply, the White House wasn't worth it. As Jesse Grant observed, for his son "to accept the Presidency would be to him a sacrifice of feeling and personal interest. He could not well stand the trial of being a candidate for public favor."[21]

But this did not mean that he would never accept the nomination under any circumstances. Grant had never trusted politicians. He believed that their short-sighted maneuvering for advantage had cost the country dearly and had contributed to the outbreak of the war. Now he worried that similar tactics could sacrifice the peace on the altar of political expediency and partisan extremism. Indeed, as one correspondent told the general, "The extreme lengths to which party politics are being carried into the United States is seriously endangering, and if not checked, will eventually overthrow our Republican System of Government." Politicians were obscuring the clear vision of the peace at Appomattox. Obstructionism by the administration had inspired and encouraged Southern intransigence. Republican factionalism might pave the way for a Democratic resurgence, a prospect Grant found intolerable. It seemed inconceivable that the party that had opposed the war in 1864 might actually regain the White House in 1868, but it was becoming more of a possibility every day.[22]

Nor were Grant's concerns merely those of a disinterested man who was above politics. He was aware that his own fame and reputation were intimately entwined with the war. He had led the Union to victory on the battlefield. Should the nation repudiate in peace what it had achieved in war, it would be repudiating Grant as well. He was

not about to let his reputation fall victim to the petty intrigues of politicians. His ambition was indeed sparked by talk of the presidency,
but it was an ambition to preserve the reputation and respect he had
gained, not to advance to higher office. Only slowly and reluctantly
did he come to accept the fact that to achieve the former he might
have to resign himself to the latter.

The general was caught in a paradox. Hating politics because of the
crass nature of partisan life, he had to consider that perhaps the only
way to restore a much-needed statesmanship to public affairs was to
take politics and the presidency out of the hands of such people. De-
ciding to run for president would open him to criticism, yet perhaps
it was the only way to preserve the basis of his reputation as the savior
of the Union. In such moments, he came to understand that he
shared much more with George Washington than the rank of lieutenant general, for the Revolutionary War hero had faced a similar situation in the 1780s. Grant's distaste for politics and the aversion to the
presidency remained, but it was essential for him to prove that the
thousands of brave Union dead had not died in vain, their achieve-
ment—and his—forfeited to the unseemly and short-sighted squabbling of selfish politicians out to secure partisan advantage at the expense of all else. Nor would he allow such people to place his
reputation in jeopardy. He was determined to make sure that he had
not served in vain.[23]

Grant chose not to share his political opinions with people outside
his circle of friends and trusted associates. Like Sherman, he was suspicious of the press and marveled at its ability to mislead and distort.
But his silence was not absolute. Washburne and Rawlins were assumed to be his authorized spokesmen; he granted interviews; and,
as in the release of his letter about Sheridan, he leaked his views to
the press with the best of them. As associates understood, his silence
was a calculated strategy, grounded in learning from the experiences
of garrulous generals like McClellan and John C. Frémont. To speak
out frequently would erode his image as a soldier superior to the
political fray. Silence would be not only golden but also safe, easy,
and wise.[24]

Grant's "reticence," as some papers termed it, soon took on comic
proportions. The curious and the clever alike entered the War Department determined to extract some opinion from him. The gen-

eral, recalled Badeau, "would simply look at them with no expression whatever on his face, and say not a single word." Unnerved, the visitors "stammered and blushed," mumbled and stumbled about, and finally took their leave. "Sometimes, as the door closed," Badeau added, "Grant would look up at me with a quizzical expression that showed he enjoyed their confusion." Yet there was method to Grant's remaining mum. One observer, responding to his colleague's complaint about Grant's closemouthed behavior during an interview, thought the general "as smart as a whip": Grant had "got our opinion, but I can't say we got his; yet I am sure he has one, if he don't tell it."[25]

But silence was not Grant's only strategy. "Sherman, what special hobby do you intend to adopt?," he asked his old friend one day. When Sherman inquired what he meant, Grant replied that he had chosen horses as his hobby, "so that when anyone tried to pump him he would turn the conversation to his 'horse.'" Soon Grant's references to horses became legendary. Gruff old Ben Wade once fumed, "As quick as I'd talk politics, he'd talk horses, and he could talk for hours on that without getting tired." The "reticence" question was a major topic of discussion in the press; some papers commended the general, others condemned him, and a few expressed the opinion that perhaps Grant simply had nothing to say. The curiosity increased as it became apparent that the best way for the Republican party to secure the White House in 1868 was to nominate the man some called "the American Sphinx."[26]

The elections of 1867 proved critical to the future of Republican reconstruction. Northern voters delivered a stunning rebuke to the Radical program at the polls, as Democrats regained power in several states and sharply reduced their margins of defeat to Republicans in others. Northerners apparently were not ready to grant the black man equal political rights in their own states, even if they supported such a policy for the South. Kansas rejected a black suffrage amendment. New York and Pennsylvania, two key states, went Democratic. The biggest blow came in Ohio, where voters defeated black suffrage and elected a Democratic state legislature, assuring the unseating of Wade. Only Rutherford B. Hayes's narrow victory in the gubernatorial race saved the Republicans from complete defeat in the Buckeye State.[27]

The voters' verdict discredited the Radical program by demonstrating that the weak link in the Republican coalition over reconstruction issues was black equality in the North as well as the South. The *Independent* attributed the result to a human "liability to weariness of any high or intense mood of the emotions or the will. . . . Indifferency and relaxation are wont to succeed the strain of extraordinary passion and purpose." The pragmatism of moderate Republicanism was back in fashion. Even Grant said that the result would "compel moderation on the part of the extremists." Moreover, most Republicans were convinced that they knew why the party had recently suffered setbacks at the polls. From Pennsylvania came the word that defeat was "owing simply and purely to the question affecting our sable brothers." In California a Republican observed, "Negro suffrage hurt us here very considerable. A great many of our party here are mean enough, to want it in the south & not in the North."[28]

Shocked at the Democratic resurgence, most Republicans realized that only one man could assure them victory in the upcoming presidential contest—Ulysses S. Grant. The Democratic gains left Grant "the man of the hour." "The more unanimous the public sentiment is in his favor," William E. Chandler told Grant's brother-in-law Frederick Dent, and "the more evident it becomes that he cannot refuse to be a candidate[,] the better and safer for the country." Republican adviser John Binney told House Speaker Schuyler Colfax that the party "cannot do better than have General Grant as our next President *as the surest mode* of retaining the Government of the nation in loyal hands." As Samuel Bowles, editor of the Springfield *Republican*, observed, people looked to Grant because he "has led them to final victory over the rebellion; they look to him to lead them in the equally essential work of allaying animosities and restoring unity and fraternity among the people, reestablishing the reign of civil law, and bringing order and peace out of the present confusion."[29]

Without Grant at the head of the Republican ticket, the future of Reconstruction, and perhaps the nation, could be in jeopardy in 1868. The general's nomination was a necessity. "Grant is the only man living who can carry this state next year on present issues," proclaimed

Pennsylvania's Andrew Curtin. "It is neither wise nor *prudent* to nominate any one but Grant," Henry B. Stanton added. And Grant owed it to the country to accept the nomination. "He must not, by refusing to run, endanger the loss of all that the Nation struggled & sacrificed to gain," declared one of Washburne's correspondents. As one Republican concluded, "We can only win with Grant." Now, as Washburne put it, it was time to push Grant, "not only as the most available but the best man for President."[30]

"The real victims of the victory of the Democrats are Mr. Wade and Mr. Chase," concluded Georges Clemenceau in his column for the Paris *Temps*. As the New York patrician George Templeton Strong put it, "The recent elections have killed off a score of aspirants for the next presidency—Chase among them—and . . . Grant is now sure to be nominated." It was clear why this was so. "The elections show, beyond all controversy, a revulsion in public sentiment against the measures and policy with which Judge Chase is most clearly defined," editorialized the New York *Times*. "Mr. Chase is too radical to be an acceptable candidate," observed Clemenceau, "and the Republican Party will have to fall back on Grant." John Sherman, who had expressed a preference for Chase, conceded defeat. "Grant, I think, is inevitably a candidate. He allows himself to drift into a position where he can't decline if he would, and I feel sure he don't want to decline."[31]

James G. Blaine breathed a sigh of relief. He had feared that Radicals—armed with schemes to revolutionize not only the South but also, through inflation, the currency system—would ride to victory in 1868 in the aftermath of a smashing triumph in the fall elections. "Now Grant looms up as the savior alike of country and party—a necessity to both." Party discipline was also on the mind of a New Hampshire Republican. "Of course I always dislike to see the party beaten, but in this case the defeat will assure the nomination of Grant," he told Washburne. "The fact is the party did need a little wholesome discipline!" Carl Schurz concluded that Grant's nomination was "rendered practically certain" by the election results.[32]

As Republicans rushed to embrace the "Savior of the Union" as the savior of their party, Montgomery Blair and his Democratic associates abandoned plans for a Grant candidacy. In November Blair made one last direct plea to Grant to run on the Democratic ticket, but the general chose not to reply. The result pleased Frank Blair, who noted that at last all the Blairs agreed that "Grant will not answer our purpose. . . . Grant has long since given up all idea of acting with us." The former postmaster general was disappointed, for he had hoped that a Grant candidacy would "prevent the war of races" that would follow a Democratic victory in 1868. The general was "the most dangerous opponent they can put up against us," but his moderation would foil the Radicals' "scheme of usurpation." Still, as Democratic leader S. S. Cox complained, "If we can't get Grant (as I suppose he is gone to the D——l or the Rads) what is to be done?"[33]

Some conservatives suggested that if Grant would not join them it was time to beat him over the head with the accusation that he favored black suffrage. Doolittle recalled how in 1865 Grant had warned against the immediate adoption of black suffrage to avoid racial conflict. Now he believed, based upon Washburne's statements, that "Grant would accept the Republican nomination on the platform of negro suffrage." With this information in hand, Doolittle urged Marble to expose Grant's earlier stand in the New York *World*, the leading Democratic journal. Marble decided to hold back, however, replying that Grant, "unpracticed in civil affairs," might yet be saved to the Democratic cause. Even if Grant was now for black suffrage, Marble saw no reason to counter Radical reservations about his candidacy "by persuading them that he *is* in sympathy with them." Bowing to Marble's decision, Doolittle nevertheless grumbled that "Grant is committed body and soul to the Radicals."[34]

Several Radicals remained unreconciled to a Grant candidacy. One Southern black, still committed to Chase, denounced a Grant nomination as "a disgraceful back-down—a cowardly retrogradation." Phillips continued his attacks. Sumner predicted that the party would go into decline should it choose Grant as its standard-bearer. The Massachusetts senator found himself in a minority, however, when he made his sentiments known at a Republican leadership meeting just after the election.[35]

Democratic and die-hard Radical papers took turns questioning Grant's commitment to Radicalism in an effort to deny him the Republican nomination. In November 1867, Congress issued Grant's testimony at the impeachment inquiry before the House Judiciary Committee in the summer of 1867. In that testimony, Grant had tried to

steer a middle course between extremist camps, although several portions were damaging to Johnson. But this was of no account to the
press. After reviewing the testimony, the New York *World* followed
Marble's strategy of exacerbating the differences between the general
and the Radicals and concluded that, if Grant was now a Radical, "he
has undergone a surprising transformation." Other Democratic papers followed suit, tweaking Radical noses and hoping to inject discord into Republican ranks. They calculated wisely, for those Radical
journals still searching for an alternative to Grant also seized upon
the testimony to attack him. Greeley's *Tribune* published a transcript
in order to discredit his Radical credentials, and the *National Anti-
Slavery Standard* concluded from a review of the testimony "that upon
the question of the negro's rights Gen. Grant is in no sense a radical."
It was a strange minuet indeed, with Radical papers engaged in a last-
gasp effort to denounce Grant and a chorus of Democratic journals
chiming in, knowing that if they did not have to face Grant they had
a good chance of victory in 1868.[36]

Grant rejected any effort to cubbyhole him. Whether or not he was
a Radical depended on how one defined the term. His advocacy of
black suffrage in the South had been slow in coming but was now
firm. In January 1867, he had characterized the hesitancy of Republicans to enfranchise Northern blacks as hypocrisy. Most Democrats
characterized such measures as Radical; Radicals deemed them necessary but not sufficient for membership in their group, for many
moderates shared Grant's position. Grant also supported congressional reconstruction, a position that seemed to most Democrats
ample proof of Radicalism, although many Radicals did not believe
that current policy went far enough. Grant broke ranks with most
Radicals over impeachment and the extent to which Southern social
change should be mandated through federal legislation. Despite his
differences with Johnson, he did not favor impeachment and believed
that such a step would only make things worse. Nor had he spoken
out in favor of land confiscation and redistribution, two favorite Radical proposals. The general was too radical for most Democrats but not
radical enough for most Radicals. The controversy simply obscured
his position, and Grant deemed it unnecessary to clarify where he
stood.

The New York *Times*, perhaps the leading moderate Republican journal, sounded the themes of the Grant movement in the aftermath of the 1867 elections. "The recent elections mean *you*, and not much else," editor Henry J. Raymond informed Grant, advising the general to remain silent on political issues. Raymond's paper would do the talking for him. It portrayed Grant as a moderate, selfless soldier, whose primary concern was to restore peace to a troubled country. Above the narrow-mindedness and selfishness of partisanship, he was a man whose election would ensure "harmony and prosperity" at a time "when men are glad to seek again the peace and rest to which they have been strangers so long."[37]

Additional editorials developed these themes. Grant's election "will put an end to the war of parties and of factions, by which peace has been repelled and the restoration of the Union discouraged and delayed." After all, true peace "implies not only a cessation of hostilities between belligerents, but the renewal of a partnership." Obviously, Grant's career fitted him for this task. "He can reconcile conflicting feelings, soothe exasperated resentments, mediate between contending parties, and thus open the way to a reconciliation full of the spirit of peace and involving all its highest and best results, better than any man in the nation." The *Times* concluded, "What the country needs now more than anything else is pacification."[38]

One of the first signs of this antiparty theme, which could appeal to conservatives as well as moderates, was a meeting at Cooper Union on December 4, 1867, to nominate Grant for president. The attendees, "sickened with politics and politicians, and anxious alone for the prosperity of the country, and the perpetuity of the Union," had "taken into their own hands the business" of nominating Grant. That those who gathered that night linked pacification with prosperity was obvious from a glance at the list of the meeting's committee, consisting of moderate and conservative Republicans and businessmen. A closer look revealed that many of those in attendance had once supported the Johnson administration. For all the talk of nonpartisanship, advocates of this movement were really conservative Republicans who had always employed antiparty rhetoric, as one incident revealed. Following the Cooper Union meeting, several papers printed a letter purportedly from Grant's brother-in-law, saying that Grant wished to be elected without reference to party. The letter was quickly revealed as a forgery, and the *Times* hastened to assure its readers that Grant was in fact a Republican.[39]

Whether this would be good enough for the Radicals was another matter. "Is Grant a Radical—has he any opinions worth the name?," asked one Pennsylvania Radical. The *Independent* thought so, reporting that Grant supported black suffrage. Others disagreed. "Refuse to endorse Grant until Grant has endorsed Radicalism," announced the Philadelphia *Morning Post*. "Meet his silence with silence more profound." Montgomery Blair, noting that "the pressure on old Grant is tremendous for a showing of his hand," attempted "to stir old Ulysses if possible" on the question of black suffrage. Despite several indications of his support for enfranchising blacks in the North as well as in the South, Grant had made no public statement on the issue, and until he did he was still suspect in the eyes of many Radicals. "Has Grant yet, by word or deed, spoken of where he stands, on what side, or for whom?," asked Phillips. Moderates still believed that silence was the best course. "General Grant is wise in keeping reticent in present circumstances," argued Binney. "Should he give any disclosure of his views prematurely, his political enemies would endeavor to destroy him as a Presidential candidate." Welles, concurring, grumbled, "His reticence is all a matter of calculation; he fears to commit himself lest he should lose votes."[40]

Jesse Root Grant surveyed the political landscape with an eye to his son's future. To a friend, he astutely observed that some Radicals "seem determined to kill him by forcing him to come out and avow himself a Radical. The truth is he is a little too Radical & has given sufficient proof of that. If the Republican candidate comes out & avows himself for negro suffrage he fails." Clemenceau summed up the situation best for his French readers: "The question is whether General Grant will consent to stand on [a black suffrage] platform and to accept such a program. No answer to this is possible because Grant carefully avoids on all occasions expressing his opinion on any subject whatsoever. . . . Up to now, Grant's unfailing silence has only alienated the extreme radicals from him. . . . The mass of the party, however, has remained loyal to him, but on condition that he open his mouth when the right moment comes."[41]

10

"IN SPITE OF MYSELF"

As 1867 ended, it appeared obvious to all but the most die-hard Radicals that Ulysses S. Grant would be the Republican nominee for president in 1868. But that question would not be answered definitively until May; meanwhile, there was still the matter of the fate of Edwin M. Stanton before Congress as it reconvened in December 1867. Andrew Johnson, following the procedures set forth in the Tenure of Office Act, sent his explanation for Stanton's suspension to the Senate. Congressional Republicans were slow to respond, and reports circulated that Stanton, once he was vindicated through reinstatement, would resign. Johnson plotted his next move. To his private secretary, he confided that "Grant had served the purpose for which he had been selected, and it was desirable that he should be superceded in the War office by another." This was just what Republicans feared: the only way to thwart the president was to reinstate Stanton and then keep him in office.[1]

On January 11, 1868, Grant and William T. Sherman sat down to discuss the situation. Grant wanted nothing more to do with the War Department, and he was alarmed to discover upon rereading the Tenure of Office Act that he was subject to a fine and imprisonment if he

held to his October 1867 promise to help Johnson keep Stanton out
of office—although the chances of this happening were virtually nil.
Moreover, the act's wording rendered Johnson's intentions irrelevant,
for should the Senate fail to concur in the suspension "such officer so
suspended shall forthwith resume the functions of his office," leaving
no discretion to be exercised by Grant. Sherman asked Grant if he
had told Johnson of his change of heart; Grant agreed that he had to
meet the president. Anxious to avoid another fiasco that might draw
him into the whirlpool of Washington politics, Sherman hurried to
the White House ahead of Grant to try to reason with the president.
Just as he was about to broach the subject, Grant walked in, ready to
deal with Johnson one more time. Sherman left, possibly aware that
he was meddling a little too much and thankful that Grant seemed to
have matters in hand.[2]

This proved wishful thinking. Perhaps it would have been better had
Sherman stayed; Grant and Johnson always would disagree about what
they had discussed, and the disagreement proved crucial to the course
of later events. Grant informed Johnson that he had changed his mind
about holding on to the office and that in any case the wording of the
act left him with no other option. When Grant pointed out that he
would be subject to prosecution if he resisted the Senate's attempt to reinstate Stanton, Johnson blithely ignored the legal realities and grandly
proclaimed that he would pay the fine and serve the jail term![3]

Then Johnson engaged in a bit of double-talk. Until now, he had
followed the procedures set forth in the Tenure of Office Act, and he
spoke of setting up a judicial test of the act's constitutionality. That
reasoning had induced him to get Grant to agree to hold on to the
position in the first place. Now he told Grant that he had not suspended Stanton under the terms of the Tenure of Office Act but had
simply followed normal procedures outlined in a 1795 statute on ad
interim appointments. Grant dismissed this argument, replying that
the Tenure of Office Act was binding until it was declared unconstitutional. He wanted out of the War Department and suggested that
the president had better plan on finding a replacement, thus fulfilling
his promise to notify Johnson of his change of heart prior to the Senate's action. He added that "on no account could he consent to hold
the office after the Senate should act." By this point, the two men were
talking past each other. Johnson apparently heard only what he

wanted to hear; he later maintained that Grant had reaffirmed his previous promise to hold on to the office or to vacate it prior to the Senate's decision. They parted, each thinking that the other wanted to continue the discussion on Monday, January 13, the day that the Senate would act on Stanton's suspension.[4]

Both men were at fault for what ensued. Grant failed to resign outright; had he quit the job at once instead of trying to help Johnson out, he would have avoided the controversy that followed. Johnson should have seen that Grant, wishing to avoid the coming conflict, was giving him due notice. At the very least, the president should have discerned that the general could not be relied upon to uphold any action that he might take. Had he wanted to avoid trouble, he should have taken Grant's advice and replaced him. Moreover, although the evidence suggests that both men agreed to talk again on Monday, Grant thought that he had conveyed his decision to quit the office, and Johnson apparently considered this still an open question. The intensity with which both men defended their recollections suggests that a serious mutual misunderstanding had taken place. Johnson failed to understand Grant's decision and Grant failed to make sure that Johnson comprehended his position.[5]

On Sunday, January 12, Grant and Sherman conferred once more and agreed that Johnson should be urged to appoint as Grant's replacement Jacob D. Cox, a moderate Republican. Cox stood a good chance of confirmation, ridding Johnson of Stanton while keeping Grant out of trouble. Sherman's father-in-law Thomas Ewing, Sr., lent a hand, telling Johnson that chances for Cox's confirmation were excellent and that the proposal "will avoid unpleasant complications, of which we have had as many as the country can well endure." The generals spent the rest of the day sounding out other politicians, and Maryland senator Reverdy Johnson went to the White House to persuade the president to accept the proposal.[6]

Why did Andrew Johnson fail to embrace this idea? Previously, he had privately expressed his belief that Grant was unreliable; the general's behavior on Saturday should have reinforced that impression, regardless of Johnson's understanding of what had been resolved. With Cox's nomination almost certain to be ratified, Johnson could still keep Stanton out of the War Department. His failure to accede to this proposal might be attributed to sheer stubbornness, but it is more likely that more than merely Stanton's status or the possession of the War Department was at stake. Johnson probably wanted to force a confrontation with the Senate and in the process smoke Grant out. It was time to pin the general down in public and make him choose sides. If Grant would not cooperate with the president, then Johnson would mount a campaign of his own, designed to discredit the general and stifle his chances for the presidency. This was a shrewd move. With Grant out of the running, Republicans would have a hard time finding a candidate who could unite the party and stand a good chance for victory. In turn, such chaos might enhance Johnson's own chances for the Democratic nomination.

On Monday, January 13, Sherman visited the White House to second the Cox proposal. Much to his surprise, the president made no mention of the idea, nor did he say that he expected Grant to call. Sherman left, suspecting that "there must be something behind the scenes." Grant, in the telegraph office responding to events in Alabama and Texas, did not meet the president. That night, Johnson hosted a reception at the White House. At the Grant house, some of Julia's friends expressed a desire to visit the Executive Mansion, and Julia asked her husband to accompany them to the levee. Grant knew that the Senate was at that hour debating whether to reinstate Stanton but reluctantly assented. As the party was leaving the house, a messenger from the Capitol arrived. Grant read the note: although he did not reveal its contents, it probably reported that the Senate had reinstated Stanton by a vote of thirty-six to six. According to Grant's interpretation of the Tenure of Office Act, his tenure had terminated with the vote. This made a visit to the White House even more embarrassing. Only the earnest entreaties of the ladies overcame his disinclination to appear in public with the president at this crucial juncture. At the reception, however, Johnson grasped the general's hand cordially. He did not inquire about Grant's failure to resume their discussion that day. Neither man spoke of what had happened on the Senate floor.[7]

The next day, Grant appeared at the War Department at 9:00 A.M. Locking the secretary's office, he handed Asst. Adj. Gen. Edward D. Townsend the keys and said that he could be found at army headquarters. Grant next notified Johnson that the Senate's reinstatement of Stanton terminated his tenure as secretary ad interim. However, he reasoned that Stanton would contact him before assuming his post, permitting the general to gather his papers and close out business—just as Grant had done the previous August. That would give Johnson enough time to name a successor, allowing Grant to comply with the law while assisting Johnson in his desire to replace Stanton.[8]

Unfortunately for Grant, Stanton was in no mood for such courtesies. Upon receiving notice of the Senate's action, he made preparations for a swift return to the War Department. No sooner had Townsend received the key from Grant than the returning secretary seized it. Had Grant known that this was to happen, he probably would not have surrendered the keys. Instead, he was surprised to receive a brusque summons "in the 'old style,'" from Stanton. Upset by this unanticipated turn of events, Grant made his way to the War Department.[9]

Gen. Cyrus B. Comstock had delivered Grant's letter to Johnson and returned from the White House to inform Grant that Johnson expected him to attend that afternoon's cabinet meeting. Not until Comstock had departed did Johnson explode at what he termed "Grant's duplicity." Several hours later, Grant arrived at the cabinet meeting, doubtless expecting that the main topic of discussion would be what to do about Stanton. Johnson opened the meeting in the usual manner, asking each department head to make a report. When it came time for the War Department report, all eyes turned to Grant, who stated that he had come as Johnson's invited guest, not as a department head. This was the moment Johnson had been waiting for. Orville H. Browning noted that the president was "evidently excited and indignant, but maintained perfect self control." In a series of interrogatories, he reviewed his discussions with Grant and insisted that the general, notwithstanding what had occurred on Saturday, had failed to keep his promise to hold on to the office or to return it to Johnson before the Senate acted. Only now, in the aftermath of Stanton's reinstatement and return, was Grant's failure to visit the White House on Monday noted by Johnson, who characterized the general's nonappearance as a major breach of faith.[10]

Grant reeled in the face of this skillful, lawyerly interrogation. Johnson's questions were carefully worded and calculated to force the unwitting and unprepared general to make damaging admissions. Grant admitted that he had once promised Johnson that he would hold on to the office and allow a court test, and he admitted that he had expected to visit the White House on Monday. In explaining his failure to do so, he claimed that Sherman's visit was designed to settle the dispute; furthermore, the Senate's speedy action had caught him by surprise—a feeble excuse, for it had been known for some time that the vote could take place momentarily. He conceded that Johnson might have persisted in believing that Grant would either resign the War Department or resist Stanton's reinstatement, despite the Saturday conversation. Johnson's questions were framed so deftly that Grant was unable to present his side of the story, and they seriously distorted the facts; after the Saturday meeting between the general and the president, it was clear that Grant would not assist Johnson in his effort to defy Congress. But they were very effective. Unprepared for Johnson's tactics, already nettled by Stanton's behavior, and aware that he was being embarrassed in front of a hostile audience, Grant excused himself and, as Gideon Welles put it, "slunk away to the door in a manner most humiliating and pitiable."[11]

Grant returned to headquarters furious at both Johnson and Stanton. To Sherman he complained that Stanton's action in reoccupying the office had "compromised" him, and he "did not like it at all." The two generals made plans to visit the White House the next day to try to straighten things out. Sherman, upset at what had happened to his old comrade, told Browning that Johnson was to blame for the whole affair because he had failed to send Cox's name into the Senate.[12]

Grant was troubled by what had happened at the cabinet meeting. Even more disturbing, and somewhat suspicious, was the account of the meeting that appeared in the *National Intelligencer* the following day. Grant sensed that the details of the meeting had been leaked to the reporter. With Sherman, he went to the White House, where Johnson pleaded ignorance about the newspaper report and claimed disingenuously that he had not yet read the paper. "Well," Grant responded, "the idea is given there that I have not kept faith with you." Once more, he explained that he had hoped to give Johnson enough time to make another nomination to the War Department, but that Stanton's unanticipated hasty return had upset everything. Sherman noted that "the President expressed himself gratified and pleased" with this information. Furthermore, Grant pointed out "that Mr. Stanton's being in the office did not make him Secretary of War any more than if he were to make his office in his own Library Room at his own private house." But Johnson would conveniently overlook this point both then and later. At the conclusion of the conversation, Grant suggested that the president issue an order "that we of the Army are not bound to obey the orders of Mr. Stanton as Secretary of War," and Johnson assented.[13]

This conference should have cleared the air between the general and the president, but it did not; as subsequent events revealed, Johnson had no intention of reaching a peaceful accord. Grant was furious with Stanton and willing to work with Johnson, but the president deliberately threw this opportunity away because he did not want to reach an understanding with Grant. William S. Hillyer, a former Grant aide and Johnson adherent, informed the president that "General Grant never had any conversation or collusion with Stanton in regard to his restoration of the war office." But Johnson stubbornly persisted in accusing Grant of betrayal, although he never offered evidence of collusion between the general and Stanton. The breach could not be mended because Johnson wished to widen it. No sooner had Grant and Sherman left than Johnson read to his personal secretary the newspaper article in question and approved its contents. Later, to Welles, he commented that Grant's conversation "only reaffirmed the fact that he had not been true to his understanding." He remained silent about Grant's explanation lest he weaken his case.[14]

Over the next several days, both Grant and Sherman contemplated how to get Stanton to resign, but, despite several opportunities, neither man broached the matter directly to Stanton. Sherman wanted simply "to get out of this political maelstrom. . . . I am made the depository of the secrets and plans of all, and unless I get away I may be embroiled between the factions." Nor was Johnson willing to resolve things, preferring to watch Stanton and Grant fight it out. In the meantime, rumors about a falling-out between Grant and Johnson circulated through the press—including one wild story that Johnson had smashed a chair over Grant's head.[15]

On January 19, Grant visited Stanton again, intending to advise the secretary to resign. Stanton put off the inquiry by talking of various topics in a "loud and violent" manner, and after some thirty minutes Grant left convinced that Stanton would not heed any suggestion of resignation. Returning to the White House, Grant repeated that he would obey Stanton's orders only when he knew they emanated from the president. He then left for a meeting at Richmond. There, he told John M. Schofield of his disgust with Stanton and spoke of resigning if Stanton did not leave.[16]

Upon his return to Washington, Grant requested that Johnson issue his directive regarding Stanton's orders in written form. Rather than comply, Johnson offered the War Department to Sherman: Sherman, determined to avoid trouble, declined. Thomas Ewing, Sr., and Sherman both advised Johnson to direct military commanders to ignore Stanton's orders. Sherman wondered why, if Stanton's claim to office was illegitimate, cabinet members were still addressing Stanton as secretary of war. On January 28, Grant renewed his request for written instructions, notifying Johnson that he would suspend action on his verbal ones. He knew that his and Johnson's recollections had differed before, and he would not be held accountable for another divergence.[17]

Once more, fine lines were drawn. Johnson distinguished between an order "authorized by the President" and one issued explicitly "by the direction of the President"; judging from the actions of other cabinet members in communicating with Stanton in his official capacity, Johnson was concerned only with orders falling under the latter category. Grant's request had to do with all orders issued by Stanton, and he felt that the president had drawn a distinction without a difference. Since Johnson had failed to issue an order to Stanton "limiting or impairing his authority to issue orders to the Army," Grant had to assume that those orders were "authorized by the Executive." Otherwise, upon what grounds could Grant make the distinction that Johnson asserted? To Johnson, Grant's response was insubordinate; to Grant, Johnson was once more trying to entrap him in a violation of the law: not only had he failed explicitly to strip Stanton of his authority, but also he had allowed other cabinet members to conduct transactions with him as secretary of war, thus recognizing his authority. This squabble, rooted in mutual distrust and suspicion, showed how ridiculous and alarming the whole affair had become. Neither man was making any attempt to understand the other. "I do not know between the parties, where the truth lies," Thomas Ewing, Sr., commented, adding that for "open truth and frankness not with either."

The basic framework of civil-military relations at the highest level of government was about to collapse.[18]

Meanwhile, Grant assembled evidence supporting his account of his conversations with Johnson. On January 28, he presented his case, reciting his previous arguments in a letter to the president that also touched on the orders controversy. After consultation with cabinet members, Johnson replied, reaffirming the correctness of his own account. Grant could not let this go unchallenged and began to compose another response. Sherman provided a set of notes and a reminder that a letter of resignation was superfluous, "as the law itself terminated the tenure of the Secretary of War *ad interim*." In a last effort to patch things up, Sherman visited Johnson once more to plead Grant's case, reiterating Grant's surprise at Stanton's actions. The president ignored the explanation; exasperated by politics, Sherman escaped to St. Louis.[19]

Grant worked on his letter for several days, spurred in part by a series of newspaper leaks inspired by the White House, which promised to make a bad situation worse. By February 3, he had composed a draft that once more sought to explain his actions, accepted the possibility that Johnson may have misunderstood what was going on, and requested that in the future the president complain directly to him rather than through the press. Once finished, he handed it to John A. Rawlins. The chief of staff had watched the events of the past weeks patiently, letting Sherman serve as Grant's chief confidant. But, now, Sherman was gone and all attempts at reconciliation had failed. The time had come to make a clean break. "This will not do; it is not enough," Rawlins declared. After all, he reminded Grant, Johnson had challenged his honor and reputation. Instead of trying to explain what had happened to someone who would not listen, why not take up the challenge? The moment for breaking with the president had arrived. Grant agreed and with Rawlins drafted a response directly confronting the president on the issue of the commanding general's veracity.[20]

The result was a letter that left no doubt in anybody's mind that Grant was at odds with the president. In it, Grant charged that Johnson had tried to involve him in "a resistance to law," denied outright that in the January 11 meeting he had made any promise to hold on to the War Department in the face of the Senate's action, and stated that he had originally accepted the position to keep the department out of hostile hands and not to assist Johnson in his maneuvers against Stanton and Congress. "And now, Mr. President," Grant wrote in closing, "when my honor as a soldier and as a man have been so violently assailed, pardon me for saying that I can regard this whole matter, from the beginning to the end, as an attempt to involve me in the resistance of law, for which you hesitated to assume the responsibility in orders, and thus to destroy my character before the country."[21]

This exchange was not private for long. On February 4, Stanton responded to Congress's call for all correspondence between Johnson, Stanton, and Grant on the incidents of the last month. Included was Grant's February 3 letter, indicating that the general had been providing him with copies of his exchanges with the president. Johnson had done what no one else had been able to do—he made Ulysses S. Grant a hero to Radical Republicans. "Gen. Grant has driven his pen through the President like a spear," reported the *Independent*. "Won't it do now to let Grant into our church?," someone asked Thaddeus Stevens. "Yes," replied Stevens; "open the doors and let him in. He is a bolder man than I thought him to be!" As Adam Badeau later stated, the letter "made the rupture with Johnson personal, and reconciliation impossible. It was a stroke of political genius, for it also made any candidate other than Grant impossible for the Republicans."[22]

Throughout the country, Republicans celebrated. One told Elihu B. Washburne that the exchange "has imparted a ground *swell* to the tide of his popularity." "That letter to Andy is a knock down argument," enthused another. Even the abolitionist *National Anti-Slavery Standard* praised the general: "The correspondence is altogether creditable to the great soldier. It will relieve the anxieties of the American people as to his real status." Last-gasp efforts by some extreme Radicals to discredit Grant by spreading new stories of his intoxication proved ineffective. "Gen. Grant's heavy guns . . . have almost completely silenced the small artillery of his traducers," reported the New York *Times*, still in the forefront of the Grant-for-president movement.[23]

Johnson heatedly responded, charging Grant with bad faith for his failure to call on Monday, January 13, and asking why Grant had failed to submit his resignation—matters to which Grant had already offered explanations. But no matter. The president concluded, in the face of abundant evidence to the contrary, that Grant had been "in collusion, if not in conspiracy, with the Secretary of War and his confederates" for months. As before, Johnson was more interested in winning debating points than in resolving a dispute. He offered the statements of the other cabinet members in support of his recollection of the cabinet meeting of January 14. Welles, Hugh McCulloch, and Alexander Randall simply signified concurrence; the longer letters of Browning and especially William H. Seward showed that, although they agreed in the main with Johnson's account, they could not corroborate all its details. These letters may have been effective politically, but they were less valuable as evidence: Johnson had provided his cabinet with his account of what had happened to help jog their memories. Furthermore, none of the cabinet had attended the critical January 11 meeting, which left that dispute unresolved. The package's impact on public opinion was minimal; congressmen laughed out loud as the clerk read the short missives of Welles, Randall, and McCulloch. "Up to now, the only result of this affair has been to define more clearly the political situation of Grant, and to draw him closer and closer to the radicals, who are now proclaiming him on every side to be their candidate," observed the French newspaper correspondent Georges Clemenceau. One happy Republican celebrated the exchange: "The straight forward, candid statements of the General outweigh with the people, the labored pettifogging of the President, backed by the diplomatic dodging of the Secretaries."[24]

Having lost Grant, Johnson turned once more to Sherman, despite Welles's warning that Sherman would not cross Grant. After withdrawing one set of orders directing Sherman to take command of a new Military Division of the Atlantic with headquarters at Washington, the president decided to go ahead with the plan on February 12, sweetening it with the offer of a promotion to brevet general. Upon receiving the proposal, Sherman immediately telegraphed his brother to oppose the promotion and threatened to resign if his desires were ignored. He made it clear to Johnson that under no circumstances would he allow himself to be brought into conflict with Grant. Foiled, Johnson decided to let Sherman remain at his post, much to Sherman's relief. George H. Thomas also declined the position.[25]

Had Johnson stopped here, he would have saved himself much

trouble. Efforts to revive impeachment had failed, leaving the president to figure out a way to circumvent Stanton. But this was not the end of the crisis. On February 21, Johnson defied the Tenure of Office Act and appointed aging Adj. Gen. Lorenzo Thomas as secretary of war ad interim. Stanton, with Grant's support, refused to abandon his office. Congressional Republicans exploded at yet another sign of the president's intractability. On February 24, the House of Representatives impeached Andrew Johnson.[26]

One might have thought that the momentous events that took place in Washington during January and February occupied all of Grant's time, but events in the South also demanded his attention. At the end of 1867, Johnson directed Grant to replace John Pope with George G. Meade as head of the Third Military District, comprising Alabama, Florida, and Georgia. At the same time, Edward O. C. Ord's request for transfer was granted; Alvan C. Gillem, a Johnson supporter, was placed in charge of the Fourth Military District. By now, some Republicans in Congress were aware that Johnson could use his power to reassign commanders to thwart the intent of their Southern legislation and decided to take the administration of the Reconstruction Acts completely away from Johnson and give it to Grant. Thus they rendered the then-sputtering impeachment movement unnecessary. On January 13, the day the Senate reinstated Stanton, Ohio representative John Bingham reported from the Committee on Reconstruction a bill doing just that: it stripped Johnson of the power to appoint or remove the district commanders and vested it solely in Grant. The bill passed the House on January 21 and moved on to the Senate. Grant would have welcomed such a bill the previous July but now opposed this measure as too extreme. Perhaps he concluded that it lent a measure of validity to charges that he was working toward a military dictatorship. The Senate never acted on it.[27]

Of more concern to Grant was the suit of William McCardle, a Mississippi newspaper editor who had been arrested by Ord on the grounds that his editorials against the election for delegates to the state's constitutional convention were obstructing the reconstruction process. McCardle's counsel challenged Ord's authority (and ultimately the legitimacy of congressional reconstruction) and sought a writ of habeas corpus in U.S. Circuit Court. This effort failed, but, under legislation passed by Congress on February 5, 1867, McCardle could now appeal the Circuit Court's decision to the Supreme Court —thus allowing the Court to rule once more on the constitutionality of the Reconstruction Acts.

Grant, who was still secretary of war ad interim when McCardle's appeal was filed, appointed Lyman Trumbull to represent the government in place of Attorney General Henry Stanbery. Trumbull did what he could to get the Court to dismiss the case for want of jurisdiction but failed. McCardle's attorneys, Jeremiah S. Black, William L. Sharkey, and David Dudley Field, pressed the *Milligan* precedent on the Court. Various delays, including Chief Justice Salmon P. Chase's attendance at Johnson's impeachment trial as presiding officer, drew out arguments until March 9, when the Court took the case under advisement. Three days later, in a rather sharp piece of legislative tactics, Congress repealed the relevant section of the 1867 legislation, which allowed the Court to hear McCardle's appeal. Johnson, already embroiled in a fight for his political life, vetoed the bill on March 25; the veto was overridden two days later. This raised the question of whether the Court still had jurisdiction in light of Congress's action. On April 6, the Court continued the case to the December term —thus ending, at least for the time being, the threat that the Reconstruction Acts would be overturned by judicial decision.[28]

But Washington was not the only stage on which the drama of Reconstruction was being played out. During the winter and spring of 1868, conventions met in the ex-Confederate states to draft constitutions as directed by the Reconstruction Acts. Northern Republicans watched these deliberations carefully. In the aftermath of the setbacks suffered by the party in the 1867 elections, many of them were concerned that the Southern constitutions, should they reflect Radical principles, would damage the Republicans' electoral chances for victory in 1868. To some extent, this was a problem of their own making; Republicans had shown a desire to reinstate the former Confederate states by the time of the presidential contest, and Grant himself was determined to expedite the process of readmission. In several states, Grant and his subordinates had to take action to resolve problems in the process; in others, their actions shaped the course of events.

When Meade replaced Pope in command of the Third Military District, people supposed that Meade's conservative nature ensured tranquility in Georgia, Alabama, and Florida. Instead, his actions in all three states sparked controversy, despite his pledge "to execute the law . . . fairly and impartially." The first problem concerned Georgia's constitutional convention. According to the Reconstruction Acts, each state could levy taxes to pay the operating expenses of the convention, but, as such taxes had not been collected, Meade had to look elsewhere for such funds. Both state treasurer John Jones and Governor Charles Jenkins refused to use funds from the state treasury as an advance to pay the expenses. Grant approved Meade's decision to remove Jones, and Meade removed Jenkins as well. Unfortunately for Meade, the governor escaped from the state with the official records and the treasury funds and then filed a bill of complaint in the Supreme Court against Grant, Meade, and the officers appointed by Meade to replace Jenkins and Jones. He alleged illegal seizure—the military had seized a state-owned railroad as an alternative source of revenue—and imprisonment.[29]

The case came before the Supreme Court during the McCardle controversy. Once more, the Court had an opportunity to rule on the constitutionality of the Reconstruction Acts and, once more, deftly evaded it. The Court demanded that subpoenas be served to each defendant personally, and Stanton advised Meade and acting governor Gen. Thomas Ruger to take separate tours of inspection to elude being served. Such precautions proved unnecessary. On the next day, the Court refused to hear a motion for an injunction against Grant, Meade, and the others and let the case sit until the following December term, at which time it was dismissed. Had the Court ruled otherwise, the reconstruction process in Georgia would have been damaged, and other Southern states might have sat back and waited for a ruling on the constitutionality of the Reconstruction Acts.[30]

In Florida, the factious Republicans caused Meade and Grant severe headaches. The Republican party was divided nearly equally into moderate and Radical wings, and the two wings were bitter enemies. Such conflict augured ill for the convention, which met on January 20. Grant refused to resolve any debates over the legality of the elections for delegates, advising that the matter be left to Congress. After two weeks of wrangling, the moderates failed to seat a delegate with irregular credentials and bolted the convention. Radical Republicans

submitted a constitution to Meade, and the moderates quickly reconvened the convention and followed with their own document. Tensions became so great that Meade directed federal troops to prevent
a Radical effort to storm the moderate meeting with black volunteers.
For a week, it looked as if Floridians would have two constitutions
presented to them, until Meade, with Grant's approval, hurried to
Tallahassee and called for the reorganization of the convention. The
reconstituted convention drafted a constitution resembling the earlier
moderate draft. Eventually, this document received the sanction of
Congress and was ratified in May.[31]

In Alabama, the convention did its work without much trouble, and
Grant instructed military authorities to refrain from interfering in the
election, "unless very satisfactory reasons exist for doing so." Within
days, however, Grant discovered "satisfactory reasons" to interfere
with the election: Alabama's conservatives were staying away from the
polls in an effort to ensure that a majority of those registered failed
to vote. Should this occur, the constitution would not be ratified. At
first Grant wondered whether the election should take place at all;
then he urged Meade to keep the polls open "to give full opportunity
to all who register to vote." When this did not boost turnout, Grant
attributed the sparse vote to reports of bad weather and "embarrass-
ments thrown in the way of voters getting to the polls by opposers of
reconstruction" and again asked Meade to extend the time for voting.
Yet, although the vast majority of those who voted approved the new
constitution, the total turnout again fell short of a majority of the
state's registered voters, resulting in the defeat of the constitution.
Grant was disappointed but realized that he had done all he could.
"We have nothing to do with defeat or success of the constitution of
Alabama," he told Meade, "but it is the duty of the military to see that
all who are entitled to should have an opportunity to express their
will in the matter at the polls." Fortunately for Grant, Congress
quickly realized that other Southern states might frustrate the readmission process by following Alabama's example, and at the end of
February it passed a Fourth Reconstruction Act proclaiming as ratified any constitution that received a majority of the votes cast.[32]

But trouble was not limited to states under Meade's supervision. In
Virginia, the convention that assembled in December 1867 was controlled by the Radicals. This circumstance alarmed most Northern

Republicans, who believed that the more radical their Southern cousins were the less chance the party's Southern wing had to survive in the long term—and the more difficult it would be to defend those governments in the North. District commander Schofield believed that "great reforms require time for their development" and pushed for a centrist Republican movement over the Radicals and blacks, who advocated stringent voting and officeholding qualifications. He appointed "respectable and competent" Republicans to offices over "the lower class of men who have acquired control over the mass of colored voters." On April 4, he went one step further, removing Governor Francis Pierpoint and installing Henry H. Wells in his place. Grant, after some vacillation, endorsed the change, although he cautioned Schofield not to make removals a habitual practice.[33]

But this was not enough for Schofield, who deplored signs of Radical influence over the delegates. "The same baneful influence that secured the election of a majority of ignorant blacks and equally ignorant or unprincipled whites to the convention," he told Grant, "has proved sufficient to hold them firmly to their original purpose." The district commander made no secret of his displeasure with empowered blacks, who elected to office "persons of their race who can neither read nor write." With this in mind, he opposed the adoption of the proposed constitution—named the Underwood Constitution after presiding officer John C. Underwood—which made local offices elective, not appointive, and disfranchised and barred from office a significant number of whites. Noting the prospect of black officeholders, Schofield exclaimed, "Will the Country at large endure such a government?" He refused to pay the expenses of an election to ratify the document, and when congressional Republicans followed suit the constitution lay inactive for the remainder of the year. As Schofield reminded Grant later on, he believed that "the stability of the government might be endangered" by "forcing upon the country extreme radical theories."[34]

Grant had to tolerate many of Schofield's actions and attitudes, for under the Third Reconstruction Act he could intervene only in certain circumstances. Still, his lack of criticism of Schofield's course suggests that building stable Southern governments was uppermost in his mind. Doubtless, the Underwood Constitution, which drew the disapproval of many Northern Republicans, might well have proved an

unnecessary burden in an election year. Although Grant did not endorse his subordinate's rantings about the incapacity of blacks, neither
did he rebuke them, at least not directly. Subsequently, he urged
Schofield's successor, George Stoneman, to appoint blacks to local offices and endorsed Stoneman's call for an election on the constitution
with the officeholding restrictions submitted separately. But the social and economic revolution that the Underwood Constitution portended for the Old Dominion was stopped in its tracks, and Grant did
nothing to prevent this outcome. The extent to which he was influenced by the advice of Northern Republicans, who were afraid of the
impact of such radical constitutions on the Northern electorate or opposed to the rigorous disfranchisement provisions, is hard to say. He
remained silent on the matter, although such considerations probably
played some role in his decision.[35]

Louisiana, a center of controversy in 1867, was a surprise: its convention did its work quietly and the ensuing election took place without disturbance. But Grant and the new district commander, Winfield
Scott Hancock, found other things to fight about. Upon taking command in November 1867, Hancock declared that "the military power
should cease to lead and the civil administration [should] resume its
natural and rightful dominion." Such words, appearing in a formal
order, implied a rebuke of Philip H. Sheridan's administration. For
all of his talk, however, Hancock soon proved that he would intervene
as much as possible in Louisiana politics, this time on the side of reactionary forces in the state. Radicals were replaced with conservatives. Sheridan's orders outlining qualifications for jury duty and voting registration were revoked, which helped exclude blacks from
juries and increased the registration of whites who had held minor
local posts during the war. Such measures revived the state's Democratic party while eroding the newly laid foundation of the Republican organization.[36]

Grant watched Hancock's actions with dismay, but he was ham-
pered by the Third Reconstruction Act from overruling them. But,
finally, Hancock stumbled in the matter of removals, in which Grant
did possess oversight authority. In February, Hancock removed nine
New Orleans city councilmen for filling a municipal office in violation
of the Reconstruction Acts. Seven of the nine men removed were
black; all had been appointed by Sheridan. Grant responded errati-

cally and uncertainly, perhaps reflecting his discomfort at making such decisions in an election year. After first ordering Hancock to suspend the removals, he backed off his request; after ten days, he reversed course again and ordered Hancock to reinstate Sheridan's appointees. Distrustful of Hancock's motives, Grant dispatched his aide, Horace Porter, to New Orleans. Porter reported that Grant's action had angered Hancock but was supported by Republicans. Hancock asked to be relieved of duty, and on March 28 he was reassigned to the Military Division of the Atlantic, the post originally intended for Sherman in February. At least in this case, Grant had thwarted Johnson's plans.[37]

In these varied circumstances, Grant sought to follow a middle course between reaction and revolution. Standing firm against the attempts of conservative whites to thwart the process in Georgia and Alabama, he shared with many moderate Republicans an aversion to Radical regimes in Florida and Virginia, reasoning that their extreme methods would eventually overturn efforts to establish a more durable biracial Republican organization in those states—especially when the Radicals threatened to employ violence to gain their ends. He supported black participation in politics in Louisiana and—after Schofield's departure—Virginia, but he did not accept the efforts of Southern Radicals to bar significant numbers of Southern whites from voting or holding office. Nor did he always move with assurance, revealing some confusion about the actual state of affairs and the consequences of decisions. Unable to control the actions of his subordinates under the terms of the Third Reconstruction Act, he gave advice and support when possible, tolerated dissent when he had to, and moved to block decisions with which he did not agree when he could.

Crucial as these decisions were to the future course of Southern Republicanism, most Northerners were much more interested in the presidency. Two questions about the White House would be resolved in the spring of 1868: would Andrew Johnson be ejected from it? Would Ulysses S. Grant reside there after March 4, 1869? Grant still hesitated about running, telling Sherman that he would avoid the nomination if at all possible. But Chase's chances were fading, and Grant dreaded the possibility of a November victory by

Democratic front-runner George H. Pendleton, "because he was an open enemy of the war, which we *must* maintain was right," as Sherman put it. Sherman believed that his friend would forgo the race "if any real good man can be elected in his stead. . . . Grant dont want to be a candidate, and will only consent in my opinion if he judges that his acceptance is necessary to the peace of the country." But the key consideration was Grant's fear of a Democratic victory. Should the party that Grant believed opposed the war succeed in winning the White House less than four years after Appomattox, the achievements of Northern arms and of Grant himself would be repudiated. The men who had given their lives on many a battlefield would have died in vain. The struggle between president and Congress would continue, dragging the army into politics. Sherman understood his comrade's concern: "My notion is that he thinks that the Democrats ought not to succeed to power," he told his brother, "and that he would be willing to stand a sacrifice rather than see that result."[38]

Of more immediate concern to Grant was the impeachment of President Johnson. Many Grant supporters had resisted this step for some time, for fear that it might jeopardize the general's own chances in the next presidential contest. Impeachment was "an anti-Grant movement," Horace White of the Chicago *Tribune* concluded back in August 1867, "the object being to get Wade into the Presidency long enough to give him prestige & patronage to control the next National Convention." Although the elections in 1867 and Grant's break with Johnson had virtually destroyed the Chase and Wade movements, some of these concerns remained. Grant himself had become fairly settled on the matter. "Impeachment seems to grow in popularity," he observed in March 1868, "and indications are that the trial will not be protracted." He supported conviction, believing it necessary to preserve peace, and remained alert to the possibility that violence might break out.[39]

Despite his advocacy of conviction, Grant took a step that helped persuade wavering senators to vote for acquittal when he supported Schofield's nomination as secretary of war. Schofield's statements describing black inferiority doubtless pleased Johnson, while his support for moderate Republicans made him acceptable to Congress. Arriving in Washington days after the end of Virginia's constitutional convention, he discussed the offer with Grant, who made clear his support for Johnson's conviction but at first advised Schofield to accept the position. Within days, Grant realized what he had done and urged Schofield to decline, but it was too late. Grant's slipup was costly. Several senators were worried about the fate of the War Department should Johnson be acquitted. By following in April the strategy he had rejected in January and naming a moderate military officer acceptable to the majority of Republicans, Johnson had erased that fear.[40]

Grant lobbied for conviction with several doubtful Republicans. He succeeded in winning over New Jersey's Frederick T. Frelinghuysen but failed with William Pitt Fessenden, a disappointing setback because of the Maine senator's influence over others. His efforts to persuade Trumbull proved unavailing. To Missouri's John Henderson, Grant gave his gut reason for detesting Johnson. "I would impeach him," Grant said, "because he is such an infernal liar." This summed up his private sentiments, but it would not do as a public justification. On May 16, Grant was quoted as advocating conviction "because the Government cannot go on practically or safely in its present demoralized condition." That day, the Senate convened once more as a court of impeachment, this time to render judgment. The issue had come down to seven Republican moderates, including Fessenden, Trumbull, and Henderson. In the end, these seven joined the twelve Democrats to acquit Johnson by one vote: thirty-five to nineteen. Grant may have been disappointed at the result at the time, but some of his supporters expressed relief, not so much because they desired Johnson's acquittal as because they worried about the consequences of Wade becoming president. Henderson, for one, called acquittal a pro-Grant measure, asserting that "the seven Republican Senators voting for the acquittal of the President were the *true original Grant* men."[41]

The taste of failure did not linger long in the mouths of either Grant or the Republicans. Within days of Johnson's acquittal, a soldiers' and sailors' convention in Chicago, "believing that the nation's victories under his guidance in war will be illustrated by him in peace by such measures as shall secure the fruits of our exertion and the restoration of the Union upon a loyal basis," endorsed Grant for president. On May 20, the Republicans convened in the same city to nominate their candidate. On the first day, the party adopted a platform supporting congressional reconstruction, calling for mandatory black suffrage in the South while leaving such a decision with each state in the North, and blasting Johnson as a traitor.

The next day, John A. Logan nominated Ulysses S. Grant as the Republican candidate for president of the United States of America. The convention ratified the nomination unanimously. When the result was announced, bedlam broke loose in the hall. Doves, released from the ceiling, soon found themselves dodging the top hats delegates tossed in the air; doubtless, the delegates soon found themselves dodging the return offerings of the doves. Behind the platform a large curtain opened, revealing a portrait of Liberty standing between two scales. Grant was pictured standing on one scale, and Liberty pointed to the empty scale, challenging the Democrats: "Match Him!" In the skirmish for vice president, it took five ballots for House Speaker Schuyler Colfax to emerge victorious over Wade and Henry Wilson.[42]

Grant heard the result from a panting Stanton, who had run from the War Department across the street with the news. The general took the news calmly, betraying no emotion. "There was no shade of exultation or agitation on his face, not a flush on his cheek, nor a flash in his eye," recalled Badeau. Grant had been resigned to accepting the nomination for some time. "If this were simply a matter of personal preference and satisfaction I would not wish to be President," he told a Republican party official. "The people speak kindly of me—even our fellow-citizens of the South, many of them. . . . To go into the Presidency opens altogether a new field to me, in which there is to be a new strife to which I am not trained." This was not exactly ambition speaking.[43]

Cynics might find it hard to accept Grant's reluctance at face value. After all, many other politicians utter similar statements in a weak attempt to veil their ambition. But there were plenty of reasons for Grant not to run for president. To leave the security of the position of general-in-chief for the uncertainties of politics was not an easy decision, and certainly not one dictated by personal preference. His hard-won reputation and fame would be placed at risk in the partisan arena. But Grant's concern for his personal reputation contributed to his final decision to seek the office. He was very concerned lest the achievements of the war be jeopardized, even lost, by the course of postwar partisan politics. He had been just as angry with Radical Republicans as with Andrew Johnson for twisting national concerns into topics of partisan controversy. Statesmanship had been in short supply in the years leading to the war, and there was no evidence that this situation had changed since the end of hostilities. Now the possibility of a Democratic victory in the fall contest threatened to spoil the fruits of Northern victory and to destroy all that Grant had achieved. Americans, argued John Sherman, "demand that our candidate should be so independent of party politics as to be a guarantee of peace and quiet. You," he told Grant, "are the only man in the Nation who can give this guarantee." Grant had heard from so many people that he was indispensable to a Republican victory that he had come to believe it. And perhaps he was.[44]

Grant revealed his reasoning for accepting the nomination to William T. Sherman. "I could not back down," he explained, "without . . . leaving the contest for power for the next four years between mere trading politicians, the elevation of whom, no matter which party won, would lose to us, largely, the results of the costly war which we have gone through." Sherman agreed: "The war, no matter what its course or conduct, was an epoch in our national history that must be sanctified, and made to stand justified to future ages." As both men understood, Reconstruction required statesmanship, not partisanship; it was in some sense tied to the war itself, for it would determine the ultimate outcome and legacy of that bloody struggle.[45]

In his formal letter of acceptance, Grant called for an end to bickering and disharmony: "Let us have peace." These four deceptively simple words were susceptible to a wide variety of interpretations, all of which reinforced Grant's appeal. They promised an end to a long, tiring, bitter conflict. They signaled a halt to the petty partisan bickering and carping that at times had overwhelmed a need for dispassionate, calm statesmanship. They offered reconciliation to those white Southerners who were willing to accept defeat and its consequences and wanted to work for reunion. At the same time, they warned that violence would not be tolerated. Finally, with peace came prosperity. Sectional harmony would be wise, wonderful, and profitable. Coming from the hero of Appomattox, "Let us have peace" was an expression of the innermost desires of many Americans and, therefore, an ideal campaign slogan.[46]

The general's trusted subordinates embraced his candidacy. "My own opinion is that, considering the state of the country, Grant will make the best President we can get," Sherman concluded. "What we want in national politics is quiet, harmony and stability, and these are more likely with Grant than any politician I know of." Schofield, newly installed as secretary of war, declared, "I have always believed that the Union could be fully restored only by the man who put down the rebellion." Oliver O. Howard, who believed that Grant's sympathies were "on the side of loyalty, reconstruction, and freedmen," urged a veterans' convention: "Let him who led us to the completeness of victory during the war lead us safely to a complete triumph in peace." Sheridan was also pleased, immediately congratulating his commander: "I believe you are sacrificing personal interest and comforts to give to the country a civil victory which will be fatal to the Rebels north and south." To Sheridan, the presidential campaign was an extension of the war: "Two solutions were necessary for the settlement of the rebellion. The first was to take away from it its military strength. That was done at Appomattox. The second, to take away its political strength. That will be done next November. It will be a short campaign, but as decisive as Appomattox."[47]

The deed done, Radicals accepted the result. "Gen. Grant, an apt pupil of events, has at last learned to be a radical," decided the *Independent*. Some Radicals had believed that on the great issues the general was with them all along. Wilson asserted that his "fidelity to his country and to the equal rights of all countrymen cannot be questioned." Swallowing hard, Phillips declared that Grant had not "travelled far, but his face is zionward. . . . Grant's election means progress." More interesting was the reaction to the platform's ambivalence over black suffrage. Grant had denounced such prevarication as hypocrisy back in 1867, but he remained silent about it now. Reports circulated that his father had advised him that to endorse black suffrage for the entire nation might well cost him the election. Perhaps discretion was better now; valor would have to wait until victory was secured.[48]

Grant believed that his nomination would force the Democratic party "to adopt a new platform, and put upon it a reliable man who, if elected will disappoint the Copperhead element of their party." He was wrong. Disappointed with the Republicans' decision "to take up small men," Chase began making overtures to the Democratic party.

Hancock, Pendleton, Senator Thomas Hendricks, and even Andrew Johnson entered the Democratic sweepstakes. At the nominating convention in July, however, the Democrats followed the Republican example by nominating a man who professed he didn't want to run —Horatio Seymour, New York's former governor. Before he could be nominated, Seymour had been forced to leave the hall. "Pity me, Harvey, pity me," he cried to a friend as he left. Then, in what can only be termed a fit of absent-mindedness, the convention nominated as Seymour's running mate Frank Blair.[49]

The Seymour-Blair ticket proved to be a serious mistake: it allowed Republicans to wave the bloody shirt vigorously. Seymour had addressed antidraft rioters as "my friends," while Blair, ignoring the warnings of his brother Montgomery to keep his mouth shut, spoke of his fears of a military dictatorship and argued that a Democratic president would declare the Reconstruction Acts "null and void," permitting white Southerners to regain control of state governments on their own terms. A disappointed Chase observed that questioning the constitutionality of the Reconstruction Acts made the Democrats appear to counter "Let us have peace" with "Let us have war." As one observer noted, "Grant can do nothing for himself, but Seymour and his men rarely open their mouths that they do not strengthen Grant's hand."[50]

Republicans attacked the Democrats right and left. "General Blair has relieved the Republican party of a good deal of labor," declared Indiana's Oliver P. Morton. "He has unmasked the enemy with whom we have to deal, and he has placed before the country the very issue—peace or war." In contrast, the Republicans were the party of "peace, repose, stability." Relieved of having to confront the race issue, Republicans could replay the war once more, and at the same time contrast Blair's promise of conflict with Grant's quest for peace. Grant's pose as a dispassionate statesman was enhanced by such comparisons. One New York businessman thought that Grant would "rise superior to all party considerations. . . . The only real matter at issue is the reconstruction of the South, and will not its rights be better recognized under Grant, who, at the collapse of the Confederacy, gave its soldiers as liberal terms as he could, and far better ones than they hoped for[?]" Democrats could have expected this from Republicans. But it caught them by surprise when John Quincy Adams II, the Democratic candidate for governor of Massachusetts, said that Grant "finished the war, and that is enough to entitle him to my respect and admiration." As if this wasn't bad enough, Adams went on to say, "I do believe he is an upright, honorable man, who will try, if elected, to do his best, not for a party only, but for the whole people of the country."[51]

Silence had worked wonders for Grant up to now, so it was only logical that he stay quiet during the election campaign. After a trip through the West along the Union Pacific Railroad, he returned to Galena and left Rawlins in Washington to handle routine army business. As a result, he had little to do with Southern affairs during the fall of 1868. In part, this was because Congress's readmission of seven Southern states left only Texas, Virginia, and Mississippi under his authority according to the Reconstruction Acts; in those states, the lack of elections considerably reduced the incidence of political violence. Indeed, after the readmission of the Southern states that had complied with the Reconstruction Acts, Grant asked Johnson to remit the remaining penalties imposed by military commissions in those states. The commanding general was also understandably reluctant to give advice to his Southern commanders lest it be interpreted as an attempt to manipulate the election results and thus confirm Blair's predictions of military dictatorship. He drew up instructions defining the use of military force in the South, directing that the express approval of the War Department (and thus the Johnson administration) be obtained beforehand. In Georgia, however, the signs of organized violence and intimidation by white reactionaries were all too obvious, and Grant worked with Meade to assist Governor Rufus Bulloch to maintain order. But these efforts proved ineffective, as Democrats ousted black legislators from the State House and employed violence effectively to ensure their victory in the fall contest.[52]

In other states, Johnson placed loyal pawns in power. Lovell Rousseau, who had once spied on Sheridan, now headed the military forces in Louisiana. He showed no interest in protecting Republican voters, telling Governor Henry Warmouth to warn blacks to stay away from the polls because of the possibility of violence. Incredibly, he charged Republicans with instigating violent incidents in the weeks before the election, a weak attempt to conceal his desire to assist the Seymour ticket. In November, the Democrats won the state, in part due to the fall in Republican votes from some 69,000 in April to 33,225. Since Mississippi voters had failed to ratify their constitution in July, the state did not participate in the presidential contest, which in turn reduced the possible incentive for political violence. Gillem, another Johnson crony, headed the federal military forces in the state; he had done his best through his appointments and deployment of soldiers to help Mississippi conservatives to beat back the proposed constitution.[53]

"It is more unlikely than ever that the presidential elections can take place without the necessity of suppressing some outbreak in the South," Clemenceau had concluded in August. "In all events of this kind, the remarkable feature is that according to telegraphic reports, there is always a band of heavily armed negroes attacking a handful of harmless whites. Then when it comes to counting the dead, a few negroes are always down, but of white men, not a trace. . . . Whatever the facts, it is practically impossible to know the truth, for both sides are interested in exaggerating the reports." Even Johnson admitted as much in September, when he allowed federal troops to assist civil authorities in their efforts to put down the Ku Klux Klan in Tennessee.[54]

Riots in St. Landry, Louisiana, and Camilla, Georgia, seemed to many Republicans the South's response to Blair's irresponsible speechmaking. "Grant will surely be elected," John Sherman predicted. "If not, we shall have the devil to pay, and shall have to fight all our old political battles over again. . . . The election of Grant seems our only salvation from serious trouble." George Templeton Strong agreed. "Should Seymour succeed (which Heaven forbid!) we should have a new rebellion on our hands within thirty days." Yet, despite some serious outbreaks of violence, the elections of 1868 did not produce the bloodbath Clemenceau feared, thanks in large part to the October elections in Ohio, Pennsylvania, and Indiana, where the Republicans carried the day. With these crucial states in the Republican column, the election seemed a sure thing. As John Sherman noted, "Grant is much stronger than our State or Congress ticket, and will get thousands of floating and Democratic votes."[55]

Panic in Democratic ranks following these Republican triumphs clinched Grant's victory. A movement inspired by New York Democrats to dump Seymour and Blair in favor of Chase misfired, and everyone had a good laugh when the administration organ, the *National Intelligencer*, called on the party faithful to line up in support of the president. Seymour rebuffed these efforts and took to the campaign trail in a last-gasp effort that only highlighted his fading chances. It looked as if the Republican party was about to win its third straight presidential election.[56]

On election night, 1868, Grant strolled over to Washburne's house to wait for the returns to come in. He did not seem too interested in the result; Badeau had seen him more excited over a game of cards. As the evening wore on, it became evident that Grant had won, carrying twenty-six states to Seymour's eight. His vote totals exceeded by over 110,000 those of the Republicans running with him, suggesting that he was more popular than the party and may have been essential to its triumph. It was early Wednesday morning when he finally walked back home with some friends. When he saw Julia in the doorway, all he could say was, "I am afraid I am elected."[57]

EPILOGUE

THE FRUITS OF VICTORY

Many observers believed that Grant's election as president constituted the end of Reconstruction. The New York *Times*, anticipating the general's victory, declared, "Peace—a settled, just and permanent peace—not merely the end of war, but the end of the discord, resentment and hatred which survive the war,—is what the American people, without distinction of section, of party, or of race, most of all, at this moment, most fervently desire." Grant promised peace. But there was no peace. Far from ending Reconstruction, Grant's inauguration marked a new stage in the process—one that would end with reunion achieved at the cost of racial equality.[1]

But the Republican triumph in the 1868 election marked a point of transition, both for Grant and for the nation. With Grant in the White House, Republicans no longer had to worry about battling the nation's chief executive. Nor was there much remaining over which to battle. At the time of Grant's inauguration, only Texas, Virginia, and Mississippi had failed to complete the process set forth in the Reconstruction Acts, and with Grant's assistance they did so within a year. As a result of political violence and the ejection of several black representatives from the state legislature, Georgia was remanded to military supervision, but even this measure merely delayed final full readmission until 1871, terminating the Reconstruction Acts. Finally, with the election out of the way, Republicans moved to abolish racial barriers to voting with the ratification of the Fifteenth Amendment in 1870.

For Ulysses S. Grant, the presidency presented new challenges. Newspaper reporter Mary Clemmer Ames watched him at a reception in early 1868. "The first life of this man has passed, like a tale told, or a dream gone by," she told her readers. "He has already entered upon another, so opposite and so bewildering in experience that his whole being is awakening to meet unknown demands, undreamed of opportunities and responsibilities." His declaration that he would have "no policy of my own to enforce against the will of the people," meant to reassure Americans after four years of Andrew Johnson, is usually misunderstood as betraying a flawed conception of the office he held for two terms. In coming years, others would note the differences between Grant the general and Grant the president as he struggled to excel in the very trade he had once despised. Whether he mastered those skills has remained a point of some dispute among historians. Recent scholarship has begun to challenge the traditional tale of incompetence. His poor reputation as president is partly due to the image Americans had of Grant in 1869 and the high expectations he had to fulfill. As James Schouler put it, "Grant, the General, as first beheld in military dress, appeared to me quite a different person from Grant the President, rigged out at a ball in white tie and regulation black suit, or when seen standing alone in early dusk at the White House gate, with glossy top hat, smoking a fragrant cigar." Such a comment reveals as much about the observer as the observed.[2]

As president, Grant faced some of the same problems he had confronted as general-in-chief. Political terrorism continued to shape Southern politics; Republicans proved fractious at both the state and national level; Northern racism and constitutionalism placed limits on the extent to which he could bring peace and justice to the South. But the means of intervention changed. New legislation enforcing the right to vote and the invocation of the guarantee clause of the Constitution replaced the general orders and congressional legislation of the Johnson years. Other concerns—the need to build up Southern Republicanism, shore up party ranks against dissidents, and respond to new issues—transformed the nature of the problems confronting the new president. Although Grant continued to hold fast to his ultimate objectives of reunion and racial justice, during the 1870s he realized and reluctantly came to accept the fact that the combination of Southern terrorism, Northern apathy, and constitutional conservatism (exacerbated by an economic depression, divisions within the Republican party, and the emergence of other issues) meant the postponement of racial equality and the admission by Republicans that the price of sectional reconciliation was justice toward the freedpeople. By the time he left the White House in 1877, Grant was a disappointed man. The vision of peace glimpsed at Appomattox Court House had been dissipated by twelve years of frustrating struggle.

In later years, one of the most popular interpretations of the Grant presidency was that Grant's undoubted skills as a general did not translate into political savvy. On the level of partisan politics, this was doubtless true, although some historians think that Grant as president came to practice politics rather skillfully. But, on the level of politics in its larger sense, as policy, such critics overlook the fact that Grant had been practicing politics for years; the Civil War and Reconstruction inevitably mixed together political and military questions. At the close of the war, William T. Sherman noted "how intermingled have become civil matters with the military, and how almost impossible it has become for an officer in authority to act a purely military part."[3]

From the beginning of armed conflict, Grant understood that a civil war was fundamentally different than a war between alien nations. One had to calibrate operations against the enemy with an eye on the impact of such operations on prospects for peace and reunion. In the first year of hostilities, Grant's belief that the war would be of short duration, in addition to his understanding that the primary goal of reunion could be best achieved through conciliating a population haunted by notions of abolitionist hordes, led him to wage a limited war that would not touch any forms of Southern property—including slaves—not directly involved in resisting reunion. Once convinced that Southerners were willing to do everything in their power to secure independence, Grant accepted the fact, as Adam Badeau later explained, that "he was engaged in a people's war, and that the people as well as the armies of the South must be conquered, before the war could end." Yet, at the same time, he kept in mind that the primary object of the war was reunion. If he could destroy Confederate morale, he could reduce the chance of the war becoming a guerrilla conflict, which in turn would avoid the obstacles to peace that such a conflict would engender.[4]

This was never clearer than during the Appomattox campaign. As Grant later explained, "My campaign was not Richmond, not the defeat of Lee in actual fight, but to remove him and his army out of the contest and, if possible, to have him use his influence in inducing the surrender of Johnston and the other isolated armies." For a week, he pursued his quarry, and the Army of the Potomac marched as it never had before. "There was no let up," recalled Badeau, but just "fighting and marching, and Grant negotiating and fighting all at once." The cornering of Lee at Appomattox capped his efforts. In terms astonishing for their generosity, the Union commander cut short attempts at vengeance and punishment as he offered the surrendered Confederates a new start in life. In Wilmer McLean's parlor that Palm Sunday in 1865, Ulysses S. Grant demonstrated that he could make peace as well as war.[5]

If, as T. Harry Williams has claimed, "Grant was capable of grasping the political nature of the war," so, too, it must be added, did John C. Frémont, George B. McClellan, and William T. Sherman. What made Grant distinctive was his understanding of the political role of the soldier. He knew that soldiers must exhibit due subordination to civil authorities—a lesson never absorbed by either Frémont or McClellan—and accept the limitations placed upon military operations by political considerations—a notion against which Sherman railed. Much the same can be said about how these generals viewed emancipation as a war aim. Frémont hungered for emancipation so much that he outdistanced Lincoln; McClellan resisted it even when it was becoming obvious that Lincoln and Congress were moving in that direction; Sherman cared little for the fate of black Americans, slave or free. Grant, who saw from the beginning that the conflict would disrupt slavery and perhaps deal the peculiar institution a mortal wound, let events dictate whether emancipation would become an avowed war goal. Once liberty and union were one and inseparable, Grant not only struck at slavery but also enlisted blacks in the fight for freedom.[6]

Diagnosing the reasons for the success or failure of many of his fellow generals, Grant pointed to politics as a primary cause. "What interfered with our officers more than anything else," he commented, "was allowing themselves a political bias. That is fatal to a soldier. War and politics are so different." He claimed that he did not know of any officer "who went into the war with political views who succeeded." When many of his colleagues spoke "of conciliation, and hurting brethern, and states rights, and so on, they made a fatal blunder." Nor were such failures confined to those favoring a conservative policy. "The generals who insisted upon writing emancipation proclamations, and creating new theories of State governments . . . all came to grief as surely as those who believed that the main object of the war was to protect property, and keep the negroes at work on the plantations while their masters were off in the rebellion."[7]

Grant was not arguing that generals should not have political opinions. "I had my own views on all of these subjects, as decided as any man, but I never allowed them to influence me." Commanders might hold opinions on the outstanding political issues of the day, but they should never let their views interfere with their judgment. Of course, foremost among those political issues was the future of slavery. That Grant vacillated over the proper policy to pursue toward fugitive slaves reflected his desire to stay out of political questions rather than any misbegotten love for the institution itself. Anyone who thought he valued slavery had forgotten his heated arguments with his father-in-law. Yet, of course, any action he took regarding slavery carried with it political implications, and the reaction of blacks to the presence of an invading Union army guaranteed that Grant would have to take some action. Moreover, Grant, like Lincoln, always viewed the question of slavery without regard to his personal inclinations and within the larger context of the war effort. Not until it became obvious that the South was willing to wage total war did Grant respond in kind by attacking slavery. When he did so, he went at it with a will. His enthusiasm about enlisting blacks spoke his desire to destroy the Confederacy and to give blacks a chance for freedom. His refusal to allow

Confederate authorities to distinguish between black and white prisoners of war testified to his growing acceptance of black equality.[8]

In his attitude toward slavery as an issue of wartime policy, Grant resembled Abraham Lincoln. In many ways, the two men pursued parallel courses. Both men let policy, not personal preference, guide their actions. They hesitated to expand the scope of the conflict lest, as Lincoln put it, the war degenerate into a remorseless revolutionary struggle. Both embraced emancipation as a war measure brought about by the intensity of Southern resistance, and both came to endorse the enlistment of blacks. If on some issues Lincoln expressed himself more forcefully and eloquently, on others—such as the mistreatment or murder of black prisoners—it was Grant who took the more advanced ground. One reason that Lincoln came to regard Grant as his general was that he kept in step with administration policy all the way through Appomattox.

T. Harry Williams suggests that one reason for this harmony between Lincoln and Grant was the general's understanding that "it was not his job to propose policy to the government." Yet this statement also deserves qualification. As Grant advanced in rank, he became more explicit in advocating military operations, in part because of their political consequences. He also proved more willing to express his own opinions about the proper means and ends of peacemaking. By the last months of the war, Grant had come to interpret his military responsibilities rather broadly, and at Appomattox he clearly crossed the line between military and civil policy. But Grant also understood that, although soldiers might assume some of the functions of civil authorities, they should not scheme to supplant those authorities. While McClellan and Frémont entertained notions of a political future—both men would become candidates to succeed Lincoln in 1864—Grant not only dismissed such notions but also wisely reassured Lincoln of his position.[9]

Probably the closest relationship Grant forged during the war was his friendship with Sherman. Despite his resistance to emancipation and his distrust of politicians, Sherman followed Grant's lead on many issues. But the two men differed in their interpretation of the relationship between war and politics. Sherman damned the press, but Grant, who also had occasion to grumble about how he was portrayed in print, understood it as a necessary evil. Sherman cared little about the popular will (his statement, "Vox populi, vox humbug," sums it up pretty well), but Grant understood the importance of retaining public support. Moreover, Sherman never came to accept, as did Grant, that the only way that the soldiers were going to preserve the peace they had done so much to secure was to become involved in the politics of postwar policymaking. Indeed, Sherman's refusal to become engaged in the process preserved his friendship with Grant. The two men disagreed deeply on the place of blacks in postwar America, and, as Southern resistance intensified, Grant showed more concern about countering it than did Sherman. By refusing Johnson's offers of office and concerning himself with frontier policy, Sherman avoided a clash with Grant over Reconstruction.

In 1865, Grant the warmaker became Grant the peacemaker. But the struggle to subdue the South did not end at Appomattox. During the next four years, in fact, Grant faced challenges that equaled those he had overcome during the war. In a brief comment on these years, E. B. Long once remarked that this was a time "where Grant seems to have been on unstable ground and where, to me, he is not at his best." But those scholars who have come to understand the particularly malevolent impact of Andrew Johnson's presidency on Reconstruction are more likely to concur with Harold Hyman's assessment that "Grant's reliability provided such stability to American governmental relations at this crucial time as to warrant great praise." [10]

Had Lincoln lived, Grant believed, it would have been possible to enact "a speedy reconstruction in terms that would be the least humiliating to the people who had rebelled against their government." He argued "that besides being the mildest, it was also the wisest, policy," for Southerners "would not make good citizens if they felt that they had a yoke around their necks." Nor did such a statement necessarily mean that he overlooked the problems of racial readjustment in the aftermath of emancipation. Sooner or later, he reasoned, Southern blacks would have to deal with their white counterparts, and to engender bitterness among the defeated certainly would not enhance the prospect of harmonious race relations. Yet, like Lincoln, Grant was not willing to sacrifice any of the fruits of victory, including emancipation and its consequences, to conciliate Southern whites. He understood that the president's chief desire was "to see all the people of the United States enter again upon the full privileges of citizenship with equality among all." And "all the people" included the freedmen.[11]

But it was not to be. Whatever else Lincoln's assassination meant for the fate of Reconstruction, it severed the productive team of president and general that had done so much to win the war. Grant would not work nearly as well with Lincoln's successor. Indeed, he came to believe that Andrew Johnson presented the greatest obstacle to a just and lasting peace. Johnson's early boisterous remarks about treason and traitors worried the general, for such rhetoric forecast a policy that would repel Southerners "and make them unwilling citizens; and if they became such they would remain so for a long while." For some time, Grant mistakenly thought that Johnson might ally with Republican Radicals, who seemed bent on vengeance or at least showed no interest in conciliation. Such fears seemed confirmed when the president tried to put Robert E. Lee on trial for treason.[12]

Having unsettled Southerners by his initial tough talk, Johnson then further complicated the chances for reunion by his about-face in policy. The new president, said Grant, soon came "to regard the South not only as an oppressed people, but as the people best entitled to consideration of any of our citizens." Such a stance encouraged white recalcitrance, which expressed itself most vividly in acts of harassment, intimidation, violence, and murder against friends of the Union, black and white. Aware that white Southerners were not yet to be entrusted with civil government, Grant sought to insulate blacks, white Unionists, and army personnel from the mockery of justice as administered by Southern civil government; he issued a series of general orders that replaced civil processes with military intervention where necessary. In striking at the Black Codes through General Orders No. 3, Grant demonstrated a commitment to black civil equality. Before long, he came to accept black suffrage as well.[13]

It increasingly became apparent to Grant that Johnson's obstructionism threatened all that had been won at Appomattox. "It tried the patience of the most patient man to see all the results of the war deliberately laid at the feet of the South by the man we trusted," he recalled. Johnson's willingness to placate Southern whites regardless of their behavior shocked many Northerners. "This was more than the people who had secured to us the perpetuation of the Union were prepared for," Grant recounted, "and they became more radical in their views." Among those Northerners who became more radical was Grant himself. Dismayed at the president's tolerance of Southern intransigence, he became disgusted when Johnson treated the momentous issue of Reconstruction merely as a partisan issue. Moreover, Johnson's attempts to affiliate Grant with his policy enraged the general, who detested such manipulation.[14]

Unable to find in the president someone who would support a statesmanlike approach toward the South, Grant turned to Congress to buttress his position. In the process, he became a maker of policy, whatever his protestations to the contrary. The resulting legislation, designed "to stay the hands of the President," sought to insulate the process of reconstruction from presidential interference by placing it in the hands of the military, who would act under guidelines set by Congress. Whether or not the policy of Congress was wise, Grant later observed, "It became an absolute necessity . . . because of the foolhardiness of the President and the blindness of the Southern people to their own interest." Conceding that much of the resulting legislation may well have been unconstitutional—certainly the Army Appropriations Act and the Tenure of Office Act were subject to question on those grounds—Grant explained that "it was hoped that the laws enacted would serve their purpose before the question of constitutionality could be submitted to the judiciary and a decision obtained."[15]

The obsession with checking Johnson's course overshadowed other concerns. Opportunities were lost, and time and energy that might have been used to address the problems of racial readjustment and economic recovery were expended on controlling the president. Indeed, the extent to which Johnson made his own behavior the focal point of Republican policy would be a mark of his success in retarding the impact of emancipation and defeat on Southern society. Similarly, Grant's decision to give top priority to the protection of blacks and white loyalists caused him to neglect other problems encountered by the freedmen. He did not delve deeply into the issues of land redistribution or the role of the Freedmen's Bureau in constructing the postwar economic order. To be sure, he dabbled with wartime redistribution in Mississippi and intervened in Florida land sales, but he did not pursue these openings to revolution and remained silent in the political debate over postwar redistribution. He had a blind spot when it came to such issues, suggesting the limits of his vision; although one must add that perhaps historians have overestimated the possibilities of unrealized economic transformations and underestimated the impact of violence and intimidation on the course of Reconstruction. To the pragmatic Grant, pursuing economic change was fruitless unless one first guaranteed civil (and eventually political) rights.

One might well wonder why, if Grant disagreed with presidential reconstruction, he did not defy Johnson earlier. Might not a man of his personal popularity have checked the president's course? Some scholars, in fact, point to Grant's continued association with Johnson as evidence of acquiescence, much as Radicals did at the time. But it is difficult to see what purpose a confrontation would have served. The general would have sacrificed whatever influence he had on Johnson; defiance would have violated his obligation to obey the president and might have even led to his removal. Critics of Grant's behavior during this period also place a rather low priority on sectional reconciliation. These historians emphasize the drive for racial equality as the criterion for judging policy during Reconstruction. But the true task of the just policymaker during the years following Appomattox was to achieve a balance between restoration, readjustment, and revolution. It proved a difficult task, possibly beyond any person's capacity. Grant deserves credit because he at least understood the problem and tried to address it. Indeed, the problems presented by race and racism in today's America suggest that there are no easy answers.[16]

Moreover, Grant's opposition to Johnson was tempered by several considerations. In the first months of the new administration, Grant did what he could to work with Johnson in order to wean him away from his rhetoric of retaliation. It did not become apparent for nearly a year how intent the president was on restoring white supremacy in the South, nor that Southerners would respond so avidly to his encouragement. Only then did Grant shift his position. Recognizing the subordination of military to civil authority, he was not eager to reveal any difference of opinion with the president. The best way to check Johnson was from within the administration, a notion Grant acted upon when he accepted the post of secretary of war. Nor did he think it appropriate for soldiers to engage in political bickering. At times his resulting silence, a product of principle as well as pragmatism, proved troubling. As the New York *Tribune* commented, it placed him "too often in a questionable position." But his silence was not total, and when he finally broke with Johnson in 1868 the *National Anti-Slavery Standard* described the resulting correspondence as the product of a "strong, irate man, who has forborne until endurance ceased to be a virtue, but . . . rather became a hindrance of a most embarrassing character."[17]

Eventually, Grant had to redefine his concept of duty as he resisted Johnson. Congressional legislation defining the role of the military—legislation that Grant helped frame—allowed him to justify resisting Johnson by claiming that he was doing his duty under law. He embraced Congress as a new source of authority even as he shaped its mandates. Grant also overcame his professed reluctance to become involved in a political dispute by reminding himself of the stakes involved. As John Pope remarked to Grant, "It is a misnomer to call the question in the South a political question." Rather, the issue before the nation was, "Shall the Union men & Freedmen, be the slaves of the old negro rebel aristocracy or not?" Having been responsible for achieving the military triumph that brought the war to a close, Grant now felt it was his duty to make sure that what was gained through bloodshed and valor would not be sacrificed in the chaotic clashes of politics. Asserting that Reconstruction was not a partisan issue but a question of policy requiring statesmanship, Grant could come to justify his involvement in politics by claiming that the issues involved were too important to be left to the politicians.[18]

Once Grant had made that conceptual leap, the presidency beckoned anew. Inclination and interest had led him to dismiss all talk of a presidential candidacy before, but he came to believe that perhaps the only way to ensure that Reconstruction would follow its proper course was to accept the highest office in the land. At the conclusion of hostilities, there was talk that only the men who had made war could be trusted to make peace. The *Army and Navy Journal*, deploring "the ignorance, want of training, and natural ineptitude of most of our statesmen," concluded that "it is clear that our best soldiers are peculiarly fitted for public life." And nobody seemed better prepared than Grant. As Henry Adams commented, "Grant represented order." Many Americans, sharing Grant's distaste for the methods and motives of professional politicians, looked to the hero of Appomattox to put an end to vicious partisanship and to bring peace to the land. Eventually, Grant accepted that responsibility. That, eight years later, he left the White House having reluctantly accepted the perpetuation of racial injustice as the price of sectional reconciliation was his tragedy and the nation's failure.[19]

NOTES

ABBREVIATIONS

AJ	Andrew Johnson
AJP	Andrew Johnson Papers
ISHS	Illinois State Historical Society
JDG	Julia Dent Grant
LC	Library of Congress
LR	Letters Received
LS	Letters Sent
OR	*Official Records of the War of the Rebellion*
PMJDG	*Personal Memoirs of Julia Dent Grant*
PMUSG	*Personal Memoirs of Ulysses S. Grant*
PU	Princeton University
PUSG	*Papers of Ulysses S. Grant*
RG	Record Group
TR	Telegrams Received
TS	Telegrams Sent
SIU-C	Southern Illinois University-Carbondale
USG	Ulysses S. Grant
USGP	Ulysses S. Grant Papers
WSHS	Wisconsin State Historical Society
WTS	William T. Sherman
WTSP	William T. Sherman Papers

Note: Wherever possible, the original spelling and punctuation of quoted material have been retained throughout the manuscript.

INTRODUCTION

1. Adams, *Education of Henry Adams*, p. 262.

2. McFeely, *Grant*, p. 216. Even then, McFeely could not resist adding a little nudge: "Perhaps so."

3. Catton, *U. S. Grant and the American Military Tradition*, p. 131.

4. T. H. Williams, *Lincoln and His Generals*, p. 324; T. H. Williams, *McClellan, Sherman, and Grant*, pp. 101–2; Keller, *Affairs of State*, pp. 259–62; Donald, *Liberty and Union*, p. 246; Brock, *Conflict and Transformation*, pp. 402–4; Gillette, *Retreat from Reconstruction*, pp. 174–79; Hesseltine, *Ulysses S. Grant*; Catton, *U. S. Grant and the American Military Tradition*, p. 131. Ulrich, "Northern Military Mind," and Farnen, "Ulysses S. Grant," also address these issues. The argument that Grant as general displayed political savvy has been questioned by Ludwell Johnson, who taunted, "One may perhaps be pardoned for asking what happened to that political acumen after Grant became president. Was this great gift somehow taken away? Or is it possible he never had it?" Johnson, "Civil War Military History," pp. 15–16.

5. Philip H. Sheridan to USG, September 15, 1867, Sheridan Papers; WTS to Adam Badeau, February 12, 1882, in Badeau, *Grant in Peace*, pp. 63, 589.

6. Clausewitz, *On War*, pp. 87–88. As the political scientist Bernard Brodie points out in an analytical essay (ibid., p. 646), the opinion that Clausewitz was the apostle of total war "is likely to be confined to those who have never touched the book." Although *On War* was not translated into English until after the American Civil War, the prewar writings of Henry W. Halleck reflect some familiarity with the book. Nevertheless, Grant seems to have been unaware of him, at least during the war; but, as Peter Paret puts it, "Some people reached conclusions similar to Clausewitz's without reading *On War*; on the other hand, many of his readers either did not understand or did not agree with him." Paret, "Clausewitz," p. 211. For previous comparisons of Grant and Clausewitz, see Donald, *Lincoln Reconsidered*, p. 102; T. H. Williams, "Military Leadership of North and South," where the point is made implicitly; Weigley, *History of the United States Army*, p. 252; Weigley, *American Way of War*, chapter 7, which argues that Grant pursued a strategy of "annihilation"; Weigley, "American Strategy," p. 432; Hattaway and Jones, *How the North Won*; Beringer et al., *Why the South Lost*.

7. Howland, *Grant as a Soldier and Statesman*, p. 417; Clausewitz, *On War*, p. 111.

8. Clausewitz, *On War*, p. 92 (italics omitted).

9. Dana and Wilson, *Life of Ulysses S. Grant*, p. 417.

10. Lloyd Lewis perceived this over forty years ago. "Grant was circum-

spect and said very little, and for the sake of peace and unity, which were his passions, glossed over Johnson's acts when speaking in public, but he evidently was worried deeply in private lest the accomplishments of the war be negated. He wanted the slave free and a citizen; he didn't want the issue revived, and he evidently thought Johnson was getting in bed with the reactionaries who wanted the negro kept down and the old order reestablished in the South." Lewis, *Letters from Lloyd Lewis*, p. 52. Harold M. Hyman and Martin Mantell have developed this insight in their work, and it informs this study.

11. USG to Jesse Root Grant, April 21, 1861, *PUSG*, 1:6–7; Gettysburg Address, November 19, 1863, Lincoln, *Collected Works*, 7:23.

PROLOGUE

1. Lewis, *Captain Sam Grant*, pp. 9–10, 45–55, 120.

2. Ibid., pp. 27–29, 34–35.

3. Ibid., pp. 35, 47, 53–54, 80, 82, 91.

4. Young, *Around the World*, 2:447–48; *PMUSG*, 1:53–54.

5. Heth, *Memoirs*, p. 111; McWhiney, *Southerners and Other Americans*, pp. 61–71.

6. Lewis, *Captain Sam Grant*, pp. 102–4, 283–332.

7. Ibid., pp. 340–41; Emerson, "Grant's Life in the West," p. 213; Richardson, *A Personal History*, p. 140; Garland, *Ulysses S. Grant*, p. xxiii; Casey, "When Grant Went a Courtin'," Lewis-Catton Research Notes. Lewis insists that Uncle Jason, along with the two blacks Grant hired later on, were free; William McFeely claims they were slaves (McFeely, *Grant*, p. 62). For more extensive discussions of this issue see Simpson, "Butcher? Racist?," pp. 74–77; Simon, "Grant at Hardscrabble," pp. 191–201.

8. *PMJDG*, pp. 75–76, 78–79, 82–83, 91; Lewis, *Captain Sam Grant*, p. 341; Casey, "When Grant Went a Courtin'," Lewis-Catton Research Notes; Simpson, "Butcher? Racist?," pp. 74–77.

9. Simpson, "Butcher? Racist?," p. 76; Lewis, *Captain Sam Grant*, p. 365.

10. USG to Jesse Root Grant, October 1, 1858, *PUSG*, 1:344.

11. Garland, *Ulysses S. Grant*, pp. xxii–xxiii; *PUSG*, 1:348–49, and USG to Jesse Root Grant, September 23, 1859, *PUSG*, 1:351–52; Lewis, *Captain Sam Grant*, pp. 366–68.

12. USG to Jesse Root Grant, September 23, 1859, *PUSG*, 1:352; *PMUSG*, 1:212–13.

13. Lewis, *Captain Sam Grant*, p. 351; *PMUSG*, 1:214–15. Others preferred his more succinct statement of why he voted for the Democrat: "I voted for Buchanan because I didn't know him and voted against Fremont because I did know him."

14. Fehrenbacher, *Dred Scott Case*, pp. 254, 569; Lewis, *Captain Sam Grant*, p. 343.

15. Emerson, "Grant's Life in the West," pp. 321–24; Young, *Around the World*, 2:446.

16. Lewis, *Captain Sam Grant*, pp. 369–71; Garland, *Ulysses S. Grant*, pp. xxii–xxiii; USG to Jesse Root Grant, March 12, 1859, *PUSG*, 1:346. Julia recalled that the slaves were hired out to other employers. *PMJDG*, p. 82.

17. Lewis, *Captain Sam Grant*, pp. 383–85; New York *Tribune*, July 26, 1885; USG to Mr. Davis, August 7, 1860, *PUSG*, 1:357; *PMUSG*, 1:217.

18. Lewis, *Captain Sam Grant*, pp. 386–87; *PMJDG*, p. 87; *PMUSG*, 1:222.

19. Richardson, *A Personal History*, pp. 175–76; Lewis, *Captain Sam Grant*, pp. 392–93.

CHAPTER ONE

1. Lewis, *Captain Sam Grant*, pp. 394–400.

2. Ibid., pp. 401–2.

3. USG to Frederick Dent, April 19, 1861, *PUSG*, 2:3–4; USG to Jesse Root Grant, April 21, 1861, ibid., 2:6–7.

4. USG to Dent, April 19, 1861, ibid., 2:3–4; USG to Mary Grant, April 29, 1861, ibid., 2:13–14.

5. USG to Dent, April 19, 1861, ibid., 2:3–4; Crane, "Grant as a Colonel," p. 44.

6. USG to Jesse Root Grant, May 6, 1861, *PUSG*, 2:20–22.

7. Ibid.; USG to JDG, May 6, 1861, ibid., 2:23–24; Nevins, *War for the Union*, 2:329.

8. USG to JDG, June 17, 1861, *PUSG*, 2:42–43; on McClellan, see ibid., 2:41; USG to Jesse Root Grant, May 2, 6, July 13, 1861, ibid., 2:18, 21, 67.

9. USG to JDG, July 19, 1861, ibid., 2:72–73.

10. USG to Jesse Root Grant, August 3, 1861, ibid., 2:80–81; USG to JDG, August 3, 1861, ibid., 2:82–83. On Missouri, see Fellman, *Inside War*.

11. USG to JDG, August 10, 1861, *PUSG*, 2:96–97.

12. Woodward, *Meet General Grant*, p. 187; Rachel Tompkins to Clara Grant, June 5, 1861, in Grant, *Letters to His Father and Sister*, pp. 159–82.

13. USG to Mary Grant, August 12, 1861, *PUSG*, 2:105; USG to Capt. John C. Kelton, August 14, 1861, ibid., 2:111; USG to Col. William H. Worthington, August 26, 1861, ibid., 2:139–40.

14. Crane, "Grant as a Colonel," pp. 43–44. USG to Kelton, August 30, 1861, *PUSG*, 2:154–55. Slaveholders who visited Grant's headquarters in pursuit of fugitives found themselves forced to take an oath of allegiance before they were allowed to depart.

15. Cornish, *Sable Arm*, pp. 12–15; Col. John L. Cook to USG, September 11, 1861, *PUSG*, 2:220, and USG to Cook, September 12, 1861, *PUSG*, 2:243–44. On September 11 Frémont issued a new proclamation in line with Lincoln's policy.

16. USG to John C. Frémont, September 4, 1861, *PUSG*, 2:186. Grant soon came to trust blacks as sources of information. See USG to Charles F. Smith, September 11, 1861, ibid., 2:234.

17. USG, "Proclamation," and USG to Gen. Eleazer A. Paine, September 6, 1861, ibid., 2:194-95.

18. Garland, *Ulysses S. Grant*, p. 182.

19. USG to Gen. Lorenzo Thomas, September 21, 1861, *PUSG*, 2:291 and annotation. For Kentucky, see Howard, *Black Liberation in Kentucky*, especially chapter 2.

20. USG to Thomas, September 21, 1861, *PUSG*, 2:291 and annotation; K. Williams, *Lincoln Finds A General*, 3:106-12. Halleck's order reflected a shift in emphasis in policy toward fugitive slaves, moving away from Benjamin F. Butler's "contraband" solution. See the exchange of correspondence between various commanders in *OR*, ser. 2, 1:776-802.

21. USG to Jesse Root Grant, November 27, 1861, *PUSG*, 3:227. Grant's concern about the press was justified. One Chicago *Tribune* reporter informed Secretary of War Simon Cameron that Grant, who was "perfectly inebriate under a flag of truce with rebels," was unfit for command. "Until we can secure pure men in habits and men without secesh wives with their own little slaves to wait upon them, which is a fact here in this camp with Mrs. Grant, our country is lost." Ibid., 4:118-19.

22. USG to Cook, December 25, 1861, ibid., 3:342-43; comment on General Orders No. 3, dated 1862, Grant Family Papers.

23. William S. Hillyer (USG staff officer) to Col. Leonard F. Ross, January 5, 1862, *PUSG*, 3:373-74; Smith to USG, January 4, 1862, ibid., 3:431. Halleck, responding to the same officer's inquiry, offered different advice that echoed Grant's previous dispatch on returning slaves to loyal masters: "The military are neither slave-stealers nor slave-catchers. . . . Let the question of ownership be settled by the civil tribunals." *OR*, ser. 2, 1:802.

24. J. G. Wilson, *Life and Public Services*, p. 24.

25. USG to Paine, January 11, 19, 1862, *PUSG*, 4:32, 68-69.

26. Grant to Col. Richard J. Oglesby, November 3, ibid., 3:108-9; General Orders No. 3, District of Cairo, January 13, 1862, ibid., 4:45-46. Henry W. Halleck to USG, February 8, 1862, and USG to Halleck, February 11, 1862, ibid., 4:193-94; New York *Tribune*, February 22, 1862; see *PUSG*, 4:291; USG to John A. McClernand, February 18, 1862, *PUSG*, 4:243; USG to Kelton, February 22, 1862, *PUSG*, 4:267-68; USG to McClernand, February 22, 1862, *PUSG*, 4:270.

27. General Orders No. 14, District of West Tennessee, February 26, 1862, *PUSG*, 4:290-91; Cooling, *Forts Henry and Donelson*, p. 248.

28. USG to Elihu B. Washburne, March 22, 1862, *PUSG*, 4:408; USG to Col. Philip B. Fouke, March 16, 1862, ibid., 4:377; USG to Col. Marcellus M. Crocker, March 17, 1862, ibid., 4:384; USG to WTS, March 17, 1862, ibid., 4:382-83; USG to JDG, March 29, 1862, ibid., 4:444.

29. McClernand to USG, March 29, 1862, ibid., 4:438n.

30. Article of War No. 102, March 13, 1862, *OR*, ser. 2, 1:810; USG to Capt. Nathaniel H. McLean, March 31, 1862, *PUSG*, 4:453-54; Fouke to USG, March 30, 1862, *PUSG*, 4:454. Other observers disagreed with such optimistic reports of Clarksville's Unionism; one townsman told a reporter that there were only six Unionists in the town. Cooling, *Forts Henry and Donelson*, p. 247.

31. USG to Gen. George W. Cullum, February 23, 1862, *PUSG*, 4:276; USG to JDG, February 24, 1862, ibid., 4:284; USG to Cullum, February 25, 1862, ibid., 4:286; USG to WTS, February 25, 1862, ibid., 4:289; General Order No. 7, District of West Tennessee, February 22, 1862, ibid., 4:265; USG to Col. William W. Lowe, March 15, 1862, ibid., 4:372-73; USG to Fouke, March 16, 1862, ibid., 4:377; USG to McLean, March 15, 30, 1862, ibid., 4:368, 447-48; USG to JDG, March 18, 1862, ibid., 4:389; Simplot, "General Grant and the Incident at Dover," pp. 83-84. Not everyone shared Grant's optimism about the loyalty of Tennesseans: see Cooling, *Forts Henry and Donelson*, p. 248. One reason for Grant's cockiness may have been his relief at resolving a conflict with Halleck in the aftermath of Donelson, which nearly led to Grant's removal from command.

32. *PMUSG*, 1:368-69.

33. USG to Washburne, June 19, 1862, *PUSG*, 5:146; USG to JDG, April 15, May 31, June 3, June 12, 1862, ibid., 5:47, 134, 138, 142-43; Geer, *Civil War Diary*, p. 38. At this time, Grant also had to deal with the question of slavery in his own family. Colonel Dent was breaking up his slave holdings under the pressure of debt, and Grant, aware that creditors might seize and sell the family slaves, told Julia, "I would not give anything for you to have any of them as it is not probable that we will ever live in a slave state again but [I] would not like to see them sold under the hammer." USG to JDG, May 16, 1862, *PUSG*, 5:124. See note 58.

34. The best studies of the transformation of the Confederate war effort are Emory Thomas's *Confederacy as a Revolutionary Experience* and *Confederate Nation*.

35. USG to Washburne, June 19, 1862, *PUSG*, 5:146; John A. Logan to Col. Garrett Nevins, July 24, 1862, *OR*, ser. 1, 17 (pt. 2):115; Edward Kittoe to Washburne, June 24, 1862, Washburne Papers.

36. USG to JDG, June 16, 1862, *PUSG*, 5:144; *PMUSG*, 1:395.

37. USG to Hillyer, July 1, 1862, *PUSG*, 5:181-82 and annotation; General Orders No. 60, July 3, 1862, ibid., 5:190-91 and annotation; "Union" to USG, July 12, 1862, Hillyer Papers; see *PUSG*, 5:192-94.

38. USG to Halleck, July 28, August 9, August 20, 1862, *PUSG*, 5:243, 278, 312. As Manning Force, who was serving under Grant at the time, pointed out, the failure of Union commanders to secure their lines against raiders stifled loyalty. The departure of bluecoats "would crush the dawning spirit of loyalty, and be very hard, almost treacherous, to the men who have

taken the oath. . . . A permanent body of troops would bring out enough loyal citizens like the sun drawing plants from their winter hiding place." Manning F. Force to Mrs. Perkins, July 20, 1862, Force Papers.

39. George B. McClellan to Abraham Lincoln, July 7, 1862, McClellan, *Civil War Papers*, pp. 344–45; Appeal to Border State Representatives, July 12, 1862, Lincoln, *Collected Works*, 5:317–19.

40. Sherman, *Personal Memoirs*, 1:285; WTS to USG, August 17, 1862, WTSP; WTS to Ellen Ewing Sherman, July 31, 1862, Sherman Family Papers; Walters, *Merchant of Terror*, p. 63; on the Union response to guerrilla war, see Hartigan, *Lieber's Code*, pp. 2, 11, 17. In his letter to Grant, Sherman added that Southerners were "much more resigned and less presumptuous than at first. Your orders about property and mine about 'niggers' make them feel that they can be hurt."

41. Thompson, *Recollections of the 3rd Iowa*, p. 275; Lyon, *Reminiscences of the Civil War*, p. 53; Kittoe to Washburne, June 24, 1862, Washburne Papers.

42. USG to Halleck, July 19, 1862, and Halleck to USG, July 19, 1862, *PUSG*, 5:218–19. See also USG to Halleck, July 8[7], 1862, ibid., 5:199. That military commanders viewed these issues as distractions is suggested by General E. O. C. Ord's letter to John A. Rawlins, July 24, 1862: "I have been anxious to inspect the works now nearly completed for the defense of this place—but my time has been principally occupied in mulatto girl investigations [Union officers commandeering women for their own purposes]." *PUSG*, 5:390–91.

43. Belz, *Emancipation and Equal Rights*, pp. 36–40; Force to Mrs. Perkins, July 20, 1862, Force Papers; General Orders No. 72, District of West Tennessee, August 11, 1862, *PUSG*, 5:273–74; Halleck to USG, August 2, 1862, *PUSG*, 5:244.

44. USG to Halleck, July 28, 1862, and Halleck to USG, August 2, 1862, *PUSG*, 5:243–44; USG to Gen. William S. Rosecrans, August 10, 1862, ibid., 5:282; USG to Gen. Isaac F. Quinby, July 26, 1862, ibid., 5:238–41 and annotation; USG to Salmon P. Chase, July 31, 1862, ibid., 5:255–56; USG to Rosecrans, August 7, 1862, ibid., 5:271; WTS to Chase, August 11, 1862, quoted in Sherman, *Personal Memoirs*, 1:294.

45. Washburne to USG, July 25, 1862, *PUSG*, 5:226.

46. USG to Jesse Root Grant, August 3, 1862, ibid., 5:264; General Orders No. 72, District of West Tennessee, August 11, 1862, ibid., 5:273–74.

47. Newton, *A Wisconsin Boy in Dixie*, pp. 27–28; Force to Mrs. Perkins, July 20, 1862, Force Papers.

48. WTS to John A. Rawlins, August 14, 1862, *PUSG*, 5:272; WTS to John Sherman, September 3, 1862, WTSP.

49. USG to Mary Grant, August 19, 1862, *PUSG*, 5:311.

50. Byers, *With Fire and Sword*, p. 45; Eaton, *Grant, Lincoln and the Freedmen*, p. 2; WTS to John Sherman, September 3, 1862, WTSP; Rosecrans to USG, September 10, 1862, *PUSG*, 6:32.

51. USG to Gen. Thomas J. McKean, September 16, 1862, *PUSG*, 6:54; Gen. James M. Tuttle to Edwin M. Stanton, September 18, 1862, ibid., 6:317 and annotation; Voegeli, *Free but Not Equal*, pp. 60–61; Eaton, *Grant, Lincoln and the Freedmen*, pp. 3–9.

52. For discussions of this question, see Gerteis, *From Contraband to Freedman* and Berlin et al., *Destruction of Slavery*. Although both of these works point to the primacy of military necessity, they overlook the fact that it would be difficult to justify a wartime policy involving such drastic changes on any other grounds.

53. Eaton, *Grant, Lincoln and the Freedmen*, pp. 9–15.

54. Ibid., pp. 18–32; Andrus, *Civil War Letters*, pp. 27–29; Knox, *Camp-Fire and Cotton-Field*, pp. 225–27.

55. USG to Halleck, November 15, 1862, and Halleck to USG, November 16, 1862, *PUSG*, 6:315.

56. Lincoln to AJ and USG, October 21, 1862, ibid., 7:3.

57. General Orders No. 4, Department of the Tennessee, November 3, 1862, ibid., 6:252–53; Lowe to Rawlins, August 18, 1862, ibid., 5:314; Andrus, *Civil War Letters*, pp. 25–26; Catton, *Grant Moves South*, p. 336. Andrus also reported (p. 28) that Grant had made a speech at Grand Junction, Tennessee, in late November 1862 stating that the Confederacy had asked for a forty-day suspension of hostilities. No record of such a speech has been found, and I have failed to discover mention of such a proposal. Given Grant's distaste for public address, perhaps Andrus had confused his commander with someone else.

58. "Proclamation," December 9, 1862, *PUSG*, 7:3–4; USG to Halleck, December 14, 1862, ibid., 7:29–32; Knox, *Camp-Fire and Cotton-Field*, p. 233. It is not clear exactly when Julia Dent Grant's slaves were freed. In her memoirs, she recalled that they were freed by the Emancipation Proclamation; John Y. Simon, pointing out that the Emancipation Proclamation did not apply to Missouri, argues that they became free upon the ratification of the Thirteenth Amendment in 1865. *PMJDG*, pp. 83, 88 n. 17, 126; Simon, "Grant at Hardscrabble," p. 194.

CHAPTER TWO

1. *PMUSG*, 1:443.

2. USG to Gen. Stephen A. Hurlbut, January 3, 1863, *PUSG*, 7:167–68; USG to Henry W. Halleck, January 6, 1863, ibid., 7:186 and note.

3. USG to Col. George W. Deitzler, February 2, 1863, ibid., 7:278–79; Catton, *Grant Moves South*, p. 377; Eaton, *Grant, Lincoln and the Freedmen*, p. 44. Eaton later recalled this instance as an illustration of Grant's "sincere and humane interest in the welfare of the most subordinate laborer dependent on him."

4. Special Field Orders No. 2, Department of the Tennessee, February 12, 1863, *PUSG*, 7:339; USG to Halleck, February 18, 1863, ibid., 7:338−39; USG endorsement of February 16, 1863, on John Eaton to John A. Rawlins, February 12, 1863, ibid., 7:339; USG to James B. McPherson, March 13, 1863, 7:415. These problems continued to mount over the next month. On April 1, McClernand complained that the refugees outside his picket lines were disrupting "the discipline and police of my camp"; Grant endorsed Hurlbut's decision to enroll blacks as pioneers and teamsters to evade the problem. John A. McClernand to USG, April 1, 1863, *PUSG*, 8:21−22; Charles A. Dana to Edwin M. Stanton, April 2, 1863, *OR*, ser. 1, 14 (pt. 1):70.

5. Col. Silas Noble to Lyman Trumbull, January 6, 1863, Trumbull Papers; USG to Elihu B. Washburne, February 15, 1863, *PUSG*, 7:332; Joseph Medill to Washburne, February 13, 1863, Washburne Papers.

6. Catton, *Grant Moves South*, pp. 388−403; *PMUSG*, 1:458−59; USG to Halleck, April 12, 1863, *PUSG*, 8:53−54; USG to JDG, April 6, 1863, *PUSG*, 8:29−30; USG to Thomas W. Knox, April 6, 1863, *PUSG*, 8:30−31.

7. Dana, *Recollections of the Civil War*, p. 49; Catton, *Grant Moves South*, p. 389; Anderson and Anderson, *Generals*, pp. 282−83.

8. Stanton to Lorenzo Thomas, March 25, 1863, *OR*, ser. 3, 3:100−1; Lincoln to AJ, March 26, 1863, ibid., ser. 3, 3:103. On the topic of Grant and black enlistment, see Westwood, "Grant's Role in Beginning Black Soldiery," which depends heavily upon Thomas's orders and reports.

9. Halleck to USG, March 30, 1863, *PUSG*, 8:93.

10. Ibid., 8:93−94.

11. Ibid., 8:94.

12. USG to Gen. Frederick Steele, April 11, 1863, ibid., 8:49. He added that "Gen L Thomas is now here, with authority to make ample provision for the negro." Within ten days, Steele reported to Sherman: "The negroes continue coming in, and many of them seem quite pleased at the idea of becoming soldiers." Steele to WTS, April 20, 1863, WTSP.

13. Cornish, *Sable Arm*, pp. 115−18; Geer, *Civil War Diary*, pp. 88−89; Newton, *A Wisconsin Boy in Dixie*, pp. 60−63. Sherman preferred to complain about black refugees obstructing military movements, although he added, "I won't trust niggers to fight yet, but don't object to the government taking them from the enemy." After the war, James H. Wilson recalled, "The speech of General Thomas's may not have removed anybody's convictions but it certainly silenced all cavil." James H. Wilson to Adam Badeau, March 30, 1867, James H. Wilson Papers.

14. Geer, *Civil War Diary*, pp. 88−89; Newton, *A Wisconsin Boy in Dixie*, pp. 60−63; Glatthaar, *Forged in Battle*, pp. 37−38; WTS to John Sherman, April 26, 1863, WTSP; Thomas to Stanton, April 12, 1863, *OR*, ser. 3, 3:121.

15. Geer, *Civil War Diary*, p. 89.

16. Cadwallader, *Three Years with Grant*, pp. 69, 86; Cornish, *Sable Arm*,

pp. 144–45; Capt. Abraham Strickle to USG, June 9, 1863, *OR*, ser. 1, 25 (pt. 2):455–56. USG to Thomas, June 16, 1863, *PUSG*, 8:328.

17. USG to Gen. Richard Taylor, June 22, 1863, *PUSG*, 8:400–1 and annotation.

18. USG to Taylor, July 4, 1863, ibid., 8:468–69 and annotation. Grant received no further evidence of the execution of black prisoners. See USG to Halleck, August 29, 1863, ibid., 9:210–11.

19. Cornish, *Sable Arm*, pp. 165–68; Rawlins to USG, July 30, 1863, *PUSG*, 9:81. Dana reported that the stories of the execution of Union prisoners were false. Dana to Stanton, June 26, 1863, Dana Papers.

20. USG to James B. McPherson, July 5, 1863, *PUSG*, 8:483; USG to McPherson, July 7, 1863, ibid., 9:3; USG to Thomas, July 11, 1863, ibid., 9:24.

21. General Orders No. 51, Department of the Tennessee, August 10, 1863, ibid., 9:135–36; General Orders No. 53, Department of the Tennessee, August 23, 1863, ibid., 9:136–37; USG to Gen. Marcellus M. Crocker, August 30, 1863, ibid., 9:215–17 and annotation. Thomas authorized the enlistment of any able-bodied blacks on August 16. Grant's directive, although it did not conflict with Thomas's order, was intended more to encourage blacks to enter camps or go to work than to draft blacks into the army. Westwood, "Grant's Role in Beginning Black Soldiery," p. 210; Cimprich, *Slavery's End in Tennessee*, p. 85.

22. USG to Crocker, August 28, 1863, *PUSG*, 9:207–8; Thomas to USG, June 26, 1863, and USG to Thomas, July 11, 1863, ibid., 9:23–25; Statement of Joseph L. Coppic and Robert Campbell, July 18, 1863, Berlin et al., *Black Military Experience*, pp. 148–49; USG to Halleck, August 31, 1863, *PUSG*, 9:219–20.

23. Byers, *With Fire and Sword*, p. 101; Newton, *A Wisconsin Boy in Dixie*, p. 91; Currie, *Enclave*, pp. 59–60; USG to Thomas, July 11, 1863, *PUSG* 9:23–24, 26; Westwood, "Grant's Role in Beginning Black Soldiery," p. 210.

24. David D. Porter to USG, July 24, 1863, *PUSG*, 9:591; Theodore S. Bowers to McPherson, July 22, 1863, ibid., 9:112; USG to Halleck, July 24, 1863, ibid., 9:110; Gerteis, *From Contraband to Freedman*, p. 122.

25. Eaton to USG, July 23, 1863, *PUSG*, 8:343–44. The chaplain also suggested that in the future Grant should call the black refugees freedmen, not contrabands, since Lincoln preferred the former term. At least the president was more tolerant than Secretary of the Treasury Salmon P. Chase, who refused to even read documents containing the word "contraband."

26. Lincoln to USG, August 9, 1863, Lincoln, *Collected Works*, 6:374; USG to Lincoln, August 23, 1863, *PUSG*, 9:196; Chase, *Inside Lincoln's Cabinet*, p. 178 (August 29, 1863); Lincoln to James C. Conkling, August 26, 1863, Lincoln, *Collected Works*, 6:406–10.

27. Welles, *Diary*, 1:387 (Welles usually revised his initial contemporary comments in light of subsequent events. These revised comments, clearly indicated in Howard K. Beale's edition, have been excluded unless otherwise

indicated); Dana to USG, August 18, 1863, *PUSG*, 9:147–48; Henry Wilson to Washburne, July 25, 1863, *PUSG*, 9:219; Edward O. C. Ord to WTS, August 14, 1863, WTSP.

28. USG to Washburne, August 30, 1863, *PUSG*, 9:217–18.

29. Ibid.; *PMUSG*, 1:570; J. J. Giers to USG, January 26, February 6, 1865, *OR*, ser. 1, 49 (pt. 1):590–92, 659; Brooks, *Grant of Appomattox*, p. 206.

30. Cadwallader, *Three Years with Grant*, pp. 124–26; WTS to USG, July 20, 21, 1863, *PUSG*, 9:68, 90.

31. USG to Hurlbut, August 4, 1863, *PUSG*, 9:139; see ibid., 9:589; USG to Halleck, August 11, 1863, ibid., 9:173–74; General Orders No. 50, Department of the Tennessee, August 1, 1863, ibid., 9:133; USG to WTS, August 6, 1863, ibid., 9:155; Currie, *Enclave*, p. 30. Grant also encouraged the renewal of loyalty in Memphis, where a group of businessmen tendered him a public reception. His response, drafted by an aide, approvingly noted "the existence of sentiments which I have so long and so ardently desired to see manifested in this Department." Linking reunion to emancipation, he added that such loyalty marked the replacement of "the despotic rule of the leaders of the rebellion" by men "*who acknowledge human liberty as the only true foundation of human government.*" USG to Ruel Hough and others, August 26, 1863, *PUSG*, 9:202–3; Richardson, *A Personal History*, p. 349.

32. Halleck to WTS, August 29, 1863, and WTS to Halleck, September 17, 1863, Sherman, *Personal Memoirs*, 1:363–70; WTS to John Sherman, September 9, 1863, WTSP. Halleck agreed with Sherman: "I have always opposed the organization of a civico-military government under civilians. It merely embarrasses the military authorities without effecting any good." Halleck to WTS, October 1, 1863, WTSP.

33. WTS to Rawlins, September 17, 1863, Sherman, *Personal Memoirs*, 1:370–71; USG to Halleck, September 19, 1863, *PUSG*, 9:221–22.

34. Cadwallader, *Three Years with Grant*, pp. 22–23; USG to Salmon P. Chase, July 21, 1863, *PUSG*, 9:94–95.

35. Catton, *Grant Takes Command*, pp. 14–32.

36. Ibid., pp. 59–60; Porter to his mother, September 13, 1863, Porter Papers.

37. Catton, *Grant Takes Command*, pp. 67–92; General Orders No. 4, Military Division of the Mississippi, November 5, 1863, *PUSG*, 9:633. Nor did Grant entirely abandon hope for Mississippi's restoration; he encouraged the efforts of Armistead Burwell to "do all in his power to mould the public mind in that state to desire a speedy restoration of the Union." USG to McPherson, November 20, 1863, *PUSG*, 9:419.

38. WTS to John Sherman, December 29, 1863, WTSP.

39. New York *Tribune*, September 2, 1863; New York *Independent*, March 17, 24, 1864; T. H. Williams, *Lincoln and the Radicals*, p. 336; USG to Crocker, August 30, 1863, *PUSG*, 9:215–16; General Orders No. 6, Military Division of the Mississippi, February 25, 1864, and USG to John A. Logan, February

26, 1864, *PUSG*, 10:107; Gerteis, *From Contraband to Freedman*, pp. 154–56; Cimprich, *Slavery's End in Tennessee*, pp. 82–86; Westwood, "Grant's Role in Beginning Black Soldiery," pp. 210–12; Eaton, *Grant, Lincoln and the Freedmen*, pp. 86, 121, 142–66.

40. New York *Herald*, December 9, 1863; Catton, *Grant Takes Command*, p. 103; T. H. Williams, *Lincoln and the Radicals*, p. 336; USG to Washburne, December 12, 1863, *PUSG*, 9:522.

41. New York *Herald*, December 9, 1863; Crouthamel, *Bennett's New York Herald*, pp. 146–48; Fermer, *Bennett and the Herald*, pp. 254–55; Jesse Fell to Lyman Trumbull, August 11, 1863, Trumbull Papers.

42. USG to Barnabus Burns, December 17, 1863, *PUSG*, 9:541; John M. Palmer to Trumbull, January 24, 1864, Trumbull Papers; Rawlins to Washburne, January 20, 1864, Catton, *Grant Takes Command*, pp. 118–19. Grant would not have entertained a Democratic nomination in any case. "Disloyalty in the North should not be tolerated whilst such an expenditure of blood and treasure is going on to punish it in the South," he told one Democrat. USG to John G. Thompson, August 29, 1863, *PUSG*, 9:211–12.

43. J. H. Wilson, *Life of Charles A. Dana*, p. 299; Washburne to USG, January 24, 1864, *PUSG*, 9:522–23; J. Russell Jones to USG, January 14, 1864, *PUSG*, 9:542–43.

44. USG to I. N. Morris, January 20, 1864, *PUSG*, 10:52–53; USG to Daniel Ammen, February 16, 1864, ibid., 10:132–33; USG to Jesse Root Grant, February 20, 1864, ibid., 10:148–49; Catton, *Grant Takes Command*, p. 110.

45. Badeau to James H. Wilson, February 16, 1864, Badeau Papers, PU; Catton, *Grant Takes Command*, p. 108.

46. USG to Frank Blair, February 28, 1864, *PUSG*, 10:166–67.

47. Catton, *Grant Takes Command*, pp. 111–12.

48. Ibid., p. 134; Hattaway and Jones, *How the North Won*, pp. 516–18.

49. T. H. Williams, *Lincoln and His Generals*, pp. 304–10; USG to Halleck, January 15, 19, 1864, *PUSG*, 10:14–17, 39–40.

50. Compare the evaluations of the plan in T. H. Williams, *Lincoln and His Generals*, pp. 295–97, and in Hattaway and Jones, *How the North Won*, pp. 511–15.

51. Hattaway and Jones, *How the North Won*, pp. 515–30.

52. James H. Wilson to USG, February 25, 1864, *PUSG*, 10:142; USG to WTS, February 18, 1864, ibid., 10:139–40; USG to Halleck, March 28, April 22, 1864, ibid., 10:232, 340.

53. J. G. Wilson, *Life and Public Services*, p. 105; Palmer to Trumbull, January 24, 1864, Trumbull Papers; Chetlain, *Recollections of Seventy Years*, p. 100; USG to Halleck, January 24, 1864, *PUSG*, 10:59; USG to David Hunter, April 17, 1864, *PUSG*, 10:305–7.

54. USG to WTS, April 14, 1864, *PUSG*, 10:284–85; Sherman, *Personal Memoirs*, 2:12; Welles, *Diary*, 2:23–24 (May 3, 1864); Lincoln to Stanton, May 17, 1864, Lincoln, *Collected Works*, 7:345–46.

55. J. McPherson, *Battle Cry of Freedom*, pp. 792–800; Thomas and Hyman, *Stanton*, p. 374. Catton (*Grant Takes Command*, p. 372) claims that the suspension of exchanges was Stanton's idea.

56. USG to Benjamin F. Butler, August 18, 1864, *PUSG*, 12:27; USG to William H. Seward, August 19, 1864, ibid., 12:38.

57. No first-rate account of Grant's 1864 campaign exists. See Catton, *Grant Takes Command*, pp. 179–254; J. McPherson, *Battle Cry of Freedom*, pp. 718–34.

58. Catton, *Grant Takes Command*, pp. 246–50, 255–305; J. McPherson, *Battle Cry of Freedom*, pp. 722–24.

59. J. McPherson, *Battle Cry of Freedom*, pp. 713–17, 741–43, 771.

60. USG to Lincoln, July 19, 1864, *PUSG*, 11:280; Catton, *Grant Takes Command*, pp. 368–70; USG to Halleck, July 19, 1864, *PUSG*, 11:281; USG to Butler, July 19, 1864, *PUSG*, 11:281; USG endorsement, August 15, 1864, *PUSG*, 11:459; USG to Stanton, July 20, 1864, *PUSG*, 11:284; USG to Halleck, August 15, 1864, *PUSG*, 11:424; USG to Stanton, September 13, 1864, *PUSG*, 12:158–59.

61. Cornish, *Sable Arm*, pp. 272–73; USG to Halleck, June 23, 1864, *PUSG*, 11:111–12.

62. USG to Butler, June 17, 1864, *PUSG*, 11:68–69; USG to George G. Meade, June 19, 1864, ibid., 11:82; Catton, *Grant Takes Command*, pp. 318–20; Cornish, *Sable Arm*, pp. 273–74.

63. Cornish, *Sable Arm*, p. 274.

64. Grant's later testimony is in *PUSG*, 13:142.

65. Pleasants, *Tragedy of the Crater*, pp. 75–84.

66. H. Porter, *Campaigning with Grant*, pp. 218, 262–65, 268; Lyman, *Meade's Headquarters*, pp. 199–200; Wainwright, *A Diary of Battle*, p. 447.

67. Catton, *Grant Takes Command*, pp. 325–29; Badeau to James H. Wilson, July 7, 1864, Badeau Papers, PU; Sears, *George B. McClellan*, pp. 365–67.

68. USG to Hunter, August 5, 1864, *PUSG*, 11:378; Catton, *Grant Takes Command*, pp. 326–49, 361. As Sheridan made clear, Grant's instructions, originally issued to Hunter, were turned over to Sheridan. Sheridan, *Personal Memoirs*, 1:464.

69. Ibid., pp. 352–53; USG to Washburne, August 16, 1864, *PUSG*, 12:16–17.

70. J. McPherson, *Battle Cry of Freedom*, pp. 772–780.

71. Sommers, *Richmond Redeemed*, pp. 75, 482.

72. Robert E. Lee to USG, October 1, 1864, and USG to Lee, October 2, 1864, *PUSG*, 12:258; Lee to USG, October 2, 1864, and USG to Lee, October 3, 1864, ibid., 12:263.

73. This interpretation straddles the difference between those who argue that the issue of black POWs was simply a cover to justify the no-exchange policy and James M. McPherson's recent assertion that it was central to the issue. McPherson's reading of Grant's offer overlooks the qualification Grant

placed on which prisoners were available for exchange. After the election of 1864, exchanges resumed because the Confederates agreed to exchange black prisoners, the pressure was off after Lincoln's reelection, and Grant was now confident that most exchanged Confederates would desert. See J. McPherson, *Battle Cry of Freedom*, pp. 799–800; Grant's testimony before the Joint Committee on the Conduct of the War, February 11, 1865, *PUSG*, 13:410–12. For Lee's desperation to secure replacements, see Freeman, *Lee*, 3:505–7.

74. USG to Butler, October 12, 1864, *PUSG*, 12:295–96; Sommers, "Dutch Gap Affair," pp. 51–64.

75. Lee to USG, October 18, 1864, *PUSG*, 12:325–26; Sommers, "Dutch Gap Affair," pp. 60–61.

76. USG to Lee, October 20, 1864, *PUSG*, 12:323–24. Sommers argues ("Dutch Gap Affair," p. 62) that Grant "had always regarded the issue as solely one of treatment of prisoners." However, Sommers fails to note the connection between this incident and the discussion of prisoner exchange several weeks earlier, although he quotes a letter from Secretary of War James Seddon to Jefferson Davis in which the Confederate war minister pointed out that "the issue is therefore made in regard to recaptured slaves, though the necessity of pressing it for the present is avoided."

77. USG to Stanton, October 24, 27, November 1, 9, 10, 1864, in *PUSG*, 12:339–40, 353, 369, 395–96, 398; USG to Meade, November 5, 1864, ibid., 12:382; USG to Alfred H. Terry, November 7, 1864, ibid., 12:394–95. This discussion is in marked contrast to Adam Badeau's comment that "not a shadow of interference with politics in or out of the army has been attempted with his knowledge or sanction." Badeau to James H. Wilson, November 10, 1864, Badeau Papers, PU. Grant did not vote. Meade to wife, November 22, 1864, Meade, *Life and Letters*, 2:245.

CHAPTER THREE

1. Catton, *Grant Takes Command*, p. 463; WTS to USG, November 6, 1864, *PUSG*, 12:373–75; USG to WTS, October 11, 12, November 2, 1864, *PUSG*, 12:289–90, 298, 373. Grant instructed Sherman to arm blacks encountered during the march: "Give them such organization as you can. They will be of some use." Sherman ignored this advice. His behavior toward blacks during his 1864 campaigns in Georgia drew criticism from Stanton and others. Grant, aware of Sherman's prejudices, disagreed with his close friend about black refugees and troops. Eventually, he sought a middle road that would separate Sherman from the mobilization of blacks. WTS to John A. Spooner, July 30, 1864, Berlin et al., *Black Military Experience*, pp. 110–11; USG to Henry W. Halleck, January 1, 1865, and USG to Stanton, January 6, 1865, *PUSG*, 13:200–1, 237–38.

2. WTS to Lincoln, September 17, 1864, and discussion, Sherman, *Personal Memoirs*, 2:137–40; Alexander H. Stephens to Linton Stephens, September 22, 1864, Stephens Papers. Sherman had expressed his disgust with previous efforts in two letters to his brother. "I repeat, all efforts to form civil governments till all the armies of the South are beaten are absurd and actually embarrass us," he declared in May. "They are a nuisance." The following month, he offered that "years must elapse before the People of the South can have a voice in a Government that they now hate with a hate you can hardly measure." WTS to John Sherman, May 26, June 9, 1864, WTSP.

3. Linton Stephens to Alexander H. Stephens, October 10, 1864, Stephens Papers; Schott, *Alexander H. Stephens*, pp. 427–28; USG to Edwin M. Stanton, September 20, 1864, *PUSG*, 12:174–75.

4. USG to JDG, September 30, 1864, *PUSG*, 12:250–51.

5. USG to Stanton, January 4, 1865, ibid., 13:223; Maddex, *Virginia Conservatives*, p. 28; Philadelphia *Press* clipping, scrapbook, Underwood Papers; Catton, *Grant Takes Command*, p. 403; USG to Stanton, February 7, 1865, *PUSG*, 13:383–84.

6. USG to George H. Thomas, November 23, 1864, *PUSG*, 13:17–18; J. J. Giers to USG, January 26, February 6, 1865, *OR*, ser. 1, 49 (pt. 1): 590–92, 659.

7. USG to Benjamin F. Butler, January 2, 1865, *PUSG*, 13:209; USG to Irwin McDowell, January 8, 1865, ibid., 13:250–51; Lew Wallace to USG, January 14, March 14, 1865, *OR*, ser. 1, 48 (pt. 1):1276–79, 1281.

8. *PMUSG*, 2:424–27.

9. Ibid., 2:420.

10. McFeely, *Grant*, pp. 198–99; E. W. Clarke to Henry Wilson, January 31, 1865, Henry Wilson Papers.

11. Catton, *Grant Takes Command*, p. 420.

12. Ibid., 421; McFeely, *Grant*, pp. 200–2; *PMJDG*, pp. 137–38.

13. Catton, *Grant Takes Command*, p. 421. George G. Meade did not follow Grant's example of refraining from political discussions. He told the commissioners that reunion and "a settlement of the slavery question as should be final" would satisfy the North. Meade was quite willing to devise some sort of labor system "which would not be so obnoxious as slavery." George G. Meade to wife, February 1, 1865, Meade, *Life and Letters*, 2:259.

14. McFeely, *Grant*, pp. 203–4; Catton, *Grant Takes Command*, pp. 421.

15. McFeely, *Grant*, p. 208; *PMJDG*, pp. 137–38.

16. USG to Isaac N. Morris, February 15, 1865, *PUSG*, 13:429; USG to William H. Seward, February 19, 1865, ibid., 13:443–44.

17. Long, *Civil War Day by Day*, pp. 634–36.

18. Cresap, *Appomattox Commander*, pp. 163–64.

19. Ibid.

20. Robert E. Lee to USG, March 2, 1865, *PUSG*, 14:99.

21. *PMJDG*, p. 141; USG to Stanton, March 3, 1865, *PUSG*, 14:90–91. In

the original draft, Grant explicitly requested Stanton to show Lincoln the telegram but excised this suggestion in the final draft.

22. Catton, *Grant Takes Command*, p. 424; Cresap, *Appomattox Commander*, pp. 166–67; Lincoln to USG, March 3, 1865, Lincoln, *Collected Works*, 8:330–331; Stanton to USG, March 3, 1865, *PUSG*, 14:91.

23. USG to Stanton, March 4, 1865, and to Lee, same date, *PUSG*, 14:98–100. Stanton took Grant's retort in stride, replying, "No apprehension is felt that you will ever exceed your authority and your object in applying for instructions was understood. . . . It was believed the enemy had a purpose in desiring to enter into political negotiations with Military officers." Stanton to USG, March 5, 1865, ibid., 14:103n. Grant's disappointment could have only been increased weeks later at Appomattox, when Lee asserted that had the March negotiations taken place he would have been willing to surrender all of the Confederate forces in the field. Ten days later, Grant corresponded with Lee concerning reports of the attempted murder of a captured white officer commanding black troops and the murder of several other whites. USG to Lee, March 14, 1865, and Lee to USG, March 23, 1865, ibid., 14:154–55.

24. *PMJDG*, pp. 141–42; USG to Lincoln, March 20, 1865, *PUSG*, 14:215; WTS to USG, March 23, 1865, *PUSG*, 14:206.

25. Sherman, *Personal Memoirs*, 2:325–31; Welles, *Diary*, 2:269 (March 30, 1865—revised version). Later, Welles claimed that Lincoln told Grant to "give Lee anything he wants if he will only stop fighting." Flower, *Edwin McMasters Stanton*, p. 259.

26. D. Porter, *Incidents and Anecdotes*, p. 314.

27. USG to Jesse Root Grant, March 19, 1865, *PUSG*, 14:186–87.

28. Lincoln to Stanton, March 25, 1865, Lincoln, *Collected Works*, 8:373; USG to Philip H. Sheridan, March 29, 1865, *PUSG*, 14:253.

29. Catton, *Grant Takes Command*, p. 441.

30. H. Porter, *Campaigning with Grant*, pp. 450–51.

31. *PMUSG*, 2:463–64, 469; Sheridan to USG, April 4, 1865, *PUSG*, 14:345; Lee to Jefferson Davis, April 20, 1865, DeButts-Ely Collection.

32. *PMUSG*, 2:477–78; Lincoln to USG, April 6, 1865, Sheridan to USG, April 6, 1865, and Lincoln to USG, April 7, 1865, Lincoln, *Collected Works*, 8:388, 389, 392.

33. Catton, *Grant Takes Command*, p. 456; New York *Herald*, April 10, 1865; USG to Lee, April 7, 1865, *PUSG*, 14:361.

34. Lee to USG, April 7, 1865, *PUSG*, 14:361; USG to Lee, April 8, 1865, ibid., 14:367.

35. H. Porter, *Campaigning with Grant*, p. 462; Lyman, *Meade's Headquarters*, p. 354.

36. Lee to USG, April 8, 1865, *PUSG*, 14:367.

37. Young, *Around the World*, 2:455; Cadwallader, *Three Years with Grant*, pp. 318–19.

38. H. Porter, *Campaigning with Grant*, pp. 463–64. According to Ely Parker, a Grant staff officer, Grant expressed his displeasure with Lee more strongly: "I am sorry that General Lee is so obstinate. He seems determined to continue the fighting. If that is his wish he shall have all he wants." "Ely Parker's Narrative," USGP, LC.

39. USG to Lee, April 9, 1865, *PUSG*, 14:371; Sheridan to USG, April 8, 1865, ibid., 14:369.

40. Porter, *Campaigning with Grant*, p. 466; Cadwallader, *Three Years with Grant*, pp. 320–22. Lee rejected the guerrilla warfare option. "A partisan war may be continued, and hostilities protracted, causing individual suffering and the devastation of the country," he told Jefferson Davis, "but I see no prospect by that means of achieving a separate peace." Lee to Davis, April 20, 1865, DeButts-Ely Collection. On this issue, see Beringer et al., *Why the South Lost*, pp. 339–51, 435–39.

41. H. Porter, *Campaigning with Grant*, p. 468; Cadwallader, *Three Years with Grant*, pp. 322–23; Parker, "Ely Parker's Narrative," USGP, LC; USG to Lee, April 9, 1865, *PUSG*, 14:372–73.

42. H. Porter, *Campaigning with Grant*, pp. 472–75; Adam Badeau to James H. Wilson, May 27, 1865, James H. Wilson Papers.

43. *PMUSG*, 2:492; USG to Lee, April 9, 1865, *PUSG*, 14:373–74.

44. USG to Lee, April 9, 1865, *PUSG*, 14:373–74.

45. *PMUSG*, 2:492–94; H. Porter, *Campaigning with Grant*, pp. 486–88.

46. Lyman, *Meade's Headquarters*, p. 358; H. Porter, *Campaigning with Grant*, p. 486.

CHAPTER FOUR

1. Cauble, *Surrender Proceedings*, pp. 72–80; H. Porter, *Campaigning with Grant*, p. 490; Adam Badeau to James H. Wilson, May 27, 1865, James H. Papers.

2. Young, *Around the World*, 2:458; *PMUSG*, 2:497; Freeman, *Lee*, 4:8–9; Catton, *Grant Takes Command*, p. 472.

3. Cauble, *Surrender Proceedings*, pp. 80–82.

4. Ibid., pp. 103–5; Alexander, *Fighting for the Confederacy*, p. 540; New York *Herald*, April 15, 1865; Wainwright, *A Diary of Battle*, p. 523 (April 10, 1865).

5. H. Porter, *Campaigning with Grant*, pp. 491–92; Burr, *Life and Deeds of Grant*, p. 813; E. McPherson, *Political History*, p. 300; USG to Edwin M. Stanton, April 10, 1865, *PUSG*, 14:379.

6. Badeau, *Grant In Peace*, p. 22; H. Porter, *Campaigning with Grant*, p. 493; *PMJDG*, p. 153; Pollard, *Lost Cause*, p. 712.

7. D. D. Porter, *Incidents and Anecdotes*, p. 314; Sherman, *Personal Memoirs*, 2:329; John Gibbon to USG, April 13, 1865, *PUSG*, 14:384; Randall and

Current, *Lincoln the President*, 4:351–52.

8. Washington, D.C., *Intelligencer*, April 14, 1865; New York *Times*, April 12, 14, 1865; New York *Herald*, April 11, 12, 15, 1865.

9. New York *Times*, April 11, 1865; Washington, D.C., *Star*, April 13, 1865; New York *Herald*, April 14, 1865, citing the New York *Tribune*; George G. Meade to wife, April 18, 1865, Meade, *Life and Letters*, 2:273; Blaine, *Twenty Years of Congress*, 2:8; Gougeon, *Virtue's Hero*, p. 314; Trefousse, *Andrew Johnson*, p. 192. LeRoy P. Graf suggests (Johnson, *Papers*, 7:lxii–lxiii) that no such conversation between Johnson and Lincoln took place, yet he admits that the two men met on April 14. At that meeting, Johnson expressed concern about the lenient treatment of the Confederates. Blaine's report is consistent with Johnson's later actions. This account of northern ambivalence about the Appomattox terms contrasts with the description in Turner, *Beware the People Weeping*, pp. 18–24.

10. Welles, *Diary*, 2:280–83 (April 14, 1865); Catton, *Grant Takes Command*, p. 474.

11. *PMJDG*, pp. 155–56, 167 n. 6; Catton, *Grant Takes Command*, p. 474; Hamilton Fish Diary, December 12, 1869, Fish Papers.

12. *PMJDG*, pp. 155–57, 167 n. 7; Bolles, "General Grant," pp. 309–10; J. Grant, *In the Days of My Father*, pp. 37–38.

13. Young, *Around the World*, 2:355; *PMUSG*, 2:509; *PMJDG*, p. 156.

14. *PMUSG*, 2:509.

15. USG to Edward O. C. Ord, April 15, 1865, *PUSG*, 14:391. Johnson later directed Grant to order the arrest of Campbell and Hunter. USG to Henry W. Halleck, May 7, 1865, ibid., 15:8.

16. Catton, *Grant Takes Command*, pp. 478–79; H. Porter, *Campaigning with Grant*, pp. 218–20; Cornish, *Sable Arm*, p. 281; Theodore S. Bowers to Ord, April 16, 1865, USGP, LC.

17. Meade to wife, January 14, 1865, Meade, *Life and Letters*, 2:256; T. H. Williams, *Lincoln and the Radicals*, pp. 360–69.

18. USG to Meade, February 9, 1865, *PUSG*, 13:399; Johnson, "Remarks on the Fall of Richmond," April 3, 1865, Johnson, *Papers*, 7:544–45; T. H. Williams, *Lincoln and the Radicals*, pp. 369–75; Chambrun, *Impressions of Lincoln*, pp. 92, 106, 118.

19. USG to Charles W. Ford, April 17, 1865, and to Silas A. Hudson, April 21, 1865, *PUSG*, 14:405, 429–30; Memphis *Bulletin*, April 21, 1865; Nashville *Dispatch*, April 19, 1865.

20. WTS to USG, April 15, 1865, *PUSG*, 14:418; Browning, *Diary*, 2:22 (April 18, 1865).

21. WTS to USG, April 18, 1865, *PUSG*, 14:419–20; USG to Winfield Scott Hancock, April 19, 1865, ibid., 14:410 and note. To his wife, Sherman stated, "There is a great danger of the Confederate armies breaking up into guerrillas, and that is what I most fear." WTS to Ellen Ewing Sherman, April

18, 1865, Sherman Family Papers.

22. WTS to USG, April 18, 1865, *PUSG*, 14:419–20; Nevins, *Ordeal of the Union*, 8:349–53.

23. WTS to USG, April 12, 1865, *PUSG*, 14:375; USG to Stanton, April 21, 1865, ibid., 14:423.

24. Welles, *Diary*, 2:294–95 (April 21, 1865); H. Porter, *Campaigning with Grant*, pp. 503–4; Thomas and Hyman, *Stanton*, pp. 405–7.

25. Thomas and Hyman, *Stanton*, pp. 405–7; Badeau, *Grant in Peace*, p. 120. The New York *Herald* published reports that Grant had dealings with Jefferson Davis and Joseph Johnston over terms, but there is no evidence whatsoever to substantiate these stories. New York *Herald*, April 14, 29, 1865.

26. USG to JDG, April 21, 1865, *PUSG*, 14:428–29.

27. Hand, "Reminiscences of an Army Surgeon," p. 306; Hitchcock, *Marching with Sherman*, p. 309. One correspondent noted that Grant "looks careworn, and from all appearance the sad bereavement of our country in the assassination of President Lincoln has greatly disturbed the otherwise placid and collected chieftain." New York *Herald*, April 25, 1865.

28. USG to Stanton, April 24, 1865, *PUSG*, 14:431–32; New York *Herald*, April 30, 1865; Catton, *Grant Takes Command*, pp. 486–87.

29. USG to JDG, April 25, 1865, *PUSG*, 14:433; New York *Tribune*, May 3, 1865; USG to JDG, May 9, 1865, *PUSG*, 15:30.

30. Welles, *Diary*, 2:295 (April 22 and 23, 1865).

31. WTS to USG, April 28, 1865, USGP, LC.

32. WTS to Stanton, April 25, 1865, Sherman, *Personal Memoirs*, 2:362; Thomas and Hyman, *Stanton*, p. 411.

33. WTS to USG, May 10, 1865, WTSP; John M. Schofield to WTS, May 5, 1865, *OR*, ser. 1, 47 (pt. 1):39.

34. E. McPherson, *Political History*, pp. 300–4; Sheridan, *Personal Memoirs*, 2:209; Niven, *Gideon Welles*, p. 501.

35. Schofield to USG, May 10, 1865, and USG to Schofield, May 18, 1865, *PUSG*, 15:64–65; Cyrus B. Comstock to Schofield, May 25, 1865, ibid., 15:66; USG to Frederick Steele, May 22, 1865, ibid., 15:87.

36. Cresap, *Appomattox Commander*, pp. 220–21; Ord to USG, April 29, 1865, USGP, LC; George L. Hartsuff to Godfrey Weitzel, May 13, 1865, Berlin et al., *Black Military Experience*, pp. 737–38.

37. Cresap, *Appomattox Commander*, pp. 220–21; Weitzel to USG, May 16, 1865, and endorsement Ord, May 18, 1865, Berlin et al., *Black Military Experience*, p. 738.

38. *National Anti-Slavery Standard*, October 7, 1865. On the subject of black troops on occupation duty, see Simpson, Graf, and Muldowny, *Advice after Appomattox*.

39. Catton, *Grant Takes Command*, p. 489; Romero, *Mexican Lobby*, p. 69; Glatthaar, *Forged in Battle*, p. 219.

40. Catton, *Grant Takes Command*, p. 491. No black troops participated in the review, according to the *National Anti-Slavery Standard*, drawing criticism from some abolitionists. If true, this was probably because the two armies reviewed—Sherman's army and Meade's Army of the Potomac—were composed of white units. The Army of the James and other organizations with black units were on occupation duty. However, Horace Porter reports that black pioneers did march with Sherman's army. *National Anti-Slavery Standard*, June 3, 1865; H. Porter, *Campaigning with Grant*, pp. 510-11.

41. New York *World*, June 8, 1865; Badeau to Wilson, May 27, 1865, James H. Papers; McFeely, *Grant*, pp. 234-35. McFeely fails to mention the resolutions, which misleads the reader as to the result of the meeting.

42. Halleck to USG, April 29, 1865, and Frederick T. Dent to USG, May 2, 1865, USGP, LC; John W. Turner to Benjamin F. Butler, May 7, 1865, Butler, *Private and Official Correspondence*, 5:616.

43. Halleck to USG, May 5, 1865, *PUSG*, 15:7; Freeman, *Lee*, 4:195-96; Meade, *Life and Letters*, 2:278-79.

44. USG to Halleck, May 6, 1865, *PUSG*, 15:11.

45. New York *Times*, April 19, 26, June 4, 17, 1865; Butler to AJ, April 25, 1865, Johnson, *Papers*, 7:234-37.

46. Freeman, *Lee*, 4:202-3; New York *Tribune*, June 5, 1865; New York *World*, June 12, 1865. A list of those indicted, including Lee, Longstreet, Ewell, and others, appears in the New Orleans *Tribune*, June 25, 1865.

47. Badeau, *Grant in Peace*, pp. 25-26; Cresap, *Appomattox Commander*, p. 228.

48. USG endorsement to Stanton, June 16, 1865, forwarding Lee to Grant, June 13, 1865, *PUSG*, 15:149; Badeau to Wilson, June 16, 1865, James H. Wilson Papers; Young, *Around the World*, 2:460. Gideon Welles dismissed stories that Johnson would have executed Lee. Gideon Welles to Montgomery Blair, February 10, 1877, Blair Papers.

49. Browning, *Diary*, 2:32 (June 7, 1865); Badeau, *Grant in Peace*, p. 26; E. McPherson, *Political History*, pp. 299-300; Seipel, *Rebel*, p. 162. See Grant's comments in Young, *Around the World*, 2:460-61. Hans Trefousse mentions that Joseph Fowler, one of Johnson's Tennessee associates, said that Grant's intervention did not save Lee, although he offers no opinion on the matter. But Johnson and his colleagues had ample opportunity to deny Grant's account, which first appeared in print in 1867, and did not. See Trefousse, *Andrew Johnson*, p. 420 n. 36.

50. USG to Robert E. Lee, June 20, 1865, *PUSG*, 15:210-11; James Speed to Lucius Chandler, June 20, 1865, LS, RG 60. In August the press reported that Johnson had directed that nolle prosequi be entered against Lee. *National Anti-Slavery Standard*, August 5, 1865. John S. Wise later recounted a confrontation between Grant and Stanton over the fate of Lee and Wise's father, a former governor of Virginia and a brigadier. Grant never mentioned such a confrontation. New York *Tribune*, July 24, 1885.

51. *PMUSG*, 2:509.

52. USG to Stanton, June 20, 1865, *PUSG*, 15:164–206.

CHAPTER FIVE

1. Philip H. Sheridan to John A. Rawlins, October 7, 1865, USGP, LC; Sheridan to AJ, November 26, 1865, AJP; George H. Thomas to USG, July 1, 1865, USGP, LC. Perman, *Reunion without Compromise*, pp. 132–43, Coffman, *Old Army*, pp. 234–42, and Sefton, *United States Army and Reconstruction*, pp. 25–59, provide an overview of these issues.

2. WTS to John Sherman, September 21 and November 4, 1865, WTSP; Meade quoted in Coffman, *Old Army*, p. 240.

3. Hesseltine, *Ulysses S. Grant*, pp. 56–58; Badeau, *Grant in Peace*, pp. 180–81; Romero, *Mexican Lobby*, p. 65.

4. USG to Sheridan, October 13, 1865, *PUSG*, 15:333–34; Nashville *Republican Banner*, October 5, 7, 1865; Mosby, *Memoirs*, pp. 389–90; *Army and Navy Journal*, October 14, 1865; USG to AJ, November 7, 1865, *PUSG*, 15:401–2; Badeau, *Grant in Peace*, pp. 27–29.

5. USG endorsement to Edwin M. Stanton, November 2, 1865, forwarding Jackson to USG, October 30, 1867, *PUSG*, 15:615–16; Browning, *Diary*, 2:48–49 (November 3, 1865).

6. USG to George G. Meade, November 6, 1865, and Meade to USG, November 8, 1865, *PUSG*, 15:398–400; USG to Stanton, October 20, 1865, ibid., 15:357–58; USG to Thomas, August 21, 1865, ibid., 15:307; for Meade's report on his summer inspection tour, see Simpson, Graf, and Muldowny, *Advice after Appomattox*, pp. 229–37.

7. USG to John Pope, October 14, 1865, *PUSG*, 15:337–38; USG to WTS, October 31, 1865, ibid., 15:377; USG to Thomas, November 4, 1865, ibid., 15:390; regarding the refusal to sell black veterans their rifles, see Rawlins to Sheridan, October 26, 1865, ibid., 16:447; Berlin et al., *Black Military Experience*, pp. 733–35; Cresap, *Appomattox Commander*, pp. 220–22.

8. USG to Stanton, August 28, 1865, *PUSG*, 15:310; Nieman, *To Set the Law in Motion*, p. 13.

9. Chicago *Tribune*, June 14, 1865; *Army and Navy Journal*, October 14, 1865.

10. Richmond *Times*, quoted in the New York *World*, August 14, 1865; New York *Times*, September 11, 1865; Badeau, *Grant in Peace*, p. 257; Adam Badeau to James H. Wilson, July 12, 24, 1865, James H. Wilson Papers; Brooks, *Grant of Appomattox*, pp. 280–81; USG to Henry Heth, November 15, 1865, New York *Times*, January 6, 1866; USG to Lyman Abbott, November 10, 1865, *PUSG*, 15:413–14; Augusta *Constitutionalist*, December 6, 1865. Badeau believed "that the South accepts the situation fairly and fully, and all that Southerners want is to be allowed to come back and be good citizens."

11. See McKitrick, *Andrew Johnson and Reconstruction*, pp. 153–213; Perman, *Reunion without Compromise*, pp. 95–109; Trefousse, *Carl Schurz*, pp. 152–360; Simpson, Graf, and Muldowny, *Advice after Appomattox*, pp. 61–77.

12. Badeau to Elihu B. Washburne, October 20, 1865, Washburne Papers.

13. James Scovel to Thaddeus Stevens, October 9, 1865, Stevens Papers; Washburne to Badeau, October 25, 1865, *PUSG*, 15:403.

14. Badeau to Washburne, November 24, 1865, and Orville Babcock to Washburne, November 24, 1865, Washburne Papers; USG to Washburne, November 9, 1865, *PUSG*, 15:403; Comstock Diary, November 12, 22, 27, 1865, Comstock Papers; New York *Times*, November 26, 28, 1865.

15. Comstock Diary, November 29, 1865, Comstock Papers; USG to JDG, November 28, 29, 1865, *PUSG*, 15:422–24. Later reports, issued after Congress had refused to seat the Southern representatives, noted Grant's approval of such action, undoubtedly because the vast majority of the Southern members-elect could not take the test oath. Springfield, Mass., *Republican*, December 22, 1865. One newspaper noted that Grant did not necessarily include all Southerners in that category. The general-in-chief "is not satisfied with the growth of loyalty at New Orleans," the correspondent wrote, due in part to the rapid revival of pro-secession newspapers. New York *Times*, November 30, 1865.

16. New York *Times*, December 11, 1865; Comstock Diary, November 30, 1865, Comstock Papers.

17. Badeau, *Grant in Peace*, p. 383; Comstock Diary, December 1, 1865, Comstock Papers.

18. Ibid., December 2, 1865; New York *Times*, December 11, 1865; Cyrus B. Comstock to Daniel E. Sickles, December 2, 1865, *PUSG*, 15:428. When Sickles and Aiken visited the latter's plantation, Aiken's former slaves were unwilling to enter into labor contracts with their old owner, due to anticipation of a division and redistribution of lands. The next month, Grant approved the restoration of Aiken's plantation, but, since Congress had yet to act on the status of lands set aside for the freedmen under General Sherman's Special Field Order No. 15, he added: "I would say leave all land, to which Freedmen have obtained possessionery titles, until such settlement is had." Augusta *Constitutionalist*, December 29, 1865; USG to Sickles, January 26, 1866, *PUSG*, 16:33.

19. New York *Times*, December 11, 12, 1865; Comstock Diary, December 2–11, 1865, Comstock Papers; Swint, *Dear Ones at Home*, p. 186. William McFeely points to Grant's failure to visit the Sea Islands as a sign of his alleged apathy toward the freedmen. However, as several accounts make clear, Grant did visit the islands. McFeely, *Grant*, p. 238; see the J. W. Saxton Diaries, December 1, 2, Saxton Family Papers; the New York *Times* report of December 11; and Comstock's diary entry for December 3.

20. *Army and Navy Journal*, December 16, 1865; New York *Herald*, August 2, 1886; USG to JDG, December 4, 1865, *PUSG*, 15:428–29.

21. Trowbridge, *Desolate South*, p. 263; Comstock Diary, December 5, 1865, Comstock Papers; Gordon's comments in *Testimony Taken by the Joint Select Committee*, 6:305; Columbus, Ga., *Sun and Times*, December 12, 1865. Contrary to Gordon's recollection, Grant took his time withdrawing black troops. See USG to Stanton, March 14, 1866, and USG to Thomas, March 28, 1866, *PUSG*, 16:115, 139–40.

22. Atlanta *Journal*, July 1, 1934, clipping in Ulysses S. Grant III Papers; Nashville *Republican Banner*, December 14, 1865; J. H. Wilson, *Under the Old Flag*, 2:37.

23. Columbus, Ga., *Sun and Times*, December 24, 1865; Comstock Diary, December 6–11, 1865, Comstock Papers; Garland, *Grant*, pp. 344–45.

24. Welles, *Diary*, 2:396–97 (December 15, 1865).

25. Ibid., 2:397–98 (December 16, 1865).

26. Johnson, Message to Congress, December 18, 1865, E. McPherson, *Political History*, pp. 66–67.

27. USG to AJ, December 18, 1865, Simpson, Graf, and Muldowny, *Advice after Appomattox*, pp. 212–14. Grant's recommendation about black soldiers was not illustrative of his sentiments about their ability as combat troops. *Army and Navy Journal*, March 31, 1866.

28. USG to AJ, December 18, 1865, Simpson, Graf, and Muldowny, *Advice after Appomattox*, pp. 212–14.

29. Ibid. See note 8.

30. Ibid. Grant had received several reports about discipline problems with black troops. Theodore S. Bowers to Charles R. Woods, December 13, 1865, RG 393, Department of Alabama, LR, 1865–66.

31. Pierce, *Memoir and Letters of Charles Sumner*, 4:272; Welles, *Diary*, 2:400 (December 20, 1865).

32. Clemenceau, *American Reconstruction*, pp. 61–62; WTS to USG, December 22, 1865, *PUSG*, 15:635; *Army and Navy Journal*, December 23, 1865.

33. Nashville *Republican Banner*, December 20, 1865; New York *Times*, December 22, 1865; Springfield, Mass., *Republican*, December 20, 1865; Mobile *Register*, December 27, 1865; Milledgeville *Federal Union*, January 2, 1866; New York *World*, December 21, 1865.

34. Francis W. Bird to Benjamin F. Butler, December 26, 1865, Butler Papers; George F. Granger to Stevens, January 11, 1866, and John L. Ketcham to Stevens, December 24, 1865, Stevens Papers; New York *Tribune*, December 23, 1865; Chicago *Republican* quoted in Memphis *Daily Appeal*, January 4, 1866.

35. Springfield, Mass., *Republican*, December 23, 1865; Boston *Advertiser*, December 21, 1865.

36. New York *World*, December 18, 1865; Chicago *Tribune*, December 14, 1865.

37. USG to Thomas et al., December 25, 1865, *PUSG*, 16:69–70.

38. Sefton, *United States Army and Reconstruction*, pp. 66–68.

39. Carl Schurz to wife, January 12, 1866, Schafer, *Intimate Letters of Schurz*, p. 356; Alfred H. Terry to USG, January 1, 1866, USGP, LC; Sickles to USG, January 6, 1866, USGP, LC; Sefton, *United States Army and Reconstruction*, p. 57; USG endorsement, January 9, 1866, on Robert Patton to George H. Thomas, December 30, 1865, *PUSG*, 16:54; New York *Tribune*, January 15, 1866. Two years later, Schurz wrote his wife that Grant said, "I traveled as the general-in-chief and people who came to see me tried to appear to the best advantage. But I have since come to the conclusion that you were right and I was wrong." Schurz to wife, December 20, 1868, Schurz, *Intimate Letters*, p. 457.

40. General Orders No. 3, January 12, 1866, *PUSG* 16:7-8; Barnes, *History of the Thirty-ninth Congress*, pp. 119-23. In February Grant pushed for extending General Orders No. 3 to include Kentucky, Missouri, and other border states. See *PUSG*, 16:82-83.

41. Nieman, *To Set the Law in Motion*, pp. 78-79, 91; Wharton, *Negro in Mississippi*, pp. 90-91; Sefton, *United States Army and Reconstruction*, pp. 71-72.

42. Comstock Diary, January 15, 30-31, and February 1-10, 1866, Comstock Papers.

43. Comstock Diary, January 30, 31, February 2, 6, 7, 10, 1866, ibid.; Comstock to Rawlins, February 1, 3, 4, 1866, AJP; Ely S. Parker to Theodore S. Bowers, January 27, 1866, *PUSG*, 16:458-59. "Many Colored Citizens" to USG, January 31, 1866, *PUSG*, 16:445-46. Comstock's letters were forwarded by Stanton to Johnson on February 15.

44. USG to AJ, February 9, 1866, *PUSG*, 16:52-53; USG to Thomas, March 28, 1866, ibid., 16:139-40.

45. Richmond *Dispatch*, February 17, 1866, quoting the Philadelphia *Ledger*; Grant endorsement on H. Rives Pollard to AJ, February 14, 1866, reprinted in Richardson, *A Personal History*, p. 521.

46. Pollard to AJ, February 17, 1866, in Richmond *Dispatch*, February 21, 1866; Richmond *Dispatch*, February 23, 1866, quoting Cincinnati *Commercial*; Bowers to Terry, February 19, 1866, and Bowers to Southern commanders, February 17, 1866, *PUSG*, 16:71-72. Pollard continued his attacks on the military, and at one point Terry prepared charges. See "Charges & Specifications Against H. Rives Pollard," March 22, 1866, RG 107, LR, President and Executive Branches; Terry to Rawlins, March 19, 1866, and Badeau to Terry, March 23, 1866, *PUSG*, 16:72-73. At the same time, Grant did not want to promote chaos, as when he approved Terry's advice to Richmond blacks to restrain their celebration of the first anniversary of the city's fall on April 3. USG to Terry, March 29, 1866, *PUSG*, 16:142.

47. Richmond *Dispatch*, February 21, 1866; Richmond *Dispatch*, February 23, 1866, quoting Cincinnati *Commercial*; USG to AJ, February 17, 1866, *PUSG*, 16:69.

48. Richmond *Dispatch*, February 21, 23, 1866; USG to Terry, March 29,

1866, *PUSG*, 16:142; Rachleff, *Black Labor in the South*, pp. 39–40; J. G. Wilson, *Life and Public Services*, pp. 97–98; USG to AJ, March 30, 1866, *PUSG*, 16:143.

49. E. McPherson, *Political History*, pp. 15–17. Gideon Welles noted on April 3 that Johnson's proclamation was a total surprise. "A sudden determination seems to have influenced the president. He did not state his reasons, but it is obvious that the Radicals are taken by surprise and view it as check-mating some of their legislation." Welles, *Diary*, 2:473–74 (April 3, 1866). On the day after Johnson issued his proclamation, the Court issued its ruling, stating its judgment that the military commission in question had been without jurisdiction without revealing its reasoning. Fairman, *Reconstruction and Reunion*, 1:143–44.

50. Welles, *Diary*, 2:477–78 (April 6, 1866—revised version); Stephens, *Recollections*, p. 545; Hayes, *Diary and Letters*, 3:22.

51. John Sherman to WTS, March [?], 1866, Thorndike, *Sherman Letters*, p. 269; Taylor, *Destruction and Reconstruction*, pp. 242–43; Mantell, *Johnson, Grant, and the Politics of Reconstruction*, p. 28.

CHAPTER SIX

1. Alfred H. Terry to John A. Rawlins, April 3, 1866; George H. Thomas to USG, April 9, 1866; Gen. John W. Turner to Rawlins, April 7, 1866; USG to Turner, April 9, 1866; and USG to Thomas, April 10, 1866, all in *PUSG*, 16:149–50; E. McPherson, *Political History*, p. 17. Thomas and Hyman (*Stanton*, p. 473) incorrectly assert that Grant and Stanton issued secret orders in direct contradiction of Johnson's proclamation. That Grant wanted to restrict the army's role in certain areas is evident in his advice that the courts would determine the eligibility of former Confederates to civil office. Ely S. Parker to Gen. Thomas Ruger, April 5, 1866, USGP, LC.

2. E. McPherson, *Political History*, p. 17; Edward D. Townsend to Thomas J. Wood, May 4, 1866, cited in Nieman, *To Set the Law in Motion*, p. 118. Penelope K. Majeske's assertion that the proclamation had minimal impact on military authority is vitiated by her selective quotation of the order. The "acts of Congress" mentioned in her quote are those "above cited," namely Section Sixteen of the Second Confiscation Act and Sections One and Two of the 1863 Habeas Corpus Act—not the legislation passed in early 1866. See Majeske, "Johnson, Stanton, and Grant," p. 345 n. 11.

3. Fairman, *Reconstruction and Reunion*, 1:148–49.

4. Rable, *But There Was No Peace*, pp. 33–39.

5. George Stoneman to USG, May 12, 1866, *PUSG*, 16:235–36; USG to Edwin M. Stanton, July 7, 1866, ibid., 16:233–34.

6. USG to Turner, April 27, 1866, ibid., 16:498; USG to Stanton, May 16, 1866, ibid., 16:199–201, 197 (two letters of the same date).

7. New York *Times*, May 24, 1866.

8. Mrs. L. E. Potts to AJ, June 28, 1866, and subsequent endorsements, Sheridan Papers. The troops finally arrived in mid-July, according to Horatio G. Wright's endorsement of July 21.

9. Oliver O. Howard to USG, July 3, 1866, *PUSG*, 16:228–29; USG to Thomas, July 6, 1866, ibid., 16:230–31; E. McPherson, *Political History*, p. 124.

10. USG to Stanton, July 7, 1866, *PUSG*, 16:233–34; *Opinions of the Attorneys General*, pp. 531–32; Thomas to USG, August 15, 1866, and USG to Thomas, August 18, 1866, *PUSG*, 16:231–32. See also Townsend to USG, July 7, 1866, and Townsend to Thomas, July 7, 1866, *PUSG*, 16:231. On the same day that he issued General Orders No. 44, Grant sent several companies of cavalry to north Mississippi "to suppress outrages" and prepared to arrest the Memphis rioters. USG to Thomas, July 6, 1866, *PUSG*, 16:230–31. Commenting on this incident, James E. Sefton argues that Grant "must have either been exceptionally weak-willed or else doubtful of the legality of No. 44 in the face of Johnson's April proclamation." Sefton, *United States Army and Reconstruction*, p. 84. It is more likely that Grant wished to test administration reaction to the order, for he did not revoke it and adhered to Speed's ruling only as it applied to the Memphis riot. In addition, Grant's concern was not over Johnson's April proclamation but with General Orders No. 26, which had a far more serious impact on the scope of military authority. He hoped his subordinates would act on their own to enforce General Orders No. 44, rather than consulting headquarters. Unfortunately for Grant, George H. Thomas was not in the habit of taking the initiative: Grant was often embarrassed by his requests for advice, which served only to alert Johnson to a delicate situation. Moreover, by August, with Tennessee back in the Union, Grant may have felt that his directive no longer applied to the state.

11. Terry to George G. Meade, August 5, 1866; Meade to Terry, August 6, 1866; and Meade to USG, August 6, 1866, all in RG 108, TR and USGP, LC; John G. Foster to George Lee, July 26, 1866, Sheridan Papers; General Orders No. 46 (July 13, 1866), in *National Anti-Slavery Standard*, July 21, 1866; New York *Tribune*, July 18, 1866; Thomas endorsement to USG, August 3, 1866, on Maj. William A. Wainwright to Gen. James L. Donaldson, July 26, 1866, *PUSG*, 16:536.

12. On the Fourteenth Amendment, see James, *Framing of the Fourteenth Amendment*, and Nelson, *Fourteenth Amendment*.

13. Thomas to USG, July 14, 1866, Stanton to USG, July 17, 1866, and USG to Thomas, July 18, 1866, *PUSG*, 16:243 (Grant's headquarters received Thomas's telegram at 4:00 P.M. on July 15); Welles, *Diary*, 2:554–55, 557 (July 17, 19, 1866). Later, Johnson suspected that Thomas was at fault and wanted Grant to remove Thomas's headquarters from Nashville to Louisville. Browning, *Diary*, 2:94 (September 20, 1866).

14. The text of the bill is in E. McPherson, *Political History*, pp. 149–51; Johnson's veto is to be found in ibid., pp. 147–49. The president was ambiguous over whether the war had ended. At one point, he spoke of this "time of peace"; at another, he declared that the "war has substantially ceased"; later, he concluded that "the war has been brought to a close." He asserted that the courts "are now in full practical operation." Yet Johnson never quite brought himself to declare formally that hostilities were at an end, and the modifying terms "substantially" and "practical" suggest some caution. Although Johnson noted in the same document that the March 3, 1865, bill stated that the Bureau "is to terminate within one year of the close of hostilities and the declaration of peace," he declined to say whether this point had been reached and formally recognized. The April proclamation declared that the "insurrection" was "at an end" everywhere but in Texas; but in his August proclamation, which concerned Texas, he felt it necessary in a separate paragraph to "proclaim that the said insurrection is at an end, and that peace, order, tranquility, and civil authority now exist" throughout the nation. Ibid., pp. 16–17, 196.

15. Badeau, *Grant in Peace*, p. 37; Parker, *Life and Public Services of Justin Smith Morrill*, p. 230; Hesseltine, *Ulysses S. Grant, Politician*, p. 67; Garland, *Ulysses S. Grant*, p. 356–57. Sheridan was not exactly pleased with the army appropriations bill, with its preference for less expensive infantry over more expensive cavalry. The bill "did not give a force sufficient for the wants of a country so extensive as ours, and which will have many elements of discord for a long time." Philip H. Sheridan to Henry Wilson, June 29, 1866, Henry Wilson Papers.

16. James H. Wilson to Adam Badeau, April 6, and July 18, 1866, James H. Wilson Papers; James H. Wilson to Elihu B. Washburne, July 5, 1866, and Badeau to Washburne, July 3, 9, 1866, Washburne Papers.

17. James, *Ratification of the Fourteenth Amendment*, p. 84; Milledgeville *Federal Union*, May 29, 1866. That Brown was willing to shade the truth a bit when circumstances required it is suggested by his report that Grant said to Lee at Appomattox, "You are not conquered, but overpowered by superior numbers and resources"—an interpretation of Northern victory that Grant was always quick to reject.

18. New York *Independent*, July 19, 1866; Chicago *Tribune*, September 2, 1866; A. P. Granger to Washburne, June 3, 1866, Washburne Papers.

19. New York *Times*, August 3, 1866; Fields, *Slavery and Freedom on the Middle Ground*, p. 152.

20. Dawson, *Army Generals and Reconstruction*, pp. 36–38.

21. Sheridan to USG, August 1, 2, 3, 1866, *PUSG*, 16:288–90.

22. Stanton to USG and USG to Sheridan, August 3, 1866, ibid., 16:289; Welles, *Diary*, 2:570 (August 3, 1866) and 572 (August 7, 1866); Sheridan to Rawlins, August 9, 1866, *PUSG*, 16:291; USG to Sheridan, August 12, 1866, *PUSG*, 16:292. Whether Grant knew that either Johnson or his private sec-

retary was responsible for the editing is unknown. See the copy of the tele-gram in AJP as well as the discussion in McKitrick, *Andrew Johnson and Recon-struction*, pp. 426-27 and note.

23. E. McPherson, *Political History*, pp. 194-96.

24. Sefton, *United States Army and Reconstruction*, p. 79; Foster to George L. Hartsuff, September 18, 20, 1866, *PUSG*, 16:390-91; Sheridan to USG (en-dorsement), October 6, 1866, *PUSG*, 16:391; George K. Leet to Sheridan, October 17, November 1, 1866, USGP, LC. The Cincinnati *Enquirer* reported in October that General Orders No. 44 was still being enforced. Cincinnati *Enquirer*, October 14, 1866.

25. Shofner, "Florida," pp. 18-19; Shofner, "Andrew Johnson and the Fernandina Unionists," pp. 211-23. Actually, Grant retreated from his pre-vious position on August 18, two days before the proclamation, when he al-lowed state courts to hear disputes arising out of the tax sales. USG to Sheri-dan, August 18, 1866, *PUSG*, 15:410.

26. Welles, *Diary*, 2:581 (August 17, 1866).

27. McFeely, *Grant*, pp. 249-50; newspaper accounts in Johnson Scrap-books, 1:155, AJP; New York *Times*, August 19, 20, 1866; Badeau, *Grant in Peace*, p. 38; New York *Independent*, August 30, 1866; Welles, *Diary*, 2:582 (August 18, 1866); New York *Herald*, August 19, 1866; Beale, *Critical Year*, p. 323; Chicago *Tribune*, September 14, 1866. Benjamin F. Butler com-mented, "If it is true that the President trapped Gen. Grant into an apparent endorsement of the Philadelphia Convention by having him present to re-ceive its delegates then it is equally true that Grant is an unfit man to be depended upon in a crisis lest he should [be] trapped again." Benjamin F. Butler to Horace Greeley, September 20, 1866, Butler Papers.

28. Badeau, *Grant in Peace*, pp. 38-39; Hesseltine, *Ulysses S. Grant, Politi-cian*, p. 74; Welles, *Diary*, 2:584 (August 23, 1866). Horace Porter later as-serted that "General Grant, at first regarding it merely as an invitation, en-deavored to decline it as politely as possible, but it was put in the form of an order, and he had to obey." Chicago *Inter-Ocean*, October 24, 1885.

29. Cadwallader, "Four Years with Grant," p. 804, Cadwallader Papers; Chicago *Tribune*, September 8, 14, 1866; Welles, *Diary*, 2:591-92 (September 17, 1866); McFeely, *Grant*, pp. 250-51; Chicago *Inter-Ocean*, October 24, 1885.

30. Welles, *Diary*, 2:593 (September 17, 1866); New York *Tribune*, Septem-ber 3, 1866; Cadwallader, "Four Years with Grant," pp. 786-87, Cadwallader Papers; Rawlins to wife, September 1, 1866, J. H. Wilson, *Life of John A. Rawlins*, pp. 335-36.

31. Welles, *Diary*, 2:593 (September 17, 1866); Niven, *Gideon Welles*, p. 552; Browning, *Diary*, 2:115 (December 3, 1866); USG to JDG, August 31 and September 4, 1866, *PUSG*, 16:306-7; Cadwallader, "Four Years with Grant," pp. 786-87, Cadwallader Papers; New York *Tribune*, September 4-6, 1866; Ammen, *Old Navy and the New*, p. 427. Benjamin C. Truman, a news-

paper correspondent and Johnson associate, denied that Grant was drunk. Truman, "Anecdotes of Andrew Johnson," p. 438. The New York *Herald*, September 4, 1866, noted that Seward reported Grant sick at Buffalo, and Johnson reported to the crowd at Cleveland that Grant was "extremely ill." See also note 38. Whether this was one of Grant's famed migraine headaches, a bout with the bottle, or some combination of the two with the latter employed as medication is hard to determine.

32. Garland, *Ulysses S. Grant*, p. 355; Richardson, *A Personal History*, pp. 528–30; *Army and Navy Journal*, September 22, 1866; New York *Times*, September 13, 1866; Chicago *Tribune*, September 14, 1866.

33. Romero, *Mexican Lobby*, pp. 138–44; Chicago *Inter-Ocean*, October 24, 1885; Beale, *Critical Year*, p. 323; Chicago *Tribune*, September 14, 1866.

34. Rawlins to wife, August 31, 1866, J. H. Wilson, *Life of John A. Rawlins*, p. 334; Johnson Scrapbooks, 1:155, AJP.

35. James H. Wilson to Orville E. Babcock, September 10, 1866, Babcock Papers; Badeau to L. Edwin Dudley, September 18, 1867, *PUSG*, 16:547; USG to William S. Hillyer, September 19, 1866, *PUSG*, 16:310; New York *Times*, September 29, 1866.

36. Ammen, *Old Navy and the New*, pp. 427–28; Richardson, *A Personal History*, pp. 528–31; USG to JDG, September 9, 1866, *PUSG*, 16:308; Cadwallader, "Four Years with Grant," p. 788, Cadwallader Papers; New York *Herald*, September 7, 1866.

37. James H. Wilson to Washburne, October 13, 1866, Washburne Papers; James H. Wilson to Babcock, September 10, 1866, Babcock Papers.

38. John Defrees to Washburne, August 23, 1866, and L. H. Funk to Washburne, September 1, 1866, Washburne Papers; Flower, *Edwin McMasters Stanton*, pp. 310–11; see also H. Price to Washburne, August 30, 1866, and David Sankey to Washburne, September 3, 1866, Washburne Papers. One writer informed Washburne, "It is now getting to be understood that Seward got the General tight once or twice on the way once at Buffalo Johnson told the Gen'l in the presence of 5 or 6 persons if he would openly take the right ground he, Johnson, would throw the whole influence of the Govt for his election to the Presidency." District Attorney Bass to Washburne, September 9, 1866, Washburne Papers.

39. Flower, *Edwin McMasters Stanton*, pp. 310–11; Bartlett, *Wendell Phillips*, p. 304; W. Jones to Butler, September 23, 1866, Butler Papers.

40. Butler to Greeley, September 20, 1866, Butler Papers.

41. Welles, *Diary*, 2:615–16 (October 11, 1866); Baltimore *American and Commercial Advertiser*, October 10, 11, 1866; Badeau, *Grant in Peace*, p. 51; U. S. Grant III, *Ulysses S. Grant*, pp. 279, 292. A careful reading of Grant's testimony to the House Judiciary Committee investigating impeachment in 1867 confirms this story, although many contemporaries thought otherwise. In 1885 reports appeared of another conversation between the president and the general. Johnson purportedly said, "General, I am very anxious to know,

in case there should be an open rupture between myself and Congress, with which side you will be found." Grant replied, "That will depend upon which is the revolutionary party." E. McPherson, *Political History*, p. 303; Burr, *Life and Deeds of Grant*, p. 855.

42. Badeau, *Grant in Peace*, pp. 51–52; USG to Sheridan, October 12, 1866, *PUSG*, 16:330–31; USG to Alexander B. Dyer, September 22, 1866, *PUSG*, 16:331–32; USG to Cyrus B. Comstock, September 24, 1866, *PUSG*, 16:314. Comstock found nothing to substantiate the rumors, and Grant informed Johnson that "no cause for apprehension exists, at least not for the present." Comstock to USG and USG to AJ, October 12, 1866, *PUSG*, 16:314–15. For talk alluding to the possibility of two governments, consult Gideon Welles's diary for April 16, 1866; both Montgomery Blair and Tennessee congressman Horace Maynard had discussed the possibility. Welles, *Diary*, 2:484 (April 16, 1866).

43. Myers, *Self-Reconstruction of Maryland*, p. 69; Andrew Aitken to AJ, October 20, 1866, AJP.

44. Thomas and Hyman, *Stanton*, p. 504; Welles, *Diary*, 2:606–7 (October 1, 1866).

45. Badeau, *Grant in Peace*, p. 195. Schoonover, *Dollars over Dominion* pp. 220–35, contains a very interesting discussion of the Mexican mission proposal.

46. Welles, *Diary*, 2:606 (October 1, 1866); Badeau, *Grant in Peace*, pp. 40–41; Moore Diary Typescript, pp. 13–14, AJP; Moore, "Notes," p. 101.

47. Baltimore *American and Commercial Advertiser*, October 18, 1866; USG to WTS, October 18, 1866, *PUSG*, 16:337–38.

48. WTS to John Sherman, October 20, 1866, and John Sherman to WTS, October 26, 1866, Thorndike, *Sherman Letters*, pp. 277–78; WTS to USG, October 20, 22, 1866, *PUSG*, 16:338–39; WTS to Ellen Ewing Sherman, October 26, 1866, Sherman Family Papers. John A. Rawlins was pleased by this development, because he was afraid that his boss was falling prey to Radicalism. See Browning, *Diary*, 2:104 (October 25, 1866).

49. Badeau, *Grant in Peace*, pp. 53–54; Moore, "Notes," pp. 100–101; Browning, *Diary*, 2:102 (October 23, 1866).

50. Badeau, *Grant in Peace*, p. 54; Comstock Diary, October 23, 1866, Comstock Papers; USG to Washburne, October 23, 1866, *PUSG*, 16:349; Stanton to William Pitt Fessenden, October 25, 1866, quoted in McFeely, *Grant*, p. 253.

51. Edward R. S. Canby to USG, October 23, 1866, and USG to AJ, October 24, 1866, *PUSG*, 16:350–54.

52. Baltimore *American and Commercial Advertiser*, October 17, 18, 23, 1866; Baltimore *Sun*, November 1, 2, 3, 1866; AJ to Stanton, October 25, 27, November 1, 2, 1866, AJP. For Missouri, see Parrish, *Missouri under Radical Rule*, pp. 91–96, and Frank Blair to Montgomery Blair, December 21, 1866, Blair-Lee Papers.

53. Sherman, *Personal Memoirs*, 2:415; USG to Stanton, October 27, 1866, *PUSG*, 16:357–58. Unlike other historians, Thomas Schoonover (*Dollars over Dominion*, pp. 220–35) does not believe that the plan to have Grant accompany Campbell was intended simply to get the commanding general out of Washington. However, Schoonover goes too far when he asserts that Mexican policy, not Reconstruction, precipitated the break between Johnson and Grant and that the Campbell mission was unrelated to the growing Grant-Johnson dispute over Reconstruction politics. This was a case where Johnson could kill several birds with one stone. Grant's change of heart regarding the mission suggests that he made the connection between domestic and foreign policy. That Grant would have supported such a mission, could it have been detached from domestic politics, is suggested by his comments in Romero, *Mexican Lobby*, pp. 144–47.

54. Comstock Diary, October 24, 31, 1866, Comstock Papers; WTS to John Sherman, October 31, 1866, Thorndike, *Sherman Letters*, 280–81; Sherman, *Personal Memoirs*, 2:414–15. Johnson's private secretary traced Grant's resistance to the Mexican mission to his fear that Sherman would take over the War Department, an explanation Sherman discounted. Moore, "Notes," p. 101.

55. Browning, *Diary*, 2:103–4 (October 25, 1866); Baltimore *American and Commercial Advertiser*, November 2, 1866.

56. Comstock Diary, November 1, 1866, Comstock Papers (He also noted, "The Union party of course have all our b[est] wishes."); Thomas Swann to AJ, November 2, 1866, AJP. Johnson replied: "The Constitution and the law must be observed. Riot and insurrection, if possible, must be prevented, and peace and order preserved." AJ to Swann, November 2, 1866, AJP.

57. Comstock Diary, November 2, 1866, Comstock Papers; Samuel Harris to Zachariah Chandler, November 5, 1866, Chandler Papers; AJ to Stanton, November 2, 1866, AJP (see also AJ to Stanton, November 1, 1866, AJP); Browning, *Diary*, 2:106 (November 2, 1866).

58. Baltimore *Sun*, November 5, 6, 1866; Baltimore *American and Commercial Advertiser*, November 6, 1866; E. McPherson, *Political History*, p. 306; USG to Canby, November 2, 1866, *PUSG*, 16:362–63; T. M. Cook to AJ, November 4, 1866, AJP.

59. Baltimore *Sun*, November 6, 1866; McFeely, *Grant*, p. 256; Harris to Chandler, November 5, 1866, Chandler Papers.

60. AJ to Swann, November 6, 1866, AJP (Johnson's telegram, celebrating "so glorious a result," made it clear that he was no disinterested spectator concerned only with preventing "riot and bloodshed" in Baltimore); Baltimore *American and Commercial Advertiser*, November 4, 1866.

61. New York *Independent*, October 18, 1866; Mantell, *Johnson, Grant, and the Politics of Reconstruction*, pp. 29–30.

CHAPTER SEVEN

1. Strong, *Diary*, 4:123 (January 23, 1867); Mantell, *Johnson, Grant, and the Politics of Reconstruction*, pp. 30−31.

2. USG to AJ, November 9, 1866, *PUSG*, 16:376; USG to Edwin M. Stanton, November 22, 1866, ibid., 16:389−90. A letter from Florida carpetbagger Daniel Richards confirms the uncertain status of General Order No. 44. "I see there is some doubt about Gen Grant's order No 44 being revoked," he wrote Washburne, "and by the whining tone of Governor Walkers Message I think he is of the opinion that it may be enforced in Florida yet." November 23, 1866, Washburne Papers.

3. Raum, *Existing Conflict*, p. 223; USG to Stanton, November 21, 1866, *PUSG*, 16:387; Ammen, *Old Navy and the New*, pp. 533−34.

4. USG to Richard Taylor, November 25, 1866, *PUSG*, 16:394−95; Richardson, *A Personal History*, pp. 534−35.

5. USG to Taylor, November 25, 1866, *PUSG*, 16:394−95; Richardson, *A Personal History*, p. 535; USG to Stanton, November 21, 1866, *PUSG*, 16:387.

6. Elias Baxter to John Sherman, January 3, 1867, John Sherman Papers; New York *Tribune*, January 8, 1867; Welles, *Diary*, 3:8 (January 5, 1867). McFeely, *Grant*, p. 258, omits Grant's advocacy of black suffrage. Other papers soon reported a somewhat different version of Grant's advice. On January 14, the New York *Times* reprinted a column from the Cincinnati *Gazette* of January 11. Grant, according to this report, "declined to express any opinion as to [the amendment's] justice, constitutionality, or expediency." He added that he wanted Congress to guarantee readmission upon ratification, saying that if Republicans "did not take some such step, they could not expect the Southern people to take a step which might be preliminary to others that would lead them they know not where." But the essential part of the *Gazette* report had to do with black suffrage. Grant was quoted as stating that it "was a question that should be left wholly and entirely with the people of the several States," and that he would vote against black suffrage in Illinois. "But he said, smiling, if he were in one of the Southern states, he believed he would vote for it, for he was satisfied that he could march the negroes up to the polls and vote them as he pleased, and would thus be gaining instead of losing political power." Reports such as these caused some second thoughts. The *Independent's* Washington correspondent's report, published ten days later, stated: "Gen. Grant favors the adoption of the Constitutional Amendment; but, since my last letter, I have heard that which convinces me that he is not exactly right on the great question of equal rights. I fear that he is opposed to colored suffrage, except on conditions such as he would not impose upon white men." Such reports not only run counter to reports of Grant's private conversations at the time but lose credibility when one recalls that the New York *Tribune* was run by Horace Greeley, who favored Chase over Grant for the next presidential race. Surely a *Tribune* reporter would have picked up

such comments and publicized them instead of filing the report that appeared on January 8. It is also likely that McCulloch would have mentioned such a statement to Welles. New York *Times*, January 14, 1867; New York *Independent*, January 24, 1867.

7. Badeau, *Grant in Peace*, p. 44.

8. USG to Philip H. Sheridan, November 15, 1866, and Sheridan to USG, November 23, 1866, *PUSG*, 16:381–82; USG to Edward O. C. Ord, December 6, 1866, Porter Papers; Cresap, *Appomattox Commander*, p. 246.

9. Cramer, *Ulysses S. Grant*, pp. 65–66; Richardson, *A Personal History*, p. 535.

10. USG to Stanton, November 21, 22, 1866, USGP, LC; Fairman, *Reconstruction and Reunion*, 1:208–10. What exactly was at stake in *Milligan* is still a topic of debate among historians. In his closing argument, David Dudley Field, counsel for Milligan, explicitly excluded the question of "military interference" in the South from the case at hand (Fairman, *Reconstruction and Reunion*, 1:206). Justice Davis told his father-in-law in February 1867, "Not a word [was] said in the opinion about reconstruction & the power [of establishing military commissions] is conceded in the insurrectionary states" (Ibid., p. 232). Stanley Kutler (*Judicial Power*, p. 67) cites this letter as proof that the Reconstruction Acts were not unconstitutional under *Milligan*. Furthermore, as Kutler and others have pointed out, *Milligan* referred to the executive's use of martial law, not to the exercise of legislative power, although Davis had added in a "totally unnecessary bit of dicta" that Congress also lacked the power to establish military courts in peacetime (*Judicial Power*, pp. 68, 93). Penelope K. Majeske takes issue with Kutler (while overlooking Fairman), arguing that his point is "meaningless" since Congress had no clearly defined policy in December 1866. In support of this, she cites Kutler's own admission that at that time "there was, as yet, no definite, agreed-upon Republican program for reconstruction and certainly no general intention to institute military commissions and control in the South" (*Judicial Power*, p. 94). See her "Johnson, Stanton, and Grant," pp. 346–47 n. 16. Several points should be kept in mind. First, Davis's comment is taken from private correspondence, so one may assume that it did not circulate widely, although one may also speculate that its import was transmitted to Lyman Trumbull and others: see Kutler, *Judicial Power*, p. 69. Second, although the April preliminary decision may have occasioned little public comment, it—taken in conjunction with Johnson's proclamation and *In re Egan*, decided in May 1866—did concern Stanton, Grant, and others, for military commissions and martial law were already, contrary to Kutler's inference, part of existing policy under General Orders No. 3 and the Freedmen's Bureau Bill of March 3, 1865. On this point, see McFeely, "Accomplices to Failure." Third, *Milligan* preceded consideration of the legislation that in time would become known as the Military Reconstruction Acts, so it is hard to judge how the decision could rule on the constitutionality of nonexistent legislation. Davis's comment came on Febru-

ary 24, 1867, four days after the First Military Reconstruction Act had passed both houses of Congress and had been sent on to Johnson for his signature. One supposes that legislators framed legislation with the decision in mind. Finally, President Johnson's action in the Watson case, discussed below, coming as it did within a week of the publication of the Court's full decision, justified Grant, Stanton, and Republican supporters of Reconstruction in their fear of the potential for mischief in the decision.

11. Nieman, *To Set the Law in Motion*, p. 144; Kaczorowski, *Politics of Judicial Interpretation*, pp. 42–43, 48 n. 32–33; Fairman, *Reconstruction and Reunion*, 1 : 214–15.

12. Fairman, *Reconstruction and Reunion*, 1 : 222; Nieman, *To Set the Law in Motion*, p. 146. Johnson submitted a copy of General Orders No. 44 in his response to the Senate's demand for information on violations of the Civil Rights Act of 1866.

13. Latham, *Black and White*, p. 65. Two days later, Thaddeus Stevens repeated the same story. Barnes, *History of the Thirty-ninth Congress*, p. 504.

14. Sheridan to USG, January 25, 1867, Sheridan Papers; USG to Stanton, endorsement, January 29, 1867, RG 107, LR.

15. USG to Oliver O. Howard, January 18, 1867, Badeau, *Grant in Peace*, p. 59; USG to Stanton, February 8, 1867, Stanton Papers; Welles, *Diary*, 3 : 42 (February 15, 1867), 46 (February 16, 1867).

16. Browning, *Diary*, 2 : 122 (January 4, 1867); Welles, *Diary*, 3 : 5 (January 4, 1867); New York *Independent*, January 17, 1867; New York *Times*, August 4, 1867.

17. Welles, *Diary*, 3 : 15 (January 10, 1867); Browning, *Diary*, 2 : 115 (December 3, 1866).

18. USG to WTS, January 13, 1867, Lewis-Catton Research Notes.

19. WTS to Grenville M. Dodge, January 22, 1867, Dodge, *Personal Recollections*, pp. 197–98; Comstock Diary, February 14, 1867, Comstock Papers.

20. J. R. Grant, *In the Days of My Father*, p. 49; Latham, *Black and White*, p. 63.

21. Browning, *Diary*, 2 : 126 (January 26, 1867); Boutwell, *Reminiscences of Sixty Years*, 2 : 86; Comstock Diary, January 24, 1867, Comstock Papers; Rutherford B. Hayes to Sardis Birchard, February 7, 1867, Hayes, *Diary and Letters*, 3 : 41.

22. Richardson, *A Personal History*, p. 535; Coolidge, *Ulysses S. Grant*, p. 249; New York *Independent*, February 14, March 7, 1867.

23. Boutwell, *Reminiscences of Sixty Years*, 2 : 107; Comstock Diary, January 23, 1867, Comstock Papers; USG to Stanton, January 29, 1866, USGP, LC.

24. Majeske, "Johnson, Stanton, and Grant," pp. 348–49; E. McPherson, *Political History*, p. 178. Majeske's argument—that Section Two of the Army Appropriations Act was meant to restrict Stanton—overlooks the fact that it was Stanton who introduced the idea. Perhaps Stanton was concerned that Johnson might replace him with a secretary more compliant with his wishes

and thus defined the relationship not only of the president but also of the secretary of war in the act. Of course, as worded, the act did restrict Stanton as well, but that was a necessary consequence of such legislation.

25. E. McPherson, *Political History*, pp. 191–92.

26. Ibid., pp. 176–77, 185–86.

27. Comstock Diary, March 1, 1867, Comstock Papers.

28. E. McPherson, *Political History*, p. 178.

29. USG to Elihu B. Washburne, March 4, 1867, USGP, ISHS; WTS to USG, March 11, 1867, USGP, LC. McFeely, in *Grant*, p. 259, incorrectly states that Grant was designated to make these appointments.

30. Welles, *Diary*, 3:60 (March 6, 1867), 62 (March 8, 1867), 65 (March 13, 1867). See also Browning, *Diary*, 2:135 (March 9, 1867); Sefton, *United States Army and Reconstruction*, pp. 113–15.

31. E. McPherson, *Political History*, pp. 192–94.

32. USG to Charles W. Ford, March 24, 1867, USGP, LC; USG to Isaac N. Morris, March 27, 1867, USGP, SIU-C; Welles, *Diary*, 3:74 (March 29, 1867).

CHAPTER EIGHT

1. USG to Elihu B. Washburne, April 5, 1867, USGP, ISHS; Badeau, *Grant in Peace*, p. 62.

2. Fairman, *Reconstruction and Reunion*, 1:370–96.

3. New York *Times*, July 24, 1885.

4. John Pope to USG, May 22, 1867, RG 108, TR; USG to district commanders, May 22, 1867, E. McPherson, *Political History*, p. 311; Philip H. Sheridan to USG, May 10, 1867, RG 108, TR; General Orders No. 31, First Military District, May 28, 1867, cited in McDonough, *Schofield*, p. 174; Sefton, *United States Army and Reconstruction*, pp. 118–24; USG to John M. Schofield, June 3, 1867, USGP, LC.

5. Badeau, *Grant in Peace*, p. 102; Dawson, *Army Generals and Reconstruction*, pp. 46–47; Sheridan to USG, April 1, 1867, Sheridan Papers.

6. Conway, *Reconstruction of Georgia*, p. 143; USG to Pope, April 21, 1867, USGP, LC; USG to Edwin M. Stanton, April [22], 1867, E. McPherson, *Political History*, p. 311.

7. USG to Sheridan, April 5, 1867, Sheridan Papers; Sheridan to USG, April 19, 1867, Sheridan, *Personal Memoirs*, 2:254–55; Sheridan to USG, April 26, 1867, Sheridan Papers; Daniel E. Sickles to Edward D. Townsend, June 14, 1867, Stanton Papers; Mantell, *Johnson, Grant, and the Politics of Reconstruction*, pp. 31–32.

8. USG to Pope, April 21, 1867, USGP, LC; USG to Sheridan, April 7, 1867, RG 108, TS; USG to Sheridan, April 21, 1867, Sheridan Papers.

9. Welles, *Diary*, 3:94 (May 14, 1867), 96 (May 21, 1867), 98 (May 23, 1867), 99 (May 27, 1867), 104 (June 8, 1867); Sheridan to USG, June 4, 7, 10, 13,

19, 21, 22, 1867, and to Stanton, June 5, 1867, Sheridan Papers; USG to Sheridan, June 6, 1867, Sheridan Papers; Badeau, *Grant in Peace*, pp. 86, 103.

10. Welles, *Diary*, 3:105 (June 11, 1867), 107 (June 14, 1867), 109–14 (June 20, 1867).

11. Hyman, *Radical Republicans and Reconstruction*, pp. 393–400.

12. James H. Wilson to Adam Badeau, July 5, 1867, James H. Wilson Papers; Springfield, Ill., *State Journal*, June 10, 1867, cited in *National Anti-Slavery Standard*, June 22, 1867.

13. Sickles to Stanton, June 16, 1867, Stanton Papers; New York *Times*, June 17, 20, 1867; Sheridan to USG, June 22, 27, 1867, Sheridan Papers; Horace Porter to Sheridan, June 25, 1867, Sheridan Papers; Mantell, *Johnson, Grant, and the Politics of Reconstruction*, pp. 33–34. Sickles was playing a double game, also assuring Johnson of his support. Sickles to AJ, June 10 and June [?], 1867, AJP.

14. Welles, *Diary*, 3:117 (June 24, 1867); *National Anti-Slavery Standard*, June 29, 1867; Sheridan to USG, June 13, 1867, Sheridan Papers; USG to Sheridan, June 24, 1867, USGP, LC.

15. USG to Edward O. C. Ord, June 23, 1867, USGP, LC; Porter to Sheridan, June 25, 1867, Sheridan Papers; Pope to USG, June 27, 1867, USGP, LC; USG to Pope, June 28, 1867, and to Sheridan, June 28, 1867, Sheridan Papers; Badeau, *Grant in Peace*, p. 71.

16. Pope to USG, July 24, 1867, New York *Times*, August 19, 1867; USG to Ord, July 30, 1867, RG 108, TS; Frederick Dent to Ord, August 20, 1867, USGP, LC; USG to Pope, August 14, 1867, RG 108, TS.

17. New York *Times*, July 13, 1867; drafts of the act are in the Stanton Papers. In calling Grant to Washington, Stanton was afraid that others might be watching the wires and sent his message through one of Grant's staff officers because he did not want his name mentioned. George K. Leet to USG, July 11, 1867, and Leet to Porter, July 11, 1867, RG 108, TS.

18. Hyman, *Radical Republicans and Reconstruction*, pp. 403–7; Mantell, *Johnson, Grant, and the Politics of Reconstruction*, pp. 33–34.

19. New York *Times*, August 19, 29, 1867; *National Anti-Slavery Standard*, July 27, November 9, 1867.

20. New York *Times*, August 4, 19, 1867.

21. USG to Stanton, July 20, 1867, USGP, LC; New York *Times*, July 24, 31, 1867.

22. Stanton to USG, July 22, 1867, RG 108, TR; USG to George H. Thomas, July 23, 1867, USG to Stanton, July 23, 1867, Leet to Porter, July 26, 1867, USG to Thomas, July 26, 1867, and USG to Stanton, July 26, 1867, RG 108, TS; Thomas to USG, August 2, 1867, USGP, LC. Within a week, Thomas demonstrated once more that he was unable to take the initiative, and Grant had to issue explicit instructions. "If civil authorities will not protect union men from the violence of paroled rebels arrest the guilty for violation of their paroles." USG to Thomas, August 7, 1867, RG 108, TS.

23. Welles, *Diary*, 3:140 (July 26, 1867).

24. USG to Stanton, July 24, 1867, Stanton Papers.

25. Browning, *Diary*, 2:152 (July 23, 1867); New York *Times*, August 2, 1867.

26. Sheridan to USG, July 3, 20, 23, 24, 1867, Sheridan Papers.

27. Sheridan to USG, July 25, 1867, ibid.; Richter, *Army in Texas*, pp. 66–69; Dawson, *Army Generals and Reconstruction*, pp. 56–57; USG to Sheridan, July 30, 1867, RG 108, TS.

28. R. King Cutler to AJ, July 30, 1867, Lovell Rousseau to AJ, July 24, 25, 1867, AJP; Castel, *Presidency of Andrew Johnson*, p. 132; Mantell, *Johnson, Grant, and the Politics of Reconstruction*, p. 35.

29. Moore, "Notes," pp. 103–7; Castel, *Presidency of Andrew Johnson*, p. 133. Johnson later told Welles that the general "appeared to have come off a debauch." Welles, *Diary*, 3:154 (August 3, 1867).

30. USG to AJ, August 1, 1867, USGP, LC.

31. Welles, *Diary*, 3:149 (August 2, 1867), pp. 153–54 (August 3, 1867—revised version); Mantell, *Johnson, Grant, and the Politics of Reconstruction*, p. 35. A telegram dispatched by Grant that day revealed that he held firm to congressional intentions: "It is certainly the duty of District Commanders to study what the framers of the reconstruction laws wanted to express as much as what they do express and to execute the law according to that interpretation." He promised to uphold any actions his commanders took in accordance with that law. USG to Pope, August 3, 1867, USGP, LC; see also USG to Ord, August 5, 1867, USGP, LC.

32. Welles, *Diary*, 3:167 (August 11, 1867); Moore Diary, August 11, 1867, AJP; Castel, *Presidency of Andrew Johnson*, p. 136.

33. Castel, *Presidency of Andrew Johnson*, p. 136; Thomas and Hyman, *Stanton*, pp. 549–50; *PMJDG*, p. 165; Burr, *Life and Deeds of Grant*, p. 851. It was at Blair's suggestion that Johnson sent for Grant. Montgomery Blair to wife, August 10, 1867, Blair Family Papers.

34. Badeau, *Grant in Peace*, pp. 92–94, 139–40; *PMJDG*, p. 165.

35. Welles, *Diary*, 3:169 (August 13, 1867); Browning, *Diary*, 2:158 (August 16, 1867); Maj. James Forsyth to Sheridan, August 14, 1867, Sheridan Papers; Montgomery Blair to wife, August 13, 17, 1867, Blair Family Papers.

36. New York *Independent*, August 29, 1867; Carl Schurz to wife, August 20, 1867, Schurz, *Intimate Letters*, p. 388; George S. Boutwell to USG, August 17, 1867, Grant Family Papers; Henry D. Cooke to John Sherman, August 19, 1867, John Sherman Papers; John Lothrop Motley to Mary Motley, August 14, 1867, Motley, *Correspondence*, 2:282–83. For reports leaked by Johnson suggesting Grant's support for the administration, see the New York *Tribune*, August 15, 24, 1867.

37. Forsyth to Sheridan, August 12, 14, 1867, Sheridan Papers. Sheridan agreed that Johnson was the source of his trouble. Sheridan to A. V. Kautz, August 4, 1867, ibid.

38. AJ to USG, August 17, 1867, AJP; USG to AJ, August 17, 1867, ibid.; AJ to USG, August 19, 1867, ibid.; Porter to wife, August 22, 1867, Porter Papers; Mantell, *Johnson, Grant, and the Politics of Reconstruction*, p. 36. Although Grant failed to protect Sheridan and Stanton, he did help to prevent the removal of Oliver O. Howard from his position as head of the Freedmen's Bureau. In July 1867, Johnson sought out Frederick Douglass to replace Howard; when Douglass declined, the president turned to John M. Langston. After conferring with Johnson, Langston, who did not want to supplant Howard, visited Grant. The general made clear his support for Howard; he criticized Johnson's policy "in severe and earnest terms" and described "in emphatic and eloquent manner . . . what the negro had a right to expect of the government in the way of protection and support, even to the extent of the bestowal of full citizenship, including the ballot." Douglass, *Life and Writings*, 4:33–35; Langston, *From the Plantation to the Capital*, pp. 276–77; New York *Times*, August 29, 1867.

39. Welles, *Diary*, 3:177–80 (August 22, 1867—last quote in revised version).

40. Ibid., 3:180–81 (August 22, 1867).

41. E. McPherson, *Political History*, p. 203; USG to Sickles, August 13, 14, 17, 1867, RG 108, TS.

42. Moore, "Notes," p. 111; Welles, *Diary*, 3:182–83 (August 23, 1867).

43. USG to Sickles, August 24, 1867, deCoppett Collection.

44. Badeau, *Grant in Peace*, pp. 109–10. The surviving evidence does not suggest whether Grant, as commanding general, considered another way of exercising authority over the district commanders in his office. Grant distinguished, sometimes with ludicrous exactitude, between his functions as secretary of war and general-in-chief. Since the law only covered the opinions of civil officers, Grant could argue that, although as secretary of war he might be barred from exercising oversight authority, no such restriction attached to his position as general-in-chief. For all of the vagueness attached to the drafting of the Third Reconstruction Act, one must recall that when it was passed Grant was not in the War Department and therefore could not be considered a "civil officer." Whether this was part of Johnson's motivation for appointing Grant is unknown, but the president soon realized that he could interpret the law to his advantage.

45. Welles, *Diary*, 3:184 (August 26, 1867).

46. Dawson, *Army Generals and Reconstruction*, p. 58; Moore, "Notes," p. 111; Badeau, *Grant in Peace*, pp. 566–67; Jordan, *Winfield Scott Hancock*, pp. 101–2.

47. General Orders No. 77, August 19, 1867, E. McPherson, *Political History*, p. 345; AJ to USG, August 26, 1867, ibid., p. 308.

48. Badeau, *Grant in Peace*, pp. 567–69.

49. Ibid., p. 568; Welles, *Diary*, 3:186–87 (August 27, 1867). In fact, Griffin soon died from illness.

50. Welles, *Diary*, 3:187 (August 27, 1867); Browning, *Diary*, 2:159 (August 27, 1867); General Orders No. 81, August 27, 1867, E. McPherson, *Political History*, p. 345. Sefton (*United States Army and Reconstruction*, p. 157) claims that General Orders No. 81 contained the "same restricting provision," but the provision does not appear in the order as reprinted in McPherson.

51. Moore, "Notes," p. 111; Welles, *Diary*, 3:188–89 (August 29, 1867); Badeau to Washburne, September 5, 1867, Washburne Papers.

52. *Independent*, August 29, 1867; Joseph Medill to USG, August 23, 1867, and "A Radical Republican" to USG, August 16, 1867, Grant Family Papers; Philadelphia *Daily Bulletin* quoted in the New York *Tribune*, August 23, 1867.

53. *Army and Navy Journal*, August 31, 1867; Philadelphia *North American* and Hartford *Courant*, in New York *Times*, August 30, 1867; James Sheldon to Washburne, August 26, 1867, Washburne Papers; John Binney to William Pitt Fessenden, September 10, 1867, Fessenden Papers; Welles, *Diary*, 3:196–397 (September 5, 1867).

54. Special Orders No. 420, August 29, 1867, E. McPherson, *Political History*, p. 314; Welles, *Diary*, 3:193 (September 2, 1867), 196–97 (September 5, 1867).

55. E. McPherson, *Political History*, pp. 342–43.

56. Clemenceau, *American Reconstruction*, pp. 104–6, 119–20.

57. New York *Tribune*, September 7, 1867; Henry D. Cooke to Jay Cooke, September 2, 5, 1867, Oberholtzer, *Jay Cooke*, 2:66–67.

58. USG to Ord, September 22, 1867, Badeau Papers, LC. In response to Ord's request for a transfer, Grant replied that he would accede when "reconstruction has progressed so far . . . that a change of commanders will not be interpreted as a disapproval of the course of the commander removed."

59. USG to Thomas, September 24, 25, 26 (two telegrams), 1867, RG 108, TS; Thomas to USG, September 26, 27, 1867, RG 108, TR.

60. Welles, *Diary*, 3:214 (September 27, 1867).

61. Ibid., 3:221–22 (October 4, 1867); Henry D. Cooke to Jay Cooke, October 7, 1867, Oberholtzer, *Jay Cooke*, 2:67; WTS to Ellen Ewing Sherman, October 7, 1867, Sherman, *Home Letters*, p. 361; see also WTS to John Sherman, October 11, 1867, Thorndike, *Sherman Letters*, p. 297. Both letters state that no actual offer of office was made.

62. Browning, *Diary*, 2:161–63 (October 8, 9, 1867); Welles, *Diary*, 3:232 (October 8, 1867), 233–34 (October 10, 1867); WTS to Thomas Ewing, Sr., October 18, 1867, Sherman, *Home Letters*, p. 363.

63. Sherman to Thomas Ewing, Sr., October 18, 1867, Ewing Papers; Welles, *Diary*, 3:234–35 (October 19, 23, 1867). The wording of Welles's October 19 entry suggests that the two men may also have discussed what Grant would do if the Senate reinstated Stanton. Grant had made it clear in a previous meeting that he would uphold the Tenure of Office Act. Welles, *Diary*, 3:186 (August 27, 1867).

64. Montgomery Blair to Frank Blair, November 30, 1867, Blair Family Papers; Milton, *Age of Hate*, p. 737 n. 37.

65. *Army and Navy Journal*, October 12, 1867; *National Anti-Slavery Standard*, October 5, 12, 1867; Clemenceau, *American Reconstruction*, p. 121; Burr, *Life and Deeds of Grant*, p. 855; Moore Diary Typescript, pp. 61–62, AJP; Castel, *Presidency of Andrew Johnson*, pp. 150–51; memo on military organizations in Maryland, October 8, 1867, Grant Family Papers.

66. *Independent*, October 3, 1867; Welles, *Diary*, 3:189 (August 29, 1867).

CHAPTER NINE

1. John Sherman to WTS, August 7, 1867, Thorndike, *Sherman Letters*, pp. 292–93; Welles, *Diary*, 3:185 (August 24, 1867).

2. USG to WTS, July 21, 1866, *PUSG*, 16:246; Benedict, "Rout of Radicalism," pp. 138–40; see also Abbott, *Republican Party and the South*.

3. J. McPherson, *Struggle for Equality*, p. 419; Henry D. Cooke to John Sherman, September 9, 1867, and A. B. Mullen to John Sherman, August 29, 1867, John Sherman Papers; James A. Hamilton to Salmon P. Chase, January 11, 1867, and William P. Mellen to Chase, June 27, 1867, Chase Papers. Thomas Ewing, Jr., agreed with Hamilton, observing that the Radicals were "expecting to be strong enough to elect an ultra man." Thomas Ewing, Jr., to Thomas Ewing, Sr., February 13, 1867, Ewing Family Papers.

4. Simpson, Graf, and Muldowny, *Advice after Appomattox*, p. 4; Benedict, *A Compromise of Principle*, pp. 50–51. Of course, defining who the Radicals were and what Radicalism was has become a question of interest to several historians. For the postwar period, Benedict's study is most useful, and I have followed his categorization in most cases.

5. *National Anti-Slavery Standard*, September 14, 1867; Mellen to Chase, July 21, 1867, Chase Papers; W. Jones to E. Delafield Smith, August 15, 1867, Butler Papers.

6. *National Anti-Slavery Standard*, May 18, June 8, August 24, September 7, 1867.

7. New York *Tribune*, July 25, 30, 1867; Hesseltine, *Ulysses S. Grant, Politician*, pp. 65, 89, 92.

8. W. Boardman to Benjamin F. Wade, April 16, 1866, Wade Papers; Cramer, *Ulysses S. Grant*, pp. 66–70; New York *Times*, November 8, 1867; *PMUSG*, 2:568; Montgomery Blair to wife, August 9, 1867, Blair Family Papers; Orville E. Babcock to Elihu B. Washburne, August 13, 1867, Washburne Papers; Benjamin F. Butler to Jones, August 20, 1867, Butler Papers.

9. Benedict, *A Compromise of Principle*, p. 281.

10. *National Anti-Slavery Standard*, June 15, September 14, 1867; J. McPherson, *Struggle for Equality*, p. 418.

11. New York *Times*, June 11, 1867.

12. Charles F. Adams, Jr., to Charles F. Adams, Sr., August 3 and September 14, 1867, Adams Papers; Richmond *Dispatch*, July 30, 1867.

13. Washburne to Adam Badeau, October 25, 1865, *PUSG*, 15:403; Washburne to USG, September 9, 1867, Grant Family Papers; Boston *Advertiser*, October 8, 1867; E. J. Sherman to Butler, September 9, 1867, Butler Papers.

14. Benedict, "Rout of Radicalism," pp. 142–43; Horace Greeley to Zachariah Chandler, August 25, 1867, Chandler Papers.

15. McJimsey, *Genteel Partisan*, pp. 109–25; Reverdy Johnson to USG, June 4, 1867, Grant Family Papers; Mantell, *Johnson, Grant, and the Politics of Reconstruction*, p. 55.

16. James S. Rollin to Montgomery Blair, September 16, 1867, Blair-Lee Papers; Welles, *Diary*, 3:121 (June 27, 1867), 184 (August 26, 1867); Frank Blair to Montgomery Blair, August 22, 1867, and to Francis P. Blair, Sr., August 2, 1867, Blair-Lee Papers; U. S. Grant, *Speeches*, [p. 16]. Although Frank Blair had served under Grant at Vicksburg, he turned on his old commander soon after the war, spreading stories that in St. Louis Grant sent Julia "to reside at a house of ill-fame . . . and lived openly with a woman who was known as a prostitute." John Potter to Washburne, March 4, 1866, Washburne Papers.

17. Babcock to Washburne, October 9, 1867, Washburne Papers. Babcock added that Horace Porter and Badeau agreed with him.

18. None of Grant's letters to Washburne in the collection of correspondence at the Illinois State Historical Society mention the general's presidential aspirations, although Washburne was away from Washington a good deal of the time in 1867.

19. USG to WTS, January 13, September 18, 1867, WTSP; WTS to Ellen Ewing Sherman, September 13, 1867, Sherman Family Papers; WTS to John Sherman, September 12, 1867, Thorndike, *Sherman Letters*, p. 295; WTS to Thomas Ewing, Sr., October 18, 1867, Ewing Family Papers; Philip H. Sheridan to USG, July 14, 1867, Sheridan Papers.

20. Badeau, *Grant in Peace*, pp. 73, 142–43; Washington *Daily Intelligencer*, September 14, 1867, in Johnson Scrapbooks, 4:58, AJP.

21. Badeau, *Grant in Peace*, p. 141; Jesse Root Grant to E. A. Collins, July 10, 1866, in New York *Times*, September 24, 1866. Of course, by publishing this letter, the *Times* added to the image of Grant the selfless soldier-statesman.

22. George E. Cole to USG, July 25, 1867, Grant Family Papers. Cole added that Grant was "the man who as President can restore this Union and give peace to this distracted country. Is it not your duty to do it?"

23. My reading of Grant's motivations is pieced together from various comments made by Grant and his associates. There is no evidence from such sources to support William McFeely's contrary interpretation of Grant's motives, which was capped by the statement that Grant wanted the office as early as 1864 and could not have endured it not coming to him. McFeely, *Grant*,

p. 277. More fruitful in understanding what was going through Grant's mind is a comparison to the situation in which George Washington found himself in 1787, prior to the Constitutional Convention, and 1788, when his name was presented for the presidency. See Wills, *Cincinnatus*, and Schwartz, *George Washington*, especially pp. 143–47.

24. John Binney to William Pitt Fessenden, December 30, 1867, Fessenden Papers.

25. Badeau, *Grant in Peace*, p. 142; Brisbin, *Campaign Lives of Grant and Colfax*, p. 307.

26. Sherman, *Personal Memoirs*, 2:438; New York *Times*, November 8, 1867. Wade later denied the story. Trefousse, *Benjamin Franklin Wade*, p. 293.

27. Benedict, *Impeachment and Trial*, pp. 67–71; Benedict, "Rout of Radicalism," pp. 144–47.

28. Washington *Daily Intelligencer*, October 14, 1867, in Johnson Scrapbooks, 4:58, AJP; N. R. Thayer to Washburne, October 10, 1867, and T. B. Shannon to Washburne, October 27, 1867, Washburne Papers.

29. Clemenceau, *American Reconstruction*, p. 135; William Chandler to Frederick T. Dent, December 24, 1867, Dent Papers; Binney to Schuyler Colfax, November 2, 1867, Fessenden Papers; Merriam, *Life and Times of Samuel Bowles*, 2:39.

30. Andrew Curtin to Washburne, October 17, 1867; Henry B. Stanton to Washburne, October 21, 1867, Shannon to Washburne, October 27, 1867, Washburne Papers; Benedict, *A Compromise of Principle*, p. 276; Washburne to John Russell Young, November 28, 1867, Young Papers.

31. Clemenceau, *American Reconstruction*, pp. 117–18; E. G. Blaine to Washburne, October 22, 1867, Washburne Papers; John Sherman to WTS, November 1, 1867, Thorndike, *Sherman Letters*, p. 299.

32. James G. Blaine to Israel Washburn, September 12, 1867, Hunt, *Israel, Elihu, and Cadwallader Washburn*, p. 121; Charles A. Page to Washburne, October 12, 1867, Washburne Papers; Carl Schurz to wife, October 12, 19, 26, 1867, Schurz, *Intimate Letters*, pp. 408–11.

33. Montgomery Blair to USG, November 11, 1867, Grant Family Papers; Frank Blair to Montgomery Blair, December 17, 1867, Blair-Lee Papers; Montgomery Blair to Frank Blair, December 16, 1867, Blair Family Papers; S. S. Cox to Manton Marble, November 11, 1867, Marble Papers.

34. Sylvester Mowry to James R. Doolittle, December 12, 1867, Doolittle Papers, WSHS; Doolittle to Marble, December 21, 1867, Marble Papers; Marble to Doolittle, December 29, 1867, Doolittle Papers, LC; Doolittle to Marble, January 2, 6, 1868, Marble Papers; see also Fitz John Porter to Marble, December 26, 1867, Marble Papers. Others pursued Doolittle's strategy. William S. Hillyer quoted Grant as stating in early 1866 that "this is a white man's government, and none but white men should have a voice in it." When Democratic congressman Charles Eldridge, who had questioned Grant during the impeachment inquiry in 1867, released this report in November,

Grant denied it; in turn, Hillyer and a "Conservative Senator from the West," possibly Doolittle himself, confirmed it. On the same day that Hillyer reaffirmed the story, excerpts from Doolittle's speech appeared in a pro-Johnson Washington journal. See the Washington *Daily Intelligencer*, November 20, 23, 1867, and the Washington *Chronicle*, November 22, 1867, all in Johnson Scrapbooks, 4:65–66, AJP.

35. J. Willis Howard to William D. Kelley, November 28, 1867, *National Anti-Slavery Standard*, December 21, 28, 1867; Donald, *Charles Sumner and the Rights of Man*, p. 339.

36. New York *World*, November 26, 1867; *National Anti-Slavery Standard*, November 16, 23, 30, 1867. One Radical editor did decide to come out for Grant, and the story of his decision is illustrative of the game played by the extremists on both sides. John W. Forney, editor of the Washington *Chronicle* and the Philadelphia *Press*, had once dreaded Grant's nomination but bowed to events. Enlisting the cooperation of John A. Rawlins, who by now was advocating the general's candidacy, he asked Rawlins to show Grant a lengthy article detailing Grant's adherence to Republican ideals. Upon finishing the article, Grant laconically told Rawlins that he was "surprised" to see himself "so good a Republican," especially in the eyes of a Radical. Rawlins relayed Grant's comment to Forney, who proceeded to endorse Grant's candidacy. Montgomery Blair reportedly hurried to Grant's house to inquire whether the general accepted Forney's endorsement. No, Grant said, he did not; Blair then allegedly leaked the conversation to the press, adding that Grant had denounced Washburne's meddling—a charge that Grant promptly denied. Blair also denied having confronted Grant with Forney's endorsement. Speculation as to Grant's adherence or nonadherence to Radicalism continued, generating much newspaper copy but little information, until the New York *Tribune* noted that out of twenty papers nine had declared that Grant was a Radical, nine had denied any such thing, and two had claimed that Grant was nonpartisan. Benedict, "Rout of Radicalism," p. 143; McFeely, *Grant*, pp. 265–66; Montgomery Blair to USG, November 11, 1867, Grant Family Papers; New York *Times*, November 11, 13, 1867.

37. Henry J. Raymond to USG, October 13, 1867, Grant Family Papers; New York *Times*, October 17, 1867.

38. New York *Times*, November 8, 18, 1867.

39. New York *Times*, December 8, 18, 26, 27, 1867; an announcement of the meeting is in the Kemper Papers.

40. Theodore M. Cowan to Edward McPherson, December 17, 1867, McPherson Papers; New York *Independent*, October 24, November 7, 1867; Philadelphia *Morning Post*, quoted in New York *Times*, November 11, 1867; Montgomery Blair to Frank Blair, November 30, 1867, Blair Family Papers; *National Anti-Slavery Standard*, November 30, 1867; Binney to Fessenden, December 30, 1867, Fessenden Papers; Welles, *Diary*, 3:244–45 (December 24, 1867); 249 (December 27, 1867).

41. Jesse Root Grant to Erasus Brainerd, November 27, 1867, quoted in Lewis-Catton Research Notes; Clemenceau, *American Reconstruction*, p. 136.

CHAPTER TEN

1. Moore, "Notes," p. 115; Mantell, *Johnson, Grant, and the Politics of Reconstruction*, p. 81. Congress passed a resolution thanking Grant for his letter defending Stanton and Sheridan. Clemenceau, *American Reconstruction*, pp. 140–41.

2. WTS to USG, January 27, 1868, WTSP; McFeely, *Grant*, p. 267; Milton, *Age of Hate*, p. 480; Castel, *Presidency of Andrew Johnson*, p. 157.

3. Grant recalled the claim but was "very certain" that Johnson did not mention it until their confrontation during the cabinet meeting on January 14. USG to John Bingham, February 12, 1868, Badeau Papers, LC.

4. McFeely, *Grant*, pp. 267–68; Milton, *Age of Hate*, pp. 480–81; Badeau, *Grant in Peace*, p. 112.

5. Milton, *Age of Hate*, p. 481; USG to AJ, January 28, 1868, AJP; Badeau, *Grant in Peace*, p. 112. Grant later contended that he did not agree to call on Monday but had intended to do so, and he understood that Johnson had expected him to call—all of which drew some rather fine distinctions. In an effort to keep her husband informed, Julia Grant pumped Congressman Robert C. Schenck for information on Stanton at a party that night. McFeely, *Grant*, p. 268.

6. McFeely, *Grant*, pp. 268–69; Badeau, *Grant in Peace*, p. 111; WTS to USG, January 27, 1868, WTSP.

7. WTS to Ellen Ewing Sherman, January 13, 1868, Sherman Family Papers; Townsend, *Anecdotes of the Civil War*, p. 124; *PMJDG*, p. 166; both Castel and Thomas/Hyman claim that Grant wrote out his letter on January 13, but they attach no proof. Castel, *Presidency of Andrew Johnson*, pp. 158–59; Thomas and Hyman, *Stanton*, p. 569.

8. Townsend, *Anecdotes of the Civil War*, p. 124; WTS to USG, January 27, 1868, WTSP; USG, draft of letter, Comstock Papers.

9. WTS to USG, January 27, 1868, WTSP.

10. Browning, *Diary*, 2:173–75 (January 14, 1868). Johnson's specific statement, given later, was: "You thus, in disregard of the understanding between us, vacated the office without having given me notice of your intention to do so." E. McPherson, *Political History*, p. 285. Of course, Grant had given notice the previous Saturday.

11. Welles, *Diary*, 3:259–61 (January 14, 1868); USG to AJ, January 28, 1868; William H. Seward to AJ, February 6, 1868, AJP; Moore, "Notes," p. 116.

12. WTS to USG, January 27, 1868, WTSP; Browning, *Diary*, 2:173 (January 14, 1868).

13. Moore Diary, January 15, 1868, AJP; WTS to USG, January 27, 1868, WTSP.

14. William S. Hillyer to AJ, January 14, 1868, AJP; Welles, *Diary*, 3:262 (January 15, 1868).

15. WTS to Ellen Ewing Sherman, January 15, 1868, Sherman Family Papers; Moore, "Notes," p. 116; New York *Times*, January 21, 1868.

16. USG to WTS, January 19, 1868, in Sherman, *Personal Memoirs*, 2:424; Moore, "Notes," p. 116; Schofield, *Forty-six Years in the Army*, pp. 412–13.

17. WTS to Thomas Ewing, Sr., January 25, 1868, and WTS to Ellen Ewing Sherman, January 28, 1868, Sherman, *Home Letters*, pp. 368–69; E. McPherson, *Political History*, p. 283.

18. E. McPherson, *Political History*, pp. 292–93 (emphasis supplied); Thomas Ewing, Sr., to Ellen Ewing Sherman, January 27, 1868, Ewing Family Papers. Sherman agreed with Grant, inquiring why, if Stanton was not secretary of war, McCulloch honored his drafts. Badeau, *Grant in Peace*, p. 133; WTS to USG, January 27, 1868, WTSP.

19. Welles, *Diary*, 3:268 (January 31, 1868); Badeau, *Grant in Peace*, pp. 132–33; Moore, "Notes," p. 117. Sherman reiterated his support of Grant's version after Congress published the correspondence. WTS to USG, February 10, 1868, Grant Family Papers; WTS to Thomas Ewing, Sr., February 22, 1868, Sherman, *Home Letters*, pp. 374–75. Grant, anxious to disprove rumors that he deceived the president, offered to discuss the matter with Reverdy Johnson. WTS to Reverdy Johnson, February 1, 1868, Reverdy Johnson Papers.

20. Badeau, *Grant in Peace*, pp. 114–15. The first draft is in the Comstock Papers.

21. USG to AJ, February 3, 1868, USGP, LC. In his letter, Grant— referring back to the January 11 conference—questioned Johnson's assertion that he had acted under a 1795 statute in naming Grant ad interim, citing a 1863 act on the same question. This issue, which arose again in the impeachment trial, is discussed in Benedict, *Impeachment and Trial*, pp. 164–66

22. E. McPherson, *Political History*, p. 282; New York *Independent*, January 13, 1868; Badeau, *Grant in Peace*, p. 114.

23. Samuel Galloway to Elihu B. Washburne, February 6, 1868; H. W. Thornton to Washburne, February 10, 1868; J. Gillespie to Washburne, February 7, 1868; James Shelden to Washburne, February 6, 1868; R. Cornell White to Washburne, February 4, 1868; and W. B. Johnson to Washburne, February 13, 1868, all in Washburne Papers; *National Anti-Slavery Standard*, February 8, April 18, May 9, 1868; New York *Times*, February 6, 1868.

24. New York *Independent*, February 20, 1868; Clemenceau, *American Reconstruction*, p. 148; Lorenzo Sawyer to Washburne, March 16, 1868, Washburne Papers. Back in St. Louis, Sherman commented that Grant "regretted as much as any person could" the recent dispute, "but he felt it forced on him by publications in the New York papers, seemingly coming from the President

himself." Once again, the press had done it—a favorite Sherman diagnosis. But even he expressed impatience with Grant's silence: "I wish he was more outspoken, but he knows his own mind and opinion and will manifest them when he deems it proper." WTS to Eugene Casserly, February 10, 1868, deCoppett Collection.

25. Welles, *Diary*, 3:272 (February 5, 1868); WTS to John Sherman, February 14, 1868, Thorndike, *Sherman Letters*, pp. 305–6; WTS to AJ, February 14, 1868, AJP; WTS to Thomas Ewing, Sr., February 14, 1868, Sherman, *Home Letters*, pp. 372–73; WTS to USG, February 20, 1868, Thorndike, *Sherman Letters*, p. 307; Moore, "Notes," pp. 119–20; E. McPherson, *Political History*, p. 346.

26. Castel, *Presidency of Andrew Johnson*, pp. 171–73. Although Thomas Ewing, Sr., advised Sherman to take the post, Sherman's wife wrote of her husband's "great distress" and of his decision to resign, "for he is not fit to go to Washington as he could never be a politician." Thomas Ewing, Sr., to Ellen Ewing Sherman, February 15, 1868, and Ellen Ewing Sherman to Ellen Ewing, February 14, 1868, Ewing Family Papers.

27. New York *World*, January 17, 1868; WTS to Ellen Ewing Sherman, January 23, 1868, Sherman Family Papers; Thomas Ewing, Sr., to WTS, February 18, 1868, Ewing Family Papers.

28. Fairman, *Reconstruction and Reunion*, 1:464–65, 417–19, 464–76; Kutler, *Judicial Power*, pp. 78–84, 100–103.

29. George G. Meade to Henry Wilson, January 9, 1868, Henry Wilson Papers; Meade to USG, January 9, 1868, RG 108, TR; USG to Meade, January 10, 1868, RG 108, TS.

30. Henry Stanbery to USG, February 12, 1868, and USG to Stanbery, February 13, 1868, RG 107, LR, President and Executive Branches; Edwin M. Stanton to Meade, March 23, 24, 1868, Stanton Papers; Fairman, *Reconstruction and Reunion*, 1:434–37, 470–71. Kutler in *Judicial Power*, ignores this case. Grant later instructed Meade to watch over election judges and other officials lest they abuse their power, "intimidate the freedmen, delay the voting and otherwise interfere with the voting." Horace Porter to Meade, March 20, 1868, USGP, LC.

31. Meade to USG, January 16, 1868, RG 108, TR; USG to Meade, January 17, 1868, RG 108, TS; Meade to USG, February 12, 13, 19, 1868, RG 108, TR; Shofner, "Florida," p. 22. Shofner states that this decision marked the use of federal power "to assist the moderates in their usurpation of convention authority," when in reality it was used to preserve the peace from Radical-induced violence.

32. USG to Meade, January 13, 1868, RG 108, TS (Grant's advice related to a decision by the convention to hold elections for officials together with the ratification vote. Such officials could not take office until the state was readmitted); Fleming, *Civil War and Reconstruction*, pp. 534–41; Robert Patton

to USG, January 14, 1868, RG 108, TR; USG to Meade, January 18, 25, February 6, 12, 1868, RG 108, TS; E. McPherson, *Political History*, pp. 336–37.

33. Abbott, *Republican Party and the South*, pp. 146–47; John M. Schofield to USG, May 25, 1868, Schofield Papers; McDonough, *Schofield*, pp. 184, 186; USG to Schofield, April 3, 5, 6, 1868, USGP, LC.

34. Schofield to USG, April 18, 19, 1868, Schofield Papers; McDonough, *Schofield*, pp. 182–83; Schofield to USG, May 25, 1868, Grant Family Papers.

35. George Stoneman to USG, June 26, 1868, RG 107, LR, President and Executive Branches; USG to John A. Rawlins, August 1, 1868, USGP, LC; Hesseltine, *Ulysses S. Grant, Politician*, p. 129. The disfranchisement provisions played a part in Grant's decision; as president he would act to strike down that clause in Virginia's constitution by requesting a separate vote on it.

36. Dawson, *Army Generals and Reconstruction*, pp. 69–73.

37. Winfield Scott Hancock to USG, February 7, 1868, RG 108, TR; USG to Hancock, February 8, 11, 1868, and Rawlins to Hancock, February 21, 1868, USGP, LC; Porter to George K. Leet, February 28, 1868, RG 108, TR; General Orders No. 17, March 28, 1868, E. McPherson, *Political History*, p. 346.

38. WTS to Ellen Ewing Sherman, January 30, 1868, Sherman Family Papers; WTS to Eugene Casserly, February 10, 1868, deCoppett Collection; WTS to John Sherman, March 14, 1868, Thorndike, *Sherman Letters*, p. 314.

39. Horace White to Washburne, August 13, 1867, Washburne Papers; USG to Philip H. Sheridan, March 31, 1868, Sheridan Papers; New York *Tribune*, April 4, 1868; McFeely, *Grant*, p. 275; Oliver O. Howard to USG, March 10, 1868, Schofield Papers.

40. Schofield, *Forty-six Years in the Army*, pp. 413–18.

41. Castel, *Presidency of Andrew Johnson*, p. 191; George H. Baker to Simon Cameron, May 14, 1868, Cameron Papers; New York *Times*, May 16, 1868; Horace White to Washburne, May 1, 1868, Washburne Papers; Badeau, *Grant in Peace*, p. 136; *National Anti-Slavery Standard*, June 6, 1868.

42. Richardson, *A Personal History*, p. 546; Eaton, *Presidential Timber*, pp. 22–23.

43. Badeau, *Grant in Peace*, p. 144; Chicago *Tribune*, April 8, 1885, Lewis-Catton Research Notes. In mid-May, Julia drew him aside. "I asked him if he thought he could fill the office and [he] replied that he thought he could do so as well as most others." Chicago *Tribune*, August 30, 1880, Lewis-Catton Research Notes.

44. John Sherman to USG, June 28, 1868, Grant Family Papers.

45. USG to WTS, June 21, 1868, and WTS to USG, June 24, 1868, WTSP.

46. See, for example, New York *Times*, June 3, October 26, 1868.

47. WTS to Ellen Ewing Sherman, June 7, 1868, Sherman Family Papers; Schofield to USG, May 25, 1868, Schofield Papers; Carpenter, *Sword and Olive Branch*, p. 239; New York *Times*, October 1, 1868; Sheridan to USG, May 22,

1868, Sheridan Papers; Richardson, *A Personal History*, p. 546.

48. New York *Independent*, May 28, 1868; Wilson to James Redpath, March 30, 1868, in New York *Times*, April 18, 1868; Howard, *Religion and the Radical Republican Movement*, p. 202; New York *World*, January 18, 1868.

49. New York *Times*, May 16, 1868; Mantell, *Johnson, Grant, and the Politics of Reconstruction*, p. 127.

50. Salmon P. Chase to John Van Buren, July 3, 1868, Chase Papers; Silbey, *A Respectable Minority*, pp. 221-32; Bigelow, *Retrospections of an Active Life*, 4:200.

51. Foukle, *Life and Services of Oliver P. Morton*, 2:48-52; Coles, "Seward or Grant in 1868?," pp. 195-200; Coleman, *Election of 1868*, pp. 253, 330; Church, *Ulysses S. Grant*, p. 363.

52. Rawlins to Schofield, August 5, 1868, USGP, LC; Clemenceau, *American Reconstruction*, p. 235; Rawlins to Meade, August 22, 1868, RG 108, TS; New York *Times*, August 27, 1868; Meade to USG, July 6, 1868; USG to Rawlins, July 8, 1868; Meade to USG, July 30, 1868; USG to Rawlins, August 5, 1868; Meade to USG, October 6, 1868; and USG to Leet, October 8, 1868, all in RG 108, TR; Nathans, *Losing the Peace*, pp. 103-46.

53. Dawson, *Army Generals and Reconstruction*, pp. 84-93.

54. Clemenceau, *American Reconstruction*, pp. 228-29, 246-48.

55. John Sherman to WTS, September [?], 1868, and October 14, 1868, Thorndike, *Sherman Letters*, pp. 320-23.

56. Hesseltine, *Ulysses S. Grant, Politician*, p. 130.

57. Benedict, *Compromise of Principle*, p. 323; Badeau, *Grant in Peace*, p. 149; Ross, *General's Wife*, p. 202.

EPILOGUE

1. New York *Times*, June 3, 1868.

2. New York *Tribune*, June 1, 1868; New York *Independent*, February 13, 1868; Schouler, *History of the Reconstruction Period*, pp. 145-46.

3. Report of Operations, April 4, 1865, WTSP.

4. Weigley, *History of the United States Army*, p. 252.

5. Young, *Around the World*, 2:454; Adam Badeau to James H. Wilson, May 27, 1865, James H. Wilson Papers.

6. Williams, *McClellan, Sherman, and Grant*, p. 101.

7. Young, *Around the World*, 2:446-47.

8. Ibid., 2:290, 447.

9. Williams, *McClellan, Sherman, and Grant*, p. 102.

10. Long, "Ulysses S. Grant for Today," p. 23; Hyman, *Radical Republicans and Reconstruction*, p. 392.

11. *PMUSG*, 2:509-12.

12. Ibid.

13. Ibid.

14. Ibid., 2:510–23; Young, *Around the World*, 2:358.

15. Young, *Around the World*, 2:358.

16. Foner, *Reconstruction*, is the best synthesis of the revolution in Reconstruction historiography.

17. New York *Tribune*, February 7, 1868; *National Anti-Slavery Standard*, February 8, 1868.

18. John Pope to USG, December 31, 1867, Grant Family Papers.

19. *Army and Navy Journal*, September 9, 23, 1865; Adams, *Education of Henry Adams*, p. 260.

BIBLIOGRAPHY

MANUSCRIPT COLLECTIONS

Boston, Massachusetts
  Massachusetts Historical Society
    Adams Family Papers (microfilm)
Carbondale, Illinois
  Southern Illinois University
    Frederick T. Dent Papers
    Ulysses S. Grant Papers
    Ulysses S. Grant III Papers
  Ulysses S. Grant Association
    Lloyd Lewis-Bruce Catton Research Notes
    Lloyd Lewis Papers
Charlottesville, Virginia
  University of Virginia
    William S. Hillyer Papers
    James L. Kemper Papers
Chicago, Illinois
  Chicago Historical Society
    Ulysses S. Grant Papers
  Newberry Library
    Orville E. Babcock Papers
Madison, Wisconsin
  Wisconsin State Historical Society
    James R. Doolittle Papers
    Timothy O. Howe Papers
New Haven, Connecticut
  Yale University
    Saxton Family Papers

Princeton, New Jersey
  Princeton University
    Adam Badeau Papers
    Blair-Lee Papers
    deCoppett Collection
Seattle, Washington
  University of Washington
    Manning F. Force Papers (microfilm)
South Bend, Indiana
  Notre Dame University
    Sherman Family Papers (microfilm)
Springfield, Illinois
  Illinois State Historical Society
    Sylvanus Cadwallader Papers
    Ulysses S. Grant Papers
Washington, District of Columbia
  Library of Congress
    Adam Badeau Papers
    James G. Blaine Papers (microfilm)
    Blair Family Papers
    Benjamin F. Butler Papers
    Simon Cameron Papers (microfilm)
    Zachariah Chandler Papers (microfilm)
    Salmon P. Chase Papers (microfilm)
    William C. Church Papers
    Cyrus B. Comstock Papers (microfilm)
    Charles A. Dana Papers
    DeButts-Ely Collection
    James R. Doolittle Papers (microfilm)
    William M. Evarts Papers
    Ewing Family Papers
    William P. Fessenden Papers (microfilm)
    Hamilton Fish Papers
    Benjamin F. French Papers (microfilm)
    James A. Garfield Papers (microfilm)
    Ulysses S. Grant Papers
    Horace Greeley Papers
    Andrew Johnson Papers (microfilm)
    Reverdy Johnson Papers
    Edward McPherson Papers
    Manton Marble Papers
    Horace Porter Papers
    John M. Schofield Papers
    Philip H. Sheridan Papers

John Sherman Papers
William T. Sherman Papers (microfilm)
Edwin M. Stanton Papers (microfilm)
Alexander H. Stephens Papers (microfilm)
Thaddeus Stevens Papers
Lyman Trumbull Papers (microfilm)
John C. Underwood Papers
Benjamin F. Wade Papers (microfilm)
Elihu B. Washburne Papers
Henry Wilson Papers
James H. Wilson Papers
  National Archives
    Grant Family Papers (microfilm; private collection)
National Archives
RG 60   Department of Justice
         Letters Sent, 1865
RG 94   Adjutant General's Office
RG 105   Bureau of Refugees, Freedmen, and Abandoned Lands
         Letters Received (Microcopy 742)
         Letters Sent (Microcopy 752)
RG 107   Department of War
         Letters Received
         Letters Received, President and Executive Branches
         Telegrams Received by General Grant
RG 108   Headquarters Army of the United States
         Telegrams Received (Entry 27), 1865–68
         Telegrams Sent (Entry 17), 1865–68
RG 393   United States Army Continental Commands
         Department of Alabama, Letters Received, 1865–66

GOVERNMENT DOCUMENTS

Official Records of the War of the Rebellion. 128 books in 70 vols.
    Washington, D.C., 1880–1901.
Opinions of the Attorneys General. Vol. 11. Washington, D.C., 1866.
Testimony Taken by the Joint Select Committee to Inquire into the Condition of Affairs
    in the Late Insurrectionary States. 13 vols. Washington, D.C., 1872.

PUBLISHED PRIMARY SOURCES

Adams, Henry. The Education of Henry Adams. Boston, 1918.
Alexander, Edward Porter. Fighting for the Confederacy: The Personal

Recollections of General Edward Porter Alexander. Edited by Gary W.
   Gallagher. Chapel Hill, N.C., 1989.
Ammen, Daniel. *The Old Navy and the New.* Philadelphia, 1891.
Andrus, Onley. *The Civil War Letters of Sergeant Onley Andrus.* Edited by Fred
   A. Shannon. Urbana, Ill., 1947.
Berlin, Ira, et al., eds. *The Black Military Experience,* ser. 2 of *Freedom: A
   Documentary History of Emancipation, 1861–1867.* Cambridge, England,
   1982.
————. *The Destruction of Slavery,* ser. 1 of *Freedom: A Documentary History of
   Emancipation, 1861–1867.* 1 vol. to date. Cambridge, England, 1985–.
Bigelow, John. *Retrospections of an Active Life.* 5 vols. New York, 1909.
Blaine, James G. *Twenty Years of Congress, 1861–1881.* 2 vols. Boston, 1884.
Bolles, Charles E. "General Grant and the News of Mr. Lincoln's Death."
   Century Magazine 40 (June 1890): 309–10.
Boutwell, George S. *Reminiscences of Sixty Years in Public Life.* 2 vols. 1902.
   Reprint. New York, 1968.
Browning, Orville H. *The Diary of Orville H. Browning.* Edited by James G.
   Randall and Theodore C. Pease. 2 vols. Springfield, Ill., 1933.
Butler, Benjamin F. *Private and Official Correspondence of Gen. Benjamin F.
   Butler during the Period of the Civil War.* Edited by Jessie Ames Marshall.
   5 vols. Norwood, Mass., 1917.
Byers, Samuel H. M. *With Fire and Sword.* New York, 1911.
Cadwallader, Sylvanus. *Three Years with Grant.* Edited by Benjamin P.
   Thomas. New York, 1955.
Chambrun, Adolphe de. *Impressions of Lincoln and the Civil War.* Edited by
   Aldebert de Chambrun. New York, 1952.
Chase, Salmon P. *Inside Lincoln's Cabinet: The Civil War Diaries of Salmon P.
   Chase.* Edited by David Donald. New York, 1954.
Chetlain, Augustus L. *Recollections of Seventy Years.* Galena, Ill., 1899.
Clemenceau, Georges. *American Reconstruction, 1865–1870.* New York, 1928.
Coles, Oscar. "Seward or Grant in 1868?" *New York History* 15 (April 1934):
   195–200.
Cramer, Michael J. *Ulysses S. Grant: Conversations and Unpublished Letters.* New
   York, 1897.
Crane, James L. "Grant as a Colonel." *McClure's Magazine* 7 (June 1896):
   40–45.
Dana, Charles A. *Recollections of the Civil War.* Edited by Paul Angle. New
   York, 1963.
Dodge, Grenville M. *Personal Recollections of President Abraham Lincoln,
   General Ulysses S. Grant, and General William T. Sherman.* Council Bluffs,
   Iowa, 1914.
Douglass, Frederick. *The Life and Writings of Frederick Douglass.* Edited by
   Philip S. Foner. 5 vols. New York, 1950–75.
Eaton, John. *Grant, Lincoln and the Freedmen.* New York, 1907.

Geer, Allen Morgan. *The Civil War Diary of Allen Morgan Geer.* Edited by
Mary Ann Andersen. Denver, 1977.

Grant, Jesse R. *In the Days of My Father General Grant.* New York, 1925.

Grant, Julia D. *The Personal Memoirs of Julia Dent Grant.* Edited by John Y.
Simon. New York, 1975.

Grant, Ulysses S. *General Grant's Letters to a Friend, 1861–1880.* Edited by
James Grant Wilson. New York, 1897.

———. *Letters of Ulysses S. Grant to His Father and His Youngest Sister,
1857–1878.* Edited by Jesse G. Cramer. New York, 1912.

———. *The Papers of Ulysses S. Grant.* Edited by John Y. Simon. 16 vols. to
date. Carbondale, Ill., 1967–.

———. *The Personal Memoirs of Ulysses S. Grant.* 2 vols. New York, 1885–86.

———. *Speeches of General U. S. Grant.* Edited by Union Republican
Congressional Executive Committee. Washington, D.C., 1868.

Hand, Daniel. "Reminiscences of an Army Surgeon." *Glimpses of the Nation's
Struggle*, 1:276–307. 6 vols. New York, 1887–1908.

Hayes, Rutherford B. *Diary and Letters of Rutherford B. Hayes.* Edited by
Charles R. Williams. 5 vols. Columbus, Ohio, 1922.

Heth, Henry. *Memoirs of Henry Heth.* Edited by James L. Morrison. New
York, 1975.

Hitchcock, Henry. *Marching with Sherman.* Edited by Mark A. DeWolfe
Howe. New Haven, Conn., 1927.

Hyman, Harold M. *The Radical Republicans and Reconstruction, 1861–1870.*
Indianapolis, 1967.

Johnson, Andrew. *The Papers of Andrew Johnson.* Edited by Paul Bergeron,
LeRoy P. Graf, and Ralph W. Haskins. 8 vols. to date. Knoxville, Tenn.,
1967–.

Knox, Thomas W. *Camp-fire and Cotton-Field.* Philadelphia, 1865.

Langston, John Mercer. *From the Virginia Plantation to the National Capital.*
1894. Reprint. New York, 1969.

Latham, Henry. *Black and White.* 1867. Reprint. New York, 1969.

Lewis, Lloyd. *Letters from Lloyd Lewis.* Edited by Robert M. Hutchins. Boston,
1950.

Lincoln, Abraham. *The Collected Works of Abraham Lincoln.* Edited by Roy P.
Basler. 8 vols. Rutgers, N.J., 1953.

Lyman, Theodore. *Meade's Headquarters, 1863–1865: Letters of Colonel
Theodore Lyman.* 1922. Reprint. Edited by George R. Agassiz. Freeport,
N.Y., 1970.

Lyon, William P. *Reminiscences of the Civil War.* San Jose, Calif., 1907.

McClellan, George B. *The Civil War Papers of George B. McClellan.* Edited by
Stephen W. Sears. New York, 1989.

Meade, George G. *The Life and Letters of George Gordon Meade.* Edited by
George Meade. 2 vols. New York, 1913.

Moore, William. "Notes of Colonel W. G. Moore, Private Secretary to

President Johnson, 1866–1868." Edited by St. George L. Sioussat.
American Historical Review 19 (October 1913): 98–132.

Mosby, John S. *The Memoirs of Colonel John S. Mosby*. Boston, 1917.

Motley, John L. *The Correspondence of John Lothrop Motley*. Edited by George W.
Curtis. 2 vols. New York, 1889.

Newton, John K. *A Wisconsin Boy in Dixie: The Selected Letters of John K.
Newton*. Edited by Stephen Ambrose. Madison, Wis., 1961.

Pleasants, Henry L. *The Tragedy of the Crater*. 1938. Reprint. N.p., 1975.

Porter, David D. *Incidents and Anecdotes of the Civil War*. New York, 1885.

Porter, Horace. *Campaigning with Grant*. New York, 1897.

Romero, Matías. *Mexican Lobby: Matías Romero in Washington, 1861–1867*.
Edited and translated by Thomas D. Schoonover. Lexington, Ky., 1986.

Schofield, John M. *Forty-six Years in the Army*. New York, 1897.

Schurz, Carl. *Intimate Letters of Carl Schurz*. Edited by Joseph Schafer.
Madison, Wis., 1928.

Sheridan, Philip H. *Personal Memoirs of P. H. Sheridan*. 2 vols. New York,
1888.

Sherman, William T. *Home Letters of General Sherman*. Edited by Mark A.
DeWolfe Howe. New York, 1909.

———. *Personal Memoirs of General William T. Sherman*. 2d ed. New York,
1891.

Simplot, Alex. "General Grant and the Incident at Dover." *Wisconsin
Magazine of History* 44 (Winter 1960–61): 83–84.

Simpson, Brooks D., LeRoy P. Graf, and John Muldowny. *Advice after
Appomattox: Letters to Andrew Johnson, 1865–1866*. Knoxville, Tenn., 1987.

Stephens, Alexander H. *Recollections of Alexander H. Stephens*. Edited by
Myrta L. Avary. New York, 1910.

Strong, George T. *The Diary of George Templeton Strong, 1835–1875*. 4 vols.
Edited by Allan Nevins and Milton Halsey Thomas. New York, 1952.

Swint, Henry Lee. *Dear Ones at Home: Letters from Contraband Camps*.
Nashville, 1966.

Taylor, Richard. *Destruction and Reconstruction*. New York, 1979.

Thompson, Seymour D. *Recollections of the 3rd Iowa*. Council Bluffs, Iowa,
1865.

Thorndike, Rachel Sherman. *The Sherman Letters: Correspondence between
General and Senator Sherman from 1837 to 1891*. New York, 1894.

Townsend, Edward D. *Anecdotes of the Civil War*. New York, 1884.

Trowbridge, John. *The Desolate South, 1865–1866*. New York, 1956.

Truman, Benjamin C. "Anecdotes of Andrew Johnson." *Century Magazine* 85
(January 1913): 435–40.

Wainwright, Charles S. *A Diary of Battle: The Personal Journals of Colonel
Charles S. Wainwright, 1861–1865*. Edited by Allan Nevins. New York,
1962.

Welles, Gideon. *Diary of Gideon Welles.* Edited by Howard K. Beale. 3 vols.
New York, 1960.
Wilson, James H. *Under the Old Flag.* 2 vols. New York, 1912.

NEWSPAPERS

Augusta, Georgia, *Constitutionalist*
Baltimore *American and Commercial
Advertiser*
Baltimore *Sun*
Boston *Advertiser*
Chicago *Inter-Ocean*
Chicago *Tribune*
Cincinnati *Enquirer*
Columbus, Georgia, *Sun and Times*
Memphis *Bulletin*
Memphis *Daily Appeal*
Milledgeville, Georgia, *Federal Union*
Mobile *Register*
Nashville *Dispatch*
Nashville *Republican Banner*
New Orleans *Tribune*
[New York] *Army and Navy Journal*
New York *Herald*
New York *Independent*
[New York] *National Anti-Slavery
Standard*
New York *Times*
New York *Tribune*
New York *World*
Richmond *Dispatch*
Springfield, Massachusetts,
Republican
Washington, D.C., *Chronicle*
Washington, D.C., *Intelligencer*
Washington, D.C., *Star*

SECONDARY SOURCES

Abbott, Richard. *The Republican Party and the South, 1855–1877.* Chapel Hill,
1986.

Anderson, Nancy S., and Dwight Anderson. *The Generals: Ulysses S. Grant and Robert E. Lee*. New York, 1987.

Badeau, Adam. *Grant in Peace: From Appomattox to Mount McGregor*. Hartford, Conn., 1887.

Barnes, William H. *History of the Thirty-ninth Congress of the United States*. New York, 1868.

Bartlett, Irving H. *Wendell Phillips, Brahmin Radical*. Boston, 1961.

Beale, Howard K. *The Critical Year: A Study of Andrew Johnson and Reconstruction*. New York, 1930.

Belz, Herman. *Emancipation and Equal Rights: Politics and Constitutionalism in the Civil War Era*. New York, 1978.

Benedict, Michael Les. *A Compromise of Principle: Congressional Republicans and Reconstruction, 1863–1869*. New York, 1974.

———. *The Impeachment and Trial of Andrew Johnson*. New York, 1974.

———. "The Rout of Radicalism: Republicans and the Elections of 1867." In *Beyond the Civil War Synthesis: Political Essays of the Civil War Era*, edited by Robert P. Swierenga, pp. 137–48. Westport, Conn., 1975.

Beringer, Richard E., Herman Hattaway, Archer Jones, and William N. Still, Jr. *Why the South Lost the Civil War*. Athens, Ga., 1986.

Brisbin, James S. *Campaign Lives of Ulysses S. Grant and Schuyler Colfax*. Cincinnati, 1868.

Brock, William R. *Conflict and Transformation: The United States, 1844–1877*. New York, 1974.

Brooks, William E. *Grant of Appomattox: A Study of the Man*. 1942. Reprint. Westport, Conn., 1971.

Burr, Frank A. *The Life and Deeds of General U. S. Grant*. Boston, 1885.

Carpenter, John A. *Sword and Olive Branch: Oliver Otis Howard*. Pittsburgh, 1964.

———. *Ulysses S. Grant*. New York, 1970.

Castel, Albert. *The Presidency of Andrew Johnson*. Lawrence, Kans., 1979.

Catton, Bruce. *Grant Moves South*. Boston, 1960.

———. *Grant Takes Command*. Boston, 1969.

———. *U. S. Grant and the American Military Tradition*. Boston, 1954.

Cauble, Frank P. *The Surrender Proceedings: April 9, 1865, Appomattox Court House*. Lynchburg, Va., 1987.

Church, William C. *Ulysses S. Grant and the Period of National Preservation and Reconstruction*. New York, 1897.

Cimprich, John. *Slavery's End in Tennessee, 1861–1865*. University, Ala., 1985.

Clausewitz, Carl von. *On War*. Edited and translated by Michael Howard and Peter Paret. Princeton, N.J., 1976.

Coffman, Edward M. *The Old Army: A Portrait of the American Army in Peacetime, 1784–1898*. New York, 1986.

Coleman, Charles. *The Election of 1868*. New York, 1933.

Conway, Alan. *The Reconstruction of Georgia*. Minneapolis, 1966.

Coolidge, Louis A. *Ulysses S. Grant*. Boston, 1917.

Cooling, Benjamin Franklin. *Forts Henry and Donelson: The Key to the Confederate Heartland*. Knoxville, Tenn., 1987.

Cornish, Dudley T. *The Sable Arm: Negro Troops in the Union Army, 1861–1865*. New York, 1966.

Cresap, Bernarr. *Appomattox Commander: The Story of General E. O. C. Ord*. New York, 1981.

Crouthamel, James L. *Bennett's New York Herald and the Rise of the Popular Press*. Syracuse, N.Y., 1989.

Currie, James T. *Enclave: Vicksburg and Her Plantations, 1863–1870*. Jackson, Miss., 1979.

Dana, Charles A., and James H. Wilson. *The Life of Ulysses S. Grant*. Springfield, Mass., 1868.

Dawson, Joseph G. *Army Generals and Reconstruction: Louisiana, 1862–1877*. Baton Rouge, 1982.

Donald, David H. *Charles Sumner and the Rights of Man*. New York, 1974.

———. *Liberty and Union*. Boston, 1978.

———. *Lincoln Reconsidered: Essays on the Civil War Era*. 2d ed. New York, 1961.

Eaton, Herbert. *Presidential Timber: A History of Nominating Conventions, 1868–1960*. New York, 1964.

Emerson, John W. "Grant's Life in the West and His Mississippi Valley Campaigns." *Midland Monthly Magazine* 8 (September, October 1897): 206–20, 316–25.

Fairman, Charles. *Reconstruction and Reunion, 1864–1888*. 2 vols. New York, 1971, 1986.

Farnen, Russell F. "Ulysses S. Grant: The Soldier as Politician, 1861–1868." Dss., Syracuse University, 1963.

Fehrenbacher, Don E. *The Dred Scott Case: Its Significance in American Law and Politics*. New York, 1978.

Fellman, Michael. *Inside War: The Guerrilla Conflict in Missouri during the American Civil War*. New York, 1989.

Fermer, Douglas. *James Gordon Bennett and the New York Herald: A Study of Editorial Opinion in the Civil War Era, 1854–1867*. New York, 1986.

Fields, Barbara J. *Slavery and Freedom on the Middle Ground: Maryland during the Nineteenth Century*. New Haven, Conn., 1985.

Fleming, Walter L. *Civil War and Reconstruction in Alabama*. New York, 1905.

Flower, Frank A. *Edwin McMasters Stanton, Lincoln's Great War Secretary*. Akron, Ohio, 1905.

Foner, Eric. *Reconstruction: America's Unfinished Revolution, 1863–1877*. New York, 1988.

Foukle, William D. *The Life and Services of Oliver P. Morton.* 2 vols. Indianapolis, 1898.

Freeman, Douglas S. *Lee.* 4 vols. New York, 1933–37.

Garland, Hamlin. *Ulysses S. Grant: His Life and Character.* Hartford, Conn., 1920.

Gerteis, Louis S. *From Contraband to Freedman: Federal Policy toward Southern Blacks, 1861–1865.* Westport, Conn., 1973.

Gillette, William. *Retreat from Reconstruction, 1869–1879.* Baton Rouge, 1979.

Glatthaar, Joseph T. *Forged in Battle: The Civil War Alliance of Black Soldiers and White Officers.* New York, 1990.

Gougeon, Len. *Virtue's Hero: Emerson, Antislavery, and Reform.* Athens, Ga., 1990.

Grant, Ulysses S., III. *Ulysses S. Grant: Warrior and Statesman.* New York, 1969.

Hartigan, Richard S. *Lieber's Code and the Law of War.* Chicago, 1983.

Hattaway, Herman, and Archer Jones. *How the North Won: A Military History of the Civil War.* Urbana, Ill., 1983.

Hesseltine, William B. *Ulysses S. Grant: Politician.* New York, 1935.

Howard, Victor B. *Black Liberation in Kentucky: Emancipation and Freedom, 1862–1884.* Lexington, Ky., 1983.

———. *Religion and the Radical Republican Movement, 1860–1870.* Lexington, Ky., 1990.

Howland, Edward. *Grant as a Soldier and Statesman.* Hartford, Conn., 1868.

Hunt, Gaillard. *Israel, Elihu, and Cadwallader Washburn: A Chapter in American Biography.* New York, 1925.

James, Joseph B. *The Framing of the Fourteenth Amendment.* Urbana, Ill., 1956.

———. *The Ratification of the Fourteenth Amendment.* Macon, Ga., 1984.

Johnson, Ludwell. "Civil War Military History: A Few Revisions in Need of Revising." In *Battles Lost and Won,* edited by John T. Hubbell, pp. 3–18. Westport, Conn., 1975.

Jordan, David. *Winfield Scott Hancock: A Soldier's Life.* Bloomington, Ind., 1988.

Kaczorowski, Robert J. *The Politics of Judicial Interpretation: The Federal Courts, Department of Justice and Civil Rights, 1866–1876.* New York, 1985.

Keller, Morton. *Affairs of State.* Boston, 1977.

Kutler, Stanley I. *Judicial Power and Reconstruction Politics.* Chicago, 1968.

Lewis, Lloyd. *Captain Sam Grant.* Boston, 1950.

Long, E. B. *The Civil War Day by Day.* New York, 1971.

———. "Ulysses S. Grant for Today." In *Ulysses S. Grant: Essays and Documents,* edited by David L. Wilson and John Y. Simon, pp. 9–26. Carbondale, Ill., 1981.

McDonough, James L. *Schofield: Union General in the Civil War and Reconstruction.* Tallahassee, Fla., 1972.

McFeely, William S. "Accomplices to Failure." *Yale Law Journal* 78
(May 1969): 1092–1103.
———. *Grant: A Biography*. New York, 1981.
———. *Yankee Stepfather: General O. O. Howard and the Freedmen*. New Haven,
Conn., 1968.
McJimsey, George T. *Genteel Partisan: Manton Marble, 1834–1917*. Ames,
Iowa, 1971.
McKitrick, Eric. *Andrew Johnson and Reconstruction*. Chicago, 1960.
McPherson, Edward. *The Political History of the United States during the Period
of Reconstruction*. Washington, D.C., 1871.
McPherson, James M. *Battle Cry of Freedom: The Civil War Era*. New York,
1988.
———. *The Struggle for Equality*. Princeton, N.J., 1964.
McWhiney, Grady. *Southerners and Other Americans*. New York, 1973.
Maddex, Jack P. *The Virginia Conservatives, 1867–1879: A Study in
Reconstruction Politics*. Chapel Hill, 1970.
Majeske, Penelope K. "Johnson, Stanton, and Grant: A Reconsideration of
the Events Leading to the First Reconstruction Act." *Southern Studies* 22
(Winter 1983): 340–50.
Mantell, Martin. *Johnson, Grant, and the Politics of Reconstruction*. New York,
1973.
Merriam, George S. *The Life and Times of Samuel Bowles*. 2 vols. New York,
1885.
Milton, George F. *The Age of Hate*. New York, 1934.
Myers, William S. *The Self-Reconstruction of Maryland*. Baltimore, 1909.
Nathans, Elizabeth S. *Losing the Peace: Georgia Republicans and Reconstruction,
1865–1871*. Baton Rouge, 1968.
Nelson, William E. *The Fourteenth Amendment: From Political Principle to
Judicial Doctrine*. Cambridge, Mass., 1988.
Nevins, Allan. *Ordeal of the Union*. 8 vols. New York, 1947–71.
Nieman, Donald G. *To Set the Law in Motion: The Freedmen's Bureau and the
Legal Rights of Blacks, 1865–1868*. Millwood, N.Y., 1979.
Niven, John. *Gideon Welles: Lincoln's Secretary of the Navy*. New York, 1973.
Oberholtzer, Ellis P. *Jay Cooke, Financier of the Civil War*. 2 vols. New York,
1907.
Paret, Peter. "Clausewitz." In *Makers of Modern Strategy*, edited by Peter
Paret, pp. 186–213. Princeton, N.J., 1986.
Parker, William B. *The Life and Public Services of Justin Smith Morrill*. New
York, 1924.
Parrish, William E. *Missouri under Radical Rule, 1865–1869*. Columbia, Mo.,
1965.
Perman, Michael. *Reunion without Compromise: The South and Reconstruction,
1865–1868*. Cambridge, England, 1973.

Pierce, Edward. *Memoir and Letters of Charles Sumner.* 4 vols. Boston, 1877–93.

Pollard, Edward. *The Lost Cause.* New York, 1867.

Rable, George C. *But There Was No Peace: The Role of Violence in Reconstruction Politics.* Athens, Ga., 1984.

Rachleff, Peter J. *Black Labor in the South: Richmond, Virginia, 1865–1900.* Philadelphia, 1984.

Randall, James G., and Richard N. Current. *Lincoln the President: The Last Full Measure.* New York, 1955.

Raum, Green B. *The Existing Conflict between Republican Government and Southern Oligarchy.* New York, 1884.

Richardson, Albert D. *A Personal History of Ulysses S. Grant.* Hartford, Conn., 1868.

Richter, William L. *The Army in Texas during Reconstruction.* College Station, Tex., 1987.

Ross, Isabel. *The General's Wife: The Life of Mrs. Ulysses S. Grant.* New York, 1959.

Schoonover, Thomas. *Dollars over Dominion: The Triumph of Liberalism in Mexican-American Relations, 1861–1867.* Baton Rouge, 1978.

Schott, Thomas E. *Alexander H. Stephens of Georgia: A Biography.* Baton Rouge, 1988.

Schouler, James. *History of the Reconstruction Period.* Vol. 7 of *History of the United States of America under the Constitution.* New York, 1913.

Schwartz, Barry. *George Washington: The Making of an American Symbol.* New York, 1987.

Sears, Stephen W. *George B. McClellan: The Young Napoleon.* New York, 1988.

Sefton, James E. *The United States Army and Reconstruction, 1865–1877.* Baton Rouge, 1967.

Seipel, Kevin. *Rebel: The Life and Times of John Singleton Mosby.* New York, 1983.

Shofner, Jerrell N. "Andrew Johnson and the Fernandina Unionists." *Prologue* 10 (Winter 1978): 210–23.

———. "Florida: A Failure of Moderate Republicanism." In *Reconstruction and Redemption in the South,* edited by Otto Olsen, pp. 13–48. Baton Rouge, 1980.

Silbey, Joel. *A Respectable Minority: The Democratic Party, 1860–1868.* New York, 1977.

Simon, John Y. "Grant at Hardscrabble." *Missouri Historical Bulletin* 35 (July 1979): 191–201.

Simpson, Brooks D. "Butcher? Racist? An Examination of William S. McFeely's *Grant: A Biography.*" *Civil War History* 33 (March 1987): 63–83.

———. "'The Doom of Slavery': Ulysses S. Grant, War Aims, and Emancipation, 1861–1863." *Civil War History* 36 (March 1990): 36–56.

————. "Grant's Tour of the South Revisited." *Journal of Southern History* 54 (August 1988): 425–48.

————. "Ulysses S. Grant and the Failure of Reconciliation." *Illinois Historical Journal* 81 (Winter 1988): 269–82.

————. "Ulysses S. Grant and the Fruits of Victory." *Essays in History* 23 (1979): 23–36.

Sommers, Richard J. "The Dutch Gap Affair: Military Atrocities and Rights of Negro Soldiers." *Civil War History* 21 (March 1975): 51–64.

————. *Richmond Redeemed.* New York, 1975.

Thomas, Benjamin P., and Harold M. Hyman. *Stanton: The Life and Times of Lincoln's Secretary of War.* New York, 1962.

Thomas, Emory M. *The Confederacy as a Revolutionary Experience.* Englewood Cliffs, N.J., 1971.

————. *The Confederate Nation, 1861–1865.* New York, 1979.

Trefousse, Hans L. *Andrew Johnson: A Biography.* New York, 1989.

————. *Benjamin Franklin Wade: Radical Republican from Ohio.* New York, 1963.

————. *Carl Schurz: A Biography.* Knoxville, Tenn., 1982.

Turner, Thomas R. *Beware the People Weeping: Public Opinion and the Assassination of Abraham Lincoln.* Baton Rouge, 1982.

Ulrich, William J. "The Northern Military Mind in Regard to Reconstruction, 1865–1872: The Attitudes of Ten Leading Union Generals." Ph.D. dissertation, Ohio State University, 1959.

Voegeli, V. Jacque. *Free but Not Equal: The Midwest and the Negro during the Civil War.* Chicago, 1967.

Walters, John B. *Merchant of Terror: General Sherman and Total War.* Indianapolis, 1973.

Weigley, Russell. "American Strategy from Its Beginnings through the First World War." In *Makers of Modern Strategy,* edited by Peter Paret, pp. 408–43. Princeton, N.J., 1986.

————. *The American Way of War.* New York, 1973.

————. *History of the United States Army.* New York, 1967.

Westwood, Howard C. "Grant's Role in Beginning Black Soldiery." *Illinois Historical Journal* 79 (Autumn 1986): 197–212.

————. "The Singing Wire Conspiracy: Manipulation of Men and Measures for Peace." *Civil War Times Illustrated* 19 (December 1980): 30–35.

Wharton, Vernon Lane. *The Negro in Mississippi, 1865–1890.* Chapel Hill, 1947.

Williams, Kenneth. *Lincoln Finds a General.* 5 vols. New York, 1949–59.

Williams, T. Harry. *Lincoln and His Generals.* New York, 1952.

————. *Lincoln and the Radicals.* Madison, Wis., 1941.

————. *McClellan, Sherman, and Grant.* New Brunswick, N.J., 1962.

————. "The Military Leadership of North and South." In *Why the North*

Won the Civil War, edited by David Donald, pp. 33–54. New York, 1960.

Wills, Garry. *Cincinnatus: George Washington and the American Enlightenment.* New York, 1984.

Wilson, James G. *Life and Public Services of Ulysses Simpson Grant.* New York, 1885.

Wilson, James H. *The Life of Charles A. Dana.* New York, 1907.

———. *The Life of John A. Rawlins.* New York, 1916.

Woodward, William E. *Meet General Grant.* New York, 1928.

Young, John R. *Around the World with General Grant.* 2 vols. New York, 1879.

Zilversmit, Arthur. "Grant and the Freedmen." In *New Perspectives on Race and Slavery in America: Essays in Honor of Kenneth M. Stampp*, edited by Robert H. Abzug and Stephen E. Maizlish, pp. 128–45. Lexington, Ky., 1986.

INDEX

Abell, Edward, 180
Adams, Charles F., Jr., 211
Adams, Henry, xv, 262
Adams, John Quincy, II, 248–49
Aiken, William, 119, 286 (n. 18)
Alabama: unionists in, 70–71; Reconstruction in, 180, 239
Alexander, Edward P., 87
Ames, Mary Clemmer, 253
Ammen, Daniel, 149, 153, 163
Andrew, John A., 211
Appomattox agreement, 84–85, 94, 98, 106, 132, 282 (n. 9), 284 (n. 41); reaction to, 85, 87–90, 107–8; Grant on, 95, 107–9, 113, 132, 187
Appomattox campaign, 78–85, 255
Appomattox Court House, 83–85, 86–88, 255
Arkansas, 164–66
Army and Navy Journal, 199, 203, 262
Army Appropriations Act, 172, 173, 260, 298–99 (n. 24)
Atlanta, Georgia, 56, 60, 65, 121
Ashley, James H., 152

Babcock, Orville H., 83–84, 118, 150, 157, 213–14
Badeau, Adam, 53, 84, 104, 107, 115, 117, 118, 142, 151, 155, 165, 182, 185, 213, 215, 218, 234, 245, 251, 255, 285 (n. 10)
Baird, Absalom, 129, 143–45
Baltimore, Maryland, 153–61
Banks, Nathaniel P., 49, 55–56, 58, 71
Belmont, August, 212
Belmont, Missouri, 19
Bennett, James Gordon, 52, 212
Bingham, John, 236
Binney, John, 199, 219, 224
Bird, Francis W., 126
Black, Jeremiah S., 237
Black Codes, 116, 123, 127, 136, 140, 259
Blacks, 17, 27, 29, 31–32, 35–36, 43–44, 51, 79–80, 81, 118–19, 120, 130, 269 (n. 16), 273 (n. 4), 278 (n. 1), 288 (n. 46); violence against, xvi, 116, 136–37, 139, 144–45, 166–70, 249, 250, 290 (n. 10). *See also* Slaves and slavery
Black soldiers, 56–58, 71, 93, 120, 256–57, 273 (nn. 10, 11), 284 (n. 40); enlisted, 38–41; Grant on, 40, 44–46, 57–58, 61–63, 93, 102–4, 113–14, 120, 256–57, 287 (n. 27); in combat, 41, 61–63, 65;